Baseball and Football Pulp Fiction

Also by Michelle Nolan
and from McFarland

Archie's Rivals in Teen Comics, 1940s–1970s: An Illustrated History (2020)

Ball Tales: A Study of Baseball, Basketball and Football Fiction of the 1930s through 1960s (2010)

Love on the Racks: A History of American Romance Comics (2008; paperback 2018)

Baseball and Football Pulp Fiction

Six Publishers, with a Directory of Stories, 1935–1957

MICHELLE NOLAN

McFarland & Company, Inc., Publishers
Jefferson, North Carolina

LIBRARY OF CONGRESS CATALOGUING-IN-PUBLICATION DATA

Names: Nolan, Michelle, 1948– author.
Title: Baseball and football pulp fiction : six publishers,
with a directory of stories, 1935-1957 / Michelle Nolan.
Description: Jefferson : McFarland & Company, Inc., Publishers, 2020. |
Includes bibliographical references and index.
Identifiers: LCCN 2020029545 | ISBN 9781476677576
(paperback : acid free paper) ♾
ISBN 9781476638133 (ebook)
Subjects: LCSH: Sports stories, American—History and criticism. |
American fiction—20th century—History and criticism. |
Sports in literature. | Pulp literature, American—
Publishing—History—20th century.
Classification: LCC PS374.S76 N68 2020 | DDC 810.9/3579—dc23
LC record available at https://lccn.loc.gov/2020029545

BRITISH LIBRARY CATALOGUING DATA ARE AVAILABLE

ISBN (print) 978-1-4766-7757-6
ISBN (ebook) 978-1-4766-3813-3

Printed in the United States of America

McFarland & Company, Inc., Publishers
Box 611, Jefferson, North Carolina 28640
www.mcfarlandpub.com

To Ray and Nikol Nolan and daughters
Logan and Myka, sports lovers all.
To Bud Plant, Bob Carter and Dan Stevenson,
pulp lovers and dear friends all.
To the entire Pulp Era Amateur
Press Society (PEAPS), pulp historians all.

Table of Contents

Preface

I've always had mixed emotions about the relative lack of interest among collectors in sports pulps. Sports and romance pulps—with often by far the most realistic stories in the field—trail in general interest the pulps that cover heroes, science fiction, mysteries and detectives, horror, westerns and occasionally other genres.

On the one hand, as a collector I often find it easier to track down my sports pulp wants than it would be to pursue early issues of titles such as *Black Mask*, *Dime Detective*, *Weird Tales* and early *Short Stories*. I also generally don't have to pay as much for sports pulps as I would many other titles.

On the other hand, I sincerely believe sports pulps have been overlooked and underrated during the entire history of pulp collecting. Possibly this is because many, and maybe most, pulp collectors and enthusiasts are not sports fans.

That is one primary reason I decided to write the first book with an in-depth look at pulp baseball and football—the book you are holding—including the first catalog ever published of baseball and football fiction from 1935 to 1957 in 1,054 sports pulps published by six companies other than Street & Smith (S&S).

The other primary reason is that I finally amassed more than 1,000 of the 1,054 sports pulps published by the big six" companies other than S&S: Popular, Thrilling, Columbia, Marvel (Red Circle), Ace and Fiction House. The 1,054 issues also include the run of nine issues of *Athlete*, an S&S pulp published in 1939–1940.

To be exact, as I write this, I have 1,020 of the issues. My friends in the pulp community, along with the invaluable FictionMags website, have been able to supply the data for all but one issue of the other 34 issues, and I have partial data on that one. Only a decade ago, when McFarland published my book *Ball Tales* in 2010, I had only 750 of the issues. Thus, this book also serves as a substantial update to the pulp information in *Ball Tales*, which was the first book to cover baseball, football and basketball fiction from the 1920s through the 1970s in all media.

Since so many collectors who seek pulp sports magazines do so for the often classic covers, I decided to include as part of the listings in Part II all cover themes for the 1,054 issues.

Street & Smith's *Sport Story* overwhelmed the field with 429 issues from 1923 to 1943, including two large reprint annuals in 1942 and 1943. FictionMags lists every issue and prints most of the cover images online, so I did not want to include S&S for those reasons.

Until now, my extensive chapters on sports pulps in *Ball Tales* and *The Art of the Pulps* (2018, IDW) have been pretty much the only material of significance in books about sports pulps, along with historian John Dinan's *Sports in the Pulp Magazines* (1998, McFarland), which was the first book on the topic. But Mr. Dinan also included details on the entire pulp field in that volume, since not many books had yet appeared dealing with pulps, and he also was not as fortunate to have access to nearly as much material as I have been blessed to acquire.

This book updates and greatly expands my basic list of sports pulps in *Ball Tales,* but that list was far more accurate than anything else produced before 2010.

I am greatly in debt to many people in the pulp community for their help, including Bob Carter (who so expertly prepared the graphics for this book), Dan Stevenson, Doug Ellis and Deb Fulton, John DeWalt, Sheila Vanderbeek, Ed Hulse, Will Murray, John and Maureen Gunnison, Phil Stevenson-Payne, John Locke, Tom and Shirlee Krabacher, David Saunders, Michael Oriard, Dave and Kelli Smith, Eric and Sharan Moothart, Mark Leonard, Kevin Cook, Alex Daoundakis, Monte Herridge, Kurt and Valerie Shoemaker, Richard Hall, Anthony Tollin, Brian Earl Brown, Tim Cottrill and the late Al Tonik, Frank Robinson and Rusty Hevelin. I apologize to anyone I have not mentioned.

Several close friends have provided the inspiration needed: Patty and Bob Lundquist, Bob and Karen Carter, Bud Plant and Anne Hutchison, and Russell and Noriko Ciochon. I can't adequately express how much you have helped during a difficult time for journalists and writers of all sorts. You are my literary angels!

Introduction

When I was in junior high, high school and college in the 1960s, I would check a downtown San Jose used-book store several times a month for old books, comics and pulp magazines. (I started there with the comics when I was eight years old in 1956.) At the time, I didn't know anyone who was even close to being an avid collector like I was until I met Bud Plant in the mid–1960s, when he discovered old comics and pulps at the same store, the immense old Woodruff and Thush building, several years after I did. It was always such a joy to make a discovery, but I remember how surprised I was to find my first sports pulp about 1962.

I was not the least bit aware any such thing had ever existed!

It was always a thrill to discover a comic book I had never seen or even heard of. The same applied to pulp magazines, my favorites of which were the science fiction pulps (which I started to read at about age 10 because of the sleek spaceships and the bug-eyed monsters), the hero pulps like *Doc Savage* and *The Shadow*, the occasional romance or western-romance pulp (neither of which turned up too often) ... and a handful of sports pulps.

I grew up in a sports-loving family and my grandmother taught me to keep score of baseball games at about age 12 by watching the nationally televised "Game of the Week" on Saturdays, featuring the dulcet tones of Pee Wee Reese and Dizzy Dean. Grandma told me all about Dizzy Dean, who pitched for her beloved St. Louis Cardinals' "Gas House Gang" when she was part of a 1930s Iowa farm family. Dad told me about the legendary shortstop Pee Wee Reese and the Dodgers when they were "Dem Bums" in Brooklyn.

So I loved the sports pulps right away. I had already started reading my family's copies of *Sports Illustrated*, but sports pulps were another thing entirely. Along with series book heroes Nancy Drew, the Hardy Boys, the Dana Girls and Tom Swift Junior, I had found sports fiction with Coach Clair Bee's Chip Hilton series and the classic Blue Sox novels by former pulp writer Duane Decker. But when the surviving pulps converted to digests by the 1950s and 1960s, the sports magazines were nowhere to be found on the racks, even while I would pick up the current *Amazing Stories* and *Alfred Hitchcock's Mystery Magazine*.

Now, more than 50 years later, I am still among the few people I know who avidly collect (and read!) sports pulps. To be honest, if you don't like sports, you probably will not like sports pulps.

I have an extensive background in several areas of journalism over more than 50 years, including sports. I have covered more than 5,000 sports events—everything from high school and college sports to the major league levels of pro baseball, football and basketball. I have done numerous articles on various aspects of sports history. Thus, I have a special fondness for team sports fiction.

Sports pulps have been given a bad name by people who think they're all about the same sort of real-life heroics you can now see on television pretty much any time day or night. Why read about heroic athletes when you can watch them? That very feeling did more than anything else to make sure sports pulps did not survive beyond the 1950s.

But it's not really about game-winning heroics.... The sports pulps were all about fascinating conflict, whether between the athletes and others in their orbits, or between the athletes and their own psyches. That conflict made for great reading, just as it did in all the other genre pulps, books and comics. Of course, in the pulps, conflict was often beyond most of what was ever seen in real life.

My goal in this book is to introduce you to authors and stories you may not likely be aware of, at least in a baseball and/or football context, along with various aspects of the sports pulps that still make them unique and fun. Is there a word like the baseball insult "busher" in any other genre? Almost everything in this book has never been covered, at least in depth and with the same degree of accuracy.

That means stories, topics and cover images portrayed in my 32-page chapter on the sports pulps in my book *Ball Tales* are not duplicated here. In that 15,000-word chapter, I also mentioned sports stories in the detective, romance and anthology pulps, but I do not cover those here. Nor do I cover the 429-issue run of Street & Smith's *Sport Story Magazine* (1923–1943), including the two reprint annuals, to the same extent. Instead, this book is an in-depth story of Street & Smith's first genuine competition, all of which began in the 1935–1937 era—the "sports big six" of Ace, Columbia, Fiction House, Marvel (Red Circle), Popular and Thrilling, plus the nine issues of *Athlete* from S&S. All of the "big six" companies outlasted S&S.

If you want coverage of Street & Smith, you can find all of the sports magazines indexed on the fabulous FictionMags website and covered in depth in John Dinan's short but interesting 1998 book, *Sports in the Pulp Magazines*, from McFarland.

Other than as part of a listing of cover themes for the 1,054 sports pulps referred to above, boxing stories are not part of this book, which is devoted entirely to baseball and football. (If anyone wants to do a book on boxing pulps, there is a wealth of material, for it was the third-most popular sport in the pulps by a huge margin. Basketball was a minor sport in the pulps.) There are slightly more than 8,000 pieces of fiction in these pulps, more than 4,000 of which focus on baseball and football, which were by far America's two favorite team sports in the 1935–1957 era. Ironically, since this book reflects the real-life scene of that period, the primary story numbers involve professional baseball (there were numerous stories about the minors as well as the major leagues) and college football (pro football was nowhere near as big as it is today). Any newspaper section of the era will reveal their primacy.

I obviously have a great fondness for genres long since vanished in their pulp and comic-book incarnations. I wrote the first (and still only) in-depth 30-year study of the once-iconic mainstream American romance comics, now largely gone for more than 40 years, with *Love on the Racks* (2008, McFarland). Now here we have the first in-depth study of pulp baseball and football, never as iconic in total circulation terms as the romance comics but nonetheless a meaningful part of American pop culture.

It is true that all the sports pulps combined made up no more than about 4 percent of the nearly 40,000 rough-paper magazines published across the first six decades of the 20th century. But to the people who read them, both off the racks and taken from used-merchandise outlets, they were (and still are) gold-medal winners! The covers are especially compelling, illustrating as they do a different era of the sporting scene when men were men and (alas!) women were mostly cheerleaders on the field or in the grandstands.

I apologize if you feel I slighted any of your favorite stories or authors, but with 4,000 stories and hundreds of authors to choose from, that couldn't be avoided. They are, however, all included in the listings in Part II for the first time. I can only wonder what some of these authors, be they prolific or one-hit wonders, might think to know their stories have not been forgotten after all.

I leave it to you to determine whether I have hit a home run or scored a touchdown!

PART I

History of Baseball and Football in the Pulps

1

Pulp Baseball and Football Authors

The Top 75 and the Other 400-Plus

How many authors contributed baseball and football stories to the 1,054 sports pulps listed in this book?

The answer is 476 authors, give or take a couple. But how many of those made significant contributions, which I define as at least 20 stories? The answer may surprise you: No more than 75 authors and perhaps as few as 71!

In other words, about 15 percent of the authors came through with at least 3,153 of the stories—or well over three-quarters of the 4,065 baseball and football stories in those 1,054 sports pulps!

This shows how hard it was to break into the sports pulps in a prolific way. So, too, does the total of "Moonlight Graham" authors who saw published exactly one baseball or one football story. (Archibald "Moonlight" Graham was the New York Giants outfielder made famous in the film *Field of Dreams* for appearing in one career major league baseball game, in 1905.)

It is possible that a handful of these one-and-done authors may have had stories published under other names, but the one-shot survey totals are at least 162 for baseball and 116 for football.

When I did my one-shot pulp author survey, I did not count names that were known pseudonyms or house names, such as the two used by science fiction author James Blish, who wrote four baseball and six football stories under his own name along with single baseball stories as by V.K. Emden and Luke Torley. Thus, Emden and Torley are not listed with the 278 one-shot wonders. But it is possible that a few of those one-shot names were unknown pseudonyms for well-known authors.

That is why my author story counts can be considered close, possibly even exact, but it is frustrating that we can never know for sure. Pulp publishers almost always refused to allow more than one story to appear under the same name—or the same pseudonym, for that matter. I'm not sure if it's a sports pulp record, but John D. MacDonald had four stories in the July 1949 issue of *Fifteen Sports Stories*.

Most pseudonyms are known and listed on the FictionMags website, but that can never be true of the house names for people who never existed, such as David Crewe and Daniel Winters. Those two names appeared on 110 baseball and football stories in the four Popular Publications sports pulps. However, I did not count house names on my author lists, because they almost always substituted for the names of prolific authors who appeared in the same issue. For example, the almost unbelievably productive William R. Cox had at least six stories appear among at least 59 credited to Crewe.

Nonetheless, it is possible that some shy author wrote his or her only pulp sports stories under a house name. Some of these we're aware of; some we will never know. Don Tracy, for example, does not seem prolific with 11 bylines, all in the Thrilling pulps, but he also wrote 15 stories as by Tracy Mason, 18 as by Roger Fuller and four as by Tom Tucker for a total of 48 baseball and football stories, all for the Thrilling group.

Perhaps the best example is the extraordinary Sam Merwin, Jr., who spent the vast majority of his pulp career as a writer and editor with Thrilling. He penned an untold number of mystery and science fiction stories but he also wrote at least 80 baseball and football stories, including 14 as by Carter Sprague, 10 as by Matt Lee and four as by Tom Tucker.

In contrast, Richard Brister—best known as the author of western and mystery novels—wrote 85 baseball and football stories, including at least one story for all six of the major pulp publishers, but he used no known pseudonyms. (Remember, I am not including Street & Smith's 1923–1943 run of *Sport Story Magazine* in this survey; for the reason, see the "Introduction." But I am including the nine issues of the little-known S&S pulp *Athlete* in 1939–1940.)

When I use numbers in this book, they refer to the minimum number of such stories. It is possible there may be a few more.

More Than 300 Stories by Ford and Cox

About 8 percent of all pulp baseball and football stories were penned by two men: T.W. Ford and William R. Cox, both of whom wrote extensively in other pulp genres as well. The irony is that Ford had no known pseudonyms and no known novels published in either hardback or paperback, while Cox used at least a dozen pseudonyms in the pulps and wrote more than two dozen sports novels alone, along with many others.

Ford finished with at least 166 baseball and football stories, yet all but 10 of them were published by Columbia (101) and Thrilling (55). He also wrote extensively for Street & Smith in the 1930s. It's no coincidence that Columbia and Thrilling published by far the most sports pulps into the 1950s along with Popular, but Ford had only five bylines for Popular, three for Marvel, two for Fiction House and none for Ace.

Cox (1901–1988), whose papers are available online, was credited with 120 baseball and football stories under his own name and about 30 under other names, not to mention dozens of stories about boxing and other sports. He is even credited with ghost writing at least seven 1940s stories using Jackson V. Scholz's byline, surely with permission. Yet Cox seems never to have written a single science-fiction story.

In contrast, Will F. Jenkins (1896–1975), much better known as Murray Leinster, wrote hundreds of science fiction stories along with just about everything else, including 24 pulp baseball and football stories for Thrilling as by Joe Gregg (14) and as by Kenny Kenmare (10). Leinster "graduated" to my list of prolific sports pulp authors when FictionMags taught me about the bylines of Gregg and Kenmare. But then, I looked up Kenmare early on, since "Kenny Kenmare" could only be a pseudonym, right?

A Super Heuman

There was a third author with more than 100 baseball and football stories in the pulps: William Heuman (1912–1971). He had 125 stories appear under his own name plus five as by George Kramer, and at least one as by Wilton Hazzard of Fiction House pulp and comic-book house-name fame. (Fiction House's best-selling comic-book line of the 1938–1954 pre–Comics Code Authority period was the only comic publisher that gave house bylines on many, if not most, stories.)

John Wilson Thorburn, who wrote almost entirely under the name John Wilson, like T.W. Ford, had no known novels published, sports or otherwise. He wrote 87 football and baseball stories as by John Wilson and five as by Jay Thorburn early in his career. Wilson had no known baseball or football stories for Fiction House but he had at least 16 for Thrilling, Ace, Popular and Marvel.

This Roemer Stayed Home with Sports

Theodore Roemer, sometimes listed as Ted, is in one respect the most unusual of all the sports pulp authors who worked for the six firms covered in this book. Roemer, who apparently wrote only sports, was credited with at least 66 pulp baseball and football stories, though he may have had a few more under house names, especially at Fiction House. Amazingly, he had at least eight stories for all six firms! Not only that, but he had baseball and football stories published by each company. No other author can come close to that distinction, at least in the sports field. He obviously submitted stories to everyone and apparently he may have recycled any rejects to everyone, too. It really is a startling example of a pulp author determined to get paid throughout the field.

Like Ford and Wilson, Roemer never had a sports novel published, nor did any of the trio have any paperback novels listed in Graham Holroyd's monumental *Paperback Price Guide* (2003).

Nelson Hutto, who had a few sports novels published in the 1960s, and C. Paul Jackson, who wrote more than 50 sports novels, were the only other authors with both baseball and football stories selected by all six pulp sports publishers covered extensively in this book.

Hutto had at least six stories for all but Columbia, for which he had only two published. Hutto was also among the few with a definite balance, with at least 54 total stories divided about equally with baseball and football themes. Jackson (1902–1991), who had no known pulp pseudonyms but had several as a sports novelist, was among the pioneers in pulp sports writing. He had at least 66 baseball and football stories along with many involving basketball. If total words written in novels and pulps combined are considered, Jackson ranks with the likes of prolific novelists Jackson Scholz and Joe Archibald for the most wordage in the post–Gilbert Patten/Frank Merriwell era.

There were 11 other pulp writers with at least 50 baseball and football stories for the six publishers: Roe Richmond (78), Zene Tuttler (74), Duane Yarnell (65), William O'Sullivan (65), W.H. Temple (64), Arthur Mann (63, including 23 as by A.R. Thurman), Robert Sidney Bowen (57), Ted Stratton (56), Bill Erin (53) and Herbert L. McNary (52). Except for Mann, these writers apparently did not use pseudonyms but may have used house names. There are no complete records available for who actually wrote many of the house-name stories, in part because those decisions were made by editors, not necessarily in consultation with the writer, in the event two of any given writer's stories were chosen for the same issue. Chances are many, if not most, writers who were paid on publication would rather have received a check for two stories rather than wait to see a story published under their own names.

Richmond wrote numerous westerns, both in the pulps including the *Rio Kid* for Thrilling and in the paperbacks, and Mann later was both baseball historian and a front-office man for the Brooklyn Dodgers. Bowen wrote numerous sports novels after moving over from pulp writing. The others were almost entirely pulp writers, mostly but not entirely in the sports field. They wrote under their own names except for John Theodore Stratton, who wrote entirely as Ted for the sports pulps.

Bond, Archibald, Bishop and Tracy

Nelson Slade Bond (1908–2006) had at least 38 pulp baseball and football stories under his own name for all six publishers, plus at least seven under the Fiction House names Ralph Powers, Wilton Hazzard and John Starr along with pseudonyms Lee Bond and Don Newall. Bond, of course, went on to focus on science fiction and fantasy and became a major name in that field, especially with his *Lancelot Biggs: Spaceman* series, which were the subject of a popular 1951 collection from Doubleday. When a few of his sports stories were reprinted in the early 1950s, house names were used, perhaps because Bond by that time had become so well identified with science fiction.

Joe Archibald (1898–1986), at one time a cartoonist as well as a writer and editor, had the majority of at least 47 pulp baseball and football stories published by Thrilling, for which he worked for a few years as art director of the firm's comic-book line when it was known as Standard Comics. Archibald may have written more sports novels (44) for older teen readers and adults than anyone else (many of C. Paul Jackson's novels were directed at younger sports fans). Archibald, who wrote mostly under his own name, penned also air war, adventure, mystery, western and even a few science fiction stories, though he was not known for costumed heroes.

Jackson V. Scholz, twice an Olympic sprinting medalist in the 1920s, wrote the vast majority of his untold hundreds of pulp stories for Street & Smith, but he also had more than 30 credits for the other sports publishers, along with numerous stories in other genres. He seldom wrote under pen names, but did have a few as by Jack Volney and Royal Hall. Like Archibald, Scholz focused on a series of 33 fine sports novels for older teens and adults when the pulp market shrank and then vanished.

Don Tracy seems to have worked entirely for Thrilling in the pulp sports field, but had only 11 baseball and football stories credited to his own name. He wrote at least a combined 37 as by Tracy Mason, Roger Fuller and Tom Tucker. Under his own name, Tracy wrote five science fiction stories for *Thrilling Wonder Stories* in the early 1940s.

Curtis Bishop (1912–1967) specialized in more than 30 sports novels for young readers in the 1950s and 1960s, mostly after the sports pulp market had entirely disappeared. He was among the few pulp sports writers who was far more prolific with football stories (at least 29 for Fiction House alone) than baseball tales (9 stories for four publishers). Yet he wrote more than a dozen novels in his Little League baseball series of 14 books (1953–1968) for grade-school readers.

House Names

Eric Rober's byline appeared at least 43 times on baseball and football stories, but they were all for Columbia, so he may have been that firm's leading house name. No genuine writer with more than 30 credits for sports stories did all of his work for one publisher. Columbia's other sports house names included Mat Rand and Cliff Campbell, both of whom had at least 35 baseball and football credits.

Popular Publications used house names for sports more than anyone else, including David Crewe (at least 59 baseball and football stories), Daniel Winters (51), Roy C. Rainey (30), Lance Kermit (19) and William Hartley (14).

House names were used for all the genres, making it impossible to know the exact number of published stories for many of the prolific writers. Some left papers now housed at colleges, but even there, some writers may not have kept up with every story that appeared under a house name. No known lists have yet appeared citing every story under a prolific house name, although the admirable FictionMags online project continues to do an amazing job adding stories to house names. It would be fascinating to know the exact percentage of all pulp stories to appear under house names, but that may never be possible. It is known that of the 4,065 pulp baseball and football stories from the six publishers, well over 300 were credited to house names.

The Others with At Least 20 Stories

Some of the other prolific writers included Burgess Leonard (at least 36 pulp baseball and football stories), western novelist Giles A. Lutz (35) and Johnny Lawson (31, all for Marvel), the pseudonym for B.W. Gardner at publisher Martin Goodman's Red Circle (Marvel) pulps.

Of the authors with at least 20 football and baseball stories but fewer than 30, Judson P. Philips (at least 28), Gardner Fox (26) and Jack Kofoed (23) are by far the best known. Philips was the real name of the famed mystery novelist Hugh Pentecost, and he abandoned the sports pulps after doing work entirely for *Dime Sports* and *Sports Novels*. Fox is well known as one of the most prolific writers of comic-book heroes, mostly for what became DC Comics, and Kofoed wrote hundreds of non-fiction sports articles in both the pulps and the slicks.

The others with baseball and football credits were pulp journeymen: Cosmo Bennett (27), Alexis Rossoff (26), Tom O'Neill (24), Norman Ober (23), Sam Carson (23) and William F. Schwartz (20). Still, they appeared more often than the vast majority of authors with at least one sports credit.

2

William Campbell Gault's Football

Famed crime and mystery writers who also made significant contributions to the sports pulps were few. One such writer was William Campbell Gault.

Gault (1910–1987), one of the most readable crime novelists of the 1950s and 1960s (and beyond), also wrote more than 200 generally excellent pulp mystery stories before he began to write both adult mysteries and young adult sports novels. But his body of work also includes dozens of never-collected pulp sports stories, including 15 football tales in the 1941–1952 period, with two written as by Roney Scott. He did not write pulp baseball, but he also wrote pulp boxing, golf, auto racing and more.

Of the more than 600 mystery novelists profiled in *Twentieth Century Crime and Mystery Writers*, edited by John M. Reilly, only four have as many as 10 pulp baseball and football credits—William R. Cox, Hugh Pentecost (Judson Philips), Stewart Sterling (Prentice Winchell) and William Campbell Gault. Cox wrote hundreds of pulp mysteries, western and sports stories, including more than 120 with baseball and football themes. Philips, under his own name, contributed 21 baseball stories and seven football tales to the six publishers covered in this book, along with many more in the likes of the general-interest pulp Argosy. Sterling wrote 19 pulp football and baseball stories, with 17 for Fiction House, including 15 with football themes.

Gault's 15 football stories for Popular Publications, Thrilling and Fiction House were unique, in the sense that he wrote them very much ahead of his time, almost in the style of modern newspaper football stories with little to no slang. They had gratifying and/or happy endings, but they read more like real life than pretty much any other pulp sports stories.

Gault's protagonists inevitably learn to cope with their human flaws and failings to grow into people willing to make the sacrifices needed to be successful, or at least gratified by their efforts. They are easily among the most readable of all pulp football stories. They not only list the ongoing scores involved in game action—usually written in his unusual style of "University--14; State--10." That was a style seldom used in fact or fiction; more typical was (and still is) "University 14, State 10." But it does not detract in any way, especially because most pulp authors made it difficult to know what the exact score was.

Part of the fun of reading pulp football—but also sometimes aggravating—is the multitude of slang expressions. Running styles are hipper-dipper (a phrase long since abandoned) or razzle dazzle; passes are air mail missiles or aerial blitzkriegs; the ball is a slippery pigskin or elusive ovoid; kickers have educated toes; white lines are chalk stripes; and on and on and on.

Gault, though, does not distract. His use of standard English enhances his stories and helps the reader to focus on what is happening to the people involved in the games. While Gault wrote his share of college stories, he also did more stories of pro football than most pulp writers, even though interest in the pros when he wrote was not nearly as intense as it is now.

"The Heart Guy"

One of Gault's best stories is "The Heart Guy" in *Sports Novels* for January 1948. This short story was his first football tale since returning from three years of military service in World War II and thus his name was not among the four authors plugged on the cover.

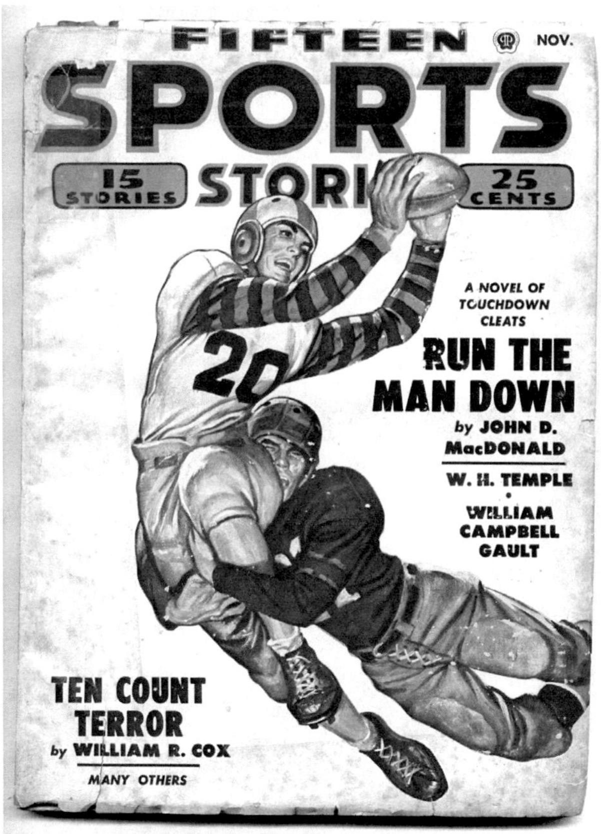

***Fifteen Sports Stories,* November 1949 (copyright 1949 Fictioneers, Inc.). Three of the best mystery writers who contributed to sports pulps are cover-featured: John D MacDonald, William Campbell Gault and William R. Cox.**

As the story opens, Steve Jessup has left the Bisons after six years as their sometimes controversial quarterback, with a divisional title the previous season. He has taken a job as a glorified bouncer at Danceland, a dance hall not far from the stadium, after finding that he and the owner of the Bisons, Walter Langdon, could not get along, in part because Steve wanted to continue to date Jean Langdon, the owner's daughter. Sports writers called Steve "the heart guy" because he was often a hunch player on the field instead of a by-the-book man, which the stubborn owner insisted he should be. Steve had more heart than head, it was suggested.

Steve loses his job at the dance hall when he is

knocked out during some trouble. At the same time, the Bisons have lost both of their quarterbacks with injuries with a playoff title game coming up. Jean invites him to dinner and he finds her father is on the scene when Steve arrives. The owner admits he is desperate; he offers Steve $1,000 to quarterback the Bisons in the playoff game, along with the possibility of returning the next season. Steve agrees, saying he "can't pass up that kind of money" (it would be more than $15,000 in today's dollars).

After returning to camp and looking good, Steve is soon offered a bribe to throw the game by a shady acquaintance, Nick Gamma, but Steve had arrived at their meeting with a couple of men from the district attorney's office in tow. Gamma is sent out of town but he has dangerous betting buddies. Steve tells his coach, Barney (no last name), about the situation. As a result, Steve tells Jean he has received death threats and she tells Barney. She still loves him, despite her loyalty to her father, and doesn't want him to play. But Steve insists on playing. "OK, Lochinvar, let's see some ball this afternoon," Barney tells him.

Steve, with plenty of help, rallies the Bisons to a 21–20 lead with three and one-half minutes to play. The Bisons are on their own 12-yard line after they recover a fumble by the favored Cougars. But he feels his exhausted team is on the verge of collapse.

What to do? Steve's head tells him a punt will likely be in order, but his heart tells him to ignore by-the-book tactics on second down after a first-down run fails to gain so much as a yard. Steve gambles, fades back and finds his fastest man, Jensen, "running with the speed of light," as Gault puts it, down field. Just like so many real-life quarterbacks do in the NFL, Steve unleashes a long pass—after all, it's like a punt, right?—and Jensen makes a fine catch in stride and scores for a 28–21 lead with the conversion kick.

The by-the-book owner, standing on the sideline with daughter Jean, immediately badgers Steve on the sideline. Langton asks him about why he so utterly defied logic. Steve responds, "A hunch ... that we couldn't control the ball for three-plus minutes. I mean that they're going to score a touchdown, as soon as they get their hands on the ball [the game is still going]. We were damned lucky, but there's no ball club safe with [Cougars flash] Cavendish on the field. That's what I mean. We got eight points, on them, now. That should be the ball game. One [point] wasn't enough." Steve then tells the stubborn owner, "You haven't got anything I want" as he walks away from father and daughter.

By "damned lucky," Steve meant they had somehow controlled Cavendish, who returns the ensuing kickoff 102 yards to score and proves Steve's point. But there was no two-point conversion in 1947 (when the story appeared).... "I knew the team didn't exist [that] could keep that boy bottled up all afternoon," he tells Barney, who nods in agreement with his "heart guy." Barney, irritated by the owner's second guessing, had seen Steve walk away from Walter and Jean Langdon and so Barney tells Steve a secret: Barney plans to accept an offer from the Lions and wants Steve to be his assistant and possibly a player the next season.

When Steve leaves the locker room, unsure of his future, he spots Jean waiting for him—without her father. She apologizes and asks Steve if he meant what he said, but he assures her he meant "almost anything." And, as the story ends, she asks, "Aren't you going to kiss me, Steve? Isn't it legal to kiss your fiancée?" Adds Gault, "And the few who remained in the stands stood and watched."

"Political Halfback"

Gault's first pulp football story was "Political Halfback" in Thrilling Publications' *Popular Football* for Winter 1941, the first issue. This short story was literally in the back of the book and appeared during Gault's first year as a pulp writer. The theme was unusual and indicative of the author's future as a solid storyteller.

An article in the campus paper opens the story with speculation that State needs a blocking back to work with brilliant ground-gainer Barry Raleigh, who is also a snooty fraternity member. The article suggests junior scholar Steve Holsom (Wholesome would have been too obvious!), who was a prep star but did not play football as a freshman and sophomore in favor of focusing on studies.

Holsom is an independent candidate for junior class president, while Raleigh has the support of the fraternities. Holsom hates the article in the paper, but he misses football and decides to turn out. Not, however, as a political move he assures Coach Gus Winkle. So the political halfback is Raleigh, who later pops off to the coach and is dismissed. But, in true pulp style, Raleigh is reinstated when Steve convinces the star to apologize. Like so many of Gault's characters, Raleigh learns the error of his ways and realizes what a great team he and Steve make.

In the end, Raleigh invites Steve to join his fraternity. Steve says he will never forget the gesture, but decides he is better off as an independent student—but also as friend and teammate. But there is no mention of the outcome of the election!

Gault often did not use full names for either people or teams. This actually helps the reader focus on the plot.

In the pulp sports era, the term "running back" was almost never used, although "blocking back" occasionally was and so was "tailback." It was often called "quarter," "half" and "full" in the backfield. What can be confusing for the modern reader is their use as defensive terms—what today are cornerbacks were called halfbacks (without the word "defensive") and what today are fullbacks were often linebackers (or backers, or backers-up, etc.). Quarterbacks almost always were the safety man (the term "safety" alone wasn't as often used). Defenses usually had more linemen and fewer linebackers and defensive backs than today.

"White Line Raider"

In this remarkable novelette of the pro game in Popular's *Fifteen Sports Stories* for January 1950, the coach is The Old Man with no other name and the team is the Cougars with no city. The league is obviously the NFL. The protagonist is Jeff Craig, a 10-year veteran Gault describes as "the greatest end in the game, they'd called him, for five of those years. [Don] Hutson was better offensively but Jeff was a sixty-minute end. In a day of specialists, of the platoon system, Jeff Craig was the last of the iron men." His buddy and eight-year teammate is tackle Lars Nelsen, "a big Swede." (Is there any other kind? Even though real Swedish spellings most often used "on" and not "en" at the end of names.)

The term "wide receiver" was not yet in use. "Split end" was often used, or "slot receiver," or "wide end," or whatever. Often, there was no distinction in pulp football between a tight end and a split end. They were all pass-catchers and blockers, as well, especially Jeff.

The entire story consists of the struggling but still effective Jeff's wise comments and bold suggestions to teammates, his frank thoughts about tactics, veterans, rookies and himself while always wondering if he had played one year too many. The story is totally about the consummate old pro and his intense loyalty to The Old Man and the Cougars. In the end, in the big game against the Bears in a snowstorm, the brilliant rookie quarterback Koski—to whom Jeff pays the ultimate compliment by calling him "a pro"—improvises a trick play to throw a game-winning touchdown pass to Jeff, whom the Bears thought could no longer run.

The ending is almost too cool for words: "I'm through," Jeff tells The Old Man. "I'm washed up. I was punchy, [during] three quarters of that game today. You didn't expect me next year, did you?" To which The Old Man responds, "Next year? Every year, I expect you, boy. You won't play, no. But you can scout, coach the ends, take tickets, sweep out the broadcasting booth! God, man, you can't quit—you are the Cougars! You've got a job as long as I live."

Gault's last line is brilliant and non-pulpy, to say the least: "It was very silly, Jeff realized. It was very silly for a man of thirty-one, weighing a hundred and ninety-six pounds, a big hulk of a jerk like him, to be crying."

"The Hard Way"

A spoiled college passing star, pro rookie Johnny Larson, joins the Cougars and his older brother Pudge, a five-year veteran in "The Hard Way," the lead story in Thrilling Publications' *Popular Sports* for Fall 1949. The coach, Jeff Talbot, expects Johnny to be a complete player, but Johnny doesn't want to block or run hard—he just figures his passing will get him by with the Cougars, who are obviously based on the Green Bay Packers. Although lazy, selfish and overconfident at the start, Johnny realizes, with the help of his gutty, oft-injured brother and his patient but stern coach, in 16 fast-paced pages that he won't have a pro career unless he becomes as tough and determined as they are. This isn't an unusual plot, but Gault's spare and unstinting writing style makes the story seem fresh.

Paul Ochem, a gutty 160-pound (!) backfield standout, is arm-in-arm with Johnny at the end of the story and the big game after being at Johnny's throat most of the way. Why? Gault's last line says it all: "Johnny was all right. Johnny was a pro."

"This Way to Glory"

Having successfully guided Northern University for six years at the top of the college game, 50-something coach Jug is back at Marlowe, where he started so many years ago, in *Thrilling Football* for Fall 1949. Jug's disagreements with the athletic policy and overemphasis on football at Northern led to his departure. Now he's back with a friend he once coached, easy-going former All-American John Sloan, now the locker-room attendant and campus philosopher. His son, Tod Marlowe, is as intense and self-centered on the football field as his father was not, but Tod has chosen Marlowe for its architectural studies program.

Tod's intensity bothers Jug's daughter, Sue, who would like to love him. Tod's headstrong attitude bothers Horse Mason, the team's other major talent, and pretty much everyone else on a potentially outstanding team. Tod is so troubled that he leaves the team, thinking he's had it with football. But when Marlowe's players find themselves up against Northern, and when Northern takes a 28–7 lead at halftime, Tod finally realizes what a heel he has been. Jug sees him suiting up in the locker room. But more important, he sees a changed man. Gault often gives athletes second and third chances via his fictional coaches and does so again.

Tod and Horse along with their inspired teammates make Jug and John Sloan—and Sue—as proud as possible, rallying for a 42–28 win with five touchdowns in the second half. As he tells Jug while heading out to play the second half, "They're [University] rough enough, but they're not 21 points better than we are. No team is."

Gault's Pulp Football Stories

All-American Football Magazine, Fall 1941, "A Pass and a Prayer"
Popular Football, Winter 1941, "Political Halfback"
Dime Sports, April 1942, "Suicide Schedule"
Sports Novels, January 1948, "The Heart Guy"
Fifteen Sports Stories, November 1948, "Touchdown Tornado" (as by Roney Scott)
Popular Sports, Fall 1949, "The Hard Way"
Thrilling Football, Fall 1949, "This Way to Glory"
Fifteen Sports Stories, March 1950, "Calamity Back"
Fifteen Sports Stories, September 1950, "Tinsel Tailback"
Popular Football, Fall 1950, "Blocking Brother"
Fifteen Sports Stories, January 1951, "White Line Raider"
Sports Novels, April 1951, "Star Bust"
Exciting Football, Fall 1951, "Glory Guy"
Sports Novels, December 1951, "The Last Big Yard"
Sports Novels, February 1952, "Fury Yard" (as by Roney Scott)

3

John D. MacDonald's Football and Baseball

In the years immediately before he began to become justifiably world famous and highly respected for his multitude of original paperback novels about mystery, crime and suspense, John D. MacDonald wrote six of the best of all pulp football short stories along with a single pulp baseball tale.

MacDonald (1916–1986) was a master of the hardboiled epic and thus his football and baseball stories were not exactly hearts-and-flowers hero worship, though they all had appropriate, satisfying endings, given all the surprises they offer.

Spoiler warning: I'm going to reveal all the clever twists and turns that make his stories so rewarding. Almost none of his sports stuff has been collected in anthologies—unlike his pulp science fiction and mysteries, the latter in *The Good Old Stuff* and *More Good Old Stuff* in the early 1980s. So you may want to skip this chapter, although it may take years to find his sport stories, which also included several under pen names and also covered boxing, basketball and other sports.

By the way, if his sports stories are ever collected, I hope they are not spoiled by updating, the way he himself insisted on modernizing details in his two volumes of mysteries. He meant well by turning a nickel into a quarter for phone booths and so much else (now he might not be able to find a phone booth!). He did not want the reader distracted by differences from the 1940s to the 1980s. But, for me, it's far more distracting to be sidetracked by the updates!

His sports stories, almost all written for Popular Publications along with a handful for Columbia, would make a great anthology in their "raw" form. I discussed one of his boxing classics involving an African American protagonist—rare in sports pulps—in my book *Ball Tales*. But here I am concerned only with football and baseball (if you skipped the "Introduction," read it now).

In one sense, MacDonald's sole known pulp baseball story, "Take the Bum Out!" in *Fifteen Sports Stories* for January 1949, may have been the most pulpish of his more than two dozen sports stories—but only because he had to contrive an unusual ball game in order to stay true to the psychological problems plaguing pitcher Johnny Lace and how he overcame them.

The story begins when Lace, back in the minor leagues after blowing a game as a rookie in the World Series, is pitching for the Bay City Sailors against the Jamison Jets. He realizes his problem: he simply can't handle the situation when two runners get on base at the same time. His father, Paul Lace, is in the stands, as MacDonald puts it so well, and soon "mourned a little death that had occurred within his son." With that phrase in the opening paragraph, I knew I could not put this story down.

After Johnny blows up and is taken out, he dreads seeing his father, who confirms that he believes Johnny should retire and join his company in his mid–20s as the graduate of an Ivy League university. Johnny's response: "Can't you see? I've got to lick it. Once it's licked, I can quit with honor. But if they drive me out I'll always carry it around with me." At the end of their discussion, Johnny concludes, "You might call it self-respect."

In the locker room the next day, hard-edged power-hitting star Tige Hancey responds to Johnny's appearance by saying, "The atomic kid! You know why he's the atomic kid?... Because he can blow up with the biggest bang in the business!" (In the wake of the two atomic bomb attacks on Japan that ended World War II in 1945, quips about atomic power became common.) Johnny feels like fighting, but backs away, and quickly is surprised to learn he is starting on the mound for the second day in a row (this was not unheard of if a pitcher was knocked out early the day before).

In the fourth inning, Johnny falls behind 11–1 when he gives up a grand slam to the Middletown Roamers, but his manager has already told him he will not be relieved, no matter what. He has struggled terribly from the start and even asked to be removed before allowing the slam. Johnny promptly walks the next three men and then—miracle of miracles—the shortstop alertly turns a bouncing ball into an unassisted triple play—the rarest feat in baseball!

The Sailors, thus inspired, score four to climb back into the game at 11–5. When Johnny returns to the mound and walks the first two hitters, he realizes his position and begins to laugh, causing his catcher to question his sanity. But Johnny has found his long-sought confidence and shouts to the two base runners, "Relax, you guys! You're going to die right there." He strikes out the side. He has found the old always-in-control Johnny that rose to the big leagues in only his second year out of college ball and shuts out the Roamers the rest of the way. In the bottom of the ninth, with the Sailors trailing 11–10 with two outs and a runner on base, Tige Hancey, second in the league in home runs, is due to bat. At that point, the entire team hears Johnny mock himself with good team humor when he asks Hancey, "How about one [a home run] for the atom kid?" The cocky, self-assured Hancey responds with a two-run homer and hysteria ensues.

Johnny now knows that whenever he leaves baseball, he will do so on his own terms. His father knows it too, having witnessed the wild game. As the story ends, Paul Lace thinks to himself, with a huge load off his mind, and MacDonald thus tells the reader, "There was little chance that the manager would talk. No, the manager would be glad to be labeled a smart man, a bush-league genius. There was a danger that, if it hadn't worked out, Johnny might hear of it. And Johnny would have resented the interference. Johnny would have been annoyed to learn that his father had convinced the manager of the wisdom of keeping Johnny on the mound—regardless." MacDonald concludes: "The manager had gambled and won—and had done Paul Lace a priceless favor. A favor which had given him back his son."

Improbable, yes. But not impossible, considering that the manager realized that

Johnny had major league ability and was pitching in a minor league game. Today, of course, a pitch count would be involved, but in 1949, that usually wasn't the case, for better or worse. Who knows what Johnny had done to his arm? But the reader knows what the manager and his father have done for his head.

Football Is Stellar, Too

Although sports pulp stories often involve the contrived and the improbable, there is almost never anything in the realm of fantasy and the nearly impossible, such as an ultra-heroic Texas Ranger or a superhero in the mold of Doc Savage or the Spider. Likewise, the villains of the piece in a sports story tend to be those with moral or ego issues, but far from the likes of the human but virtually impossible Joker in *Batman*.

So when MacDonald tries an unexpected twist and catches the reader by surprise, it's more a case of food for thought than anything else. Such is the case in "Last Chance Cleats" from *Sports Novels* for March 1949. Like he so often does, MacDonald tells the story in the first-person account of a protagonist, in this case Mike Burk, backfield coach at Harbour College, retained by new head coach Weston Walker. Burk had helped coach the team to 18 wins in a row heading into the new season, and received support from Rooney Mulligan, who took a pro job. But Walker, formerly a famous player and a spit-and-polish, no-nonsense type, received the bid from college officials.

Walker retains the coaching staff but cuts several of the returning players, including clumsy but hard-working and popular backfielder Red Rollins, who also served as something of a team mascot with his offbeat sense of humor. Harbour wins its first two games without Rollins, who is replaced by a steadier, far less quirky man. In his account of the second game, against the talented Michigan Raiders, MacDonald refers to fans thinking a 19-game winning streak (including Walker's first game the week earlier) could be at risk. But Harbour rallies to win and MacDonald states "Twenty-one wins in a row!" in a separate paragraph, which only makes it all the more obvious that the correct streak is now 20!

The big threat to the streak is the third opponent, the Gray Wave of Ohio, which is not only the favorite but hungers for redemption for Harbour's upset win the previous season. MacDonald writes far more on-field play-by-play than he usually does, if only to stress that Harbour seems devoid of defensive emotion despite leading 6–0 at the half. As the Gray Wave mows down the Harbour defenders in the fourth quarter and threatens to take the lead, Burk tells Walker that he needs help in the defensive backfield. Walker responds, "Send in anybody you think will do us some good." At which point, much to Walker's consternation and anger, he sees Red Rollins checking into the game! "As usual, Rollins refuses to wear a helmet," MacDonald writes, referring to an option in those leather-helmet days. When Walker asks how Rollins had a uniform, Burk responds, "I took one to him. He was up in the stands with a coat on over the uniform."

Rollins helps provide inspiration and on-field grit for his teammates, who finally stop the Gray Wave on the one-foot line. The Gray Wave is so dispirited that their last possession also goes for naught and Rollins and the team are next seen celebrating their real 21st consecutive win in the locker room (MacDonald does not refer to a number). Rollins is his comical self, standing on a chair warning "that next Saturday we got that tough team from Vassar coming in" (at the time, Vassar was an all-women's college). Walker ends the story by showing he has a sense of humor by telling Rollins to get some sleep because "I've got to have you in shape for the Vassar game" as the team roars with good-natured laughter. And as the story ends, Walker grins and tells Burk, "What are you going to teach me next, coach?"

Of the four authors plugged on the cover of this issue of *Sports Novels,* all have many more sports stories logged with Popular Publications than McDonald. The irony, though, is that only four months later, MacDonald would set what may have been a sports pulp record with four stories in *Fifteen Sports Stories* for July 1949! He wrote the boxing story "The Glory Punch" under his own name, but also penned the football story "Bye, Bye, Backfield" as by John Wade Farrell, the fishing story "Blue Water Fury" as by Scott O'Hara and the auto racing story "The Thunder Road" as by Peter Reed. Since Popular Publications, Columbia and Fiction House among them used more than 300 house names for stories, and relatively few of the authors published under house names have been identified by their true names, it is possible other authors may have had four stories in one issue. All publishers disliked using the same name on even two stories in the same issue, so that's a rarity in any pulp genre.

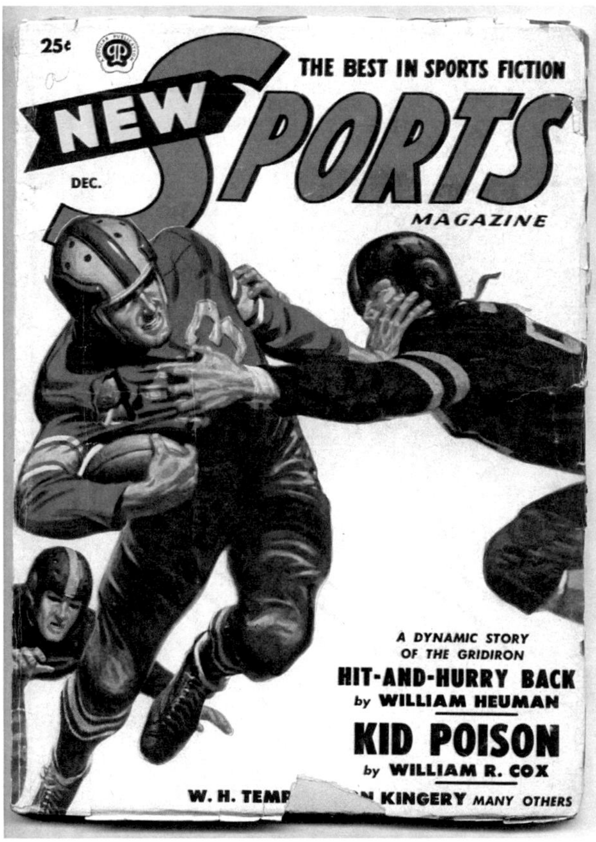

New Sports, December 1950 (copyright 1950 Popular Publications Inc.). A straight-arm directly to the mouth—in leather helmets!—would soon become a thing of the past.

"Bye, Bye, Backfield" is only six pages long, with a highly unusual setting in spring football drills for a new 29-year-old coach, former pro backfield star Bunny Hale, at successful Mideastern University. Mideastern comes off a bowl win produced by the third-year, post-war backfield of Bus Mulligan, Charlie Western, Sancho Sanchenelli and their leader Hal McKeaver, who narrates the story. Hal calls the backfield a "closed shop" heading into the foursome's senior year and talks of how anyone who threatens the status quo is made to look bad in drills. That was a common plot device in football stories, especially since it's always been the case that if one key player is made to look bad, it usually messes up the play.

Hale, however, is young enough to get into uniform when needed to teach his veteran foursome a lesson—in other words, to make them look bad in a genuine way. One can only imagine the headlines a college team would make today if a coach participated in scrimmage drills! It hasn't taken long for Hale to get wise to his backfield foursome, but at the same time, he acknowledges they are needed, even though it's important not only to develop depth for the current season, but also for the season following the graduation of the four stars.

The squad's depth is such that Hale's solution is unusual: He will play four different backfield foursomes, each with one of the returning stars! But the coach also tells McKeaver, "...I want to be able to send the four of you in as my fat-cat offensive backfield, my surprise package. I know how much you can get out of those [other three] boys."

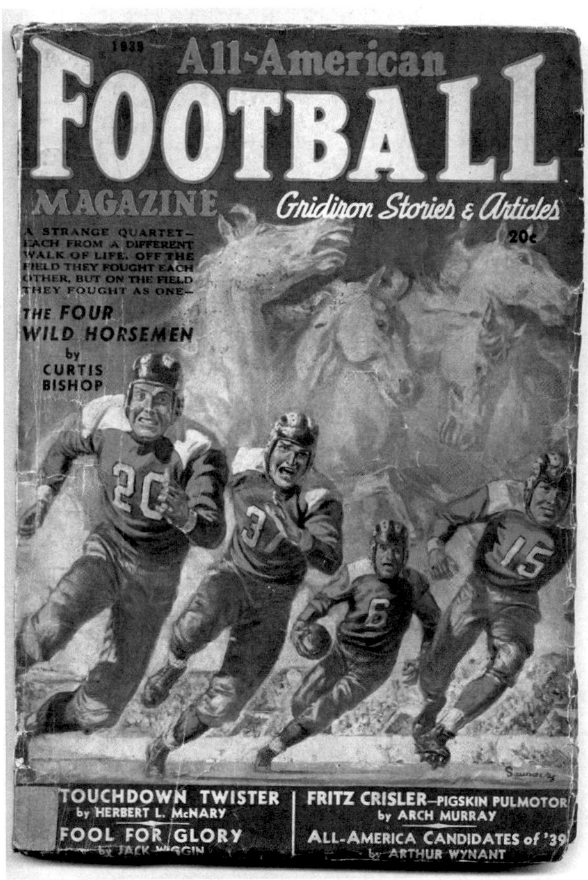

***All-American Football Magazine*, Fall 1939 (copyright 1939 Love Romances Publishing Co., Inc.). Obviously inspired by Notre Dame's "Four Horsemen of the Apocalypse" in the 1920s, Norman Saunders vividly illustrated "The Four Wild Horsemen" by Curtis Bishop.**

MacDonald adds in Hal's thoughts, "Suddenly, I liked the big guy [Hale] better than anyone I'd ever met."

In "Runaway Cleats" in *Sports Novels* for September 1948, MacDonald uses a plot often used by others—the hero with a secret past. In this case, lineman Ferris Gallahan—nicknamed "Sir Gallahan"—who says he is a transfer from Yohannus College, becomes the roommate of All-American Ed Stumpke, who narrates the story. A self-righteous teammate, Sid Raegen, eventually learns that there is no Yohannus College and that Gallahan served time in jail before cleaning up his life and seeking a fresh start.

The secret is known to the college president and the head coach, but not to the players until Raegen tells a few, including Stumpke. It doesn't take long for the players to threaten future pro Raegen with mayhem in practice unless he maintains silence, since Sir Gallahan has proven to be a talented teammate as well as popular with his teammates. As the story ends, Stumpke assures coach Mike Kaydee that the team will be just fine and Kaydee responds, "Maybe we'll play the brand of ball they do at Yohannus."

In contrast, "Six Points to Remember," in *Fifteen Sports Stories* for September 1949, features a plot unusual for the period—how a minority athlete, a Mexican running back named Juan Procuna, proves himself both on and off the field to his teammates at Northern Tech. Procuna, not a big man at 175 pounds, gets the chance to play because of injuries to teammates in a backfield dubbed "The Four Norsemen" because there was an Englishman, an Irishman, a German and a Jew. (One can only wonder how many puns were made about Notre Dame's "Four Horsemen of the Apocalypse," as named by famed writer Grantland Rice.)

As Wade, the lineman narrating the story, says, Northern Tech travels to "deep in the heart of you-know-what." (Apparently, there were concerns about alienating readers in the South.) The coach gives Procuna the option of sitting out but Procuna tells him he wants to play and, thus, is willing to take the inevitable slurs. A Big Green lineman opposite the narrator tells him, "Now send me that greaser you got back there," which is only the first in a series of slurs along with physical assaults, including an eye bruise–causing fist. When Procuna is pounded unmercifully, the team doctor tries to take him out, but Procuna shouts, "They want me out of the game, they better bring out a pistol and shoot me."

The Northern Tech players have been won over, bonding with "Juanito," as he calls himself, and shouting "Amigo!" and "Viva Villa." (MacDonald means well here, but references to Pancho Villa would not go over so well not too many years in the future.) The Mexican back eventually is rewarded. He scores one touchdown in a lopsided win and also takes out two Big Green defenders with a block—as usual, MacDonald does not overstate the heroics. And at the end of the story, when Procuna's teammates are wondering if there will be trouble, Big Green players greet Procuna with handshakes and acknowledge that his courage has taught them something. On the train ride home, the story ends with Juanito teaching his teammates how to sing "a very catchy little number called Maria Bonita."

Two Football Wives Win Out

One of the three "full-length novels" in *Fifteen Sports Stories* for November 1949 was an 18-page story titled "Run the Man Down." It's the story of Tom Lamar, a star halfback at Carvel College who married young and is having financial problems along with his wife, Carol Ann, and their toddler, Tommy. A talented teammate and Tom's primary blocker, Tide Wallinger, has succumbed to the blandishments of Southern Idaho University and leaves the Carvel team while attempting to take Tom with him to join what amounts to a pro football team in a college setting. Tom loves the study of the science of how growing food can be improved to benefit America and the post-war world and that's how he wound up at Carvel on the GI Bill following service in World War II. Carol Ann supports Tom's ambitions and is willing to sacrifice for him, but she isn't willing to see him give up his non-football dreams just to accept money to play big-time football.

She tells Tom that she and Tommy will not be joining him in Idaho. "It's the nearest thing to death I can think of," she says, talking about leaving her husband in order to keep her conscience clean. That leads to Tom's decision to stay at Carvel even though they are so poor they can't get a grocery loan from a local businessman. The story ends with Tom and Carol Ann comfortable with their decision—and then they find three 50-dollar bills left by Wallinger as a loan—part of the payment Wallinger received to go to Idaho. Wallinger's note reads, "But truly and honestly it is not a gift. It's a loan. Conscience money, you might say. And when you get to work on those green little growing things, Lamar, I want it back with interest. Adios, you second-rate athlete with the first-rate wife."

There is very little football in this story, but the morality and ethics are worth countless touchdowns.

"Fight, Scrub, Fight!" in *New Sports* for February 1949 is also billed as a "smashing football novel" even though it is only 17 pages long and takes about 45 minutes to read. It's the story of Tony Strega and his wife of eight months, Loren Quinn. Strega, a 29-year-old former college and pro player, looks at football as a no-nonsense game of angles and logic and thus approaches his first year as coach at small Adams College without emotion and without sentiment, even though Loren insists that "two and two aren't always four."

Strega intends to use Adams and his small 24-man squad as a stepping stone, but Loren likes the town, the college and the idea of raising a family in such a setting.

When a topic of sentiment involving the possible first-ever playing time in the traditional Greely game for two third-generation Adams players, third-string seniors Frank Mercer and Julius White, comes up, Tony tells Loren, "...I'm thinking of Tony Strega. First, last and all the time. Nobody but you in this wide world gives a damn about Tony Strega. So [what happens if] I put them in. So we lose the game. Am I the guy who upheld tradition? [The players' grandfathers and fathers helped beat Greely.] Not on your life! I'm the guy with a hole in his season record. Believe me!"

Loren responds, "You're hard, Tony" and decides she won't attend the game. They talk a bit more but Tony shuts off the conversation by saying, "Honey, if I spent my time worrying about the feelings of the boys on the squad, I might as well buy a pick and start looking for a construction gang."

There follows a series of events and injuries that force Mercer III and White III into the game in the fourth quarter. For a small squad, it's not that improbable. Loren changes her mind about attending the game. White plays with three broken bones in his hand and Mercer barely gets the ball over the goal line for a game-deciding touchdown. Strega is overcome with emotion about "those crazy, wonderful kids," perhaps referring to the entire squad. Loren asks him "Darling, how much is two plus two?" and he responds, "...usually four Loren, or five, or six or seven." Suddenly, life for both of them at Adams College doesn't seem so bad, after all.

MacDonald was far from the only genre author (mostly mystery and science fiction writers, but sometimes also those who penned mostly westerns and air war stories) to tackle sports pulp fiction before moving on. He never wrote a sports novel, and neither did famed science fiction author James Blish. But Blish did write sports about the same time MacDonald did, mostly for a different company. Let's tackle that next....

4

James Blish's Versatility

Most people reading this will know James Blish as a noteworthy science fiction writer. Few of Blish's fans will realize, however, that in his first decade as a professional writer, Blish turned in a remarkably prolific stretch of pulp sports stories, capped by one of the earliest to deal with the issue of race in baseball.

Three years after Jackie Robinson broke the modern Major League Baseball color line in 1947 with the Brooklyn Dodgers, the majority of the then-16 MLB teams still had not been integrated. Future African American Hall of Famers such as Willie Mays, Hank Aaron and Ernie Banks had yet to reach the major leagues. James Blish, however, perhaps inspired by Robinson's Most Valuable Player season in 1949, published "Big-Time Rookie" in Columbia's *All Sports* for April 1950, dealing with the tribulations of African American prospect Billy Trenton. (Mays played in the old Negro Leagues until his first minor league season at age 19 in 1950, so Blish may not have heard of him when he wrote "Big-Time Rookie.")

Blish (1921–1975), who sold his first science fiction story before he turned 19 in 1940, has seldom, if ever, received much credit for "Big-Time Rookie" since he wrote the story as by V.K. Emden, a pseudonym he seldom used. The story was among his final few during the 1947–1950 period when he wrote at least 20 sports stories for Columbia, Marvel, Ace and Fiction House. Blish's career in science fiction was taking off by 1950 and he may not have wanted to use his name on pulp sports stories any longer. The only such story to use his real name as late as 1950 was "Casey and the Second String," a tennis tale that appeared in Columbia's *Super Sports* for September 1950.

In a 14-month period from December 1947 through January 1949, Blish saw published no fewer than 16 pulp sports stories, including 10 dealing with either baseball or football. Not many genre writers have ever enjoyed such productivity in such a short span. Even more remarkable, Blish was a sports writing unknown. That is underscored by the fact that his only cover plug was for his unusual "Fullback Frankenstein" in Marvel's *Sports Leaders* for April 1948, the first issue. And for the story's title, Marvel's editor used "Football Frankenstein" on the cover (perhaps that was the working title).

"Big-Time Rookie" was certainly Blish's most important story, even though it was not cover featured and, indeed, was the back-of-the-book short story. Ironically, one of the three cover featured stories was "Hate That Horsehide!" written by science fiction author Lester del Rey under his favorite pen name, Philip St. John. Columbia either did not want to publicize a story dealing with race or did not realize its unusual nature, though that is hard to believe.

As the story opens, Billy Trenton is the newest man on the Cougars but is struggling, although he is batting cleanup. Manager Seamus MacMahoney wonders if *Banner* sports writer Fred Harkness could be correct: "Cougar pennant chances have lessened by half this season. With a mistaken gesture of brotherly love the club's owners have brought a negro [*sic*] boy out of the sticks who used to play phenomenal baseball—in the sticks. Billy Trenton, the new third sacker, is out of his depth on a big-league team. Manager MacMahoney, who saw his best years some years back, can't seem to find any fault with Trenton, but the men who have to play with a stumblebum can find plenty. There's trouble brewing when a good team has to buck a third-rate player's errors. Cougar fans are beginning to feel cheated...."

The manager thinks: "The kid was trying hard. Too hard, maybe?..." But soon Mears, a veteran catcher who aspires to become the manager, is thrown out when Trenton singles to centerfield with two outs. Mears bitterly complains to the manager about Trenton's seeming inability to hit to right, but the manager mutters "Stow it!" and the game continues. After the Cougars lose, the manager meets with Trenton to ask why he's so tense at bat, why he's trying too hard despite his obvious athletic ability. Trenton tells the manager that he's worried because his new bride, 17-year-old Hallie Lou, is being urged by her parents to annul the marriage. Hallie Lou has gone home but not to seek a split. She just wants to calm her parents. But that only makes Trenton press even harder because "I gotta make good!"

The manager's wife, Annie, says Harkness, a friend of Mears, is trying to start a race riot with his incendiary material in the *Banner* about players' acceptance of Trenton, but the manager has bigger trouble with three games left in the season: The doctor has told him his eye weakness including blind spells are being caused by the great tension he is under. The manager thus decides that both Mears and Trenton will have to go to save his sanity and possibly his eyesight. With both benched, MacMahoney sees his team hustle hard enough to win two close games heading into the all-important pennant-deciding contest. With Annie earlier having asked him about the unfairness involved in benching Billy, Trenton is back in the last game. Thinking he is nonetheless destined to leave the team, Billy loosens up, doubles twice and drives in a key run to keep the Cougars ahead. Late in the game, the manager calls Hallie out of her box seat to tell her that he will not release Billy after all—while Billy obviously is playing well because he has no motivation to try too hard—and Hallie's parents, attending the game, see for themselves that Hallie's husband is a worthwhile man. As the story ends, Billy legs out a triple and the future is bright for all concerned. There is no conclusive material about the final score or about Mears and the nasty writer, but Blish lets the reader assume that all will be well for Billy and Hallie.

The story is realistic enough to be believable, so Blish scored a triumph with a little-known landmark in sports fiction.

"Fullback Frankenstein"

Perhaps Blish's most interesting football story is "Fullback Frankenstein." It's a short story dealing with the puzzle of journeyman pro Henry "Freeze" Fenderson, who displays phenomenal offensive, defensive and punting ability but never shows any emotion and therefore has caused problems and confusion for his teammates.

Fenderson, who did not play in college and has drifted from team to team, performs so well and with so little boastfulness or desire for glory that player-manager Ralph Payne of the Swallows in the Mountain League (where all but one of Blish's six football stories is set) is determined to develop the patience to help Freeze.

Toward the end of the nine-page story, a nasty teammate with a hatred for Freeze shockingly kicks him during a pileup. The game is halted to attend to Freeze's possible rib injuries, but only Payne has seen the kick and immediately fires his own man. Payne, in front of the team, takes the opportunity to ask Freeze about the kick and Freeze acknowledged he suffered a similar serious injury in an accident as a boy and lost the ability to use the nerves in his facial muscles. It turns out that Freeze didn't want people to know because he sought no sympathy and had always wanted his teammates to believe he earned any success.

Payne tells his players: "This guy you've been bucking and calling a snob and a showoff has been through hells you'll never even be able to imagine. He doesn't show it on his face because he can't. Speak up, Freeze. I know it, and there's no point in keeping it a secret any longer."

Freeze's teammates apologize for their criticism and the game continues, with the Swallows showing a newfound unity and drive while winning easily.

The plot twist is so unusual that most readers were likely to have been surprised by the final-page revelations. The title is a bit of a giveaway—at least I thought so—even though Blish was more or less forced to use the solo "Frankenstein" instead of the correct reference to Doctor Frankenstein's monster. Of course, by that time the Frankenstein name had been used incorrectly in the titles of several classic movie versions from Universal.

Remarkable Sports Production

Few references to Blish's pulp sports stories exist in his biographical entries and no complete list has been compiled until now. Here's the complete list in chronological order:

Sports Fiction, June 1947: "Sabres Are for Saps" as by Luke Torley (fencing)
Sports Fiction, December 1947: "Bats for Brains" (baseball)
All Football Stories, December 1947: "Backfield Business" (football)
Complete Sports, December 1947: "Phantom Blades" (hockey)
All Basketball Stories, Winter 1947–1948: "Dribble Trouble" (basketball)
Ace Sports, January 1948: "Back Seat Hoopster" (basketball)
Real Sports, April 1948: "Touchdown Destiny" (football)
Sports Leaders, April 1948: "Fullback Frankenstein" (football)

Best Sports, May 1948: "Puck Poison" (hockey)
Big Sports, May 1948: "Ten Yards to Glory" (football)
Sports Fiction, July 1948: "Scrapple at the Crease" (hockey)
Big Baseball Stories, August 1948: "Slide, Sucker, Slide" (baseball)
Sports Fiction, October 1948: "Double-Clutch Danger" (baseball)
Super Sports, October 1948: "The Hustler" (baseball)
Sports Fiction, January 1949: "Gridiron Workhorse" (football)
Super Sports, January 1949: "The Touchdown Tenderfoot" (football)
Sports Fiction, March 1949: "Cinder Saint" (track)
All Sports, April 1950: "Big-Time Rookie" as by V.K. Emden (baseball)
Baseball Stories, Spring 1950: "The Big Hate" as by Luke Torley (baseball)
Super Sports, September 1950: "Casey and the Second String" (tennis)

Mind-Boggling Productivity

Consider this: In the 14-month span for pulps dated from December 1947 through January 1949, Blish published 15 sports stories and four science fiction stories, along with at least three western stories, one crime story and one jungle story for at least 24 stories. Granted, none were novels, but it's still production-plus, especially in the sports field. In all, in a little more than three years from June 1947 through September 1950, Blish published 20 sports stories, with six about football and six about baseball, plus others involving basketball, hockey, track, tennis and fencing, appearing in 13 different magazines.

When Blish began writing sports stories in 1947, there were only six regularly published science fiction magazines with non-reprint fiction: *Amazing Stories, Astounding Science Fiction* (which had already become a digest), *Fantastic Adventures, Planet Stories, Startling Stories* and *Thrilling Wonder Stories.* Popular's *Super Science Stories* resumed (following a long break) with its January 1949 issue, featuring a Blish story right away. But in 1947 and 1948, there were more sports titles than science fiction titles—a situation that would be massively reversed in the 1950s, with a solid market until the late 1950s, by which time the pulps were gone and the digest boom of the 1950s was over.

Blish, then, showed a noteworthy ability to adjust for a short period from one of the weakest markets in history for new science fiction—nothing but six well-established pulps—by selling sports stories at a pace only a handful of genre writers ever matched.

Robert Silverberg didn't get that chance in sports before he became a science fiction legend, since his seven sports stories all appeared in 1956 and 1957 as the genre died out, as you'll see next.

5

Robert Silverberg's Baseball

The amazingly prolific science fiction writer Robert Silverberg was among the youngest authors ever to sell a story to a sports pulp. He was also among the last, with short stories in each of the final six sports pulps.

Silverberg was 19 years old when he sold a science fiction story to Columbia's *Future Fiction* for October 1954, titled "The Silent Colony." He went on to win a remarkable number of major science fiction awards and distinctions for an equally noteworthy number of novels and shorter stories.

Not many people, however, are aware of Silverberg's sports fiction stories, which were published within little more than a year, again for Columbia, the last publisher of pulp sports magazines.

Silverberg's first published sports story appeared in *Ten Story Sports* for April 1956, meaning he wrote it before he turned 21. He was born January 15, 1935. The story was "This Isn't Last Year," a baseball tale like all but one of his seven pulp sports stories.

His other baseball stories were "Bat-Shy," in *Ten Story Sports* for July 1956; "Stretch Drive" in *Ten Story Sports* for October 1956; "Beanball Hurler" in the 1956 issue of *Super Sports*; and two in the 1957 issue of *Super Sports*: "Egghead on the Mound" and "Outfield Outlaw," the latter as by Calvin M. Knox, one of his best-known pseudonyms. (He also had a basketball story, "Goon Boy," in *Ten Story Sports* for January 1957, the last issue.) All seven baseball stories were above-average stories that forced the reader to ask quickly with interest, "So what's going to happen to this character?"

Silverberg had the distinction of having a cover-teased story in only his third appearance, "Stretch Drive." Both of his stories in the 1957 *Super Sports* annual were also teased, so he wound up being the last author to have his name on a pulp sports cover. The last issue of *Ten Story Sports* hit the stands late in 1956, but the 1957 *Super Sports* did not go on sale until the beginning of spring training in 1957. I am fortunate to have a copy with the arrival date of March 17, 1957, meaning that's when it went on sale (or perhaps a day or two later) where this particular copy was sold.

Silverberg's stories are totally accessible with grammar at a higher level than most sports stories. He used a lot less sports slang than many writers did from the 1930s to the 1950s. Anyone could read a Silverberg sports story and readily understand it.

"This Isn't Last Year" opens in May for complacent Bernie Kingston, second-year third baseman of the Stags at age 24. His rookie year for a pennant winner was good enough that in real life he would have been Rookie of the Year in many seasons with a .329 batting average, 27 homers, 92 runs batted in and 32 stolen bases—statistics many real-life winners of the honor have not matched. But, 10 pounds heavier after spending the winter on the banquet circuit, he is so complacent on the bases and in other aspects of the game that an angry teammate, grizzled catcher Charlie Gorman, tells Bernie that he is "good hit, no hustle"—a clever takeoff on the standard "good hit, no field."

Bernie's reaction to a negative newspaper evaluation—he's called a fat-cat—is merely to say, "I'm not lazy, I'm careful. I'm hitting .368; I've already hit 15 homers this season." But the manager is so frustrated by Bernie's obvious lack of effort on the bases that he benches him. Bernie finally realizes with an emotional panic that he has placed his career in danger. Gorman, who has been Bernie's most severe critic, also realizes that Bernie has learned his lesson. Gorman, called on to pinch-hit, slams a run-scoring double to tie the game 10–10 but fakes an injury, forcing Bernie into the game as his pinch-runner because he is the last available substitute. Gorman walks off with a wink at Bernie, who suddenly realizes the chance he has been given.

Bernie, who had been a daring and usually successful base runner in his rookie season, steals third base and, with a weak hitter at bat, also steals home for an 11–10 comeback victory. As the story ends, Bernie tells Gorman, "Thanks, Charlie. I was just a fake big-leaguer up to now. It took a real one to straighten me out."

In "Bat-Shy," former catcher Kelly Langston, who has switched positions because he once was hit on the head during a batter's swing, learns to conquer his fears when challenged by teammates. By the last paragraph, Langston has learned there is nothing more important than courage and agrees to help his team in an emergency by returning to play catcher. Right below the end of the story, a Columbia house ad plugs Silverberg with "Another topnotch [*sic*] baseball story by Robert Silverberg, 'Beanball Hurler,' is among the champion features in the 1956 *Super Sports*."

In "Beanball Hurler," new Bears player-manager Max Banson hates "head-hunter" Charlie Valdez of the Quakers and lets the fiery pitcher know it during a scuffle. Soon, however, the Bears' owner figures Valdez can help his team and tells an appalled Banson that he has purchased the controversial pitcher. Banson says he won't start Valdez but soon realizes he is endangering his own career with his hatred of the pitcher. Later, summoning up his courage, he challenges Valdez to tell him why he's so violent. Valdez breaks down, asks for help from Banson, and tells him that he can't control his temper when players and fans razz him. Banson tells Valdez to get the anger out of his system by firing his next throw to him at shortstop. The ploy works and Banson is convinced that Valdez has won his inner battle "and will win twenty."

"Stretch Drive," Silverberg's longest story at 20 pages, is the up-and-down tale of 31-year-old outfielder Joe Rice, who has spent almost all of his 10 years in pro baseball in the minors. He had an unsuccessful brief spell with the Flatbush Bums in 1954, and even though he loved the game, he became frustrated enough to enlist in the Navy. Unable to get a job when he leaves military service, he rejoins the Bums because by law they have to take him back for a certain amount of time. He has more bad days than good for manager Charley Lang, but both Lang and Rice eventually realize that Rice is the consummate teammate, helping the other players any way he can both off and on the field. He eventually sacrifices his body for the team and ruins his arm, but Lang won't let him leave the team to rejoin the Navy. Lang tells Joe that he will become a coach and will have a place in baseball as long as he wants it. In many ways, this is Silverberg's best story.

One oddity is that when Silverberg has the general manager talking with Joe about his lack of success in his first big-league stint, he has him going 4 for 23 at bat for a .131 average. Well, that's actually .174. In fact, any hitter with four hits cannot hit .131. He can bat .133 (4 for 30) or .129 (4 for 31), but he can't mathematically hit .131 with four hits!

The least important of Silverberg's sports stories were his last two, "Egghead on the Mound" and, as by Knox, "Outfield Outlaw." Nonetheless, they still tell the stories of appealing characters. In "Egghead," pitching bonus baby Tommy Thomas, having just graduated from college, brings a bookish approach to life and pitching, thus attracting unwelcome attention from the lesser intellects in the clubhouse. By story's end, he has not only proven himself a winning pitcher, but a brave sort with his fists and his book. In "Outlaw," talented rookie centerfielder Rex Lund learns that hogging all the plays and attention in the outfield only backfires on him when the other two fly chasers conspire to give Lund a lot more work than he ever bargained for.

These stories show how Silverberg's gain—a fabulous career in the science fiction field—was fictional sports writing's loss.

6

Michael Avallone's Baseball

Michael Avallone was among the most prolific paperback and magazine fiction writers of the second half of the 20th century, most notably for wild tales of his eccentric and most colorful private detective Ed Noon in dozens of novels and short stories.

Avallone, however, published six baseball stories in the last days of the sports pulps, leaving many readers wishing his market for them had not disappeared before he even reached age 32. Like other genre authors who were far better known for mystery and/or science fiction, such as John D. MacDonald, William Campbell Gault and James Blish, he wrote of sports well enough to tantalize readers into wondering how far he might have gone in that field as well.

Avallone (1924–1999) sold his first pulp story when he was 25 years old to Fiction House's *Baseball Stories* for Summer 1950. "Aw, Let the Kid Hit" was only four pages long (including one with an illustration), but it will still leave an impression on anyone who reads it.

It's the tale of Browns rookie Oll (no first name used), sent up as a pinch-hitter for his first major league at-bat against Roxy Carter, one of the most successful veteran pitchers in the major leagues. Carter's league-leading Hawks held a 12–1 lead. Avallone has Carter thinking, "Hmmm. Big, strong looking. Shoulders are plenty broad. Doesn't look scared either. The way most bushers look in their first at bat in the big time. Never heard of this guy before. Must be a new one."

Impressed with the rookie's poise while standing in against a called strike on a fastball and a ball on a curve, Carter decides to shake off his catcher's signal and to try "a sizzling fast ball that was all steam and no curve (meaning no movement). Just a high, hard one made to order for power hitters." Avallone follows with a nice description of the rookie's first swing:

> Oll, who had given a good imitation of still life up until then, kicked into action like a supercharger. His arms, legs and bat did a chain reaction routine and Roxy Carter's fastest delivery tore a seat apart in the upper deck.... Roxy was delighted. He'd been right, of course. Should have known by the way the kid held that right shoulder of his in the dropped position at the beginning of his swing. Batters get real power that way. Roxy knew. Hadn't he pitched against the best of them in his time?

In real life, a number of players had debuted with a home run in their first at-bats by 1950, and many more have done so since.

In the locker room, the catcher, referred to as both Deacon Boyle and Doyle (pulp editors did not always serve their writers well), expresses great anger and frustration at Carter's pitch to the rookie. Tempers eventually flare, after half a page of outrage, and Carter rams a balled-up first into Boyle's left eye. But the catcher has a reputation as a back-alley fighter and begins beating his ace pitcher unmercifully. Suddenly ... in the best Ed Noon fashion!—"a big green kid ... plucked Boyle backwards and spun him around.... He recognized Oll in the split second before the kid's huge right hand rocked him off his feet. A left hook, even harder than the right, sent him crashing to the floor."

When Carter is helped to his feet and sees his rookie rescuer from the opponent he has just beaten, he thanks him. Oll replies, "Shucks. It was a pleasure, Mr. Carter." The pitcher, after telling the kid not to call him Mr. Carter, quickly realizes how unusual it is to see an opponent in his locker room and asks him why he's there. After a bit of back-and-forth, the kid ends the story with a request: "I was wondering, seeing as how you're my first homer victim, could I have your autograph, Mr. Carter?"

"One More Miracle!"

Roxy Carter returns for another sentimental turn in "One More Miracle!," Avallone's second baseball story, in *Baseball Stories* for Spring 1952. This was a featured novelette, a realistic look at how hero worship can influence a baseball star's already-inflated ego. As the story opens, Dr. Mal Ferguson has given grade-school baseball fan Danny Montgomery only a few weeks to live and has agreed to a hospital visit by Comets slugger Biff Baxter, the Babe Ruth of his day. Everyone is agog at the hospital anticipating a post-game visit by Baxter, who is listed with a career total of 506 home runs (in real life, by 1952 only Babe Ruth's 714, Jimmie Foxx's 534 and Mel Ott's 511 had surpassed that total in regular league games).

The cynical-cum-sweet story is greatly enhanced with remarkable detail over several pages involving hospital scenes, conversations, people and commitments. Baxter has had a bad game that day, striking out with the bases loaded to end it, and is reminded by the manager Niles that he has a commitment to visit the ill-fated boy in the hospital. Baxter has forgotten and must break a date with his girl, whom Niles dismisses (correctly, as it turns out) as a gold-digger. When Baxter finally arrives at the hospital, Danny asks him to hit a home run for him in the next game in a scene possibly influenced by the 1948 film *The Babe Ruth Story*. Baxter, overwhelmed by the moment and his own ego-driven confidence, offers to hit two homers!

After much more talk and headlines informing the world of his promise—it's amazing how Avallone put so much telling detail in such a basic plot—Roxy Carter, this time pitching for the Tigers, has struck out Baxter twice. But on his third trip to the plate, Baxter lofts a ball barely over the 297-foot mark in left field for a home run he considers embarrassingly cheap. But he has at least fulfilled what Danny asked for. It was Biff who volunteered to hit two balls out.

The Tigers take a 12–6 lead with Roxy still on the mound when Baxter comes up for his final chance. By this time, Baxter has learned so much about himself and his world, having acknowledged with emotional frustration to Niles that he has promised too much and that he is filled with regret. Niles agrees, but tells him, "You'll do it, Biff. You can do anything." To which Biff responds, "You know what? I think I can too."

Carter realizes Biff's position. He throws two balls to Baxter, giving him the perfect hitter's count at two balls, no strikes. Carter throws a strike and Biff blasts the pitch into the stands. Everyone goes nuts. But Niles, realizing what may have happened, confronts Carter well after the game. Carter at first denies he served up a cripple for Baxter to hit, but Niles persists. Carter finally fesses up: "You was the one man I knew I couldn't fool, you old houn' dog," Carter tells the wise old manager. " Yup, I gave the good one to Biff. Twern't right, maybe but we were so far in front, I figured it wouldn't hurt none. Leastways, we won."

Niles thanks him, not even having to say he would never tell anyone else. "I'm sayin' Thanks, Roxy. For Biff, for me and for Danny Montgomery. One more home run can't hurt this game. Not baseball." Roxy ends it: "Miracles don't hurt none, either."

"Headache Hurler"

Avallone's third baseball story, "Headache Hurler" in Columbia's *Ten Story Sports* for October 1955, was his only cover-featured tale of the sport. This is the lead novelette and tells the tale of rookie pitcher Trimble, whose first name is never mentioned.

Trimble is obviously an extremely talented prospect as a much-needed starter for the World Series champion Hawks and for manager Hal Hollis and coach Red Burns, who already have a great starting trio. But Trimble obviously has a chip on his shoulder, not to mention a foul temper, after several seasons in the minor leagues, especially his three years in the Texas League.

When a teammate commits an error and costs Trimble his first start, the kid throws a stunning temper tantrum on the mound and, later, he shockingly walks before either the manager or relief pitcher can talk with him. Hollis demands an explanation and Trimble decides it's time to open up. He has a long talk with the manager and coach about how difficult it was to endure his less-than-stellar teammates in the minors. Even though his records were good, they would have been even better without so many tainted losses.

Hollis, portrayed as wise and filled with humanity, decides that he'll give Trimble more opportunities if only he'll promise to take the advice of his veteran pitching teammates—and he'll only realize that errors are part of the game. In the end, Trimble does just that, when he wins a game despite committing an embarrassing error of his own.

Avallone was clearly one of the best storytellers to work for Columbia in its last days as a pulp publisher, but the editors didn't always provide enough help. For example, in "Last Place Clubs Don't Die" in the 1956 issue of *Super Sports* (by then an annual), the talented young author refers to a playoff game as "the most drawn out, dog and cat fight since Bobby Thompson slew the 1950 Dodgers." Earlier in the story there were accurate references to Babe Ruth and Carl Hubbell, but in this case it was Bobby Thomson who beat the Dodgers in 1951.

Michael Avallone's Pulp Baseball Stories

Baseball Stories, Summer 1950, "Aw, Let the Kid Hit"
Baseball Stories, Spring 1952, "One More Miracle!"
Ten Story Sports, October 1955, "Headache Hurler"
Super Sports, 1956 issue, "Last Place Clubs Don't Die"
Ten Story Sports, January 1957, "Breadwinners Don't Loaf"
Super Sports, 1957 issue, "Power the Ball Plateward"

7

Duane Decker's Baseball

Duane Decker wrote one of the most collectible series of all sports novels with the same cast of characters, the 13-book Blue Sox epic published from 1947 to 1964, the year of his passing in his mid–50s. Many collectors have expressed regret that the series could not run longer, so beloved were the books in their time and still avidly collected and read today. I extensively detailed the series in a chapter in my book *Ball Tales*. But what I did not have at the time were all of Decker's pulp baseball stories. What a surprise I encountered when I finally found them all!

Decker (1910–1964) wrote only baseball stories for the pulps: just nine in all. But he was notably prolific and also contributed much fiction and non-fiction alike to the slicks for many years, far more than he ever wrote for the pulps. He wrote eight of his baseball stories for publisher Martin Goodman's line of pulps in 1947 and 1948. Those were the two years that Timely/Marvel comics publisher Goodman tried something never attempted by anyone else in such a limited time frame: he published 10 distinct sports pulp titles! Only two of them made it into the 1950s, as I've detailed in another chapter.

Three of his stories were much-abbreviated versions of his first two books: *Good Field, No Hit* (1947), the story of light-hitting, combative and intelligent third baseman Johnny Madigan, and *Starting Pitcher* (1948), the tale of converted shortstop Eddie Lasky.

Madigan's story was later published as the lead "novel"—actually a 20-page novelette—in the first issue of *Big Baseball Stories* for May 1948 and it was titled "Home Runs Don't Count." The date of the magazine is nine months later than the listed date of August 1947 that *Good Field, No Hit* was published by M.S. Mill (soon subsumed by Morrow, which reprinted the book several times). That doesn't necessarily mean Decker sold the story to Goodman's pulp line well after it saw book publication; pulp stories were often held in inventory.

The Surprise Revealed

But what was a surprise was to see that Decker's lone non–Marvel baseball story, a short titled "Last Chance Chucker," was published in Popular Publications' *Sports Novels* for November 1948. Like the pulp version of Madigan, this was an abbreviated version of the Eddie Lasky/Blue Sox story in *Starting Pitcher*. The surprise was that likely selling on the racks at about the same time was *Complete Sports* for October 1948, with the exact same Lasky plot expanded into a novelette titled "Base-Thief to Mound Marvel" but with entirely different names for all teams and players!

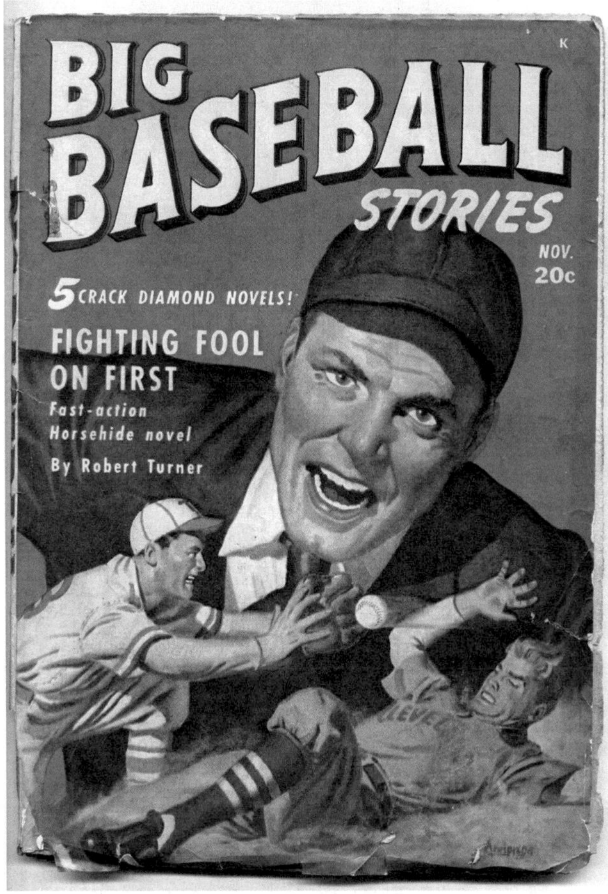

***Big Baseball Stories*, November 1948 (copyright 1948 Interstate Publishing Corp.). Allen Anderson contributes an unusually symbolic cover centered on an umpire's call on a slide for this Marvel title.**

Cases of sports plot similarities from different authors appearing in the same year, if not at virtually the same time, likely occurred more than once in the pulp era. But the same plot at the same time, right down to almost identical verbiage in some cases, by the same author may never have otherwise happened, though I can't be certain. It's as though Decker plagiarized himself on this story. I suppose it is possible that he wrote "Last Chance Chucker" earlier and then decided he could sell a version more than twice as long.

"Last Chance Chucker" is a 9-page, back-of-the-book story. The plot is how young all-star shortstop Eddie Lasky, injured rescuing a dog in an off-season vehicle accident, finds his speed on the bases and in the field limited too drastically to play at such a high level. Blue Sox manager Jug Slavin, well aware of this, offers him a utility role, but Lasky soon realizes he wants to return to stardom as pitcher. In his first start, in an emergency replacing a supposedly injured teammate, Lasky pitches a no-hitter for eight innings. But he is still so team-oriented that he injures his hand in a risky gamble to score the eventual winning run. It's then revealed that Slavin faked the teammate's injury to give Lasky more confidence—and to see how long Lasky could last on the mound if he was sent out with the idea of lasting only a few innings.

In "Base-Thief to Mound Marvel," an 18-page story, all-star outfielder and base stealer Whitey Lane is in the same position, learning that a car injury (sans the dog) now limits him from playing centerfield at the all-star level. Like Lasky, but with a lot more pitching tips and other story-expanding elements thrown in, Lane pitches a shutout (but not a no-hitter) and scores the winning run with hustle (but is not injured).

Similar Phrasing

In a paragraph describing Opening Day, it's said for Lane,

> In that morning's papers, they predicted what Big DiMag and Williams would hit and how many homers guys like Mize and Kiner would collect and how many victories the Fellers, Newhousers and Blackwells would chalk up. Then, they ventured predictions on the pennant races and a couple of them were so bold as to say Whitey Lane would probably do a whole lot to spark the Blue Sox to a pennant. They figured he'd hit his reliable .330 and collect, as he usually had, two hundred hits over the season and show that he was the niftiest center fielder and deadliest leadoff man in the major leagues.

The same day, Lane had received a doctor's letter stating that his health was OK but that his speed would be permanently limited.

In the same circumstances, it's noted,

> It was destined to be a big year for a lot of people if you took stock of the crystal-ball-gazing of the sports experts. They predicted what Big DiMag and Williams would hit; how many balls Mize and Kiner would propel out of the parks; how many wins Feller, Newhouser and Blackwell would rack up. And down among the slightly less spectacular items, they claimed that Eddie Lasky, the pint-sized speed merchant, would spark the Blue Sox to a pennant, hitting his reliable .320, collecting his bonded 200 hits, proving once more that he was the best second-spot hitter as well as the best shortstop in the business, bar none.

The same day, Lasky was sent a similar letter as in the Lane story.

Both versions of the plot are readable, like the Madigan story was half a year earlier. The Lasky and Madigan tales were the only Blue Sox–related stories of the nine published, and even though Lane also plays for a Blue Sox team, all the personnel are different. Just a mystery that will likely never be solved!

In the Madigan stories, the major difference is that his home run–hitting but nasty competition for third base is Mike Marnie in the novel and Mike Mowbray in the pulp story. There are also a lot of details about other players in the novel that are not included in the novelette. Both are highly readable and the pulp version is surely Decker's best story for the rough-paper magazines.

The Decker Pulp Stories

Here, presented for the first time for the benefit of Decker baseball collectors, are his nine pulp stories. They are all competent, but none of them are as compelling as the Madigan and Lasky stories.

Complete Sports, September 1947, "First Inning's, Worst Inning"
Real Sports, October 1947, "Foot in the Bucket"
Big Baseball Stories, May 1948, "Home Runs Don't Count"
Real Sports, June 1948, "Shadow Over Shortstop"

Complete Sports, October 1948, "Base-Thief to Mound Marvel"
Sports Novels, November 1948, "Last Chance Chucker"
Real Sports, November 1948, "The Batboy Who Won a Pennant"
Big Baseball Stories, November 1948, "Ninth-Inning Blues"
Complete Sports, November 1952, "Miracle at the Plate"

8

The Unsung William R. Cox and T.W. Ford—Nearly 10 Percent of Pulp Sports

William R. Cox and T.W. Ford were among the most prolific of all pulp writers from the 1930s to the 1950s, but today these two popular storytellers are among the least recognized. They combined to publish more than 2,000 stories, almost all in the pulps in several genres, but they have never received the credit they deserve. From the standpoint of baseball and football stories for the six publishers indexed in this book, they combined for well over 320 stories, or at least 8 percent of the slightly more than 4,000 stories indexed in this book. They both wrote many stories about other sports. The exact number can't be confirmed because of the use of pseudonyms and house names.

The amazing FictionMags website—coordinated by award-winning pulp historian Phil Stevensen-Payne—lists more than 800 stories for Cox (1901–1987), including more than 150 as by Joel Reeve and Roger Spellman as well as more than 650 under his own name. Ford published few, if any, paperback or hardback novels—unlike Cox—but Ford has more than 700 stories listed and is also surely over 1,000. The FictionMags site is not complete, but it's by far the best compilation of stories and cover images available and is always being updated by collectors around the world.

The best list of much of Cox's work is his entry in *Twentieth Century Crime and Mystery Writers* by John M. Reilly, who credits Cox with more than 1,000 stories in the mystery, western and sports fields. So little is known of Ford that he is listed only by his initials, but he was cover-featured dozens of times, as was Cox. This book indexes all of their pulp baseball and football for the six publishers for the first time. All of their work for Street & Smith is listed in FictionMags.

Cox was among the few who sold at least one or two baseball and football stories to all six publishers, with a total of 120 stories under his own name and likely more than 30 under other names. But he sold the vast majority of his sports work to Popular Publications (62 stories under his own name) and Fiction House (43), leaving the other four publishers to account for only 15 combined. His first pulp sports story was the track tale "Legs" in *Dime Sports* for October 1935 (this has incorrectly been credited as 1934, but the magazine did not exist until the July 1935 issue).

It was utterly amazing that Cox could write so many mystery and western stories concurrently with his immense sports output, which was well over 300 stories in all sports and all his names. In John Dinan's *Sports in the Pulp Magazines* (1998), Dinan quotes a letter from Cox saying there were over 50 sports pulp magazines in 1934, but such a market did not develop for several more years. While there were slightly more than 50 sports pulp titles in all from the 1920s through the 1950s including boxing pulps, there were never close to 50 at any one time in the marketplace. Cox, however, did have a market of more than 50 pulps in the 1930s if mystery and western pulps are included.

Cox wrote many western and mystery novels and penned 22 sports novels for young adults from 1956 to 1980, the year this remarkable writer turned 79.

There is no doubt that the most prolific contributor of pulp baseball and football was Ford, who contributed 101 baseball stories and 65 football tales under his own name to the six publishers, plus many for Street & Smith in the 1930s. Ford wrote well over 300 pulp sports stories in all, but he was even more prolific in the western field and more. Like Cox, Ford established a primary relationship with two publishers: Columbia (101 baseball and football stories) and Thrilling (55). He sold only 10 combined to the other four, with apparently none to Ace (which published 111 sports pulps, but only seven after 1943—seven issues of *Ace Sports* when the magazine was briefly revived in 1947–1949).

Here are three representative stories by each author.

"Tramp Athlete"

The title of Cox's fine football novelette for Fiction House's *All-American Football Magazine* for Fall 1939 (the second issue) is deceiving, since Morey Tanner was anything but a tramp, a fake, a charlatan. The unknown halfback, thanks to the recommendation of his former coach, shows up at practice for legendary coach Mickey Sheraton's college all-stars, who are preparing to play the annual all-star game against the professional league's Whales (similar to a real-life series). Tanner played for Kenton Teachers College and is just hoping to make an impression, since he plays the same backfield spot as the handsome, imposing Penn Madison. When introduced to Sheraton's young friend Ginny Gardner, Tanner is dumbstruck in a love-at-first-sight manner by the beauty of Gardner, whose brother owns part of the rival Wolverines. But Ginny is dating Madison, of course—what else would you expect from a good pulp story?

"A queer tramp athlete from nowhere" is how Madison describes Tanner to Ginny when she wonders where he is from. What Madison does not know is how confident Tanner is, both on and off the field. Naturally, the story centers around their intense, immediate personality conflict. Madison is soon outraged when he learns Tanner and Gardner have already expressed love for each other.

Sheraton, meanwhile, has noticed how intelligent Tanner is and how much he knows and cares about the game beyond just a playing role. The coach realizes that Tanner wants to make his mark in pro football because his real goal is not a long playing career, but rather a pro coaching job. With the all-stars trailing the Whales

7–0, Sheraton replaces Madison with Tanner to start the fourth quarter, enraging the prima donna star, who had insisted he would play all 60 minutes. Tanner shows the all-stars what an inspiring team player he is and scores a touchdown, but he is soon injured and replaced by Madison, who eventually scores the winning touchdown in the final seconds. "Well I'll be damned. He's the hero after all," Tanner tells himself.

Madison, who loves to mouth off but finds that Tanner will not back down, exchanges punches in the locker room with Tanner, who knocks out Madison. Not long after, Madison is outraged when he catches Ginny and Morey in a kiss. Meanwhile, Sheraton receives a coaching offer from the Whales before the league season starts and takes many of the winning all-stars with him, including both Madison and Tanner. The coach wants both—Tanner offers steadiness and insight but Madison has the flash pro fans prefer.

As the season ensues, Ginny loves Tanner but insists that he must look after Madison, whom she still cares for like a brother. Madison finds that the pros are much more of a challenge to his courage than he expected, while Tanner's injuries threaten to sideline him against the Wolverines in the title game at the end of the season. But Tanner is inherently decent and finds ways to help Madison to gain back his courage and confidence. Tanner plays the title game "on one leg" and blocks for Madison on the winning touchdown.

By the final page, Madison proves he is decent as well, just as Ginny knew he was. Madison surprises Tanner by telling him that his brother owns half the Wolverines—the half that Ginny's brother does not own—and Madison's brother wants to hire Tanner as backfield coach, since a doctor tells Tanner he has suffered career-ending injuries. Madison has long since given up on Ginny, since she wants to marry Tanner, but Madison realizes that Tanner would make a great coach for him and Tanner agrees.

It's an enjoyable story of people who all turn out well in the end. There are no villains in this one.

"The Fifth Infielder"

Shy Wade is a centerfielder from a team in Milltown—there were hundreds of those town teams all over America in those days—and his amazing speed and hustle justify the title in this compelling story by Cox in Fiction House's *Baseball Stories* for Summer 1939. Shy, it turns out, was adopted as a boy by former major league star Amby Conecky to prevent Wade from going to an orphanage. Conecky has lots of flaws—he drinks too much, for one—but he still can play, still loves baseball and has taught and loves this talented kid. As the story opens, Shy is 20 and Conecky is 36, having spent most of the previous decade out of organized baseball after being unfairly banned.

Wade has become such a promising player that Conecky sends him to the Centaurs, who are managed by hard-boiled Bullhead Pritchard, the man responsible for the ban against Conecky. The Centaurs need help, and in those days when any team could sign a free agent, Pritchard decides Wade is good enough to help him. Pritchard has no idea Conecky has sent him—and the hard-boiled Pritchard also has no idea that the resourceful, bright Wade has also been sent to investigate him.

That's the story—how Wade works his way onto the team, wins the friendship and respect of his older teammates, and how Wade and others prove that Pritchard had framed Conecky so that baseball officials thought he had thrown a game. Conecky, having gone on the wagon, is not only reinstated by baseball but with Pritchard gone is allowed to play. The Centaurs, who have several admirable stars, claim the pennant and Conecky finds he has a future as a manager. And he just might pinch-hit in the World Series.

This story is fun, with all sorts of the twists and turns that stamped Cox as a storyteller deluxe.

"Front-Page Backfield"

Malden College football coach Shag McGurn finds his third-year backfield has grown cocky and conceited in Cox's short story in Fiction House's *Football Action* for Second Fall 1949 (that's how Fiction House numbered its football pulps). There's a hysterical scene in their dorm room where the four seniors are reading all their press clippings in all the many newspapers of the era as McGurn confronts them following a less-than-stellar effort in victory the day before.

"Get a load of this, guys," says quarterback Slim Porter:

> "Again the genius of Malden's Phantom Backfield rose above the stubborn defense of a great Carter team and snatched victory from certain defeat in the closing minutes of yesterday's game. Slim Porter's grand strategic lateral to Andy Farmer scored one touchdown. His alert recovery of a Carter fumble and Toots Calhoun's amazing broken-field running scored a second. Beast Ferguson's magic toe converted both points and Malden squeezed out a well-deserved, one-point win." Now there's a writer. Got the four of us into his lead paragraph.

Talk about reading your press clippings! This inspires McGurn to respond, "Get out the scrap books, girls, and paste it in. Cut out all references to the linemen who made it possible. Be sure not to let a word creep in about the hours of painful coaching from [assistant Bo] Fielder and McGurn. Or the nursing along of four prima donnas through three tortured years."

McGurn decides to have open competition for all jobs and lets the entire team know it. Everyone starts to work harder. He shifts Beast Ferguson to the line. He lets the team know that the coaches are in charge. The players turn out to be good teammates, after all. Guess what? It all works out beautifully. After all, this is a pulp story!

"The Third Stringer"

One of the ultimate pulp football stories is Ford's "The Third Stringer" in *Exciting Sports* for Fall 1950. This novelette has so many plot convolutions that it seems unbelievable, but it's fun because the protagonist is so unusual.

Jed Chorens, having played football at Edgewater Teachers College—it's derided as "some hillbilly school"—and for two seasons with the minor league Rosemont Roosters, finds himself as an unknown backup end with the Warhawks as a throw-in in a trade from the Redbirds in what is obviously the NFL. Warhawks coach Dana Grabb knows nothing about Chorens until he spots the rookie making an unusually determined tackle against star fullback Big Tolly Emmers in a scrimmage. Right away, Jed has made an enemy. Grabb asks assistant Dave Bakis, "Who is he?"

That wouldn't happen in an NFL camp today, of course. Nor do many 176-pound defensive ends show up. But Chorens shows he's a lot more than the average third-string rookie. When Grabb asks him how he seemed to know exactly how one play was going to develop, Chorens calmly explains, "Because I saw [the halfback] patting down his helmet as they lined up." In the next day's scrimmage, the longtime coach is amazed to see Chorens playing center in place of two sidelined teammates. When asked what an end is doing at center, Grabb finally coaxes Chorens to acknowledge, "I wanted to get into some action. The C team wasn't doing much of anything."

Grabb is also quick to notice that the unruffled rookie calls him "Grabb" instead of "Mr. Grabb" or "Coach." He doesn't like it, but he lets it slide because this is not just any newcomer. When Grabb cautions him about making an enemy of Emmers, Chorens replies, "He's all right. He means well—just a trifle hot-headed. I guess it's the strain of living up to being a star." And when he's forced into action by teammates' injuries when league games start, Chorens makes a couple of serious mistakes, one of which costs his team a chance to win. When film shows that an uncalled penalty caused Jed's big mistake, he shrugs off the bad break and the press criticism that comes with it. "The rest of the team would have figured I was making up an excuse," he tells the coach, who is boggled by the maturity of this odd rookie.

Grabb is also amazed by Chorens's explanation of why he turned down a chance to fight with Tolly: He was a college boxing star. "I could take an untrained man like Big Tolly and slash him to ribbons.... We happen to have a game Sunday and Big Tolly is one fine fullback!"

The capper occurs when the team is forced to take two planes when a large one is not available.... You guessed it, Chorens took the plane that carried the starters. And when forced to play halfback—his minor league position, though he never said he had played there—he helped win a big game in the final minute with a lateral to—who else?—Big Tolly for the winning touchdown.

"I've been a dumb monkey, fella," Big Tolly tells Jed in the locker room. "I should've known when we had a real football player in our midst. If you want to hang one on my jaw. Hey, that's blood on your hand!" When the doctor begins to remove the tape covering what Jed had said was a sprain, Ford writes, "They could see the ragged piece of bone poking through the skin. And then they knew. Jed had sustained a fractured bone in the back of his hand, had played on with it even when it became a compound fracture."

Not a boring line to be found in this little epic!

"The Diamond Tramp"

As in the Cox story above, the word "Tramp" is not really appropriate in Ford's "The Diamond Tramp" in *Thrilling Sports* for Fall 1950. Rookie Louis "Spike" Austin has such valuable utility skills that he is sent by his manager at a baseball school, following his first season in the minors, directly to the Florida spring training camp of the big league Barons. There, he finds raw-boned and raw-tempered manager Mack Canly and his kind, affable coach, Hooks Obers. This was one of the pulp versions of "good cop–bad cop."

Austin wins over his teammates with his never-ending enthusiasm but his confidence takes a hit when he makes rookie mistakes. Obers cooks up a plan to help Austin by telling teammates to encourage him and by introducing Austin to Pamela Barnes, who is a friend of the daughter of Austin's baseball school coach. Austin, who has never had a girlfriend, can't believe his luck.

The plan works well and Austin seems to be on the verge of stardom until one of the veterans has too much to drink and reveals Obers's tactics. Austin is deflated and tells the girl he can't tolerate that kind of relationship. Naturally, by now she really does care for him and tells him, "You've found out how good a ball player you can be." Austin still walks away, but her comment runs through his brain over and over and he decides to keep playing despite the humiliation. He succeeds beyond his dreams and when she shows up after the big game, he takes charge with her.

"For a shy Joe, he sure has come a long way, a long way," an admiring teammate says to end the tale. It's another readable story without any villains. Far-fetched though this type of happy finish may be, the absence of a sneering bad guy somehow enhances the story in so many cases.

"Big League Fluke"

Ford creates a memorable baseball character in "Skitter" Lober in the short story "Big League Fluke" in *Exciting Sports* for Spring 1945. The light-hitting but slick-fielding Skitter lives up to his name with a constant barrage of baseball chatter at shortstop and hustle to go with it for the minor league Angels (16 years before an American League expansion team takes that name). Skitter, however, drives his teammates crazy with his never-ending chatter and inability to stand or sit still.

Skitter, though, finds he has to sit through oral surgery for two abscessed teeth. Not quite himself, Skitter gets struck by a truck on the way home. He thinks he isn't seriously injured but he eventually finds out he had a concussion. But he doesn't tell anyone and calms down so much that he starts hitting a flurry of singles, doubles and triples for the first time in his career. Shocked at his conversion to an explosive hitter, Skitter finds himself promoted to the major leagues—to the New York Sachems. But even though he wins over teammates he finds he has recovered from his concussion but is once again a weak hitter without power.

Skitter finally tells his understanding manager, Joe Brachen, "I gotta confession to make. I'm up here on false pretenses, a sorta fluke." He explains that apparently the concussion made him loose enough to hit well but now that he's totally healthy, he's back to his old, jittery self. The manager's response is a classic:

> Listen, Lober. I told you once you were my shortstop. Actually, we seldom expect a minor-leaguer to hit pitching in the majors as he did down there. Also, we were scouting you weeks before you went on the splurge. I'm telling you again. You are my shortstop. Now stop worrying. I don't like a worried player on my club. If there were any doubts in my mind they went when I saw [second baseman] Brownell begin to ride you. Brownie never bothers to ride a kid he doesn't think is worth it. So—

His first time at bat the next day, he hits a run-scoring double. As the story ends, "He knew he had plenty more of them in his system."

9

Girl Meets Boy

When Nelson Bond wrote "Front Page Backstop" in *Ace Sports* for August 1939, no women were covering Major League Baseball on a regular basis. Women weren't even allowed in press boxes, much less in a locker room or manager's office.

For Bond, who would shortly become well known for his often whimsical science fiction and fantasy, this short story, bannered on the cover, was actually one of his earliest whimsical fantasy pieces, even though it appeared in a sports pulp. So did more than 50 of his other sports stories, virtually all in the late 1930s and early 1940s, including at least 45 dealing with baseball and football.

Reporters were often key characters in pulp baseball and football, since those were the sports most likely to be covered in person and headlined in the newspapers, along with boxing and horse racing in the pulp era. But female reporters in a sports story? They were popular in the movies of the 1930s and 1940s, covering crime and other dramatic stories as a "sob sister," and there were plenty of such femme reporters in the mystery and suspense pulps. But in sports stories? They were rare indeed. But then, in retrospect, it wasn't surprising that the prolific pen of Bond, who may have written more science fictional humor than anyone, would come up with a female sports reporter on the big-time baseball beat.

Day Curtis was her name and getting good columns was her game for the *Evening Star*. That's why she decided to pursue Jack "Screwy" Sanderson, boastful second-year catcher for the Blues, in the wake of his sensational rookie season. After yet another winning effort, while Sanderson signs autographs and banters with fans in a most immodest way, Blues trainer Musty Mulligan tells manager Doc Nye, "You're just seein' the beginnin' of this show-off stuff. I know ballplayers. Give 'em a column inch, an' they want the whole damn front page!" To which Nye responds, "Which is OK by me. Sanderson can have the whole Sunday paper to hisself, as long as he keeps on startin' rallies like he did today."

When Sanderson tears himself away and returns for a nap at his hotel, he encounters newsmen in the lobby and, as he had already often done in his second season, begins to boast again. He gives them plenty, then they chase him to the door of his room, where he promises more for them that night while socializing at the Pleasure Palace. He spots a female figure in his room, thinking it might be Belle DuBois, a singer at the Pleasure Palace who has been chasing after the young celebrity. But he quickly realizes it's not the glamorous Belle, but rather a girl who has been admitted by the maid. She introduces herself and says she writes a column about sports called "The Woman's Angle." In this way, Bond enables the reader—who more than likely knows all about the male-dominated sports pages—to understand that a woman could, indeed, be seeking a word or three with the colorful Screwy. But when she challenges his change in personality from just Jack to boastful Screwy, he calls her "a lousy newspaper reporter" and chases her away so he can take a nap.

Day Curtis soon harasses her editor into letting her go on the upcoming road trip because she is convinced she wants to reveal "the why" of Sanderson's "false face." Eventually, Day corners Jack and he tells her, "This is off the record. Between you and me. Even if you are a newspaper woman, I think I can trust you. You're right in thinking that I'm not naturally talkative...." And he tells her at length about how the most successful players in their post-career days are often those who were not only solid on the diamond, but colorful off the diamond. "It's common sense ... [showmen] knew what they were doing. By building a reputation, they make sure that when they leave baseball the world will find a place for them. And meanwhile, they get big salaries...."

Day disagrees, mentioning serious real-life stars like Lefty Grove, Charlie Gehringer and Lou Gehrig (the doomed star who had played what would be his final game not long before this issue of *Ace Sports* hit the stands). But Day can't convince Screwy and they end the conversation. Much later, after Screwy's boasts have put so much pressure on himself that he has fallen into a long, deep slump, Day decides to talk with the wise old manager, Doc Nye. Day tells him that Jack-cum-Screwy has fallen under the spell of the beautiful social climber Belle DuBois. Day hatches a plan, Doc listens, and soon Belle is given free tickets to hobnob with famous fans in the box seats at the big Fourth of July doubleheader. Screwy is surprised that Belle wants to see him play rather than just socialize with him in front of crowds at night.

Screwy is then shocked that Belle is soon introduced to the Blues' stars between games, including Slugger Garrity, whom Nye gives permission to sit with Belle for the second game. Screwy objects, knowing who Slugger really is, but Belle shoos Screwy away while hoping Winchell (that's right, gossip columnist Walter) gets a gander at Belle and Slugger. It isn't until the end of the game that Belle discovers Slugger is "the best darn batboy in the league," as he calls himself (batboys were often adults in those days).

Belle realizes she has been had and will be the object of derision instead of delight. But, as Bond ends the story, "Jack Sanderson and Day Curtis did not even hear the invective hurled by the betrayed showgirl. They had forgotten her entirely. They had forgotten, also, that the grandstands were not yet empty. For it was the first time they had come together with mutual understanding in their eyes and hearts. The slow-filing crowds got a great kick out of that. For once, the public scored a 'beat' on Winchell. They knew about the Curtis-Sanderson engagement several days before he printed it in his column."

Thus ends an amusing story about an emerging star who learns that being yourself is what's most important.

This story also shows the importance of careful editing, which wasn't always the case in the pulps. In the first game of the climactic doubleheader—before Jack learns the truth about Belle—he swings wildly at an outside pitch for the first strike. Then he sees "the second and third offerings both go by for called strikes." Finally, he swings and misses at the final pitch. "Strikeout!" Bond emphasizes. But it was a four-pitch strikeout! Indeed, Jack really needed that girl reporter's help!

10

The Cover Artists and Themes

Unlike the covers for several other genres, sports pulp covers did not offer fantastic, garish scenes to tantalize the reader. Almost all the scenes could be duplicated by a newspaper or magazine photographer.

However, that doesn't mean sports covers were not attractive. On the contrary, many collectors of sports pulps search for them primarily or exclusively for the covers, which offer a unique cross-collector appeal.

It's not unheard of for baseball card and/or memorabilia collectors, for example, to be captivated by the covers of both fictional scenes in the pulps and the historic covers offered by non-fiction sports magazines.

The vast majority of pulp covers in any genre were illustrations or paintings, depending on how you wish to define them. Very few covers for the slicks—there were no exclusively sports fiction publications among the slicks—were anything but photographs. On the same newsstand of the 1930s, 1940s and 1950s, however, could be found slick magazines with photo covers of famous athletes (and they were almost always famed in those days to be chosen for a magazine cover). On the same newsstands, pulps sometimes featured real-life stars on their covers—yet only if they were featured in a non-fiction profile inside the same pulp—but the vast majority of the pulp covers portrayed fictional heroes. For the most part, these characters were pretty much interchangeable among all the publishers and titles, although it's easy to recognize the different artistic styles.

Sports pulp covers were used primarily to attract fans of a particular sport; thus pulps with a baseball cover theme tended to appear on the stands from March or April to October or November. Since pulps appeared a month or two before the cover dates, a November or December pulp could still have a baseball theme, especially if linked to the World Series, which was held in October (there were no other types of modern-day playoffs during the pulp era).

There were a handful of mixed-sport covers, but pulp covers were almost always single-sport scenes. Of all the sports, boxing was in many ways the most useful, because there were no boxing seasons. If an artist failed to make a deadline for a seasonal cover, a boxing cover could always be used, especially since most pulps contained at least one boxing story. I don't know for sure in specific instances, but I would not doubt that editors usually had a paid-for boxing cover available "just in case."

Cover Themes Vary

I uncovered (pardon the pun) cover themes for all 1,257 sports pulps published from the beginning of the competitive era in 1935 through the last sports pulp, issued in 1957. The first-of-its-kind index in this book does not include story listings and non-fiction essay data on the 157 issues of Street & Smith's *Sport Story Magazine* issued from 1935 to 1943, nor does the book include story data on the 32 issues of the *All-American Sport Story Magazine* published from 1935 to 1938, but cover themes are included because I have complete data on those, in large part thanks to the FictionMags website and to my own collection. Thus, comparisons are accurate and theme counts are complete.

Both Street & Smith (429 issues from 1923 to 1943, including reprint annuals in 1942–1943) and Fleischer's *The All-American* (45 issues from 1933 to 1938) are indexed on the FictionMags website. What is not indexed are the sports featured in all those stories. The earliest issues of both titles include a much wider variety of sporting activities than those featured on the 1935-onward covers.

The other 1,054 sports pulps in my index—not counting the all-boxing magazines—featured a tiny fraction of sports other than baseball, football, boxing and basketball on their covers. Thus, even though only baseball and football stories are indexed in this volume, all cover themes are listed, primarily because many enthusiasts advised me to do so. However, to index all the more than 8,000 stories in those issues would make this book larger than would be practical.

Here are the number of cover themes for each sport for the 1,257 issues from 1935 to 1957:

Baseball—548 (includes 49 all-baseball pulps)
Football—270 (includes 113 all-football pulps)
Boxing—130 (does not include the all-boxing pulps)
Basketball—75 (includes two all-basketball pulps)
Hockey—47
Track and field—27
Tennis—10
Mixed sports—9
Swimming and diving—7
Wrestling—4
Skiing—4
Horse racing—3
Patriotic (flag and battle)—2
Women's softball—1
Women's basketball—1
Roller derby—1
Polo—1
Bobsledding—1
Crew—1
Boat racing—1

Motorcycles—1
Waterskiing—1

Except for boxing, the top five cover-theme categories are all team sports invented in America, other than hockey from Canada, which is far more popular in America now than hockey was during the pulp era. The only other team sports represented were women's softball and women's basketball with one cover each, both from Street & Smith. Soccer then was played worldwide but to a far lesser extent than "the beautiful game," as it is known, was played in America.

Since the majority of readers were men or older teenage boys, the publishers obviously sought cover appeal for the majority of readers who had played those team sports in their youth.

The numbers show how different editors emphasized team sports a bit differently, although there were no huge differences. Fiction House, of course, successfully guessed that their industry-leading emphasis on annual or twice-annual football pulps in the fall would be the right financial move. Likewise, Thrilling/Standard figured football would lead their single-sport line, especially since baseball covers dominated their general-interest pulps. However, Thrilling published three of the leading general-interest sports pulps, while Fiction House released just three issues of their only anthology-style pulp (*Bull's-Eye Sports* in 1938–1939).

The Real Cover Boys

The first 11 issues of *Popular Sports* from Thrilling/Standard offered a distinction unique among the pulps that began from 1935 on: Their covers, all painted by Earle Bergey, showed real-life superstars in the most popular sports of the day.

The athletes were all white for two primary reasons: All the major team sports did not feature—or even have, in almost all cases—any African American athletes until after World War II, and black athletes were often thought of as commercial suicide, especially in the 1930s.

The bimonthly *Popular Sports* cover featured, to go along with biographical stories, these 11 Hall of Fame caliber athletes, from the first issue in June 1937 through the 11th issue in February 1939: Dizzy Dean (baseball), James J. Braddock (boxing), Lou Gehrig (baseball), Larry Kelley (football), Eddie Shore (hockey), Barney Ross (boxing), Joe Medwick (baseball), Don Budge (tennis), Bob Feller (baseball), Sammy Baugh (football) and Hank Luisetti (basketball).

Several pulp titles produced covers with real-life athletes, most notably Street & Smith's *Sport Story Magazine*, but *Popular Sports* offered just short of an unprecedented two years' worth of nothing but. All of these covers offer cross-collecting appeal. *Popular Sports*, though, never again featured a real-life cover boy through the end of its 63-issue run, which ended with the Spring 1951 issue.

More than 300 sports pulps were published after the war (1946–1957), but none of them featured any black athletes, in contrast to the concurrent sports non-fiction slick magazines, such as *Sport Magazine*, and the six-issue run of Fawcett's sporadically published Jackie Robinson comic-book title (1949–1952). Even before Jackie

Robinson first integrated modern Major League Baseball with the Brooklyn Dodgers in 1947, a small number of African Americans were playing pro football and basketball.

Pulps were read primarily by older teenagers and adults of all ages, but the vast majority sold much better before World War II than after the conflagration. Therefore, publishers of the sports pulps were obviously leery of publishing anything controversial on their covers, in much the same way post-war publishers dropped the soft-core porn pulps (*Spicy Detective* and the like) and the horror and terror pulps.

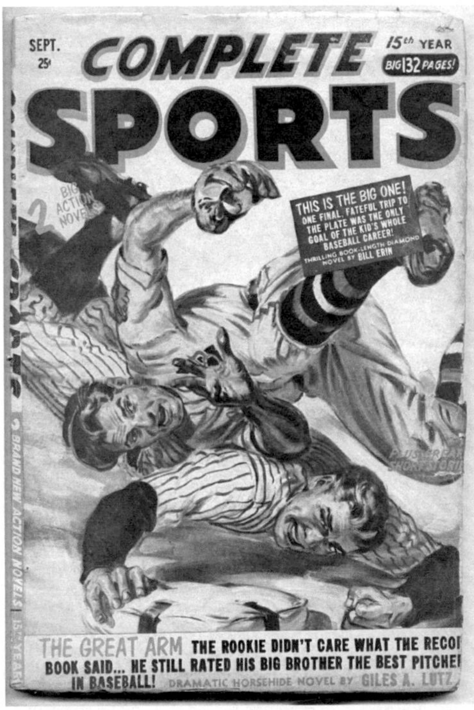

Complete Sports, September 1952 (copyright 1952 Stadium Publishing Corporation). One of Norman Saunders's best covers is this emotional portrayal of a runner sliding safely into a base as the fielder tumbles over him with the ball in his glove, but no tag yet made.

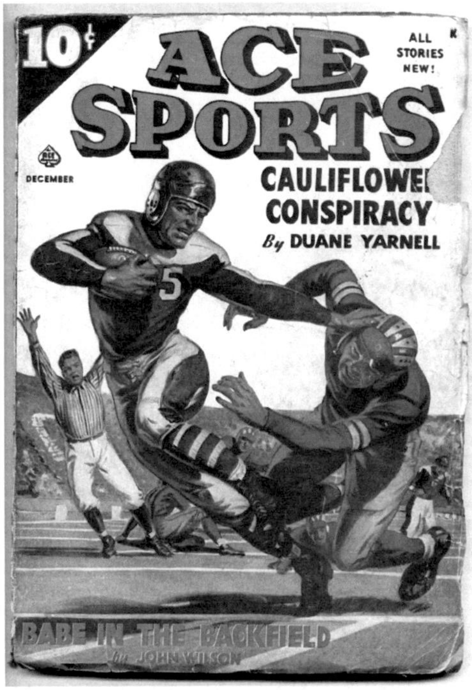

***Ace Sports,* December 1942 (copyright 1942 Periodical House, Inc.). Straight-arms by swivel-hipped halfbacks were a popular theme in the sports pulps, but nobody portrayed the action better than Norman Saunders.**

The Prolific Sports Artists

Of the more than 150 collectible artists cited for excellence by Tim Cottrill in his *Ultimate Guide to the Pulps* (2001)—the first combined pulp index and price guide—none were specialists in sports covers. Nonetheless, there were two exceptionally prolific sports cover artists, Norman Saunders and Earle Bergey, especially considering that sports was the smallest of the recognized pulp genres.

Norman Saunders (1907–1989), the father of noted pulp historian David Saunders, drew an astounding 866 pulp covers in fewer than 25 years, not to mention hundreds more covers for comic books, men's magazines, general-interest publications and much more, as detailed by David in his landmark volume *Norman Saunders.*

Norman is best known for his creative and emotionally stirring detective pulp covers, but he also did numerous western, science fiction and sports covers, among other genres. David lists 98 sports covers, most of them baseball, boxing and football covers, since those sports offered Saunders by far the most opportunities. When looking at a Saunders sports cover, you can practically feel the exertion and emotion of his subjects. More than any other pulp artist, he used faces to portray both the joy and pain of athletics.

***Ace Sports,* December 1940 (copyright 1940 Magazine Publishers, Inc.). Famed cover artist Norman Saunders, who did hundreds of pulp covers for several genres, was consistently the best at portraying emotion in sports pulps.**

Saunders painted sports covers primarily for Ace, Fiction House, Popular and Martin Goodman.

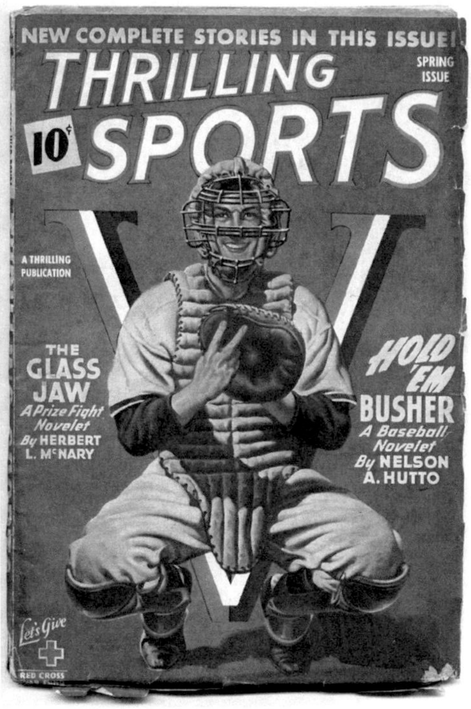

***Thrilling Sports,* Spring 1944 (copyright 1944 Better Publications Inc.). Earle Bergey beautifully portrays a catcher giving a victory sign he wants everyone to see! Thrilling Publications used patriotic covers on many pulps during World War II.**

Bergey (1901–1952) also worked in a wide variety of genres, especially romance and science fiction, and labored for all seven of the major pulp publishers, though the majority of his sports work was for Thrilling/Standard. That firm published 229 sports pulps from 1936 to 1953 and Bergey magnificently illustrated the covers for nearly 200 of them, making him the most prolific of all sports cover artists. Considering that only 1,257 sports pulps were published from 1935 to 1957—the years of competitive publication after Street & Smith began the genre in 1923—Bergey's sports total alone is remarkable. Bergey's covers frequently reflected exertion, but he also usually injected feelings of glory and humor, along with a luminous style.

George Gross was the leading artist for pretty much the entire Fiction House line, including most of its 109 sports pulps plus its long-running specialty title *Boxing Stories* (not evaluated in this book, which covers team sports). Gross's covers did much to sell his firm's pulps in all genres, but he was especially effective with his colorful portrayal of sports.

Rudolph Belarski, so well known for his drama-packed mystery/detective pulp covers, did a handful of sports themes for Thrilling/Standard. Other accomplished artists who worked in the sports genre, but were much better known for other themes, were Allen Anderson, Rafael DeSoto, Hubert Rogers, A. Leslie Ross, H.W. Scott and J.W. Scott.

Unless an artist signed his work, it is often difficult to identify many sports cover artists. The publishers rarely identified the artists on the table of contents page.

***Baseball Stories*, Summer 1938 (copyright 1938 Fiction House, Inc.). George Gross provides a classic illustration for the second issue of the first pulp to feature only baseball stories. In the late 1930s, Fiction House was the first to publish pulps devoted to team sports—football (three titles), basketball (a one-shot) and baseball (this title ran 33 issues, more than any other pulp devoted to team sports).**

How Publishers Compare

Here are cover themes from the eight sports pulp publishers of the 1935–1957 period:

Popular Publications (230 issues)
Baseball—113
Football—55
Boxing—24
Basketball—24
Track and field—8
Hockey—5
Swimming and diving—1

Thrilling/Standard Publications (229 issues)
Football—105
Baseball—92
Boxing—15
Basketball—7
Hockey—3
Track and field—3

Horse racing—2
Tennis—1
Polo—1

Columbia Publications (223 issues)
Baseball—131
Football—47
Boxing—34
Hockey—5
Basketball—3
Roller derby—1
Horse racing—1
Motor sports—1

Street & Smith Publications *Sport Story Magazine* (157 issues in 1935–1943 period)
Baseball—48
Football—28
Boxing—26
Basketball—16
Hockey—13
Track and field—11
Tennis—6
Swimming and diving—3
Patriotic—2
Wrestling—1
Women's softball—1
Women's basketball—1
Motorcycles—1

Martin Goodman Publications (143 issues)
Baseball—69
Football—36
Boxing—19
Basketball—9
Mixed sports—8
Hockey—1
Wrestling—1

Ace Publications (111 issues)
Baseball—49
Football—19
Hockey—16
Basketball—10
Boxing—6
Track and field—3
Swimming and diving—2
Tennis—2
Wrestling—2
Skiing—1
Mixed sports—1

Fiction House (109 issues)
Football—74
Baseball—34
Basketball—1

All-American Sport Story Magazine (32 issues from 1935 to 1938)
Baseball—9
Boxing—4
Football—3
Basketball—3
Hockey—3
Track and field—2
Skiing—2
Tennis—1
Swimming and diving—1
Crew—1
Waterskiing—1
Bobsledding—1
Boat racing—1

Athlete Magazine (Street & Smith) (9 issues)
Baseball—3
Football—3
Basketball—1
Hockey—1
Boxing—1

11

The Coming of Competition

Nothing ever showed how serious the competition was among pulp publishers better than the title of the first viable competitor for Street & Smith's long-running *Sport Story Magazine.*

At a time that *Sport Story Magazine* and the relatively short-lived competitor the *All-American Sport Story Magazine* were 15 cents on the newsstands, along came *Dime Sport,* Vol. 1, No. 1, for July 1935 from Popular Publications. (During the depths of the Great Depression, a dime was worth about $2 in 2018 money, so a nickel made a significant difference in sales potential.)

The new sports title was, however, no surprise, nor was the publisher. Popular produced more than 5,000 pulp magazines over more than two decades before it finally vanished in the mid–1950s, although that was still a little more than half what Street & Smith published with nearly 10,000 pulps before giving up on the rough-paper scene in 1949 (the science fiction best-seller *Astounding Science Fiction* had been a digest since 1943 and, of course, continued to dominate the fantastic fiction magazines).

Popular Publications, guided by the indomitable Harry Steeger, already had *Dime Detective* (which debuted in 1931), *Dime Mystery* and *Dime Western* (both debuted in 1932) and *Dime Adventure* (the first issue appeared one month before *Dime Sport,* but *Dime Adventure* lasted only six issues).

Dime Sports—the plural title was adopted with the fifth issue in November 1935—demonstrated that fact by running 81 issues (the most behind *Sport Story Magazine* at the time) before factors involved with World War II caused a break in Popular's sports publishing in 1944. When publication resumed with the January 1947 issue, the title became *New Sports,* since sports pulps no longer cost a dime. Like the science fiction magazines, sports pulps sold primarily as niche products to niche readers and thus cost 15 cents. *New Sports* ran 34 issues until it expired in 1951, having run 115 issues under the two titles.

Dime Sports began as a monthly, which was also no surprise, since Street & Smith's *Sport Story Magazine* had already appeared twice a month for a little more than a decade. Although several non-sports pulps ran longer than 429 issues, no sports pulp came remotely close to the Street & Smith sports monster's total, which included two annuals in its last two years, in 1942 and 1943.

Dime Sports ran monthly for three full years—through Vol. 6, No. 6, June 1938, the 36th issue. Other than Street & Smith's titles, no other sports pulp would ever run monthly for nearly that long.

Dime Sports foreshadowed the importance of baseball and football, by far America's most popular team sports in those days, by featuring baseball on two of the first three covers and football on the next three. Oddly, the second issue (August 1935) featured the start of a swimming race—one of only two such covers in the history of sports pulps (other than Street & Smith, of course). With 730 covers for baseball (439) and football (291) across 1,054 sports pulps listed in this index in this book (all but the boxing magazines), *Dime Sports* proved prescient on a commercial basis.

The first six issues of *Dime Sports*—the only real competition for Street & Smith in 1935—were a bit different when it came to the stories. Of the 43 fictional tales in those six issues, only about a third had the themes of baseball (8) or football (6). In contrast, those two sports featured the themes of more than half the 8,049 fictional stories in the 1,054 pulps from seven publishers (including the nine issues of *Athlete* from Street & Smith in 1939–1940).

Dime Sports must have been a strong seller right from the start, however, to sustain monthly appearances for so long by a new publication. Editor Joseph Cox, who wrote a brief column for the readers, purchased 43 stories for the first six issues, with 29 different author bylines and 15 distinct sports themes. No known house names were used for the bylines, although Popular Publications would come to use house names more often than anyone.

The only authors in the first six issues to achieve fictional fame were William R. Cox, who was featured once in a track story in the October 1935 issue, and Robert Sidney Bowen, who wrote four stories, all dealing with aspects of track and field. Cox went on to write at least 148 football and baseball stories along with numerous tales of other sports, to go with countless mystery and western stories, and Bowen wrote at least 57 baseball and football stories to go with many other sports stories along with tales in other genres.

Joseph Cox talked early on with the readers about the importance of variety in the magazine's fiction. He was as good as his word in the first six months, because there were not only six track tales, but three apiece about boxing, horse racing, rowing (crew) and tennis—all big in the lives of many of the nation's sports fans. Indeed, in the pulp sports era, boxing and horse racing were the sports that most gave baseball and football competition for the headlines.

There was only one story of golf and hockey, both among the eight in the first issue, and motorcycle racing, polo, lacrosse and auto racing also had one story apiece in the first six issues. Polo and lacrosse were generally much bigger in the East when it came to what held the interest of sports fans. As for basketball, there were two stories—the same number devoted to soccer. But it wasn't basketball season during the first six issues, which appeared on the stands from May through October. Very few stories in the ensuing years contained soccer themes, but there were a fair share of basketball stories, as the 56 hoop covers demonstrated (there were no soccer covers unless Street & Smith published them).

Like Street & Smith, *Dime Sports* also carried non-fiction in all of the first six issues, including a ballyhooed three-part series in issues 4–6 bylined by the famed football coach Pop Warner about aspects of playing the game. This series may well have been directed toward the high school and college athletes who read the sports pulps, although one could imagine older readers being interested in Warner's techniques, too.

The first five issues cover-featured the themes of sports in that issue in smallish type compared to how well the featured stories and authors achieved cover plugs, in the manner of virtually all pulp magazines.

By 1936, *Dime Sports* was destined to share the stands with first *Ace Sports* and then *Thrilling Sports* and *Star Sports Magazine*, all from different publishers. The sports pulp popularity race was on and the games were afoot!

12

The Competition Explodes

In the wake of the six issues of the monthly *Dime Sports* in the second half of 1935, the still-mighty *Sport Story Magazine* was going as strong as ever, with 24 issues in 1936 (two each month). But as 1936 began, a second monthly pulp arrived to make a serious challenge for the dimes of pulp sports fiction fans: *Ace Sports.*

That's right, *Ace Sports,* appearing from a firm known in the indicia as Magazine Publishers but soon dubbed Ace on the covers, also charged a dime for a package every bit as handsome as *Dime Sports.* Ace placed a very large 10-cent symbol on the upper left corner, but also placed "MONTHLY" in capital letters below the logo.

Street & Smith was well known for the serials it ran in many of its genre titles. *Dime Sports* did not run serials, but Ace made a big deal of it at the top of the table of contents: "Every Story Complete—No Serials!" That was noteworthy at the time, but it would soon become well established that none of the six publishers who unveiled competition by the end of 1937—the six publishers focused on in this book—would ever run a serial in a sports pulp.

The general-interest action/adventure pulp *Argosy* from the Frank M. Munsey Company ran a lot of team sports serials throughout the mid– and late 1930s, but the magazine had a generally older readership with the patience for serials. Not so the sports pulps, many of which were purchased by teens as well as adults.

Ace Sports began its 68-issue run with what was declared to be a football novel, but was actually a 28-page novelette about college football with the generic but alliterative title "Gridiron Grit" by the more than competent Joe Archibald, with an attractive cover to match by Rafael M. DeSoto. Stories of baseball, hockey and horse racing were also plugged on the striking green cover.

Just as the new Superman character in *Action Comics* in 1938 had no original costume hero competition in the comics for a year, Dime and Ace battled it out monthly with Street & Smith by themselves until late in 1936, when Thrilling (Better Publications) began *Thrilling Sports* and Red Circle (Marvel) started *Star Sports Magazine. Ace Sports* and *Dime Sports* remained monthly until the second half of 1938, by which time so many rivals had popped up that there were no monthly titles from the six publishers. Street & Smith itself surrendered late in 1939, when the final four issues were monthly instead of twice a month.

There has never been a truly accurate portrayal of how sports pulps grew, then shrank during World War II, expanded in the last three years of the 1940s before the explosion of television, and then slowly grew more infrequent until the last two issues appeared in 1957.

Here is a chart of the issue totals from the six publishers, along with the nine-issue run of *Athlete* from Street & Smith in 1939–1940. At the bottom of the chart are the publishers with the most issues in the 1936–1951 era of strong sales. Would you believe that five different publishers shared that honor by the end of 1944? By definition, Fiction House could not, because all of its successful titles were single-sport pulps published either once or twice each year.

1935: 6	1943: 59	1951: 58
1936: 29	1944: 36	1952: 22
1937: 62	1945: 20	1953: 18
1938: 85	1946: 31	1954: 11
1939: 87	1947: 60	1955: 9
1940: 69	1948: 109	1956: 5
1941: 73	1949: 63	1957: 2
1942: 77	1950: 66	

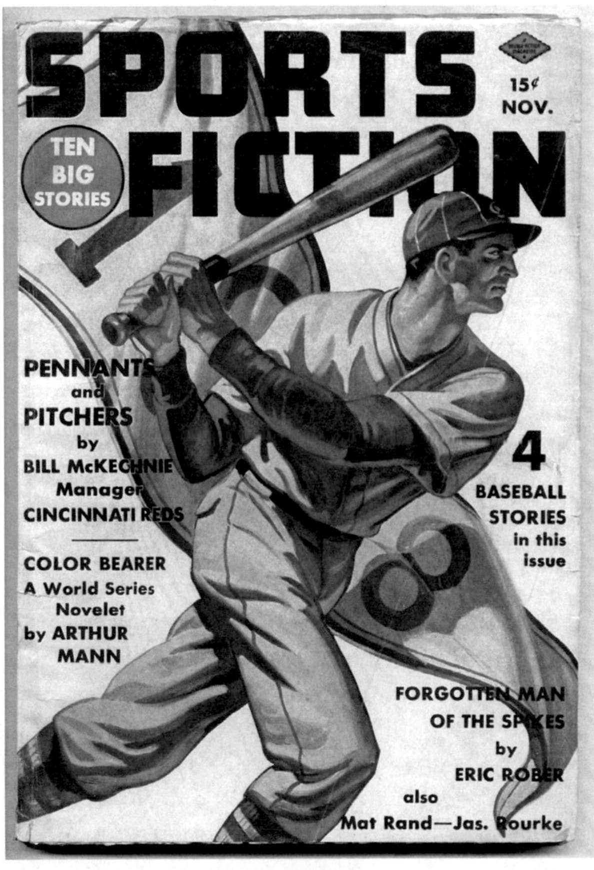

***Sports Fiction,* November 1938 (copyright 1938 Blue Ribbon Magazines Inc.). This Columbia title features a nicely symbolic World Series cover and a classic but seemingly awkward batting stance.**

Here are the issue totals for the leading publishers:

1936: Popular, 6
1937: Ace, 17
1938: Columbia and Marvel, 19
1939: Columbia, 23
1940: Popular, 18
1941: Columbia, 18
1942: Columbia, 19
1943: Columbia, 15
1944: Thrilling, 14
1945: Thrilling, 11
1946: Thrilling, 12
1947: Thrilling, 17
1948: Popular, 34; Marvel, 29
1949: Thrilling, 18
1950: Columbia and Popular, 18
1951: Columbia, 16

It's interesting to note that except for the post-war year, 1948—before the full effect of television—the 24 issues of Street & Smith each year from 1925 to 1938 were more than any leading publisher among the six in the chart above.

It's also intriguing to note that in 1937, the combined 36 issues of the four titles established in 1936 outnumbered by 26 issues the 10 titles that started in 1937. And in 1938 and 1939, only *Dime Sports* published as many as nine issues (1938), followed by eight in 1939, a year in which no other title ran more than six issues.

In the early 1940s, before the full effects of paper rationing and other wartime impacts, total issues were strong but only twice in the 1940–1943 period did any title run more than six issues: *Dime Sports* with 12 in 1940 and with 9 in 1941. All the other titles (see the index of all issues in this book) published no more than six issues in any of those years.

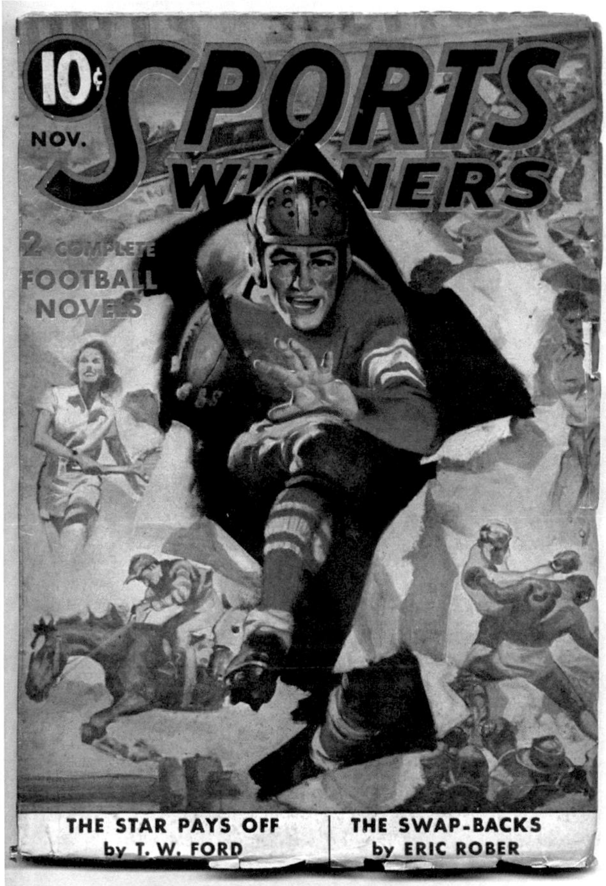

***Sports Winners,* November 1941 (copyright Columbia Publications, Inc.). This highly unusual football cover shows a halfback bursting through a medley of other scenes. Most such covers portrayed an athlete bursting through a newspaper.**

In 1944 and 1945, with many regular readers serving in the military, and with paper rationing in full force, only *Thrilling Sports* and *Popular Sports* were published as many as four times in 1944, and only *Popular Sports* and *Exciting Sports* appeared as many as three times in 1945. Indeed, by 1945, only the Thrilling (Better Publications) pulps were anything but twice-a-season single-sport pulps. Even in 1946, the first full post-war year, only Popular's *Sports Novels* appeared as many as six times. No others were produced more than three times that year.

The years 1947–1949 would be another explosive period, similar to 1937–1939. But by the 1950s, pulp totals shrank every year, as the next chapter will show in a discussion of what made each of the six companies different when it came to sports pulps.

13

The Sports Pulp Publishers

Even though sports was not a major pulp genre in the manner of the many more thousands of western and romance magazines, sports emerged as a significant market during the second half of the pulp era.

In round numbers, there were a little more than 1,500 pulps focused primarily on stories of team sports from the first (Street & Smith's *Sport Story Magazine* in 1923) to the last (Columbia's *Super Sports* annual appearing during baseball's spring training in 1957). (Remember: throughout this book the boxing magazines are not listed, but with fewer than 125 total issues across a handful of titles, they are not statistically significant except to those who collect them.) With some debates about what constitutes a pulp, close to 40,000 issues of the rough-paper largely fiction magazines appeared in the first six decades of the 20th century. If the genre digests are included in that time frame, the number is no more than about 44,000 through 1960, though digests continued far beyond the pulp era, of course.

The general public, of course, often considers the term "pulp" to encompass not only the digests such as *Fantastic Universe* and *Manhunt*, but also the bizarre and sensational detective, romance and exploitation magazines. They purported to be telling true stories, which differentiated them from the rough-paper pulps, which often carried some genuine non-fiction but were largely fictional. Stories in the likes of "slicks" such as the *Saturday Evening Post, Colliers* and *Redbook* were something of a cross between dignified popular fiction and literature.

Publishers such as Munsey, Dell and Clayton did produce a small number of genre pulps during the post–1934 era of sports pulps from multiple major companies—and some of their anthology-style pulps did include a number of sports stories—but the vast majority of those firms' pulps appeared before *Dime Sports* began real pulp sports competition in 1935. During most of the 1935–1957 era, all seven major pulp publishers produced sports pulps. Street & Smith was the first to quit sports (1943), followed by Ace (1949), Thrilling (1951, although single issues appeared in 1952 and 1953), Popular (1952), Fiction House (1954), Marvel (1955) and Columbia (1957).

Munsey, for decades the publisher of *Argosy*—always one of the best-known pulps—included numerous sports stories in that magazine, as did Dell in *Five Novels Magazine*. But they are not included along the six publishers of 1935–1957 sports pulps in the index in this book. I did include the nine issues of Street & Smith's *Athlete* magazine in 1939–1940 for a total of 1,054 issues. But I did not include the 1933–1938 run of 45 sports pulps from the publisher of *Ring Magazine*, titled the *All-American Sport Story Magazine,* because they are all listed on the Fiction-Mags website along with the entire 429-issue run of Street & Smith.

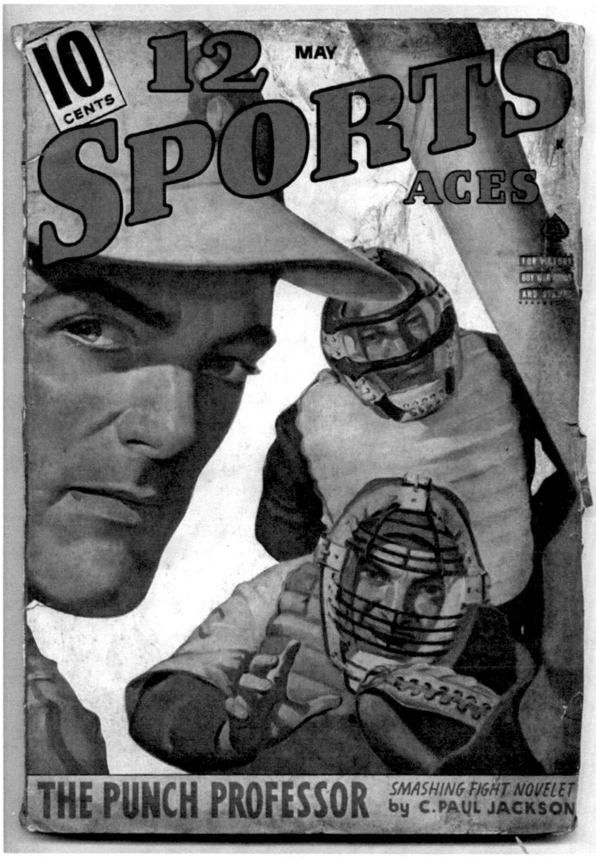

12 Sports Aces, May 1943 (copyright 1943 Periodical House, Inc.). Here's a nice perspective cover by Norman Saunders of what the pitcher sees as he readies a pitch.

In this chapter, I use numbers rounded to the nearest 50 issues, since there are enough questions remaining that we still don't absolutely know the exact pulp count from every major publisher. All six of these publishers absorbed smaller publishers, leading to minor confusion, and all six publishers produced magazines listed under various companies in the indicia for tax purposes but usually carrying the same logo on the covers.

There were eight significant genres of pulp fiction: western including western romance, love and romance, crime and detective, science fiction and fantasy, air war and military, costume heroes and assorted super characters in several genres, sports, and horror and terror, pretty much in that order of frequency. Many of these overlapped except for one genre—sports. Not that a sports story could not include a criminal or science fictional theme—a few did—but sports was far and away the most realistic of all pulp genres. Sports, in fact, was the only genre in which real life could and did surpass fiction in terms of sensations. (Love and romance stories in the rough-paper magazines almost always sanitized sexual feelings beyond any degree of realism.)

Ace

Ace, later famed for its plethora of paperbacks in the 1950s and 1960s, basically functioned as a pulp publisher from the early 1930s to 1949, when A.A. Wyn's firm departed pulp publishing except for *Complete Love* and *Ten Story Love,* which it converted to comic books in 1951. Ace published nearly 1,400 pulps, including 111 sports pulps, so sports themes occupied fewer than 8 percent of the company's market for stories.

Ace never had more than three sports titles on the stands at the same time, including 68 issues of *Ace Sports* (1936–1943, 1947–1949), 30 issues of *12 Sports Aces* (1938–1943, with the first issue titled *Variety Sports*) and 13 issues of *Champion Sports* (1937–1939).

The only major genre in which Ace was not active was science fiction.

Columbia

Except for Thrilling's *Ranch Romances* in 1961–1971 (its final decade a cross between a pulp and a digest), Columbia was the last of the major pulp publishers. From the early 1930s through 1960, Columbia published about 1,750 pulps, including magazines in all eight major genres, and many carried the Double-Action logo even though most of the indicia listings called the firm Columbia.

Famed for its Archie Series comic-book line (which began in 1939 as MLJ Comics, and which created Archie and Co. in 1941), Columbia was usually listed in pulp writers' memories as the lowest-paying major company. Although Columbia magazines are collected, especially by genre specialists, they are generally considered a cut or three below the other major publishers.

Columbia produced 223 sports pulps, all general-interest publications, so about 12 percent of its pulps had sports themes. None were continuously published through World War II, but several enjoyed long runs. They include 37 issues of *All Sports* (1939–1945, 1948–1951), two issues of *All-American Sports* (1940–1941), 10 issues of *Blue Ribbon Sports* (1937–1940), 43 issues of *Sports Fiction* (1938–1944, 1947–1951), 30 issues of *Sports Winners* (1938–1944, 1950–1952), 61 issues of *Super Sports* (1938–1944, 1946–1957) and 37 issues of *Ten Story Sports* (1937–1941, 1952–1957).

Fiction House

Fiction House produced pulps from 1921 to 1955, with some breaks for economic problems, and was by far the most popular in the comic-book field of the seven major sports pulp publishers. Fiction House produced everything from long-running titles to more one-shots than the other publishers while finishing with about 1,750 pulp issues, similar to Columbia. However, Fiction House is avidly collected, unlike Columbia, because Fiction House consistently produced many of the best covers in the field, especially in the 1940s. The firm's romance pulps almost always had a western theme, and the company did not deal with the horror/terror pulps. Nor did Fiction House pulps include costume heroes except in the small jungle genre, with Tarzan knockoff Kaanga in *Jungle Stories* and a handful of tales starring Sheena, Queen of the Jungle (who was a comic-book staple for 15 years).

Fiction House failed with its only general-interest sports pulp—three issues of

Bull's-Eye Sports (1938–1939). But no other publisher was nearly as successful with single-sport pulps—33 issues of *Baseball Stories* (1938–1954), 25 issues of *Football Stories* (1937–1953), 24 issues of *All-American Football Magazine* (1938–1953) and 23 issues of *Football Action* (1939–1953), for a total of 109 sports pulps along with 105 issues of *Fight Stories,* the long-running boxing pulp that no other publisher could compete with.

If *Fight Stories*—the only significant boxing pulp—is counted, about 12 percent of Fiction House's magazines involved sports, including about two decades of non-fiction college football annuals.

Marvel/Red Circle/Martin Goodman

Publisher Martin Goodman apparently more often than not made much more money off his comic books for about three decades beginning in 1939. His firm produced nearly 850 pulps but also a huge number of magazines and fiction in general, if all of his men's magazines, non-fiction sports publications, and thousands of comic books and paperbacks are considered. His pulps bore the Red Circle logo in the 1930s but often no logo at all the rest of the way. He finished with 143 sports pulps, close to 20 percent of his entire pulp output.

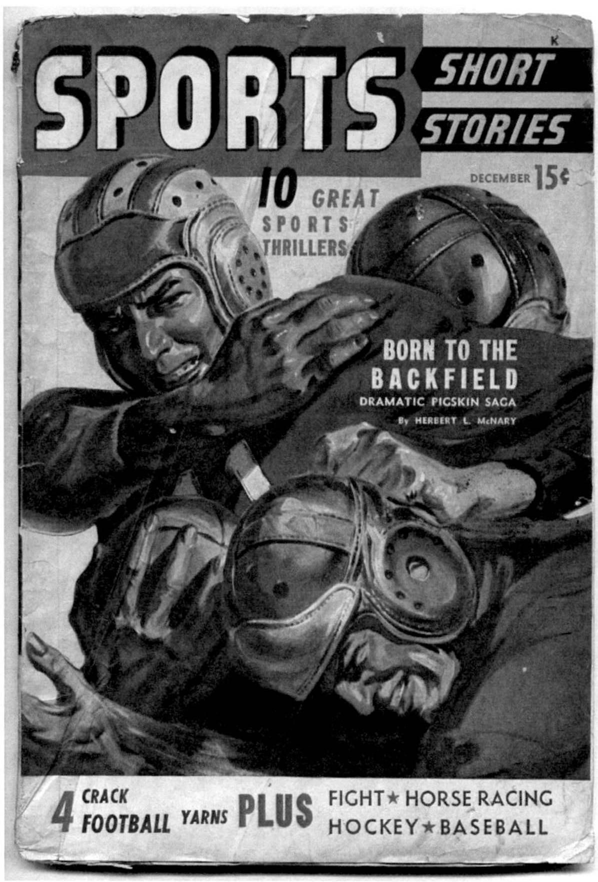

***Sports Short Stories,* December 1947 (copyright 1947 Interstate Publishing Corp.). This debut issue of a Marvel pulp shows a tackler trying to jar the ball loose. As often with this company in its post-war issues, there was no non-fiction content.**

Goodman's *Complete Sports* (1937–1943, 1946–1955) ran 60 issues across 17 calendar years—a remarkably productive run and persistent run considering the magazine's often quarterly appearances. None of his other sports pulps were especially successful, nor were most of his genre pulps, but he had amazing success in the western pulp field.

He published three

single-sport pulps in 1947—*All Baseball Stories, All-Basketball Stories* and *All Football Stories*—along with three issues of *Big Baseball Stories* (1948), four issues of *Big Sports Magazine* (1948), two issues of *Big Book Sports* (1947–1948), four issues of *Sports Short Stories* (1947–1948) and three issues of *Sports Leaders* (1948). His first sports pulp, *Star Sports Magazine,* ran 10 issues (1936–1938), and he had a long-interrupted 11-issue run of *Real Sports* (1938–1939, 1947–1948). No other pulp publisher failed with 10 titles!

Marvel's other titles were moderately successful—22 issues of *Sports Action* (1938–1942, 1947–1948) and 21 issues of *Best Sports* (1937–1939, 1947–1948, 1950–1951).

Popular Publications

Popular Publications operated from the early 1930s to 1955 and produced a little more than 5,000 pulps—more than anyone except Street & Smith's total of nearly 10,000 pulps. Popular succeeded well in every genre, the only pulp publisher to do so, but it was also the only major pulp publisher not to deal in comic books at all. Ace, Columbia, Fiction House, Marvel, Street & Smith and Thrilling all had significant success in comic books in the 1940s, which made for crowded newsstands indeed.

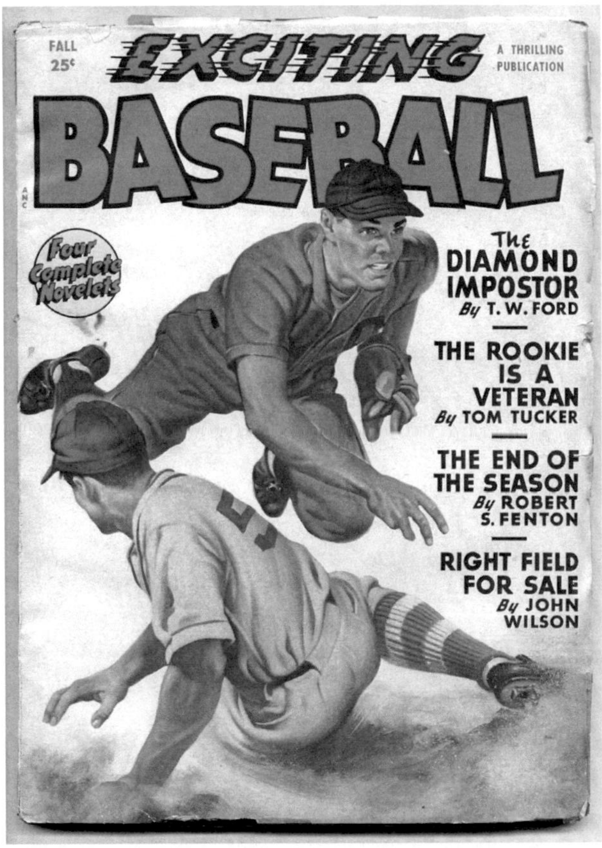

***Exciting Baseball,* Fall 1949 (copyright 1949 Better Publications Inc.). Earle Bergey vividly portrays the intensity of a double-play attempt against a high slide by the runner.**

Popular's four sports pulps all succeeded and amounted to 230 issues—one more than Thrilling and seven more than Columbia. Yet the other two publishers tried many more titles. Popular's *Sports Novels* ran 85 issues (1937–1944, 1946–1952), more than any sports pulp except Street & Smith's *Sport Story Magazine.* Popular's *Dime Sports* ran 81 issues (1935–1944), the second-most behind its sister pulp. Also successful were the runs of *New Sports,* with 34 issues (1947–1951), and *Fifteen Sports Stories,* with 30 issues (1948–1952).

However, Popular's sports output, like Street & Smith's, amounted to less than 5 percent of its pulp total. That says a lot about sports pulps, since Popular consistently featured attractive covers and numerous solid writers.

Thrilling Publications

Thrilling was the logo and Ned Pines was always the publisher, from late in 1931 to early in 1958 (and through 1971 with a quarterly version of *Ranch Romances,* filled mostly with reprints). The company produced three general-interest sports pulps, all successful, along with four football titles and three baseball publications for a total of 229 sports pulps, plus three sports stories in the one-shot *Stories Annual* (1955). It was the only company to succeed in both general and single-sport pulps and that was likely a credit to the legendary editor Leo Margulies, who guided the pulp line for nearly two decades into the early 1950s.

To compete with Street & Smith's *Sport Story Magazine, Dime Sports* and *Ace Sports,* Pines launched *Thrilling Sports* in 1936 as the fourth general-interest pulp and destined for a 74-issue run (1936–1951). *Thrilling Sports* must have succeeded nicely because it was followed by 63 issues of *Popular Sports* (1937–1951) and 38 issues of *Exciting Sports* (1941–1950), which became the largely reprint title *Five Sports Classics* for its final four issues (1950–1951). (Pines used "Thrilling," "Popular," "Exciting" and "Startling" in the titles for a large number of his pulps and comic books.)

Thrilling succeeded on three of its four all-football pulp annuals—14 issues of *Thrilling Football* (1939–1952), 12 issues of *Popular Football* (1941–1951) and 11 issues of *Exciting Football* (1942–1951) with a couple of years seeing two issues. *Best Football Novels* (1942) was a one-shot but wartime paper restrictions may have been the reason. Like Martin Goodman at Marvel, Pines did very well with his wartime comic books. Thrilling's baseball pulps seem to have started too late to run long—five issues of *Exciting Baseball* (1949–1953), four issues of *Popular Baseball* (1949–1951) and three issues of *Thrilling Baseball* (1949–1951).

14

The Phantom Issues and Oddities

In the years covered by the first-ever index of pulp baseball and football stories and of all cover themes by six major companies in this book, no pulp sports title that ran more than 10 issues ever had a consistent publishing schedule for more than three years.

Some issues, in fact, should have appeared but never did. It took many years to confirm that these are, indeed, phantom issues. Comic-book historians, including me, earlier needed many years to make many similar confirmations for the *Overstreet Comic Book Price Guide* in its first two decades (1970–1990). Now, with very few exceptions, the phantom comic books have either long since been discovered and listed in *Overstreet*—or their nonexistence has been confirmed.

Collectors and readers of pulp genres with by far the least-known magazines published and indexed—sports and romance—are still solving puzzles. Here, I am presenting for the first time the three phantom issues along with other publishing quirks that have driven collectors crazy for decades.

One: Columbia's *Sports Fiction* should have published Volume 5, No. 1, for Spring 1944, but did not, even though stories were listed in a "coming next issue" in Vol. 4, No. 6, for Winter 1943–1944. Instead, some of these stories were never published and what was to be the lead story, a baseball tale titled "Bargain Basement Ballhawk" by C. Paul Jackson, was published in the misnumbered Vol. 5, No. 2, for Summer 1944. In the same issue, "First Across the Line," a track story by Sam Carson, also appeared after being advertised for the mythical Spring issue. The Summer issue was the last before the wartime break. *Sports Fiction* resumed with Vol. 5, No. 3, for June 1947.

Two: Marvel's *Complete Sports*, Vol. 4, No. 5, for April 1943 exists; no trace has ever been found of Vol. 4, No. 6. The magazine picked up with Vol. 5, No. 1, for September–October 1946.

Three: Marvel's *Sports Action*, Vol. 3, No. 5, for October 1942 exists; no evidence of the existence of Vol. 3, No. 6, has ever turned up. *Sports Action* continued with Vol. 4, No. 1, for August 1947.

Collectors, including me, have been seriously indexing pulps from these companies for years. If these three missing numbers existed, we would surely have seen them by now. Of all types of pulp magazines that have been confirmed to exist, copies have been seen and noted of all the roughly 40,000 known issues.

It's no coincidence that all three "phantom issues" would have appeared during World War II. The war caused publication to be discontinued or frequency to be cut for every sports pulp title—except for a few single-sport pulps published once (Thrilling) or twice (Fiction House) each season. The war also caused recordkeeping errors, since many issues were likely planned but abruptly suspended or discontinued during the war, with no resulting corrections to account for issues never published.

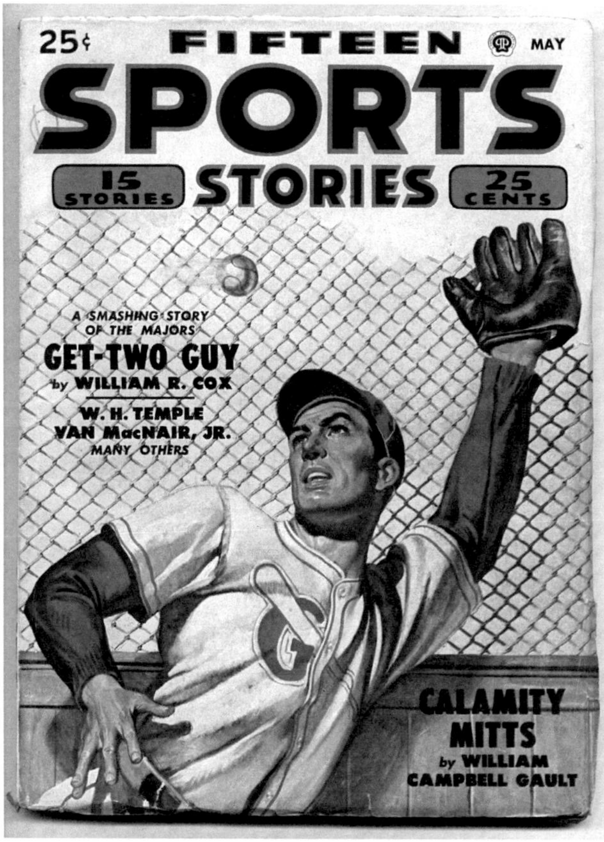

Fifteen Sports Stories, May 1950 (copyright 1950 Fictioneers, Inc.). Typical of many pulps, the cover of an outfielder making a catch does not reflect either of the two baseball stories in this issue. The cover is an oddity, in that no major league park had such a low fence. This looks more like a minor league park.

Score These as Errors!

How bad were the bookkeepers? (I'm using that term although some editors may have been required to keep publication records.) Here's an example of how bad: Fiction House began *Baseball Stories* in 1938 and continued it until 1954, with no yearly interruptions. Yet the two 1952 issues stated "11th Year" on the covers! It should, of course, have read "15th year." Isn't that amazing? They wanted to boast about their success and they under-counted the years!

Marvel, on the other hand, over-counted the years in the case of the November 1952 issue of *Complete Sports,* which began in 1937, stating "15th Year" on the cover and on the table of contents page. *Complete Sports,* as stated above about its "phantom issue," did not publish in 1944 and 1945. Therefore, the boast should have been 14th year, to be accurate, or 16th year, to be inaccurate. (How many people have you seen state something to be the 50th anniversary, when it's really the 50th whatever? It's like birthdays—on your 30th birthday, you enter your 31st year.)

But wait! When *Complete Sports* last appeared with the October 1955 issue, the statement had been revised to be correct—17th Year! (seven calendar years from 1937 to 1943 and 10 more from 1946 to 1955). One can only wonder whether a reader, a contributor, an editor or a book-keeper had called that correction. Just another pulp quirk!

I'm in no position to say which genre or even which publisher of the pulps contained the most typographical errors. I only know that I spotted dozens of typos and other mistakes when I began to collect them as a teenager. I would speculate that Columbia and Marvel had the most mistakes and Street & Smith had the least. But then, the former pair of publishers has often been said to have paid the least and S&S likely paid the most throughout its long history.

The Other Publishing Breaks

In addition to the three titles listed above, eight other major titles suffered breaks of at least two years. Here are the eight breaks:

Ace Sports (Ace Publications): Vol. 15, No. 4, for November 1943 to Vol. 15, No. 5, for November 1947 (this was an error, since Ace usually published in volumes of four issues. The next issue was Vol. 16, No. 2, for January 1948).

All Sports (Columbia): Vol. 4, No. 2, for Winter 1944–1945 to Vol. 4, No. 3, for November 1948.

Sports Winners (Columbia): Vol. 4. No. 6, for Spring 1944 to Vol. 5, No. 1, for October 1950 (Columbia usually published in volumes of six issues).

Super Sports (Columbia): Vol. 5, No. 3, for April 1944 to Vol. 5, No. 4, for July 1946.

Ten Story Sports (Columbia) Vol. 7, No. 5, for June 1941 ended the first run. The title picked up from *Sports Winners* with *Ten Story Sports*, Vol. 6, No. 2, for July 1952.

Best Sports (Marvel): Vol. 2, No. 5, for December 1939 ended the first run. The title picked up with Vol. 2, No. 1, for October 1947 and ran through Vol. 2, No. 4, for September 1948 and picked up with Vol. 2, No. 5, for February 1950, then ran six issues through Vol. 2, No. 10, for December 1951.

Real Sports (Marvel): Vol. 1, No. 6, for April 1939 ended the first run and picked up with Vol. 1, No. 7, for October 1947, in complete contrast with the *Best Sports* resumption.

Sports Novels (Popular): Vol. 11, No. 1, for July 1944 resumed with Vol. 11, No. 2, for February 1946.

Thrilling Oddities

The three Thrilling general-interest titles—*Exciting Sports, Popular Sports* and the flagship title *Thrilling Sports*—were the only general-interest sports pulps not to be either discontinued or forced to take a significant break.

Exciting Sports began as a quarterly with Vol. 1, No. 1, for Winter 1941. Then this title did something no other sports pulp ever did: *Exciting Sports* was published as an all-baseball number or an all-football number from Vol. 1, No. 2, for Spring 1941 for 16 issues though Vol. 6, No. 2, for Spring 1945. There were nine all-baseball issues and seven all-football issues.

Popular Sports went from bimonthly to quarterly publication with Vol. 6, No. 3, for Summer 1940 and was a quarterly through Vol. 17, No. 1, for Fall 1947. There was one extra issue, Vol. 8, No. 3, for November 1941, meaning there were five 1941 issues.

Thrilling Sports became a quarterly from Vol. 13, No. 1, for Summer 1942 through Vol. 19, No. 2, for Fall 1947. Vol. 14, No. 2, was dated March 1943 instead of Spring. (For this company, actual months were often listed in the indicia but the covers featured seasonal dates.)

***Popular Baseball,* Summer 1950 (copyright 1950 Better Publications, Inc.). The Thrilling Publications group copyrighted several issues of *Popular Baseball* during World War II, but the title did not begin its four-issue run until 1949.**

All of the three Thrilling general-interest pulps were interrupted several times during World War II paper rationing, meaning only two or three issues were published in some years. All three titles went from bimonthlies to quarterlies from 1949 to their demise in 1951. The last four issues of *Exciting Sports* became *Five Sports Classics,* which published mostly reprints from the 1930s and early 1940s. Unlike books, the titles of stories were unlikely to be remembered by pulp readers a decade or more later.

15

Titillating Titles, Mind-Boggling Blurbs and Terrific Terms

Of all the pulp sports titles that exploded in the 1935–1939 period from six established publishers to compete with the long-running Street & Smith's *Sport Story Magazine,* none could compare with publisher Martin Goodwin's *Complete Sports* for over-the-top verbiage to describe cover-featured stories.

Complete Sports ran 60 issues from 1937 to 1955, although it was never published monthly. Other than the quarterly *Ten Story Sports* from Columbia, the quarterly *Complete Sports* was the only regularly sports pulp on the stands by 1955 (Columbia's *Super Sports* appeared only yearly in 1955–1957). The rather prosaic title *Complete Sports* was chosen in 1937 to indicate there were no serials, which were so common in pulps of the period.

There was nothing prosaic, however, about the cover terms for story titles, unlike most descriptions used by other publishers. Other than the flamboyant Fiction House—which published almost entirely single-sport pulps—the other four publishers seldom exaggerated the merits of their cover features. *Complete Sports* was among seven titles (plus, of course, Street & Smith's 427 issues plus two annuals) that ran at least 60 issues. The others were Popular Publications' *Sports Novels* (85) and *Dime Sports* (81), Thrilling Publications' *Thrilling Sports* (74) and *Popular Sports* (63), Ace Publications' *Ace Sports* (68) and Columbia's *Super Sports* (61).

What's intriguing is that the terms became increasingly garish, if that term can be applied to words as well as art. Considering we're talking about the colorful pulps, "garish" can apply to every aspect of the rough-paper magazines.

Here are the distinctive terms first introduced for usage during each of the three publishing periods for *Complete Sports*:

For 1937–1943 (23 issues): thriller, great, smashing, winner, new, gripping, action, crack, swift-moving, thundering, big (11 terms)

For 1946–1949 (13 issues, with none in 1944 and 1945): exciting, fast-action, tense, dynamite, terrific, sensational, power-packed, thrill-a-minute, top-notch, rugged, hard-driving, amazing, feature (13 additional terms)

For 1950–1955 (24 issues): big, new (used together), riotous, starting, top, bang-up, jarring, dramatic, pulse-pounding, raw-red, hilarious, tense, timely (used together), hard-hitting, headline hot, pulse-hammering (13 additional terms)

In all, 37 different terms were used to describe cover-featured titles! A survey of Goodman's Marvel Comics in the 1960s might yield similar results.

For story titles, the other publishers would more often than not let the story titles and author names suffice along with a description like "full baseball novel," "pro football story," "college gridiron tale" and the like. No one could match *Complete Sports* for adjectival terms.

Fiction House Blurbs

Other than three issues of the general-interest pulp *Bull's-Eye Sports* in 1938–1939, Fiction House published only the long-running *Baseball Stories, All-American Football Magazine, Football Action* and *Football Stories* for a total of 106 such issues (*Fight Stories* is outside the purview of this book). Thus, Fiction House also produced many baseball stories (229 in 33 issues of *Baseball Stories*) and football stories (435 in 72 issues of the three football pulps). A handful of reprints are added to the count, since these were commercial decisions dealing with how to fill space—and also noting that few readers would remember the first publication of those stories.

Unique among sports pulp publishers, Fiction House sometimes used drama-packed full sentences as cover blurbs, just as the colorful firm did on many of its comic books from 1938 to 1954 (oddly Fiction House was among the few major comic-book publishers that did not produce any sports comics, unless a handful of the earliest *Fight Comics* counts with a boxing character). No other publisher stressed both action and sex appeal—"guns and gams"—the way Fiction House did, although women only occasionally appeared on its sports covers and guns were not a factor.

Here's a look at some of the blurbs on the covers of *All-American Football Magazine*:

Fall 1938 (first issue): For "Wise-Guy Wingman" by William R. Cox: "Irish Jim Dugan played football fun, [and] wisecracked himself off the team. But in the pinch the red-headed ball-haw proved his blarney brand of play." For "Gangway for the Iron Horse!" by William Hyliger [*sic*; it's Heyliger]: "Huge and awkward—no swivel-hipped halfback flash, but given the ball he became a non-stop football express—blasting tacklers off his path."

Fall 1939 (second issue): For "The Four Wild Horsemen" by Curtis Bishop: "A strange quartet, each from a different walk of life, off the field they fought each other, but on the field they fought as one—"

Fall 1940: For "The Galloping Ghost" by Curtis Bishop: "Shifty as a shadow—elusive as a will-o-the-wisp—but fragile as a puff of smoke—"

For First Fall 1943: For "Point-a-Minute Powerhouse" by William Heuman: "The gashouse kid made the touchdowns—the blue bloods got the glory."

For First Fall 1944: For "Pride of the Whiz Kids" by Bill Heuman (editors frequently used different first names, possibly depending on whether they personally knew the author): "Show the ex-pro a sawbuck and he'd block out the goal posts."

For Second Fall 1944: "Gangway for a Touchdown-Thief!" by William Heuman (whose name is left off the cover): "Every white stripe he crossed carried him closer to the big house bars."

For Second Fall 1946: "The Saga of Payoff Pete" by Stewart Sterling: "Was the scatback scooting for his alma mater or for Hollywood headlines?"

For Second Fall 1947: "Texas Likes 'Em Cleat-Loco" by Stewart Sterling: "If you're not razzle dazzle hep, Kid, stick to the Ivy League!"

For First Fall 1950: "The Flying Saucer Kid" by Burgess Leonard: "Jet-propelled, crazy-armed Desperate Dan was an air-express freak on a ground-anchored Dixie eleven."

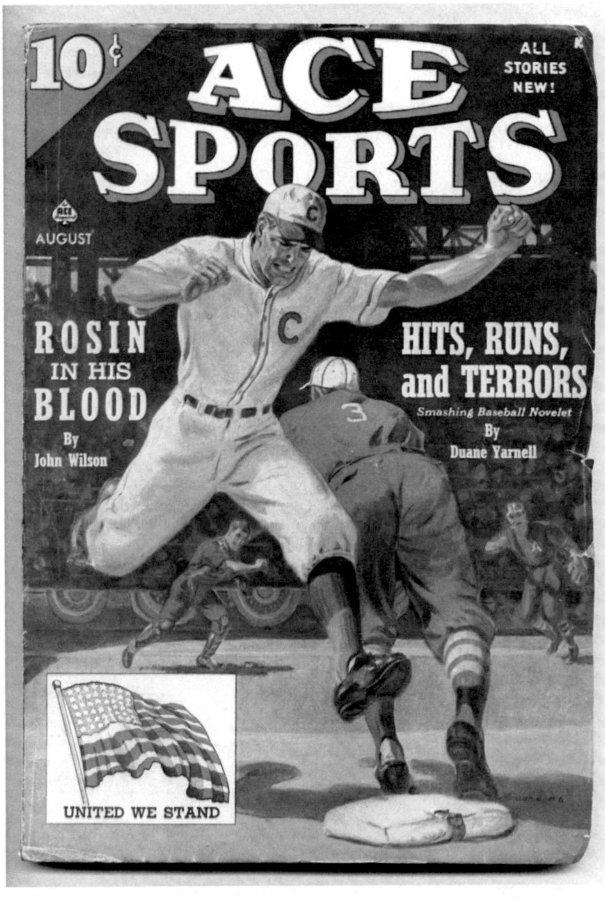

***Ace Sports,* August 1942 (copyright 1942 Periodical House, Inc.). Where is the ball? The absence of the hidden horsehide makes this cover by Norman Saunders unusual. This was actually part of the American Flag magazine cover series, which appeared on almost every United States magazine dated August.**

Story Titles

Since all the baseball and football story titles are listed in the index, the following is a handful of observations.

The story titles, not necessarily the ones submitted by the authors, ranged from generic and pedestrian to wildly imaginative, sometimes from the same publisher. In general, Fiction House and Marvel used the most colorful titles, and Columbia employed the most generic or straightforward, with the other three publishers somewhere in between.

All the publishers, though, were fond of alliteration, just as newspapers and non-fiction magazines so frequently employed alliteration (and sometimes still do).

As the chapter about the use of "busher" in baseball story titles shows, there were plenty of frequently used terms and frequent use of similar or identical story titles. For example, "Diamond Destiny" was used several times for baseball stories, as was "Gridiron Goliath" and so on.

Every now and then, a title would force a mental double-take, such as "The Fifth Base" by Joe Archibald in *Ace Sports* for April 1936. Not long after, the same author's story in *Ace Sports* for September 1936 was titled the pedestrian "Hot-Corner Guardian" for the story of a third baseman. The alliteration was clever but the story theme was obvious in *Ace Sports* for April 1939 with "Second-Chance Second Baseman" by E. Newman Eveslade.

No Hits, No Runs, No Terrors

Six years apart, Ace and Popular came up with title takes on that classic announcer's indication of a clean inning: "No Hits, No Runs, No Errors." Ace cover-featured "Hits, Runs and Terrors" by Duane Yarnell in *Ace Sports* for August 1942 and Popular came up with "No Hits, No Runs, No Terrors" by William Heuman in *Fifteen Sports Stories* for October 1948. The two stories could not have been more different.

Heuman's tale was an excellent story of Carey Ford, a high school pitching phenom brought to the big leagues and struggling with his confidence, and Al McGill, a talented veteran catcher trying to cope with alcoholism. How they help each other survive and ultimately thrive in a 14-page novelette makes for compelling reading. Here, "Terrors" has significant multiple meanings.

Yarnell's novelette is the wacky epic of how Terrors catcher Shanty Evans, a sincere player-manager with a bent for understanding psychology, is traded to the Worms and decides to hire four supremely talented but totally eccentric players, all of whom have been rejected by other teams. They all make it possible for Shanty's new club eventually to show the Terrors how the game should really be played.

Both stories are enjoyable, but the reader is left saying "That could never happen" about the Ace story but "I'm sure glad that happened and I'm happy I read that story" about the Popular tale.

16

Bushers in the Stories

If there was one word that editors loved to reflect conflict in the title of a pulp baseball story, it was "Busher!"—often used with an exclamation point. A busher, of course, was a player with major league talent and minor league attitudes/brains/habits/confidence and so on. "Bush" was an adjective slapped on a defective player and "Bushes" were a location—the minor leagues.

In the slightly more than 2,300 baseball stories in the 1,054 sports pulps indexed for this book, "Busher" or a variation of the term was used no fewer than 98 times! This wasn't necessarily the author's idea or the editor's title, but in the publishing world, editors have the final say, whether it's the title of a book or a short story. Since there were 111 all-football pulps and two basketball pulps, along with a number of general-interest pulps with no baseball stories in a given issue, "Busher" was used even more frequently than it might seem.

Some of my favorite titles involving "Busher" are "Squeeze Play for a Busher" (L.C. Lewin, *12 Sports Aces*, September 1943); "Rah, Rah, Busher" (Walt Brown, *Sports Fiction*, March 1949); "Busher with the Big League Heart" (Burgess Leonard, *Baseball Stories*, Spring 1951). But of all the dozens of different titles with the "busher" word, none was ever used more than one of my favorites, "Big League Busher"—the ultimate contradiction in terms.

From 1938 to 1951, "Big League Busher" was used 10 times! Sometimes "Big League" was hyphenated whether or not it modified a word, and sometimes it wasn't. In fact, the editing process for each publisher was erratic, to say the least, on hundreds of sports terms and even on ordinary words located in dictionaries (a while, awhile and so on). And, to be brutally honest, some pulp stories seemed if they had barely been edited, if at all.

One successful writer, John Wilson, wrote two stories titled "Big League Busher" four years apart for different publishers. (A handful of times Wilson wrote under his real name, Thorburn, using Jay instead of John, his real given name.) We'll never know if that was his title twice, an editor's title twice, or one of each, but the stories were about as different as could be.

Popular Publications and its four sports pulps used "Busher" in the title 39 times, followed by Marvel (19), Columbia (16), Thrilling (11), Fiction House (9) and Ace (4). From those numbers, you can see it was more often than not an editor's choice, since logic indicates if a writer's title were always used, the percentage of usage per publisher would be closer.

Perk Prather, Big League Busher

Wilson's first "Big League Busher" story was the more complex of his two, appearing in *Thrilling Sports* for November 1947. Like so many sports stories, it involved a secret emotion harbored by the hero—in this case, two such motivations for potential malevolence.

As the story opens, young pro rookie Perk Prather confronts Big Moose Jordan, manager of the Class C Rockets the Central League, about taking over the job a shortstop. "I'm a better ball player than the guy you got playing short," Prather bluntly says. Jordan tells him the job is not open, so Prather proceeds to tell him he looked up Jordan at the recommendation of his son, Chip, who was killed in the war while serving with Prather.

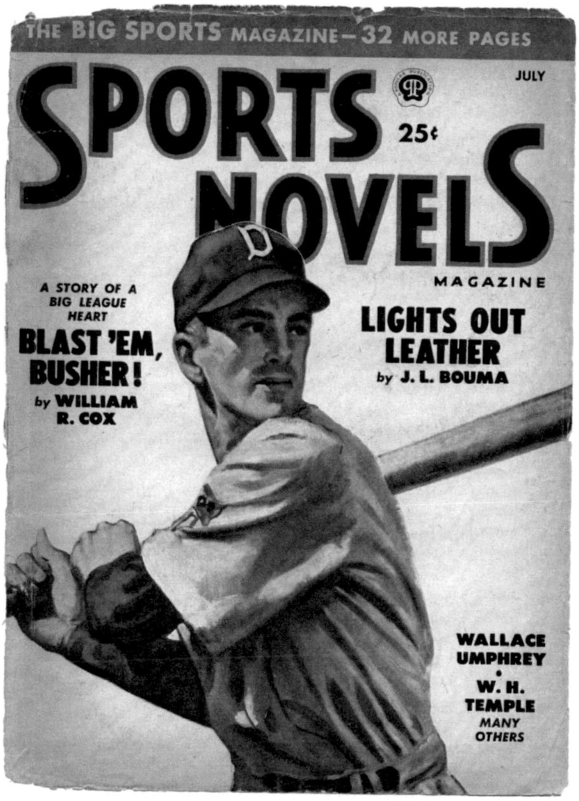

***Sports Novels*, July 1949 (copyright 1949 Popular Publications, Inc.). "Blast 'Em, Busher!" was typical of this publisher, which used "Busher" and variations far more than other publishers.**

"When the B-24 was shot from under him," Wilson relates in immediate background, "Chip had parachuted. He stood on the ground, fighting it out and taking eight Japs with him. A money player, too, Chip," written in his often clipped style, leaving out "was." (World War II ethnic epithets were common in pulps in the first few years after the war.)

Big Moose, of course, feels obligated to take on Prather, who quickly displays ability on the field and an annoying self-confidence to go with it. The team owner takes a fancy to Prather and orders Big Moose to release his shortstop, who has a family and money problems to go with less-than-stellar ability. Wilson foreshadows Big Moose's humanity when the veteran manager tips off a fellow manager lower in the minors about the shortstop's ability.

Prather proceeds to show he is a prospect, indeed, but he also seems to want to make teammates look bad after engaging in verbal spats. He is quickly on his way to pariah status, though he is playing shortstop. Finally, Big Moose confronts Prager: "Tell me the whole story, kid." It turns out that Big Moose was a ferocious but not dirty competitor in the major leagues, both physically and verbally (trash talk is not a modern development!). One of his unintended victims was rookie third baseman Dutch Prather 14 years earlier, when Perk was about six years old. Dutch was high-strung and couldn't take pressure; he gets involved with gamblers. Eventually, he takes his life when it seems he will be dubbed a failure and will not be able to pay his debts. (Why the uncommon name Prather didn't ring an immediate mental bell, Wilson does not explain.) Big Moose keeps the family's secret, dug up by a friend sports writer, again showing Big Moose's innate humanity, which Perk can finally see.

Perk, freed from seeking vengeance on Big Moose, at last realizes that seeking vengeance on Big Moose will only destroy both of them. In the final pages, Big Moose's old teammate, who has long since become highly respected scout Fog Lawler, shows up to scout the Rockets. Prather has his own problems under that pressure, but shows enough to be signed by Lawler's organization. But it turns out that what Lawler really showed up to tell Big Moose that Lawler will return to the majors as a manager and intends to take Big Moose with him as a coach. Big Moose is relieved he is no longer a "Big League Busher"—but Lawler ends the story by saying that Prather will need "a couple of more seasons in the minors." He was not the Big League Busher, after all.

Lefty Barrow, Big-League Busher

In *Sports Winners* from Spring 1951, Wilson's second short story titled "Big-League Busher" was cover-featured, hyphen and all. It's the nicely written, sentimental tale of clever 33-year-old pitcher Lefty Barrow, who has kicked around the minor leagues for 10 years but is finally getting his first genuine shot at the big leagues (he had one brief "cup of coffee," as baseball people still say, years earlier).

Cam McBride is the wise old manager of the Jay Birds in what is obviously the American League, what with references to the Clippers and an Italian star named Hap DiBello. He tells Lefty he has called him up to serve as a much-needed backup relief pitcher but most importantly to provide advice and wisdom for a potential-filled but headstrong young fastball pitcher, bonus baby Bus Harris. Lefty has a long history of helping younger pitchers. They have their ups and downs, including a hotel room fistfight, but in the end, Harris realizes from Lefty's season-long example of crafty pitching that Bus's fastball won't be enough to keep the fireballer in the majors.

The ending is contrived but not totally outrageous: Lefty and Bus both play vital pitching roles in the game that gives the Birds the pennant over the Clippers, with Lefty aggravating a serious arm problem since he knows this is likely his last shot at major league glory. Bus wins over everyone when he uses his curves in relief of Lefty to finish the win.

"Cost us your arm to win the marbles," Cam tells Lefty, informing him of a commitment from the team owner. "I figure we owe you something—plenty. You'll be back with us next year—and for as many years as you want to stay—as a tutor for the pitchers."

Wilson thus ends the story: "Lefty took a deep, wonderful breath. He'd helped a few other guys along the road, and in doing so, had helped himself. There was no better feeling."

Blurbs for "Big League Busher"

Here are the 10 blurbs that introduced the different "Big League Busher" stories:

Ace Sports, October 1938, Joe Archibald

> "The best shortstop in the league, Bill Harper was sold down the river by a hate-mad manager—for doing the kid a good turn. Then the kid came up again and took his place, and he was sold again. He was a sucker Samaritan, was Bill Harper. He cast his bread upon the turbulent baseball water and expected—cake."

Real Sports, January 1939, Johnny Lawson

> "Fandom clamored for Alonzo Hoggett and his jump ball, but the mound marvel's golden soupbone warned Hoggett that already he was on the list of unburied dead!"

Super Sports, July 1939, Mat Rand

> "When a rookie batter headed Hal Edwards toward semi-pro obscurity, Edwards demonstrated that a crippled floater and a last-place team can win a big-league pennant!"

Complete Sports, January 1941, Roe Richmond ("Bushers" is plural)

> "Blazing line drives might put Poly Marue's Lakewood Pioneers back in the league—blazing line drives and a brilliant fireballer out on the mound, and a fighting heart behind first base!"

Popular Sports, Summer 1941, T.W. Ford

> "Baseball's Wheel of Fortune Was Against Charlie Candon—But the Fighting Rookie Had the Diamond Instinct to Make the Odds Even!"

Exciting Sports, Spring 1944, W.H. Temple

> "Tough Old Catcher Crayton, in His Last Chance in Big Time, Rebels When Grandstander Storm Tries to Send Him Back to the Minors!"

Best Sports, October 1947, Orbe Bubisk

> "The kid was a powerhouse at bat, but about as capable as a Newfoundland puppy covering first base, and nobody knew better than the kid that the veteran big-leaguer he had to beat out for the keystone spot probably hit at least .400 and fielded something like 1.000!"

Thrilling Sports, November 1947, John Wilson

> "Rookie Perk Prather looked like the answer to a manager's dream but Big Moose Jordan did not realize that the dream was really a nightmare until it was just a bit too late!"

New Sports, May 1948, William Heuman

> "Snarling, bitter enemies, the two brothers spanned that vital keystone sack—a rookie who had to win, and a star who had to shine!"

Sports Winners, April 1951, John Wilson

> "Lefty Barrow had long given up hope of playing for any but bush teams. Then came the call from the Birds, and Lefty found that there was a place in big-time for a man who hadn't hesitated to help the younger players along. And Lefty was there primarily as a trouble-shooter."

17

Where Football and Baseball Numbers Prevailed

It's intriguing to note that season or career statistics were seldom used in pulp baseball and almost never in pulp football, because in real life they are such a staple of sports coverage. That was also true during the pulp sports era, although to a lesser degree.

Some statistics were never used as a fictional target in the pulps to the best of my knowledge—Babe Ruth's 714 homers in league games, Joe DiMaggio's 56-game hitting streak in 1941, Lou Gehrig's 2,130 consecutive league games played, Cy Young's 511 league-pitching victories. When the last sports pulp appeared in 1957, Ruth's career total still seemed like the stuff of baseball fantasy, since the next four players on the home run list were Jimmie Foxx with 534, Mel Ott with 511 and Gehrig with 493 (Ted Williams retired in 1960 with 521). On the other hand, Cal Ripken far surpassed Gehrig's record and both Hank Aaron and much later Barry Bonds finished with more homers than Ruth.

In 1952, when "Old Three Hundred" by Wadsworth Nealey appeared in the September issue of *Super Sports,* it was likely the most unusual pulp story ever to appear about a statistical goal. This novelette—billed as a novel but only 21 pages long—features the quest of 40-year-old Mike Timilty needing three wins to reach 300. There is a reference to the then most-recent real-life pitcher to win 300—Lefty Grove finished his career with exactly that many when he finished 7–7 in 1941—along with mentions of the others to win 300 in the 20th century with essentially the same rules that Timilty faced: Young (who pitched from 1890 to 1911), Walter Johnson, Christy Mathewson, Grover Cleveland Alexander and Eddie Plank. Apparently because rules were different in the 19th century, 300-game winners Pud Galvin, Kid Nichols, Tim Keefe, John Clarkson, Mickey Welch and Hoss Radbourn were left out.

Only 11 years after "Old Three Hundred" appeared, Early Wynn of the White Sox was 43 when he went 1–2 in 1963 to finish with 300 wins. The parallel is eerie. The only pitcher to reach that mark between Grove, the fictional Timilty and Wynn was Warren Spahn, who won No. 300 in 1961 and finished in 1965 with 363.

So Nealey's story of Timilty was remarkably true to life. But, of all things, Timilty's struggles are a lot more about his career, personality and family than his win total. There is no description—none!—of his 300th win. There is exactly one line: "...He won the three games necessary to get into that 300 club...." All of this is by way of emphasizing that what Timilty really wants is a television show for kids. He's making only $20,000 at this point—about $250,000 in today's dollars—and has been promised by a talent scout that he would be paid $6,000 per month. His wife, Lynne, has recently had twins, giving the family six children, and the aging mound star is extremely frustrated that a bonus baby pitcher, Whitey Hall, signed for $95,000. Throughout his career, though, Timulty was considered one of the good guys in baseball. He just questioned how he was being treated toward the end. His attitude did not prevent him from pitching well, including a no-hitter, but his arm health proves problematic.

Champion Sports, **July 1937 (copyright 1937 Periodical House, Inc.). Rafael De Soto, one of the best of the pulp cover artists, portrays Yankees slugger Lou Gehrig. Sports fact and fiction writer Jack Kofoed, in his article "Iron Men of Sport," said "The Iron Horse" "...had played in more than 1,800 straight games by now" on his way to a record 2,130. That was true, since he ended the 1936 season with 1,808 in a row. Since this issue likely hit the stands in May or June, what would have happened if Gehrig's streak had been halted early in the 1937 season?**

Yet Hall proves worth his money, especially the way he helps Timilty reach many wins including his 25th of the season—in the season-ending game that wins a pennant for the Brownstown Bombers. Hall pitched two great innings after Timilty, for the first time, calls for him to relieve him.

In the last few paragraphs, Timilty muses that he should be able to pitch in a more limited role the next season—but is then told he has the TV show and $8,000 per week! So the happy ending was not win No. 300, but much bigger bucks! That rang true to life then and surely does now.

"Winning Streak"

Other than a couple of plot mistakes, "Winning Streak" by Curtis Bishop in *Blue Ribbon Sports* for May 1938 is a commendable novelette involving the increasing maturity of a young major league pitching star and the growing wisdom of an old-school manager. As the story opens, manager Dan Devlin of the Amherst Angels meets in training camp 22-year-old prospect Clay Randall, a sophisticated University of Texas graduate who represents what Devlin seldom saw in his youth on any baseball team. Devlin, who began his career in 1908, claims to be 47 but most writers figure he's really over 50. What is not in dispute is his record of 17 consecutive pitching victories in 1920. Devlin is not happy when Randall requests a $500 bonus to sign (well more than $15,000 today) and incentives built into his contract regarding pitching victories, but he looks so sharp that Devlin's management agrees to the extra money.

The young pitcher impresses Devlin as a man of character as well as ability, so he decides to introduce him to his 20-year-old daughter, Mary Devlin. A relationship ensues as well as one victory after another for Randall. But manager Devlin becomes suspicious when Randall makes several excuses to delay key starts, including one against "King Carl" Hubbell of the Giants. (Numerous real-life major leaguers are named in this story.) Devlin suspects that Randall is trying to enhance his chances of breaking Devlin's record. Randall wins his 16th in a row, but Devlin figures he hasn't compiled his streak on the square, even though Mary has come to believe that he has.

"He's a four-flusher, a windbag," Devlin tells Mary at this point. "He doesn't belong to baseball. He isn't worth one of those dinky little shoes you're wearing." So Mary makes a deal with her father: If Clay does back off from any assignment that threatens his chance to tie or break the record, she won't marry him. Devlin agrees.

A key point in the story is that Devlin thinks too many modern players are soft. Ironically, some old-timers have the same opinions about today's players when compared with men who performed well after *Blue Ribbon Sports* was discontinued in 1940 after 13 issues! Devlin recalls that he set his record of 17 wins in a row in a 50-day span—a start every three days. Even in 1920, four days was more the norm. (Walter Johnson never started more than 42 games in a 154-game season in that era and usually started a number in the 30s, or about once every four days.) So the reader knows Devlin was a tough old nut.

Randall ties Devlin's record with a brilliant pitching performance against the Cubs, but it's soon discovered that he did it while suffering the pains of "acute appendicitis!" The doctor tells Devlin he should have had his appendix out a month ago. When Mary and Dan try to contact Randall's family, they learn that Clay Randall had wanted all of his extra money so he could help pay for his mother's much-needed eye operation. All of this is a bit derivative and pulpy, but it's not out of the realm of possibility.

What is fantastic is that Clay agrees to pitch only a few days after his operation in his last, late-season shot at winning his 18th in a row, since it's a single-season record. He can barely stand, but the Angels take a 4–0 lead in the top of the first inning. Clay goes to the mound—and rolls a pitch to his catcher! The umpire calls "Ball one!" and Clay walks off. The writer explains that Randall can get credit for the victory if the Angels hold the lead—which was not true of a starting pitcher then, nor is it true now. A starter must go five innings to get the win unless he is declared "most effective pitcher" by the official scorer under extraordinary circumstances. One pitch would never have been enough.

But that doesn't stop Devlin from telling his team as the story ends, "If you let them monkeys catch you and the kid doesn't get credit for this game, I'll send every damned one of you back to the bushes."

"Sun Field Slugger"

The prolific Zene Tuttler produced a fine short story dealing with a statistic in Columbia's *Sports Fiction* for Summer 1943. "Sun Field Slugger" involves the struggle of 15-year veteran Wave Seeley to avoid finishing his career with 1,999 hits. This was likely written about a year after the attack on Pearl Harbor on December 7, 1941, and player after player, regardless of age, was joining the military to serve in World War II, so it wasn't unusual to see a 34-year-old baseball player do so.

By the time Wave needs one more hit to reach 2,000, he was pretty much done as a player and his Lions had a better performer in right field in rookie Hank Flanders, who had been called up to replace an injured veteran. Seeley fails to get hit No. 2,000 in several games. Like the grand old teammate he has always been, he fakes a leg injury, so manager Joe Daugherty would not feel guilty about taking him out. Flanders thus could replace him the next day and would give the Lions a better chance to win with the pennant at stake against the Dukes. Flanders does so with his bat, but in turn he decides to fake a rib injury after he crashes into a fence making a crucial catch in the top of the 10th inning. Flanders, it turns out, has earlier noticed that Seeley seems capable of playing, after all, so Flanders asks the manager to let Seeley pinch-hit for him.

The key element is that Seeley has been willing, after all, to listen to Flanders's tip about the opposing pitcher's patterns. Flanders's teammates think it's ridiculous for the rookie to try to help the great Seeley, but when Seeley does pinch-hit, he realizes that Flanders is correct. Seeley waits for the pitch he figures to get and wins the pennant with his 2,000th hit—a home run!

When Seeley thanks Flanders in the locker room, Seeley acknowledges that what he really wanted, even more than his 2,000th hit, was to finish as a .300 hitter every season of his long career. The home run guaranteed that. Flanders, who plans to join the Merchant Marines after the season, is overheard by Daugherty, who chews him out for faking his inability to bat. Seeley acknowledges his fakery as well, mollifying the manager and making him realize that both men are unselfish teammates. As the story ends, the manager tells Flanders, with regard to the World Series, that he had better not party too late with newfound buddy Seeley.

"Flanders!" the manager yells to end the story. "No staying out later than eleven. You gotta be in perfect shape to play for us every day the rest of the season!"

When this story was written, dozens of major leaguers had finished with 2,000 hits, so it's not as strange as it might seem. But there is no reference to that milestone in context, unlike the 300 wins in "Old Three Hundred" nearly a decade later from the same publisher.

"Clutch Hitter"

C. Paul Jackson, who wrote more sports novels than anyone who started in the post 1940-era, had yet to write his first book when he came up with a twisty tale in "Clutch Hitter" in Popular's *Sports Novels* for June 1942.

As the story opens, 12-year minor league slugger Stub Kolo, 34, who has not succeeded in two major league trials, has just broken the record for an unidentified team in an unidentified minor league by hitting in his 43rd consecutive game. (Batting streaks were the talk of baseball fans after Joe DiMaggio's 56-game streak for the Yankees in 1941.) He has 39 homers—and would soon set the league record with his 40th—154 runs batted in and a batting average better than .400. But Kolo is not happy—he is bitter that Privateers owner Butch Bray has instead called up to his big league team a fine young prospect on Kolo's team, Rand Thomas. But Privateers manager Joe Manz scouts Kolo as well and insists he wants him, too.

Even so, Bray bad-mouths Kolo to Manz, informing the reader that Kolo's suspicions are correct about Bray trying not only to keep Kolo off his team, but also away from daughter Nancy Bray, with whom Kolo has long been in love. With Nancy in tow after the game in which he hits his 40th homer, Manz finds Kolo in the company of Butch Bray, who once again warns him to stay away from his daughter. Kolo explodes in bitterness against Bray, taking the better part of a pulp page to accuse him of sabotaging both his career and his love life. Manz is taken aback but not enough to abandon his desire to see both Kolo and Thomas on his big league team for the stretch run of a race for second-place money (no pennant race here!).

Kolo struggles in his third (and obviously final) crack at big league pitching but Thomas plays well. However, Kolo quickly spots a flaw in Thomas's swing and knows big league pitchers will also spot it. Sure enough, the rookie soon goes into a slump. Kolo could have kept quiet, but that's not in his character. When he offers to help Thomas, the rookie is amazed that Kolo would be such an unselfish teammate. They were never enemies in the minors, so it's not such a shock, but when Manz sees them together working on Thomas's hitting, the manager is so impressed he decides to offer Kolo a contract as a player-coach the next season. He doesn't tell Kolo, though, because he just wants to watch him for the rest of the season. Kolo, meanwhile, isn't happy to see Thomas dating Nancy after she has followed her intense, blustery father's wishes.

Getting a chance to return to the lineup when a teammate joins the Marines, Kolo hits well—and even ties a single-game record with four home runs! He also ties Tony Lazzeri's record of seven homers in a four-game span. But Butch Bray is still not convinced that Kolo has a big leaguer's team spirit, though Manz has long since realized that Kolo does have it. So, with second-place money at stake, Kolo has a chance to tie Babe Ruth's mark of five homers in eight games. Instead, he goes 4 for 4 without a homer—but drives in Thomas with the game winner with a soft, opposite field single.

Bray is finally big enough to apologize in the locker room:

> Kolo, I've got a bit of crowmeat to eat and I'm eating it. I was wrong about you. I guess I've been wrong all these years. You were big league today, Kolo. Any man who could shorten his cut on

> that short pitch when he had a chance to [swing for a homer]—Well, I'm saying I was wrong. Will you shake hands, Kolo? That's over, Thank God! Now, Kolo, do something else for me. There is a fiery bundle of girl who has just completed artistically and convincingly telling off her dad. She threatens to come in here herself if I don't send you out, and she'll do it!

Thomas assures Kolo that he is just friends with Nancy and Bray continues to talk. "I've been a complete heel, a stubborn fool, Kolo. Nan didn't want it the way I tried to arrange things. I took advantage of her loyalty to me to [cause Nancy to temporarily walk away from Kolo]."

Kolo doesn't hear any more. As Jackson's last line says, "Bray broke off and grinned. There is little use talking to thin air!"

It's a nice way to end a compelling story.

18

The Sports Plots Thicken

In the more than 4,000 fictional baseball and football stories from the six pulp publishers from 1935 to 1957 listed in this book, there is one common element in virtually all of them: conflict, more often than not far greater and more intense conflict than ever seen (or at least made public) in real life. Indeed, such conflict is seldom seen in real-life sports events.

In real-life media accounts of team sports, no matter how important the games are, the conflict is limited to team vs. team or individual vs. individual within a team framework. Non-fiction reporters, columnists and broadcasters, of course, will always look for an angle: Player vs. former team, brother vs. brother, a player who has overcome a physical or mental challenge. But the majority of real-life accounts involve a fan's emotional rooting interest and seldom too much else.

The "fans" of fictional sports did not expect to read much in the way of statistics. In fact, in some pulp stories, the score is not even mentioned, although the winning and losing teams are apparent. But, unlike real-life viewers or listeners, readers of pulp fiction almost never started the story by rooting for a particular team. Until they are given a reason to care about a team or a character, readers generally just "root" for a well-told story, especially if the outcome is not predictable.

In fiction, unlike real events, surprises abound. That is pretty much the whole purpose of fiction. Surprises in real life exist, of course, such as a .200 hitter coming off the bench to win the game. But how many times will the star athlete learn during or after the big game that the other team is coached by his father? In real life, that would be an almost unbelievable development!

Of course, far fewer secrets of all types can exist in the modern world, where the exponential increase of readily available information would have dumbfounded the athletes and fans of the 1930s and 1940s. Thus, many pulp plots seem even more far-fetched to today's readers than they did back in the day. Of all the players in the National Football League, how many would be surprised today by the type of revelations so often made or uncovered in the pulps?

The best pulp sports stories, of course, contain action and character development as well as conflict. Character development, however, was of necessity often in short supply except in longer stories. Even then, sometimes characterization develops out of surprises, such as a revelation that a coach known as a martinet actually has a heart, humanity or both.

I would estimate that hundreds of distinct plots are represented by pulp baseball and football stories. The situation is complicated by the fact that the performance of every player in a baseball game is obvious to fans but that is not the case in football, which is why many football coaches over the years have called it "the ultimate team sport." There's a lot to be said for that, since a baseball team can often overcome a poor individual performance, but that's not as often true for a football team with, for example, an offensive lineman who makes mistake after mistake.

So, let's talk about pulp plot possibilities.

In both of these most American of sports, conflict can be represented by a change in position—from quarterback to defensive back or receiver, from shortstop to outfielder. This involves the psychological challenge each individual feels, especially if he (there were very few female athletes in pulp sports) doesn't want to make the switch. Most often the switch is dictated by the needs of a football coach or baseball manager, but sometimes it's the result of a player's failure at one position, such as going from pitcher to outfielder.

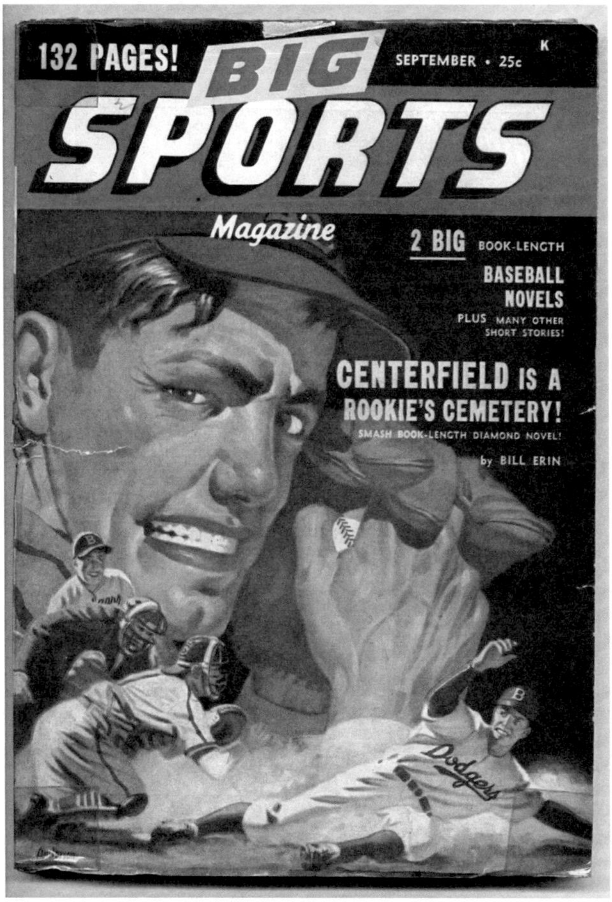

***Big Sports Magazine*, September 1948 (copyright Exclusive Detective Stories,, Inc.). Allen Anderson contributes a highly unusual combination of symbolism and reality in this portrayal for a Marvel pulp. The pitcher's emotions are portrayed, apparently before this play at the plate.**

In stories of pro sports, conflicts involving position changes aren't as common as they are in stories about college or high school athletes. In fact, many high school batting stars must become fulltime pitchers to advance to the majors, because there are many more pitching spots available on rosters as there are starting-level position places. For contrasting reasons, most high school quarterbacks wind up playing another position in college since there are several first-string receivers or defensive backs but only one starting quarterback on every level. It's often said that the toughest thing in sports is batting, but I would suggest it is winning the regular quarterback job at the major college or professional levels.

Family conflicts and/or cooperation are often plot elements. There are plenty of father-son or brother-brother stories. The best of them, of course, are more complicated than that. For example, the story of a father/head coach who is ethical enough to relegate his son to the backup quarterback job may or may not be exciting if his son wins or fails to win a game serving in emergency duty. That's a bit of a cliché, but what if the story ends with the top quarterback recovering from injury and the coach's son back on the bench? That would likely be a compelling story.

In real life, statistical goals can be vital to athletes, especially those seeking a better contract or a trade. Some pulp fiction deals with those goals, but not all that often.

Personality conflicts are at the root of many pulp plots. Coach vs. team, coach vs. player, owner vs. coach, player vs. player or players, player or coach vs. umpire, player or coach vs. reporter, player vs. love interest, and on and on. Sometimes the conflict is resolved in victory or friendship; sometimes the resolution is sad or grim. Often in stories involving conflict, one human is essentially a good guy and one has motivations involving ambition, selfishness, criminality and so on. The best stories of conflict involve real people instead of cardboard figures. In real life, seldom are athletes all good or all bad; they all have their complexities, good points and flaws.

In real life, games of all types seldom involve sensational revelations. In pulp stories, they are as likely as not.

Jealousy, that most common of human emotions, is the linchpin of many a story, especially when a teammate gets too much credit and/or another teammate gets too little. For many athletes, the situation becomes untenable. Likewise, if two men are battling for the affections of the same woman, jealousy may never go away, or at least not until both are happy. The same applies to financial circumstances. During the "bonus baby" era of the 1950s, when major league teams would pay a supposedly brilliant prospect more to sign than they would pay a proven veteran, the jealousy that resulted became a common theme.

Racial resentments and/or sheer racism—so common in the real world following the integration of big-time baseball and football teams in the post-war 1940s and 1950s—were far less often a theme in the pulps. The topic was just too difficult for many writers to handle. Especially in the 1940s and early 1950s, in the era before *Brown v. Board of Education,* integration and civil rights—racial themes were not considered good for magazine circulation in a significant part of the country. Inter-racial couples, common in today's media including advertising, were never seen in the pulp era.

It should also be noted that the real pulp sports era was essentially 1936–1953. The total number of sports pulps in 1935 and 1954–1957 was only 51 issues, meaning that about 95 percent of the 1,054 sports pulps appeared in an 18-year window (plus the powerful influence of Street & Smith's *Sport Story Magazine* until its demise in 1943, of course). That means racial themes were seldom seen.

In baseball, many stories were set in the minor leagues, leaving open endless plot possibilities involving promotions and demotions. A much smaller percentage of football stories were set in the professional ranks; the college game received far more real-life headlines until the 1950s, when the explosive growth of television steadily enhanced the appeal of both.

Fear is part of some plots, especially fear of the ball in baseball and of being badly injured in football. The "yellow" athlete is the subject of many plots, especially in an era when manhood and courage were so valued in fiction as well as real life.

Scandals, especially involving women, gambling and shady behavior, are often plot elements. Genuine crime, more often than not the "fixing" of games, is sometimes a plot element. The college basketball point-shaving scandals of the late 1940s and early 1950s were huge news, but basketball stories were far, far less common than baseball and football tales throughout the pulp era. The occasional story of an ex-con's secret would pop up, often with the reader knowing the facts before teams or fans.

Lineup versatility occasionally became a plot element, such as fielders who could not hit well—"good field, no hit"—or football players who could play well on only one side of the ball, during the seasons when they often played both ways.

The "big game" was far more often an element in baseball with the World Series and in football with the bowl game.

"Class conflict," as it were, was frequently involved in football and baseball when it came to situations involving hillbilly athletes, upper-class people from colleges and the like. It had a double meaning in football stories, in which themes were common of seniors vs. freshmen and sophomores. (In much of the pulp era, freshmen were not allowed to play on varsity teams at colleges.)

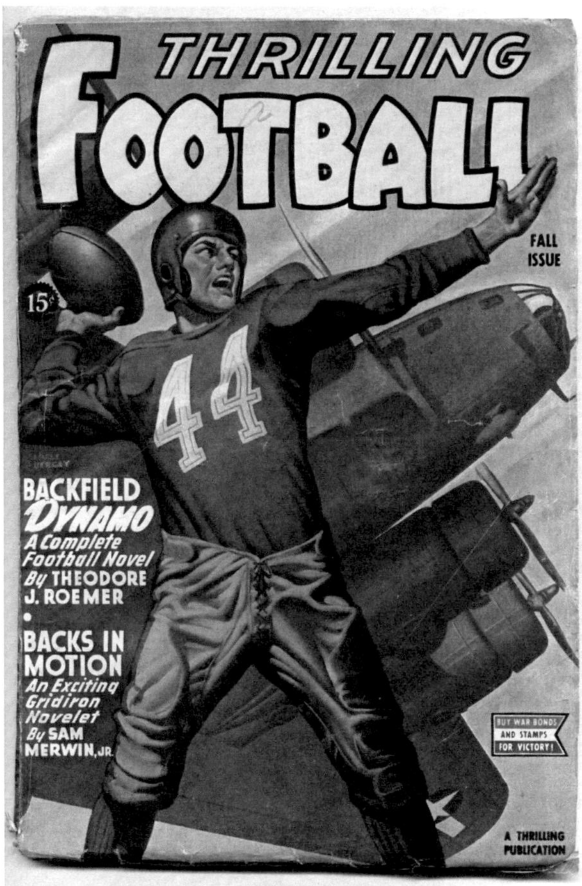

Thrilling Football, Fall 1944 (copyright 1944 Better Publications, Inc.). Earle Bergey's symbolic cover features two types of wartime bombers—a quarterback and a B-17.

During World War II, military themes were common in pulp sports. Military and camp teams, returning from the war, a veteran's courage or lack of it, and so much more provided fodder. Plot themes sometimes involved aging athletes, in some cases those who sacrificed years to military service.

Of course, some plots involved crucial decisions in big games. These are generally the closest thing to typical real-life reporting seen in a pulp story, but often what leads to the decision involved some form of conflict resolved in time to set up the necessary heroics.

19

The Few Women in Pulp Baseball

Only a handful of pulp baseball stories—and no football stories that I have seen—deal with women on the field, whether playing in their own league or against men.

One such tale, "Patience at the Plate" by J.J. Mathews in Columbia's *Ten Story Sports* for April 1955, was a piece of fluff with a happy ending and a pleasant protagonist but no real logic, internal or otherwise. It required a "suspension of disbelief" beyond almost anything ever seen in pulp sports.

At some undesignated level of organized baseball, complete with a commissioner, Jack Costain is managing the Danton Clippers in Ohio. A hustler type with whom he served in World War II brings a beautiful, highly athletic girl ("woman" was not used in those days) to Costain as a legitimate prospect. It turns out that 5-foot, 100-pound Patience Cooper Baldwin could indeed play, at least well enough both at bat and at first base in her first workout to convince Costain and his general manager to sign her. To his credit, it's not for a "dog and pony show" to attract fans, but rather because she looks good enough to help the team, as Costain tells the reader while narrating the story.

Mathews, whether a pen name or not, sold four baseball stories and one football tale to the pulps, all to Columbia. His grammar and sentence structure are as good as or better than most in this story, but he leaves an awful lot out, beginning with an explanation of why anyone five feet tall would ever be placed at first base, no matter how well he or she could hit or field. It's said that she has spent four seasons playing well in a men's semipro league and she does show superior skills while each teammate would "shake his head in awe." Costain tells the general manager, "She's the best player I have ever seen, in twenty years in baseball. She'll draw fans like honey draws flies; she's worth everything we have to give her."

When Costain's boss reminds him the commissioner probably won't allow a girl to play, the manager responds,

> I'm sick and tired of the attitude that baseball is holy. They throw a midget out of the St. Louis [Browns] because he is a midget [Eddie Gaedel after pinch-hitting once in 1951]; they won't let a club sign a girl because it cheapens the game. I'd like to ask the Commissioner why they allowed the Browns to sign Pete Gray, that one-armed ball player, during the war. [Gray batted .218 in 118 games in 1945]. He's as much a freak, or gimmick, as this girl is.... I'm going to sign her, Dick, if I have to take it to the Supreme Court.

Costain signs her for the $25,000 she requests. He tells the team there will be no more swearing in the dugout because "this girl is a lady." He says she will use his office to dress and shower.

The next day, in her first moment on the field, the opponent's leadoff batter tries a drag bunt but Patience (she's never referred to by her last name) neatly gets the out and the batter mutters, "Women! I suppose they'll be running for President next!" In 1955, that was more unlikely than a woman playing baseball with men!

In her first at-bat, Patience hits "a soft, lazy lob over the heart of the dish" for a two-run homer. But the next time the Blues come to bat, catcher Drexel (first names were not always used) singles and soon is ejected because he "had begun to get fresh with Patience and he had stepped on his toes with her spikes." Even in 1955, it seems unreal that the first player to reach first base against the girl's team gets fresh with her! But Fowler, Drexel's replacement runner—even though ejected base runners are not allowed to be replaced by pinch-runners!—tells Patience, "Miss, Drexel had it coming!" To which she replies, "Thank you. I'm here to play ball—not fool around." To which he grins and says, "Yes'm." Patience follows with a run-scoring single and a three-run triple, finishing with five RBIs in an 8–0 win!

Soon after the game ends, Costain receives a telegram from the commissioner, ordering him not to play her again and saying he is immediately flying to Danton (obviously Dayton). Reporters are frustrated because Costain won't allow them to interview Patience. But, in a move that defies logic, Jack and the general manager, along with the club's lawyer, let two reporters accompany them to a meeting that night with the commissioner and his two lawyers!

The commissioner expresses his objections to a girl playing. "Look at Drexel—he started to get fresh with her and I expect others will, too."

At this point, Costain interjects, "Mr. Commissioner, there wouldn't be any Negroes playing in the majors today if Jackie Robinson hadn't been willing to take a few digs and insults." Robinson broke the modern major league color line in 1947 with the Brooklyn Dodgers, but by 1955 Costain's noble but inaccurate logic made no sense, since all the teams except the Boston Red Sox had been integrated. He doesn't change the commissioner's mind, but Costain tells him he has tried to keep as much as possible out of the press and that they will all meet the next day. That made no sense, either; such a smashing debut for a women in baseball, quotes or not, would have been America's biggest sports story the next day.

The next day, Costain tells Patience she "played a great game. I hope the Commissioner was impressed." What impressed Costain most was how Patience avoided an argument about a hard tag! (No other details about her game were provided.) But Patience is not so enthusiastic; it turns out that most of the players have asked her out and she isn't sure what to do. "That's a problem, all right," Costain tells her. "I suppose every one of them's beginning to feel a little pang in his heart, Patience. You're a very beautiful girl, Patience. I suppose you know that." Patience responds with a grin, "Thank you, kind sir." Costain says he'll let her know about the commissioner's decision, which turns out to be negative. The manager and the commissioner verbally brawl, and when Costain says he insists on playing Patience, the commissioner leaves with a huff while saying, "Then, sir, the war is on!" Patience is heart-broken after meeting with Costain and, without telling him, checks out of the team's hotel.

Two weeks later, Costain meets with her again. She's ready to reveal her secret. She is really Patience Jackson, daughter of former major leaguer Dick Jackson, with whom Costain played in 1936. Her father wanted a boy and taught his athletic daughter how to play baseball, but she tells Costain what she really has always wanted is to become a Hollywood actress. Her baseball feats convinced a Hollywood talent scout to sign her up for Dynamic Studios, which is exactly the result she sought as a baseball player.

As the story ends, Costain tells the reader, "I just saw Patience Jackson in her first movie. She really is a wonderful actress."

"Curves Crazy"

Another of the few stories involving female players is "Curves Crazy" in Marvel's *All-Baseball Stories,* a one-shot dated October 1947. About the same time, the publisher also produced two other one-shots, *All-Football Stories* and *All-Basketball Stories.* The author was Gene D. Robinson, who sold at least 19 baseball and football stories, along with numerous other sports stories to four pulp publishers. This short story, which is spoiled by numerous typos and grammatical gaffes, was obviously not meant to be taken seriously, even thought the tale did appear during the era of the All-American Girls Baseball League in the heart of the Midwest (and in 1992 the subject of the movie *A League of Their Own*).

Forrest "Woodsy" Darwin, 45-year-old owner of the Belk City Gobblers—a team he created for his son, player-manager Bob Darwin—has hired a matrimonial agency to introduce him to potential brides, though he doesn't want anyone to know it. He's taken aback when the object of his pen-pal affections, the much younger Millie Maples, meets him at the train station and is surprised to see an older man than she expected. She has brought her "girl baseball team," as Robinson non-grammatically puts it. She and 13 teammates make up the Band Box Brunettes, "and not a blonde on the club," she says.

The elder Darwin later mutters, "A girl ball team. I'd rather she'd brought along a herd of elephants." The population of the town, including inquisitive reporter Bennie Upton, is agog with interest, notwithstanding that the Hawks are also in town to meet the Gobblers in a three-game series with the pennant at stake. The Band Box Brunettes capture attention with a pre-game workout before the Hawks move in to beat the Gobblers in the first game. Meanwhile, manager Bob Darwin has fallen hard for Millie.

The next day, Millie talks Bob into a three-inning "workout" exhibition and the women beat the Gobblers 1–0, with Millie getting a hit for the only run. The only explanation provided is that Millie says she has formed a team with the best girl players in the country. But the Gobblers are inspired enough to go on to beat the Hawks 9–1 in the second game of the series.

At this point, it's explained that the "obscure" Big Six League is not part of organized baseball and there are no hard-and-fast roster rules. This becomes the key point in the story after Bob admits to his angry father that he has, indeed, fallen in love with Millie and that they plan to be married. The outraged Forrest Darwin is so angry at his son that he fires the entire team and plans to forfeit the final game, and the pennant, to the Hawks. Millie goes to the elder Darwin and tells him that he must have mistakenly sent her a photo of his son instead of his photo, just as Millie had suspected when she saw how old Forrest was in person. Forrest agrees with son Bob that the only solution is to have the only team in town, the Band Box Brunettes, play by name as Gobblers in the final game, even though they're a "girl team."

Bennie Upton, the curious but kind reporter, learns that the Brunettes have a .745 winning record over three seasons when they have played against men on their barnstorming tour. Upton learns that star pitcher Essie Latham has lost only twice to men. He thus excites the town and tickets become a hot item, after all, resulting in "a monster crowd."

The Hawks don't take the whole thing seriously until they realize the girls can play. The girls provide lots of defense but not much hitting while falling behind 1–0 into the bottom of the ninth. Two walks and a sacrifice bunt put two runners in scoring position with two out. Then manager Millie pulls a surprise when she realizes there is no rule preventing her new love Bob from pinch-hitting for the Brunettes, a.k.a. Gobblers. Bob slams the first pitch off the right-field wall to win 2–1. "Anyhow, it took a man to beat us," mutters the Hawks manager, which would have spoiled the story if it weren't a romantic comedy.

After Millie turns the team over to Essie Latham following her marriage to Bob, he asks what caused such a beautiful young woman to try a matrimonial bureau. But the typesetter's garbled quote makes it, "Say, how come you to ever try a matrimonial bureau—with your looks?" But we know what Bob means.

"It was a lark. We girls did it for fun," Millie responds. "I did it for a lark—but I caught a Gobbler."

A Female Player Labeled "Baseball Humor"

The concept of a woman playing Major League Baseball was considered so ridiculous that the back-of-the-book short story "Pennants and Petticoats" by George Kramer was labeled "baseball humor" in the table of contents of Columbia's *Super Sports* for September 1952.

And, indeed, it was a humorous story of how super promoter Swifty Parker brings a female centerfielder to the St. Louis Lions, one year after another such promoter/owner type, Bill Veeck, brought 3'7" Eddie Gaedel to the St. Louis Browns for what turned out to be one pinch-hitting appearance.

Cookie Martin isn't a bad player but soon most of the team falls in love with her and distractions ensue. She doesn't last too long—she is beaned in what turns out to be her last game—and she disappoints the whole team when she chooses Swifty himself to be her husband.

What neither Swifty nor Cookie told anyone is that they were already married when she joined the team!

What readers never knew was that George Kramer was actually the prolific William Heuman, who wrote a handful of his multitude of stories under that name.

A Female Impersonator at Shortstop

"Wench at Shortstop," credited to house name Mat Rand in Columbia's *Sports Fiction* for December 1950, was not labeled humor, but it could have been.

It's the story of a game between a small-town team in Wyoming and the Baltimore Bloomer Girls' Baseball Club. It turns out that two of the Bloomer Girls are obviously Bloomer Boys, so to speak, but the Wyoming fellows don't let that bother them because they are all agog over beautiful shortstop Pansy DeMarr.

Pansy is anything but a pansy and even legs out a game-ending inside-the-park home run with a great slide at home to beat the Wyoming fellows 2–1. The real shocker, though, is that "she" is discovered to be a "he"—a genuine female impersonator who can play shortstop with the best of them!

20

High School Football

The vast majority of football stories during the pulp era dealt with college football, since most of the real-life headlines were devoted to the college game. There were quite a few involved with pro football, both big time and small time, along with the military version of the game during World War II. But high school football? There were only a handful of such stories, almost all published by Thrilling.

It is true that some teenagers read the pulps, especially the science fiction magazines and, yes, the sports publications. But the majority of pulp readers were adults, and thus pulp editors tailored most of their stories for high school graduates and those who didn't make it that far but still were literate. In fact, teens who read the sports pulps likely preferred to read about their "older brothers" on college gridirons. The many sports novels designed for young adult readers in the 1940–1970 era had a higher percentage of high school stories than pulps did, but these novels were designed primarily for the increasingly educated students in middle school and high school in the post-war years.

When Leo Margulies, the editor of the Thrilling line for nearly two decades, put together two of the first baseball and football anthologies in the late 1940s for Cupples & Leon with stories from his own magazines, he did not use stories of high school sports, even though both books were obviously designed to appeal to the teenage readers for whom Cupples & Leon produced so many books.

Baseball Roundup (1948) included 10 stories suitable for young-adult readers, including six of major league ball, one of the minor leagues, two dealing with the college scene and one about town ball played by high school graduates with a variety of backgrounds.

Without exception, the authors chosen were among the most prolific in pulps—John Wilson, Joe Archibald, William O'Sullivan, Sam Merwin, Robert Sidney Bowen, Jack Kofoed, Don Tracy and Bill Erin, plus the pen names Roger Fuller (Tracy) and Carter Sprague (Merwin). None of the stories contained especially adult themes. Interestingly, the Archibald story originally appeared as by Perry Dixon (apparently a Thrilling house name) as part of the eight-part Larry White series in the late 1930s in *Thrilling Sports.*

In *All-American Football Stories* (1949), seven of the nine stories Margulies selected dealt with college football and the other two involved the pro game. Again, there were no stories of high school football. Six of the names listed for authors earlier appeared in *Baseball Roundup*—Wilson, Tracy, O'Sullivan, Merwin, Sprague and Archibald—along with Richard Brister, Nelson Hutto and Robert Fenton, all well known from the pulps.

So, what about the best Thrilling Publications stories of high school football? Except for Wilson's novelette "The Touchdown Way" in 1951, they were written by lesser-known pulp writers. Two were short-short types by John Gartner: "Last Game" in *Exciting Football* for Winter 1945 and "High School Coach" in *Thrilling Football* for Fall 1944. Another was a 10-pager by Ted Stratton, "Stars Over the Gridiron" in *Popular Football* for Winter 1945. Then there was the novelette "The Junkman's Son" by Don Keene in *Thrilling Football* for Winter 1949.

Stratton's story is almost entirely a play-by-play of the high spots of an unbeaten season, with one twist: a superstitious coach. Gartner, who wrote four young-adult sports novels for Dodd, Mead in the 1950s, focused on the emotions of two different coaches in their last high school games. Keene, on the other hand, produced a well-developed story with excellent characterization.

Keene, who was credited with seven football and baseball stories, all for Thrilling Publications, may well have been a pen name or house name, just as so many were who appeared for only one company, no matter which one. Indeed, it's hard to believe a little-known writer could have produced such a well-realized story as "The Junkman's Son." In one respect, it's similar to Wilson's excellent story dealing with high school delinquents on a football team.

"Junkman's Son" begins with an explanation that this is a tale of the past, when sororities and fraternities were allowed in many high schools nationwide. Indeed, as the 1950s approached, such elite social organizations had become primarily a part of the national college scene, where they had long prevailed. This is the story of potential football star Andy Gellig, the son of a poverty-stricken junkman known as "Give-a-Nickel" Gellig. He doesn't want his son to play high school football and doesn't even want him to save the pre–high school clippings he has earned for what today would be known as youth football. Father Gellig, as he is called, insists that what he wants is to see Andy become No. 1 academically in high school so that he can get a head-start on a much better life.

What Andy doesn't realize is that Hilltown High's coach, Joe Flaherty, is dubbed "The Lucky Phoney" by his fellow coaches. It turns out that Flaherty works with the fraternities to make sure he plays their best boys in a scratch-my-back, scratch-your-back system. As Keene writes, "Flaherty, sub-consciously perhaps, realized his own shortcomings and was in constant terror of losing his job. In his slow-witted way he had arrived at the decision that the best way to insure [*sic*] his staying on at Hilltown was to make himself so popular with the portion of the student body that 'counted' that any move to replace him would be met by a students' uprising."

During rush week, the poverty-stricken Gellig makes the social mistake of asking about and comparing the initiation dues and membership fees of the four primary fraternities. He is thus formally blackballed by all four fraternities, who tell Coach Flaherty that they want nothing to do with Andy. That doesn't stop him from turning out for football, but even with a 48–0 lead in the first game, the coach refuses to play him and even sends him to the locker room early. When *Herald* reporter Jerry Banks, who doesn't cooperate with the fraternities, asks Flaherty why he did so, the coach lies and says Gellig had a "bum knee."

The next week, however, Banks observes at practice that Gellig is running well in a punt return drill. The coach observes this and panics. He schemes to have Andy badly beat up in a scrimmage, asking line star Mike Roragen to lead other fraternity members in punishing Gellig physically so that he will break his leg and either give up football or be too injured to play. Andy is battered and beaten, but soon Roragen halts the scrimmage to avoid seriously injuring Andy and orders his teammates to lay off. After reporter Banks witnesses much verbal chaos between Roragen, his teammates and the coach, Banks tells him,

> You made a mistake, Joe. You thought these kids could be as rotten as you are. They might be snobs and they might do some dizzy thinking about their fraternities, but they're basically okay. You did a good thing, Joe, when you shocked them to their senses. Yeah, you were swell, even though you didn't mean to be and even if it's going to cost you your job.

Ultimately, Roragen and the players apologize to Andy and welcome him to their team. Principal Pop Slade fires Flaherty and sets into motion a plan to end the Greek system at Hilltown. As the story ends, Keene writes that "the day was not far off when everybody at Hilltown—athlete, esthete, average kid—would have reason to be thankful for the changes that would all be due to Andy Gellig, the junkman's son."

What is so noteworthy about this story is that the protagonist engages in no game action at all, but the reader realizes that Andy is already a genuine star with remarkable courage.

"High School Coach"

In Gartner's "High School Coach" East High coach Jim Baker seeks an open job at State University in order to fund $5,000 in brain surgery for his assistant, Shorty Cook. (That much in today's dollars would be nearly $75,000.) In a college game 15 years earlier, Cook had been severely injured because of a dirty play using the knee of the mighty Buck Masters—the same man Baker must beat in Beach City's league title confrontation with West High. State athletic director Mike Horan will be on hand, admittedly to offer the winning coach the State post. That's not a particularly realistic way to offer a job, but it's a good story hook. Cook, by the way, has long since recovered enough to help Baker, but still needs the surgery.

All of that is a contrivance, but otherwise it's a touching tale. As the game goes on, Baker's star fullback, Bob Morgan, sustains a head injury caused by the knee of a West player. The technique was not ruled illegal, but Baker knows it has been taught by the unethical Masters. Morgan, backed by Cook, soon tells Baker he can return for a possible game-winning play—but Baker remains skeptical. Finally, Cook breaks down and tells Baker, "Don't put him in, Jim. I was wrong. He's not ready. I know why you want the State job so bad, Jim. But don't take a chance on the boy. Don't let Buck Masters give him what he gave me!"

Morgan begs Baker to let him play, but the coach knows what's right. "No, Morgan. It's just a game. If I put you in now you might be permanently injured. I can't take a chance on your future, boy."

Baker's team loses to Masters's team, but outside the locker room the East coaches are stunned to hear Horan turn down Masters for the State job. Masters protests vehemently, but Shorty Cook leaves the locker room and cracks the 275-pound Masters in the jaw, with Horan looking on. Masters doesn't dare attack Shorty, and Horan soon offers the job to Baker:

> There never was anyone considered but you, Jim. Masters' team played hard driving football. But yours played smart football as well. Do you know when I was real sure you were the man for us, Jim? I had the glasses on you when you made the decision not to put Morgan back in. I've been around a long time, boy, and I know how hard that choice was. We need a man like you at State, Jim, to build winning football teams. And what's more important, to build men.... One more thing, Jim. If you don't take Shorty along with you, I'm going to be real disappointed.

Of course, the vast majority of high school coaches were (and are) not cruel and unethical the way the coaching villains were in "The Junkman's Son" and "High School Coach." Most readers likely realized this, but conflict is what often made a pulp story a pulp story. Today, an athlete with a concussion would go through protocol, taking any temptation to return him to a game out of a coach's hand. Instead, the story might be whether the athlete himself returns to football or decides to retire, so "High School Coach" could not be written the same way today.

"Last Game"

Jim Devers is only 50, but he calls himself "an old, broken-down coach" who needs to retire after 25 years of high school coaching. The four-page short-short story is filled with details of preparation for his last game—his last opportunity to beat West in an unnamed part of the country. He tells nobody outside his family that he is planning to retire.

So he shocks his team just before kickoff by acknowledging this will be his last game. "I want you to win this game for me," he tells the team bluntly. "...I want you to win this game for an old broken-down coach. I want to sit in my easy chair on a winter evening and lay my head back and close my eyes and dream. Dream of the last team I ever coached—the first one to beat West! Let's go!"

How did the game go? We're never told, other than the team won for Jim Devers. Not even the score is mentioned in the five paragraphs—five!—devoted to the game. In a way, that's what makes this story so touching. More space is devoted to the post-game celebration—and a crying spell Devers endured when the locker room was finally empty—than to the game itself. Somehow, it's entirely fitting.

After dinner with his wife, Mary, and their three daughters, after "a running fire of conversation" about what a day it was, the adults settled down in their easy chairs. "Mary looked up from her knitting, started to speak, then stopped and smiled." The story then ends, "Ex-football coach Jim Devers was asleep."

"Stars Over the Gridiron"

Stratton's entire 10-page story reads like a string of newspaper play-by-play accounts of several of the eight games Coach Ben Herron's West High team wins to take the league title. There is no back story, no characterization, no real plot—except for the fact that Herron is superstitious. There is a sports writer, Del Ackers, who constantly roots for the team and writes like the all-time "homer"—like nothing that would ever be permitted today (and was seldom seen in the 1940s, as well).

After the last victory, Ackers pulls an old horseshoe out of Herron's coat pocket. "From the left hind foot of a white horse," the coach says. Then Ackers pulls out a shamrock, three rabbits' feet, a lock of baby's hair, a wisdom tooth, and another horseshoe. After such a straightforward story, this was quite a surprise ending!

21

Crime on the Diamond

Dick Friendlich was not a prolific pulp writer, but he did an amazing amount of writing as a famed sports writer and columnist for San Francisco newspapers before, during and after the period when he also wrote 18 sports novels for teen readers from 1948 through 1967.

His books were consistently among the best of their kind, so it was no surprise he wrote a unique short story in Fiction House's long-running *Baseball Stories* for Spring 1953. "The Face at First" was billed this way in the table of contents: "The hillbilly's baseball pitches were his lone defense against a conscience that gnawingly echoed: You're a murderer" with the last three words in italics.

I met Dick in the early 1970s when I was a young journalist, and a nicer guy you would be hard-pressed to find. I told him I enjoyed all of the novels he wrote on baseball. (At the time, that was the only sport I was interested in reading about, because I grew up in a family of baseball fans, from my grandmother on down.) But I surely wish I could have asked him about "The Face at First," of which I was unaware until many years later.

Friendlich obviously borrowed from the only time in Major League Baseball history, before or since, that a pitcher killed a batter with a pitch. Ray Chapman, a star shortstop for the Cleveland Indians, had played all 111 games of his 1920 season when he died after being hit by Carl Mays of the New York Yankees. Mays went 26–8 that season and turned 38 years old shortly after he last pitched in the 1929 season. His career record across 15 seasons for four teams was 208–126 and, ironically, he was also among the best hitting pitchers of his era, hitting .268 lifetime with 291 hits including five home runs.

As the story opens, Friendlich describes second-year major league pitcher Clem Bassett of the Hornets as "faster than Feller when Bob broke in [1936], some said, and just wild enough to be effective." (Like many writers, Friendlich uses a real baseball player, who was still active when the story appeared, but does not use real team names.) Six weeks earlier, Cowboys rookie shortstop Joe Cramer had died when hit by a pitch from Bassett six weeks earlier and Bassett had been sent away to recover emotionally.

"Clem had made it look good, though," Friendlich writes. As the pitch left his hand, aimed at a spot just to the right of Cramer's ear, he had shouted "Look out" in feigned apprehension. And, as he had hoped, Cramer had turned, and tried to fall away from the plate, and the gray-white deadly missile had taken him right at the base of the skull. Afterwards, Bassett had succeeded in forcing tears to his eyes as he tramped the hospital corridor in the brief death watch with the baseball writers and the other players. He kept wringing his hands and repeating wildly, "It got away from me! I knew it as soon as it left my fingers! I yelled to Joe to look out! It just got away from me!"

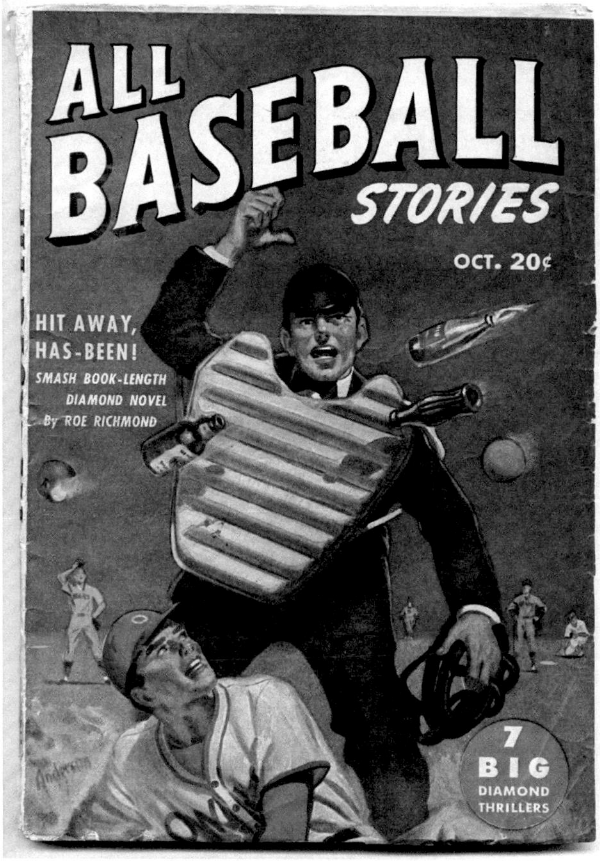

All Baseball Stories, October 1947 (copyright 1947 Interstate Publishing Corp.). Allen Anderson's portrayal of an umpire being barraged on an out call by three bottles, an orange and a half-eaten apple. This is artistic license taken to an extreme, since the runner is looking up for the call.

It's explained that four years earlier, Cramer and Bassett were both breaking into baseball in a Class D league on the same team. Bassett was so poor he had never even eaten in a restaurant until signing his first contract. Cramer caught Bassett stealing a teammate's wrist watch but told Bassett that he would not report the incident if he would put the watch back. Much later, in his second season in the majors, Bassett had already begun to steal items from teammates in the locker room when he was stunned to find Cramer in the lineup of the Cowboys. Bassett knew that once Cramer heard the stories about the thefts, his petty racket would be exposed. So Bassett killed him the best way he knew—with a fastball.

Cramer was struck in the fifth inning, but had already warned Bassett about a brushback pitch earlier: "Look, hillbilly, you try that on me once more and you'll need a new leg. I keep my spikes filed for guys like you. Look out the next time you have to cover first base."

Now, with Bassett back on the mound against a different team, the Cougars, a batter named Grant got an infield single. (It was common in pulp baseball to refer to last names only, just as newspaper accounts sometimes did.) But Bassett didn't see Grant dancing off first base—he saw Cramer! When the next batter stepped up, Bassett also saw the face of Cramer. He was so rattled that he made a couple of mistakes, allowing a run to score, and the manager took him out.

Bassett, given another start, strikes out the first three batters he faces and seems to be his old self. But when a batter singles to open the second inning and the next batter, Dick Sedgewick, hits a grounder to the first baseman, Bassett races to cover first base. Suddenly, he remembers Cramer's threat to spike him, so he turns his head toward the runner but sees Cramer's eyes, not Sedgewick's. Because he should have been looking for the throw, Bassett is struck by the ball where he had hit Cramer six weeks earlier—at the base of the skull—as Sedgewick runs down the base line. Bassett dies.

The story ends in the aftermath of what seems like a tragedy but winds up being poetic justice. In the final paragraph, Sedgewick, innocent of trying to spike Bassett, is outraged when he is asked by doctors about "two long, blood-smeared slashes on Bassett's ankle." Sedgewick cries out, "It's a damn lie! I don't care if they did look like spike wounds. I was still 10 feet away from first when the ball hit him. How the hell could I have spiked him from 10 feet away? Answer me that!"

Thus does Friendlich insert the element of supernatural—or did Bassett spike himself? This was a highly unusual ending for a pulp baseball story.

"The Eyes Have It"

In "The Eyes Have It" in Columbia's *All Sports* for March 1942, Bill (William) Heuman offers a unique take on the old gangsters-bribe-a-player theme. As the short story opens, slugging veteran first baseman Beau Bradford is in a severe slump in the final days of a pennant race, having seen his batting average drop from .360 to .310. His beloved old manager for a decade, "Uncle Hen" Whately, tells Bradford to hang in and that he is too valuable to bench, especially because he is still better than any replacement would be.

Bradford admits to himself that his eyes are not what they once were, but he has secretly ordered what he hopes will solve his problem. At this point, gangster Blackie Malone's men kidnap him at gunpoint. That was a common theme in the nickel novels of Heuman's youth, but wasn't seen too often in the pulps and films of the 1940s. Malone offers $2,000 to Bradford if he will continue to play without glasses, because he has learned of his vision problems.

Bradford is far too clean-cut to consider throwing a game, but he figures his much-loved old manager, who has encountered investment problems and is basically broke, also needs money to pay for his sudden health issues. Not just the $2,000, but shares from the World Series if the Cougars can beat the Eagles in a doubleheader that will decide the pennant. So Bradford takes the money to play without glasses, which he could have easily obtained, but makes no guarantee about his performance level. Then, in a newspaper account the morning of the crucial games, a sports writer reports that Bradford was seen at Malone's headquarters.

Bradford's sterling reputation is such that the fill-in manager expresses faith in him. He goes on a batting rampage and the Cougars sweep to take the pennant. In the final paragraphs, when he turns over the $2,000 to team officials to help Uncle Hen, he stuns his teammates by telling them that even though he did not play with glasses, he had ordered newfangled contact lenses but had to wait for their arrival. "You can't see 'em," he says. "They're contact lenses. They fit over the eyeballs on the inside. Something new they got out. I can only wear 'em a couple hours at a time.... You see, they're specially made and got to fit exact. That's why it took me a few weeks to get them."

"Modern" contact lenses were not available to most people until the late 1930s, which explains why Bradford had to explain it all. One can only wonder how many people might have read this clever little tale with contacts!

"The Diamond Murders"

In 1937, pulp mystery and crime writer William Edward Hayes made baseball murder mysteries into a cottage industry. He wrote two baseball whodunits for *Detective Fiction* weekly and one for Red Circle's (Marvel) *Best Sports* for June 1937, the third issue. Red Circle called it a "complete novel," but the 28-page story—with some of the largest type used in a pulp—was really a novelette. This was among a handful of sports stories by Hayes.

The chief protagonist is veteran catcher Hal Kerry, embattled player-manager of a team oddly referred to only as "The Appersons," named after the owner, known only as Old Man Apperson. Sports writers are asking Kerry if rumors are true, he is about to be traded to St. Louis, but Kerry doesn't yet know. The first baseman, referred to only as Crofton, is a mouthy sort and so is the third baseman, Bib Nieland, whom Kerry suspends for going over the top with his comments. It isn't long—the seventh page—before the rebellious Crofton defies Kerry's orders and swings away instead of putting down a sacrifice bunt. During that time at bat, Crofton is mysteriously shot in the back and dies. At the same time, Kerry is knocked out in the clubhouse area, and thus does not see the shooting.

There follows not a baseball story but a police procedural for 14 pages, with much confusion over Kerry's fate, since it's not certain whether Helen Apperson, the owner's daughter and seemingly Kerry's romantic interest, has legally inherited the team. It's also not certain to others if Kerry is the culprit, since Crofton was rumored to be in line to replace him as manager (although the reader knows it could not be Kerry, since he was unconscious). Not long after Crofton's murder, Old Man Apperson himself is found dead next to a canal from "a blow in the back of the head."

Kerry refuses to leave the team and, with Helen's encouragement, continues to serve as catcher/manager, all the while wondering if he might become murder victim No. 3. As the tension mounts, Kerry realizes who the murderer is—a photographer shooting the game under a hood. Instead of throwing to second base on a steal attempt against the Tribesmen, Kerry pegs the ball at the photographer and knocks him out as the camera goes flying. It turns out the camera is a disguised gun and that the photographer is actually Spud Littman, trigger man for gangster Kiss Spillane, who is located in the stands.

In the brief aftermath, it's revealed that Crofton and the financially distressed Apperson had gotten involved in a tangled web with Spillane. Crofton, befitting his reputation as a cad, tries to "put the heat on Kiss for a bigger salary" once he took over as manager. As a result, both the first baseman and the owner had to be killed. Hayes has a good line during the aftermath, describing Kiss Spillane as "a bad imitation of Edgar G. Robinson in a derisive mood." Thus does art imitate life imitating the art of being a gangster!

As the detective wraps everything up, he says, "Kerry, there's a flock of newspaper boys out there now. You want to make a statement?" To which Kerry responds, "Just one that concerns them. Tell them I'm going to win a pennant." Hayes ends with, "If you remember the end of that season you'll remember it was no boast. He led his team to a pennant."

New Sports, April 1948 (copyright 1948 Popular Publications, Inc.). This high kick by a pitcher into the logo was an unusually clever design. *New Sports* was actually a continuation of *Dime Sports,* but it began at 15 cents and soon became 25 cents.

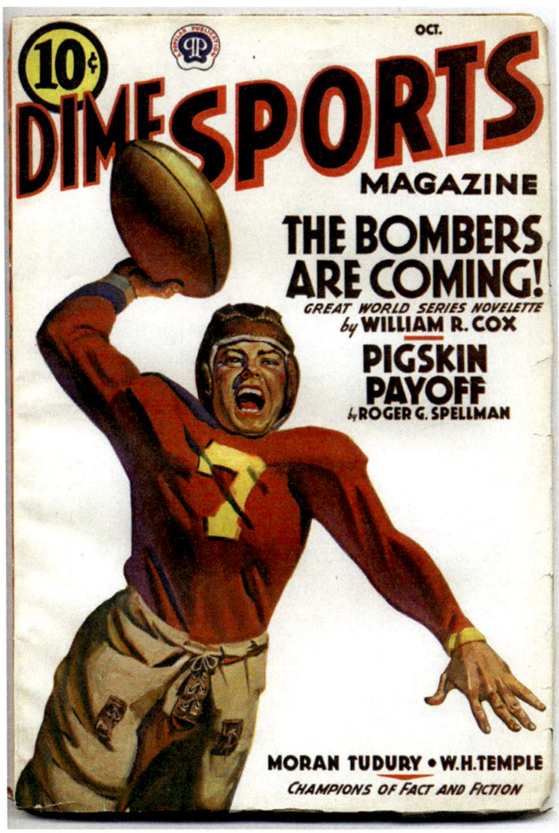

Dime Sports, October 1939 (copyright 1939 Popular Publications, Inc.) Even though the featured story is a World Series novelette, the cover features a quarterback.

Dime Sports, August–September 1939 (copyright 1939 Popular Publications, Inc.). The featured story is a World Series tale, but this issue would have hit the stands no later than July!

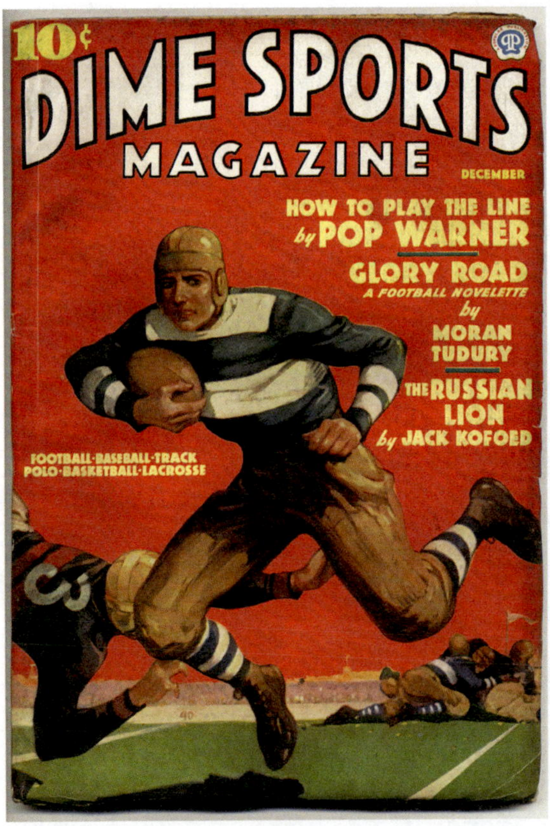

Dime Sports, December 1935 (copyright 1935 Popular Publications, Inc.). "How-to" articles such as "How to Play the Line" by the immortal coach Pop Warner soon disappeared from the sports pulps in favor of either biographical articles or more fiction.

12 Sports Aces, **May 1940 (copyright 1940 Ace Magazines, Inc.). Safe or out? On this cover by Norman Saunders, with the ball on the left side and the base on the right side, it's impossible to tell.**

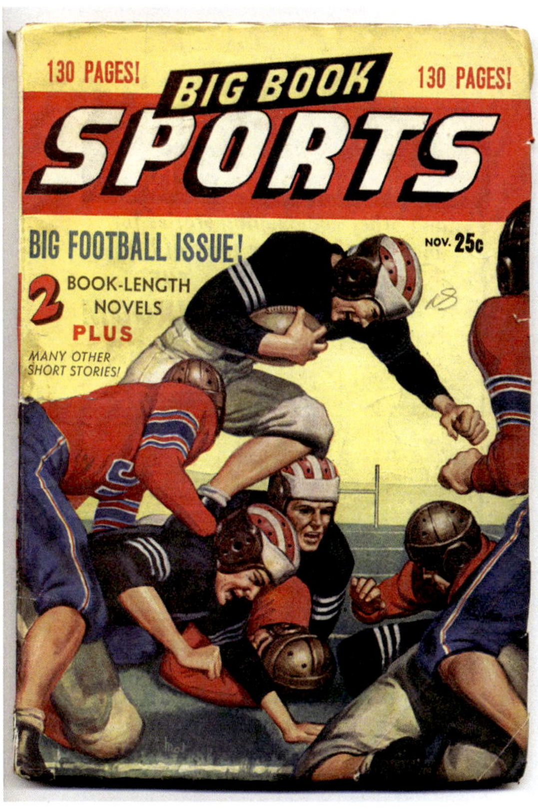

Big Book Sports, **November 1947 (copyright Exclusive Detective Stories). Eight football players are portrayed on this unusual cover for the first issue of this Marvel title. With the goalpost in the background, this is not a play in the red zone.**

All Football Stories, December 1947 (copyright 1947 Interstate Publishing Corp.). A player's smile at the goal line tells the tale of a touchdown on an unusual cover for this Marvel one-shot title. Although listed quarterly in the indicia, this went along with the contemporary one-shots *All Baseball Stories* and *All-Basketball Stories.*

Sports Action, August 1947 (copyright Stadium Publishing Corporation). C. Bloom is credited on the table of contents page of this Marvel title with this oddly symbolic cover of a pitcher, the ball and a glove.

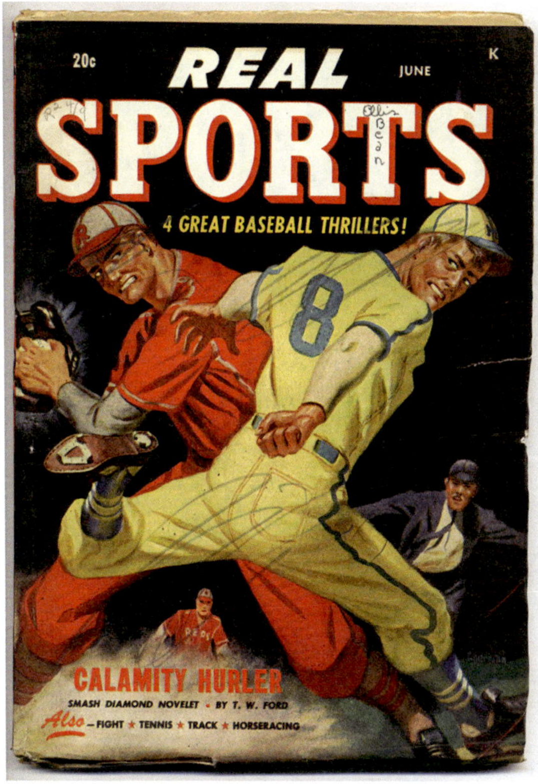

***Real Sports*, June 1948 (copyright 1948 Interstate Publishing Corp.). The umpire signals safe even though the first baseman has the ball in his glove as a runner steps on first base on the cover of this Marvel title.**

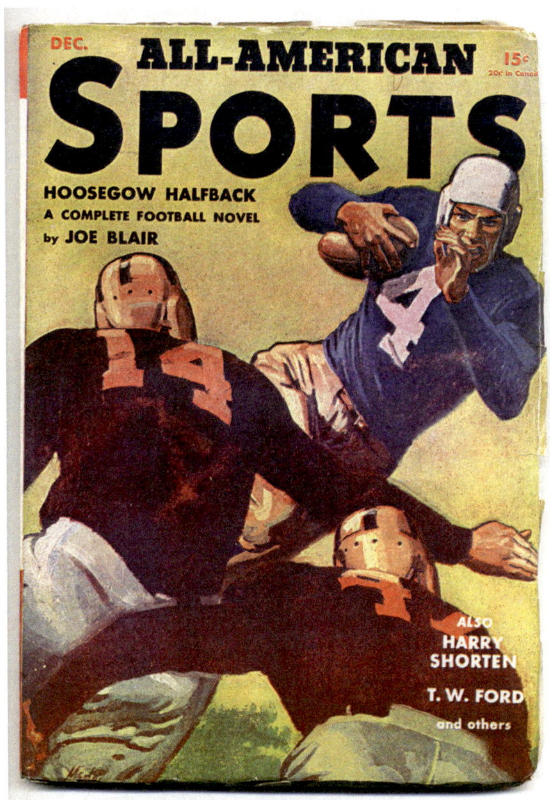

***All-American Sports*, December 1940 (copyright Atlas Fiction Group, Inc.). This muddy cover on the first issue of a Columbia title was typical of much of the company's less-than-stellar art. This title ran only two issues—the only outright failure of the company's seven pulp sports titles.**

Super Sports, December 1951 (copyright Columbia Publications, Inc.). This symbolic cover of a World Series issue features "Fury on First" by Hunt Collins (a pen name for S.A. Lombino, best known as Ed McBain and Evan Hunter). It was the only baseball story credited to Collins, a name known for science fiction in the pulps.

Football Stories, First Fall 1942 (copyright 1942 Fiction House, Inc.). Fiction House was noted for using "guns and gams" on the covers of many of its pulps and comic books, so Allen Anderson's cover reflects that with a cheerleader close to the action.

All-American Football Magazine, First Fall 1942 (copyright 1942 Love Romances Publishing Co., Inc.). George Gross didn't do too many close-ups for sports pulps, but the intensity of this leather-helmeted warrior is beautifully portrayed on this signed cover, which more resembles a Norman Saunders effort.

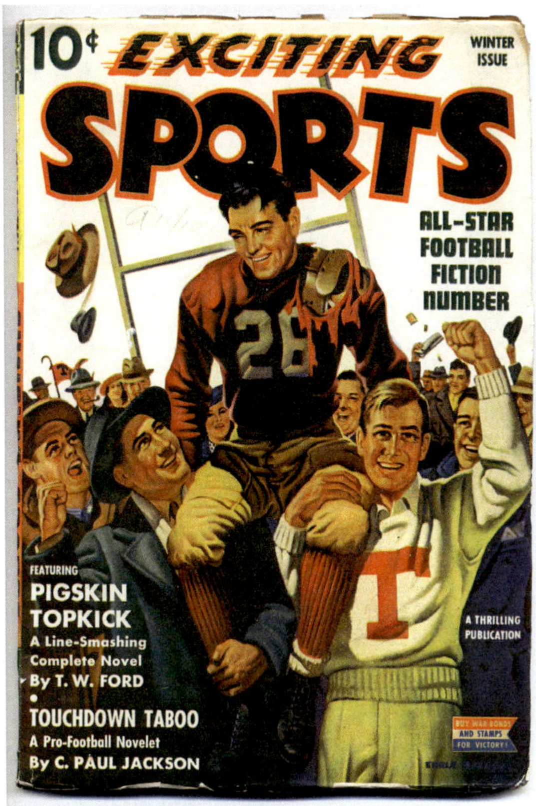

Exciting Sports, Winter 1943 (copyright 1942 Better Publications, Inc.). A college football hero, with his jersey torn apart, vividly displays the joy of victory with only fans and a falling goalpost in the background of this Earle Bergey masterpiece.

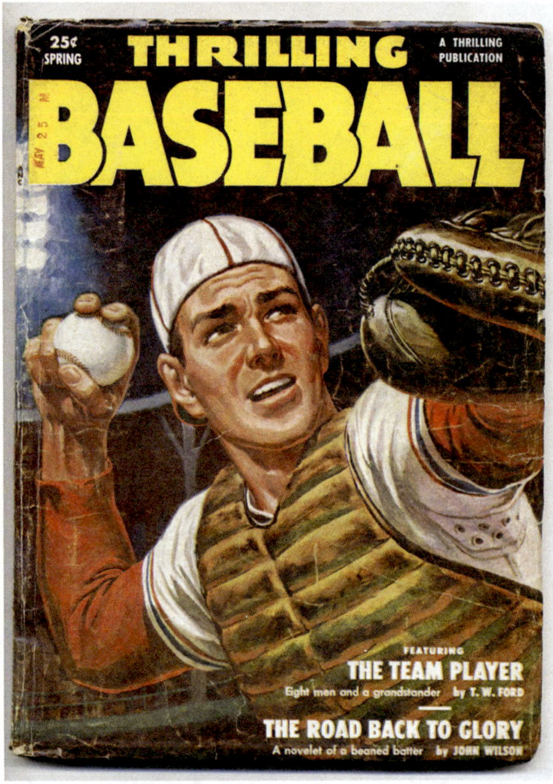

Thrilling Baseball, Spring 1951 (copyright 1951 Standard Magazines, Inc.). Thrilling Publications (as its logo always ran) tried three all-baseball magazines in the final years of its long pulp sports era, but they ran only 12 issues combined as television began to take center stage with baseball fans.

Popular Football, Winter 1945 (copyright 1944 Better Publications Inc.). Earle Bergey's great patriotic cover shows a soldier's happiness at seeing a player tackle a dummy with a caricature labeled Tojo.

22

A Bonus (Baby) for 1950s Readers

The revival of Major League Baseball's bonus baby rule in 1952 led to several intriguing stories in the last years of the sports pulps, all from competent contributors. The rule had a convoluted history beginning in 1947 until 1965, when the advent of the major league draft ensured that big league teams would never again be forced to carry players with no experience—but with at least a $4,000 bonus for signing—on their rosters for two years, as they were in the seasons from 1953 through 1957. A $4,000 bonus in those years was equal to more than $40,000 today in buying power.

Pulp writers, of course, made the stories far more dramatic with bonuses of as much as $70,000 or $80,000, since that was an easy way to make conflict between veterans and bonus babies seem more realistic and inevitable. Sandy Koufax, for example, signed for the major league minimum of $6,000 plus a $14,000 bonus in a deal brokered by his father, Irving, as related by Jane Leavy in her biography of the Dodgers' pitching Hall of Famer. Leavy wrote that the Milwaukee Braves offered him $30,000 but Koufax declined to go back on his deal with the Dodgers and never pitched in the minor leagues.

Seven Anderton (1893–1958) began writing sports stories in the final years of his long pulp-writing career, which began in the 1920s. Among the 14 baseball and football stories he wrote for Columbia and Thrilling was "Nize Bonus Baby" in Columbia's *Ten Story Sports* for July 1953, apparently in response to the 1952 rule revival. The title was a takeoff on Milt Gross's newspaper strip "Nize Baby."

This story is pure pulp, but it's captivating throughout and awe-inspiring in the sense that talented 18-year-old bonus baby Carl Sadowski succeeded on the field, but not at all off the field, and by the end volunteers to serve in the Korean War instead of trying to continue to play ball, in part because he gambles on his own team. There weren't many pulp sports stories in which a young protagonist emerges as a total loser, but this 25-page novelette of a ruthless young man who "had to win," as he always said, was one of the few.

Anderton features the manager of Rivertown Bisons, Marty Winfield, and 36-year-old shortstop Buddy Boden, a longtime fan favorite. (Even though the plural of Bison is technically Bison as well, in the 1950s there were no pro sports teams with singular names.) They are utterly baffled by the combination of cockiness, supreme self-confidence and selfishness of Sadowski, who as the story begins has batted .828 in 27 games and 133 at-bats for his high school team with 34 stolen bases. Sadowski demands a bonus of $15,000 after all taxes and other deductions—and gets it, since Boden's skills clearly aren't what they once were.

Sadowski quickly gets involved in verbal and physical scuffles with teammates and opponents. After one such fight, he tells reporters, "He was in my base path, so I ran into him. Then he jumped me—and any ape that jumps me better kill me, or he's going to get hurt. That's all I have to say." This from an 18-year-old! Winters asks Boden, the consummate team man, to room with Sadowski to try to get him straightened out.

Sadowski soon helps win a game with a run-scoring hit when he is asked to bunt and is fined $50—a cliché in lots of baseball stories and movies. But what was anything but a cliché is what Sadowski tells his manager: "Don't fine me for playing my own way. You didn't teach me the game. If you know more about it than I do, [then] you play. If you fine me again, I'll go into the damndest batting slump you ever saw—and my feet may start getting tangled up. I'm winning ball games and I'm not going to be fined for it! ... I make the difference. If you don't think so, put Boden back in my place and see what happens...." Sadowski has just played his 13th game and is batting .740 with no errors at shortstop.

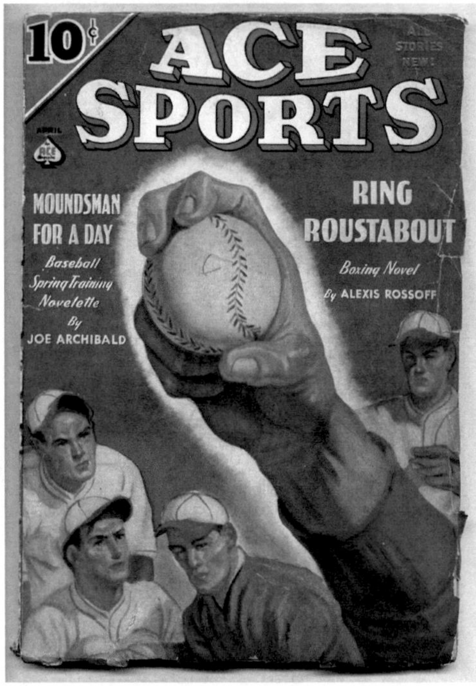

Ace Sports, **April 1939 (copyright 1939 Magazine Publishers, Inc.). When the baseball season is about to start—this issue likely hit the stands in February or March—what's better than a glowing tribute to pitchers?**

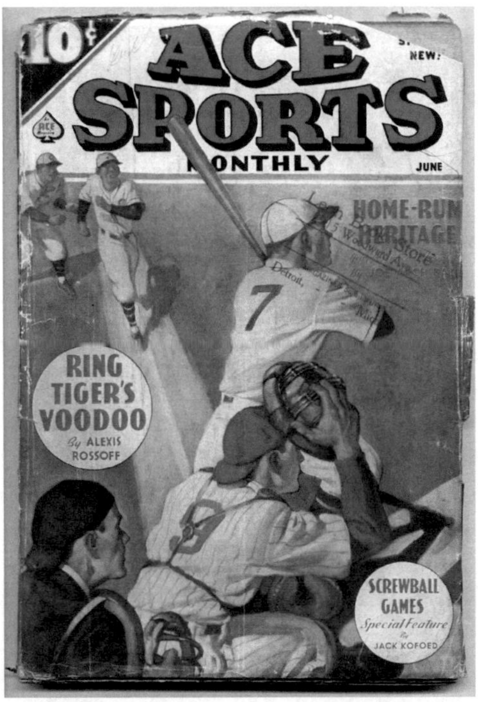

Ace Sports, **June 1938 (copyright 1938 Magazine Publishers, Inc.). The batter follows the ball he apparently hit into the right-field bleachers but the runner from third base isn't even looking at it.**

Ultimately, after many puzzling incidents involving the young phenom, Boden and a friendly sports writer, Tom Elder, learn that Sadowski is involved with gamblers, just as he had been in his home town. Sadowski tells his manager that a mob boss offered him big bucks to throw games—and when Sadowski refuses, he is forced to win a fight with two gangsters including, as he puts it, "I laid Buck out with a couple of shots." Sadowski injures his ankle in the melee, and never plays another game for the Bisons after Winfield learns of his situation.

Sadowski's teammates, with Boden back in the lineup, are inspired enough to win the pennant and World Series with Sadowski relegated to the bench. Boden is a bit amazed when he learns of the kid's military plans, but Sadowski is something of a young Ayn Rand: "Why not? What's wrong with a country where a guy can do anything he's big enough and strong enough to do. The Commies have got to be stopped or it'll get so a guy can't run his own racket."

Winfield figures the Sadowski story may be enough to force a change in the bonus baby rule: The story ends with the manager telling Boden, "The Commissioner is going to be in there pitching. Next year and afterwards, any kid that gets into the majors is going to first demonstrate that he's more interested in playing baseball than in getting rich. And contracts are going to have different wording. You watch." It took longer than "next year," but Anderton's manager was right.

"Bonus Baby"

In H.C. Butler's short story "Bonus Baby" in Marvel's *Complete Sports* for October 1954, pitching prospect Tommy Lock joins the Hornets after signing for an $80,000 bonus. Such an amount would no doubt have caused much angst in the 1950s, when that was more than most veteran players made in a four- or five-year span and the minimum pay for any player was $6,000.

There's nothing wrong with Tommy's character and manager Stubby McLean thinks he has what it takes. But burly Mike Randall, a former star who won only eight games the year before, mercilessly harasses Lock because Randall feels threatened. Lock takes some rookie lumps and eventually he and Randall have a violent locker-room fistfight. A teammate breaks up the fight but Lock feels growing pain in his pitching hand. He doesn't want the manager to know and Lock survives a relief job in the game that means a pennant, thanks to smart pitching and sheer courage on the last play, when Lock makes a great throw to first base on a tough chance to end the win.

Lock blacks out and when he regains consciousness, everyone has learned he pitched with a broken finger. Even Randall, his bitter enemy, realizes what a heel he has been. "I guess I had you wrong, kid. I guess you're one bonus baby that ain't wearing didies any more. I had that sock in the puss comin' I guess. I'm sorry I got such an iron jaw that it broke your hand."

"The Bonus Bust"

Christopher Fleming wrote only three pulp baseball stories, all for Columbia in 1952–1953. But his "The Bonus Bust" in *Ten Story Sports* for October 1953 is a sweet short story, indeed.

It's the story of Joe Keith, who signs for $75,000 with the Cod City Gold Sox, a mythical major league team that must keep the outfielder on the roster. It seems everyone bitterly resents him, especially Biggo Taylor, the popular power-hitting outfielder who "is pushing 40" but can still play. Joe incurs the anger of manager Cliff Hug when he swings away instead of bunting and brings home three runs when his long drive to the outfield is dropped. Hug gets even angrier when Keith steals home on his own to win the game. Hug and Keith eventually get into such a verbal spat that the manager fines Keith and he responds, "OK! Fine me fifty! I got plenty!" So the manager makes it $100, equal to about $1,000 today.

Eventually, the hatred for Keith, whose batting average drops to .232, grows so great that he starts drinking. But a friendly bartender coaxes Keith into seeing the wisdom of trying to respect his teammates and even asking the manager and Biggo Taylor for advice. It works! But even before then, Keith writes a check for $70,000—a donation to a home for old ball players—and gives the check to the manager, saying he'll play for the $5,000 he really deserves. It's a remarkable gesture.

As the story ends, Keith's teammates have been won over by his maturity and willingness to learn. The plot may be far-fetched but the lesson is real.

"Bonus Baby"

Another story titled "Bonus Baby" by the prolific western/sports pulpster Roe Richmond appeared in Columbia's *All Sports* for April 1950. It's the tale of a great pitching prospect named Hardister, who feels sorry for himself because it seems his teammates rarely play well when he's pitching, although he has an 11–12 major league record—pretty impressive for a 20-year-old.

The story is mostly game action, but Hardister eventually realizes he needs to take charge and stop blaming others. But he also needs to become more aggressive verbally, too. But just when it seems he is becoming better at handling his situation, his arm goes dead. So he decides to try something he once saw in high school—pitching at a variety of angles to reduce arm strain—and he finds his way into the hearts of his teammates when he wins a game that puts them into the World Series.

The story ends with no guarantee Hardister will play in the Series—or even be able to return to the team—but a teammate puts it best: "Hope your arm ain't ruined, Hardy. But hell, a kid with your guts don't need too much of an arm."

23

A Bit of Baseball in College

Almost all pulp baseball stories are set in the professional ranks, either the majors or minors, but a handful were set in college as well as high school, as you can see from the chapter on the preps.

During the primary pulp sports era from the mid–1930s to the early 1950s, the vast majority of Americans did not acquire a college degree. Since pro football did not yet have the popularity it enjoys today, most attention was focused on college football, with plenty of fans devoted to high school football as well, especially in small cities and towns. The sports sections of both metros and smaller papers were filled with stories about college football compared to the relatively small space devoted to the pro game, especially before World War II.

Baseball, though, was another story, since college baseball was played mostly by white students from well-off family backgrounds. College players like ULCA's Jackie Robinson in the late 1930s were uncommon indeed, from the standpoints of both talent and race. There was nothing in the pulps from a baseball standpoint like there was in the numerous Frank and Dick Merriwell baseball stories for pre-college readers from 1896 to 1916. The Merriwells, of course, had adventures in many other sports as well as all over the world.

One of the few Merriwell types in the pulps—the Merriwells themselves reappeared in serials and complete stories in several Street & Smith pulp titles in the late 1920s and early 1930s—was Joe Archibald's character Larry White for *Thrilling Sports* as by Perry Dixon. White appeared in six stories from 1938 to 1940, participating in baseball, football, basketball, crew, track, boxing and hockey. Today, with intense competition for both scholarships and roster sports in both colleges large and small, there are no five-sport athletes. In fact, only a tiny fraction of all college team sport athletes play even two team sports, although it's not quite so uncommon to see runners participate in cross country (fall), indoor track (winter) and outdoor track (spring).

Five sports did not seem so far-fetched in the Larry White period, since schedules were usually shorter, and truly outstanding college athletes were not as common as they are today. In "Diamond Dust" in *Thrilling Sports* for July 1939, the story opens with Larry working on his pitching for Ashhurst Prep, having enjoyed a stellar career at Springvale High. White is set to face rival Canford Prep and "pitching sensation" Chick Ormister. The two pitchers will be eyeballed by scouts Herb

Lennox—"a great old player," Larry calls him—for the Blue Sox and Lew Breen of the Lions.

Before the game starts, Ormister finds his "talisman"—a cap from Burlington High in Vermont—has gone missing. "I've never pitched without it," he says, not long before a teammate brings the cap to the pitching star.

There follows several pages of play-by-play—there is little characterization in this story—during which White and Ormister collide on a play at first base when Larry is trying to cover the bag to retire Ormister on a ground ball. Both caps fly off and Larry recovers one of them. When Ormister declares it's his cap, Larry tells him, "Listen, Ormister, you've got to forget about that stuff. You've got to find out sooner or later that you can pitch with anything on your head. I need some luck myself today."

Ormister responds, "Okay, White! I'll show you I don't need luck to beat a hot-shot sport like you! Go in and start [continue] pitching." Soon, Larry acknowledges to his coach that he cleverly copped the hat in order to examine a foreign substance, but he is convinced that it is not Ormister who is cheating. Being the fair-minded star that he is, Larry says Ormister deserves a chance to show his stuff to the scouts. But an Ashhurst home run beats Canfield 4–3 in the bottom of the ninth before the real fireworks conclude the action in the locker room.

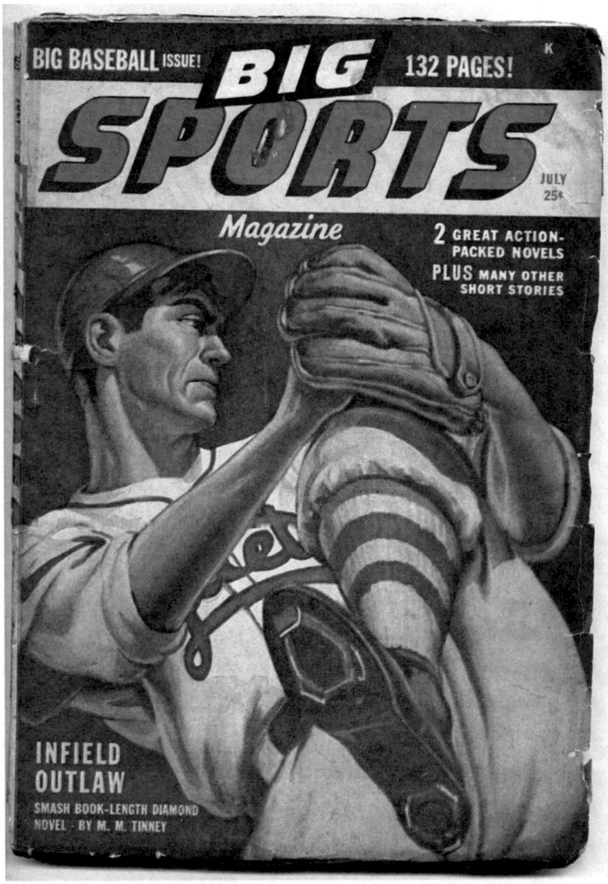

***Big Sports Magazine*, July 1948 (copyright 1948 Exclusive Detective Stories). This pitching perspective is unusual on this cover of a Marvel short-run title. Only one author is cited, and then only in small type in the bottom left corner.**

When the Canfield players go into Ashhurst's locker room to confiscate the cap, White proves that someone had applied paraffin to the cap. That someone was the shifty scout Breen, who modified the cap in hopes Ormister's chance to be signed by Lennox would be ruined. Larry is thus proven correct—no Canfield players were guilty, but the scout was. Lennox tells Breen, "You'll be run out of the big leagues for this, Breen!" The story ends with good feelings all around.

The only real characterization is Breen's ability to suss out the plot as the hero of the piece.

"The Cardboard Coach"

John Wilson (Jay Thorburn) could write about pretty much any scenario in sports, and he proves that in "The Cardboard Coach" in *Exciting Sports* for Fall 1949. Unassuming country boy Swish Semler, who had failed in his only shot at pitching in the majors due to an injury but refused to alibi for it, was enjoying great success coaching high school ball in his rustic home town of Crabbs Corners (no apostrophe) when he was tapped by a wise athletic director for a tough coaching job at King's College.

At King's, Semler discovers to his dismay that foul-talking assistant coach Hap Kirn, a former major league standout, is bitter because he wasn't promoted. Making matters much worse, the team is full of spoiled players, many of whom support Kirn. There follows many angry words at workouts and, in general, a whole lot of unhappiness expressed over Semler's coaching style from many players in the previous year's lineup, including the school paper—except the athletic director.

Semler refuses to quit as coach. He finds and develops several players with the attitudes he has been looking for and thus has created the deepest roster in the college's history. Eventually, he challenges the regulars to a game against his Yannigans—and Semler will pitch! It's not a bad idea, but his injured arm has never recovered and players on both teams begin to realize he has more courage than they ever could have imagined. The Yannigans win 7–1 and prove to everyone that Semler, indeed, deserves to be the coach of all the players.

"Swish drew a deep, wonderful breath of complete relief"—in the locker room—as the story's last paragraph reads. "The best place in the world—next to Crabbs Corners—was King's College."

24

Nice Pulp Guys Fade Away

Before he became well known as one of America's best paperback western novelists, Giles A. Lutz was among the most prolific pulpsters of the 1940s and 1950s, writing westerns and sports stories for all the major companies of his era. Lutz (1910–1982) was among the few prolific authors of westerns who also wrote dozens of sports stories, including baseball (27) and football (8). Most authors of sports stories who were best known for their work in other fields emerged from the genres of air war, science fiction and crime and mystery.

Lutz wrote about half of his sports stories for Marvel (Martin Goodman). He seems to have loved baseball the most, as reflected by his remarkably hard-boiled short novel "Nice Guys Don't Win Pennants" in *Exciting Baseball* for Spring 1953, which was the last of the 229 sports pulps produced by Thrilling Publications from 1936 to 1953. This was the fifth issue, but it surprisingly appeared after a year's lapse following the first four issues in 1949–1951.

Thrilling likely had a back load of original stories, as reflected by the observation that all nine stories in the 1953 *Exciting Sports* were new, unlike the numerous reprints used in 1951, which was the last year for the firm's sports pulps except for the final issue of *Thrilling Football* in 1952.

By 1954, the pulp rough-edge format was clearly on the way out in favor of the 25-cent digests from numerous publishers. Thrilling, though, continued to publish several pulp titles after the firm gave up on sports titles, possibly because of the ever-increasing influence of televised sports.

The intense, violent "Nice Guys Don't Win Pennants" fit in with an effort to produce a handful of hard-boiled titles in 1952–1953, well after Leo Margulies left following his nearly two-decade run as editor at Thrilling, also known as Better Publications but as Thrilling since late in 1935 for the cover logo. There were the three issues of *Mobsters* in 1952–1953, the four issues of *Texas Western* in 1953 and the five issues of *Space Stories* in 1952–1953, along with the final few issues of the long-running hero titles *The Phantom Detective, G-Men Detective* and *Black Book Detective* (starring the Black Bat). They all featured intense covers and even more intense stories, many of which had suggestive themes.

The title of "Nice Guys Don't Win Pennants" would have been immediately recognized as a takeoff on the real-life comment in 1946 by always outspoken Brooklyn Dodgers manager Leo "The Lip" Durocher. In the 1975 biography credited to Durocher

Dime Sports, **October–November 1938 (copyright 1938 Popular Publications, Inc.). There was no World Series story in this issue, but the cover expresses typical symbolism.**

and sports author Ed Linn—titled *Nice Guys Finish Last*, of course—Durocher claimed he made his real quote while talking with famed sports writer Frank Graham of the *New York Journal-American*. Durocher said he pointed to the New York Giants in the other dugout and said, "...Take a look at them. All nice guys. They'll finish last. Nice guys. Finish last." (Indeed, they did finish last that season in the eight-team National League.) Even today, probably no more recognizable comment has ever been uttered in baseball.

In the same chapter of that biography, Durocher talked about why he had so respected Eddie "The Brat" Stanky, who was famed as a remarkably combative infielder in the 1940s and early 1950s and by 1953 appeared in his final major league games as a player-manager with the St. Louis Cardinals. So it was no surprise that Lutz modeled the manager and the key player of the Wildcats—Rex Bradford and shortstop Joe Starky—on Durocher and Stanky in his story of rookie second baseman Eddie Logan.

Logan is a talented, mild-mannered 23-year-old called up from the minors to replace an injured star in the final days of a tight pennant race with the Mustangs (no cities or league were named, but this story clearly takes place in the major leagues). Eddie immediately finds the locker room filled with angry, tense players who were influenced by "a deadly effect on mind and muscle," as Lutz puts it. Most of the players eye Eddie with suspicion, since he does not have anything even remotely like a reputation as a firebrand, notwithstanding his standout statistics in batting and fielding. Logan is instantly hated by Mele, a second baseman who has failed in his attempt to replace the injured star at second base. Although real-life competitors for the same job were not always friendly, the hatred Lutz describes in Mele is as over-the-top as could be.

Eddie makes one friend in star pitcher Bert Stine, whose goal is to win the pennant while becoming a 30-game winner. (There had not been one in baseball at that point since Dizzy Dean in 1934 for the "Gashouse Gang," as the St. Louis Cardinals were then known.) Otherwise, Logan's nature is perceived as non-combative and even timid, which is especially looked at with disdain on this club.

In the hotel lobby, an attractive woman named Sue Elsinore introduces herself as a reporter. "I'm writing woman-interest stuff on baseball for the *News*," she tells him of her unusual assignment. Eddie cooperates to a point but, as Sue tells him, "You haven't given me a thing the paper didn't already have. But I'll be back at you." Eddie's response is "Swell" but he's thinking of her sex appeal, not her reporting objectives. Soon they are dating. Eddie cannot tell Sue his secret, but he soon confronts the problem in person before the Wildcats take on the Mustangs. Alan Fenton, star pitcher for the Mustangs, is Eddie's slightly older stepbrother and a major league bully. They have hated each other since childhood, when Eddie as a 12-year-old became enraged in a fight with Fenton and nearly beat him to death with a stool. Eddie spent a year in reform school and never again got into a fight, on or off the diamond.

When Logan faces Fenton in the first game of a pennant-deciding series, Eddie is so nervous that he has a terrible game both at bat and in the field, ultimately costing the Wildcats a 1–0 loss. He leaves the park early only to later receive a message from Mele in the hotel lobby that Bradford wants to see him at a drinking establishment a few blocks away. Eddie walks over but is set upon by three thugs waiting for him in an alley. Eddie escapes because Starky sees the assault, thinks Eddie is being attacked by Mustang fans, and steps in with his fists while Eddie flees. Word has spread the next day and Starky punches Eddie in the locker room. Bradford tells Eddie—but not the pugnacious Starky!—to leave the stadium because of his timidity. He listens to the Wildcats win on the radio.

The next day, Eddie can't help himself and watches the game from the stands. He is tortured when he sees Sue, in her role as a reporter, and Fenton seemingly having a grand time during an interview. Utterly discouraged, he returns to his hotel room and prepares to leave a club where he is clearly not wanted. But Bradford calls and asks him to meet in the beer pavilion at the nearby park—the same park where Eddie had so recently sparked with Sue. Eddie agrees to meet with Bradford, but when he arrives, Eddie sees only Sue and Fenton sitting together.

The reporter and the pitcher are not getting along—and suddenly Fenton slaps her. Immediately enraged, Eddie fights for the first time since beating up Fenton more than a decade earlier. Eddie scores a knockout but realizes he wants nothing to do with Sue and storms off. Realizing he has licked the fear he had always had that he might kill a man in a fight, he confronts Bradford and tells him without regard for Bradford's status as manager, "I'm playing tomorrow. You hear me?" Bradford agrees, seeing the combative new version of Eddie. Meanwhile, Eddie has told his story to Sue when she calls. When he arrives at the stadium for the pennant-deciding game, the first thing Eddie does is to deck the unpopular Mele because he realized it was Mele who set those three thugs on him. Bradford orders Mele off the team, much to the delight of everyone who is seeing the new Eddie.

Then the story really gets pulpy, which to some might ruin the tale, but made for a cathartic finish for any reader who is interested in fairness. Trailing 2–0 in the bottom of the ninth, Eddie slams a nasty curve from Fenton and legs out a three-run homer while viciously knocking the Mustangs' catcher into backup cover fielder Fenton on a wild, fearless play at the plate. A riot seems about to ensue and Eddie is ready, willing and able to scrap—until Starky runs onto the scene with a bat, threatening to kill any Mustang who goes after Eddie.

Bradford soon confesses to Eddie that he had heard of his fears from a friend, who figured Eddie could be a great player if he was just willing to fight Fenton on or off the diamond. Bradford set up the meeting at the beer pavilion between Logan and Fenton while acknowledging that Sue "is a pretty good little actress ... she's my wife's niece ... she's no reporter." Bradford tells Eddie,

> Sue and I didn't plan on this love business. I should've known. It always happens. But it worked out right for us. When you finally told her what was eating on you, I knew how to go. She picked up Fenton, and I hired that beer place for the evening. The guy who owns it is a Wildcat fan ... she kept feeding Fenton enough beers so that it was easy to make him mad ... and got so sore he slapped her. A guy in love can't stand to see his woman slapped.

Eddie goes out to find Sue. Starky, who knows he has found a combative double-play partner, tells him, "She'll ruin you. She'll soften you up. Just when I think I got me a second baseman who's tough enough, some dame steps in and louses it up." To which Eddie responds, "Don't you ever get the idea I won't be tough enough" and grins at Starky. Then Eddie goes out to answer Sue's wave.

Indeed, a nice pulp story left the reader anything but a loser.

25

Managers in the Press Box

Fans of baseball and football need to be older than 50 to have any real comprehension of how important both real and fictional print journalists were in the pulp sports era, much less in the non-pulp decades of the 1960s and 1970s. Until cable television hit the scene more than two decades after the pulp era ended in the 1950s, print was still the primary way most fans received their sports news, although network television provided an ever-increasing number of sports broadcasts in the 1960s and 1970 in contrast to the far fewer games televised on commercial TV beginning in the late 1940s and continuing with slowly expanding sports coverage in the 1950s.

Pulp sports stories were destined to vanish with all the other kinds of pulp epics. But of all pulp stories, those in the sports pulps were the closest to real life, albeit often more fanciful and dramatic than the background and action that the typical real sports event provided. In the 1930s, 1940s and 1950s, sports fiction in pulps and books rivaled non-fiction in print for readers' attention. Once real-life visual sports began to flood the television industry in the 1960s, magazine sports fiction of all types was never going to survive. Why read sports fiction when real-life drama was so readily available?

Of all the characters once so prominent in all forms of sports fiction, print sports reporters are the least remembered today. While they still function in real life with much lesser influence than they once had, they have pretty much vanished from fiction set in current times. Print reporters still show up in crime stories, just as they did so often during the era of pulp crime and mystery, but that's it. Most school-age readers of what few sports stories remain in books would not know what the nickname "Scoop" would even mean.

When I read my first pulp sports stories in second-hand magazines already decades old in the 1960s and 1970s, I fully understood what the roles of reporters, columnists and editors were in those stories, and not just because I began my journalism career not long after I read my first pulp sports stories in the 1960s. Of course, the word "journalist" almost never appeared in the pulps, sports or otherwise. "The newspaper game" was how it was described, along with more colorful expressions such as "ink-stained wretch," "knights of the fourth estate" and so much more.

More often than not, print reporters made at least cameo appearances in the sports pulps (radio reporters were not mentioned nearly as often). Occasionally, however, reporters were among the primary heroes or villains ("poison pen" was a popular expression).

Sports Writer Culbert Johns, aka Player-Manager Jim Cully

One such character was the remarkable Culbert Johns, who appeared in the highly readable short novel "Behind the Plate" in *Exciting Sports* for Spring 1941 and deemed good enough to be reprinted in *Popular Sports* for Spring 1951, the last issue. Both stories were credited to Jack Terry, who wrote all of his pulp fiction for Thrilling Publications in the 1940s, including eight baseball and football stories, and thus may have been a house name. Very few real bylines appeared for only one publisher if a dozen or more stories were involved.

Not many pulp stories were as intricately plotted as the 50-page "Behind the Plate," in which the observant young Munro City Blade sports writer Culbert Johns emerges as catcher Jim Cully, player-manager of the Class D Colonels of the Southwest League (or the Southern Valley Association, as it's later called) in an unnamed state. How this occurs forms the basis for one of the best and most unlikely combinations of comedy and drama ever to appear in any sports pulp.

As the story opens, the intense cub reporter is having loud conniption fits in the press box over the lack of both intelligent play and hustle by most members of the Colonels. He is certainly correct, based on Terry's descriptions of the action, but such verbal outbursts would not have been looked upon with favor, then or now, and his fellow writers ridicule him with expressions like "Mr. Sissy Pants" and "Mr. Bright Boy." They do not know—nor will they soon learn—that Johns was an outstanding catcher at an East Coast college. Johns is even prouder of his column "Behind the Plate" (thus giving the title a double entendre), in which he led off with the following:

> Last night, at Root Park, an alleged ball club known locally as the "Kernels" prostrated themselves with their customary indifference and presented the Marcom Blue Devils with the game. Chief complaint of the mourners who witnessed it was that it took the whole of nine long, dreary innings to perpetrate the crime. There were moments when the local club resembled ball players but most of the time it was only in their costume. If the Kernels aim to play in exclusive company, they are headed in the right direction. A few more drab exhibitions such as this and they'll have to give away a set of china with each ticket to lure a corporal's guard through the turnstiles. It was a colorless exhibition of a sparkless, wooden club marked only by mismanagement in almost every frame. Our beloved Kernels went through the motions as if they were afraid of awakening the customers. Roberts' Robots missed scoring opportunities repeatedly, most notoriously in the ninth inning.

The next morning, J.B. Frost, the publisher and managing editor, yanks the column because he is afraid the newcomer's writing will offend advertisers and stockholders of the paper. Culbert soon learns, however, that Leila Root, the daughter of the late owner of the baseball team, would like to see him manage the team, since he seems to know baseball better than anyone available. But, of course, in order to do so, he has to violate a promise to his girl Betty back home that he will no longer participate in baseball except as a reporter. He decides he wants to manage and so abandons his thick mustache and fake glasses—both designed to fool Frost into thinking's he's older. In the manner of Clark Kent and Superman, who debuted in the comics three years before this story appeared, Culbert adopts the "secret identity" of Jim Cully—but decides to continue writing his commentary in the *Blade*! This part of the story, of course, requires a suspension of disbelief on the part of the reader, although Culbert writes objectively and critically about himself and the team during a long series of both negative and positive episodes on the diamond for several weeks.

Culbert originally seeks only to manage, but injuries and misfortunes soon force him to take over as catcher. (Player-managers were common in those days, especially in the minor leagues.) As Jim Cully, he comes into the managing job as a firebrand and slowly turns around the club with a combination of fines and stern discipline, but also excellent coaching and leadership and a humanitarian approach where needed. He endures injuries but also displays real talent as both hitter and fielder, which is not far-fetched in a Class D league for a good college player. Eventually, though, his identity as the newspaper commentator is unveiled after Betty visits him and malefactors learn the truth. They break up when he refuses to abandon the team and the path is ultimately cleared for a romance with Leila Root, who concurrently finds out that her fiancé, a club official, is really a rat.

Frost thinks it's all great for circulation now that Culbert's dual identity has been uncovered, but Culbert refuses to resign as a player/manager at Frost's demands. As Jim Cully, he is determined to continue, now that the team has a shot at the league title, and makes several late-season deals, including bringing in two old college stars who were great teammates and buddies of Culbert. They help him win the pennant, thus proving he was prescient as a reporter when he said he could do a better job than the original manager. As the story ends, both he and Leila want "the winning ball" and Jim tells her, "I sure do want that ball myself, Leila. But I have a scheme whereby we can both have it. Let's drive up to the lake tonight to talk it over."

The last lines read, "The pressure of her slim hand in his was answer enough. And now he knew why he had chucked everything and kicked over his future to run that ball club. It was a matter of a blond-haired girl with very provocative lips, now that he really had time to study them…."

"Press-Box Manager"

One of the most amusing short stories about pulp baseball was "Press-Box Manager" by Hal K. Wells in the Spring 1953 issue of *Exciting Sports*, which was the last sports pulp from Thrilling Publications. Hy Hardy, sports editor of the *Morning Gazette*, writes consistently critical columns—"High Hard Ones by Hy"—and game stories dealing with embattled manager William "One Hit Too Late" Maroney, having given him the sobriquet for his none-too-successful tactics with the Cougars in an unnamed Class B league (in those days, minor league teams in organized baseball were rated Triple-A, Double-A, Single-A, B, C and D).

When Maroney has finally had enough, he goes to the newspaper office to confront Hy Hardy—which sounds more like the name of a high school hero in the comic books—but instead encounters *Gazette* manager editor Ed Whitney, a fellow member of a fraternal order. Maroney gets the inspiration to type an open letter to Hardy, inviting him to manage the Cougars, and Whitney is excited enough to play it up big along with a replay signed "Hy (I Can't Do Worse) Hardy."

Hy fervently believes in "going by the book and playing the percentages" during a wild game against the Bantams, so his lineup and tactics are distinctly unorthodox in every way anyone could imagine. A capacity crowd sees Hy manage the Cougars to a 6–0 lead, only to see the Bantams come back for a 15–12 advantage. heading into the ninth inning. Hy wants a left-handed hitter to pinch-hit for right-handed slugger Howie Rogers, who has gone 4 for 4, so he sends in the only player not yet used, pitcher Lefty Devore, who proceeds to hit a two-strike curve for a grand slam.

Or was it? The ending is sheer insanity. First, the Bantams catcher appeals that Lefty has celebrated so wildly on the bases that he missed first base, ending the game on an appeal with a new ball thrown to the first baseman and nullifying all four runs. But Hy tells Lefty to touch all the bases on another trip around the bases, because Hy has the upper hand since he knows that an appeal with a new ball can only be started by a pitcher on the mound rubber. Plate umpire Bull Grogan, no fan of Hy, nevertheless agrees that Hy is correct and that the Cougars have won 16–15. "And I hope some day you bite off too big a chunk of that rule-book and choke to death!"

The Cougars' owner decides that Hy should be his new manager and fires Maroney. But Maroney is nothing if not resourceful and realizes that old buddy Whitney will have a job opening, since Hy can't be both manager and sports columnist. Indeed, Whitney hires Maroney to cover the Cougars. The story has one of the best ending lines of any pulp tale: "Hy Hardy may find certain problems facing him in his new job," Maroney said con-

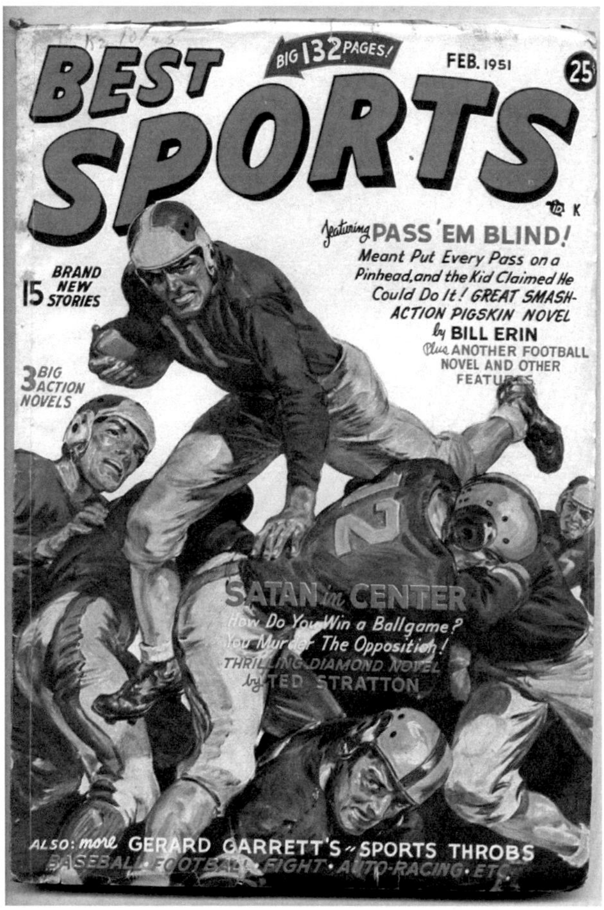

Best Sports, February 1951 (copyright 1950 Stadium Publishing Corporation). Norman Saunders nicely portrays a mighty leap over defenders on the cover of this Marvel title.

tentedly. "If so, he will find frequent and helpful hints in a new sports column that will appear, starting tomorrow, in the *Morning Gazette*. The title of the column will be 'Down the Middle with Maroney.'"

"Holdout Blues"

Arthur Mann's "Holdout Blues" in *Thrilling Sports* for September 1940 tells the nicely written tale of second baseman Lew Stewart, who was a star rookie the previous season for the New York Mets—that's right, the Mets, 22 years before the team of that name played its first season during the National League's expansion from eight teams to 10 in 1962. It was fitting that Mann nailed the future name, he was a real-life journalist, prolific fiction writer and later a front office man with the Dodgers beginning in their Brooklyn days.

Stewart wants a large contract and becomes a holdout, following a movie-making stint in Hollywood by the handsome player. He has strained his eyes temporarily under the lights on the set. Longtime reporter Charlie Dodd of the *New York Globe*, dean of the metro writers, helps Stewart hide at Dodd's home while avoiding being reachable in order to complete a trade. Dodd soon resolves the conflicts of interest for Stewart but the team gets the final say in the last paragraph, acknowledging Stewart's signing but refusing to reveal the terms!

Dodd comes across better as a person than a journalist, since he is more than willing to ignore protocol in order to help a good young person who also happens to be a standout player when healthy. Mann may well have known a real-life writer with a human side after whom he modeled Dodd for this story.

A Sports-Writing Villain

In Columbia's *Sports Winners* for Fall 1943, the prolific C. Paul Jackson presents a thoroughly reprehensible member of the press in "The Tackle Takes It." It's the story of how Del Crouse learns to love playing on the line instead of in the backfield for Middle University. It's also the story of how the shifty-eyed Scoop Gurney plays both Crouse and young feature writer Midge Bowle for suckers because he wants a cushy job at the university. The two-faced Gurney is one of the most disgusted reporters in pulp history.

Gurney and others trick Crouse into thinking Bowle is in trouble at the Tasmo Tavern, where no self-respected Middle U athlete could afford to be caught in daylight, much less late at night. In a climax right out of a nickel novel from decades earlier, Crouse, having fallen for Bowle, is knocked out and drugged into a stupor before a game. Unable to perform, he is booted off the team when he is found out. But Bowle knows the truth and the coach asks Crouse to spot players for the radio announcer at the big game, just in case he is cleared in time to play.

That's exactly what happens in the second half of the title game against Monsun University, when Crouse suits up at halftime and blocks well enough to lead Middle

U from a 20–0 halftime hole to a 21–20 victory. Crouse's block makes possible the winning conversion in the final seconds and he soon is headed for the arms of Midge, after all. Meanwhile, Gurney has been physically ejected from the locker room by the coach, who will make sure Gurney will get his comeuppance. This story is pure pulp but it's still fun.

Likewise, in Columbia's *All Sports* for Winter 1943–1944, "Winning Pitcher, Dotson" by John J. Wallace tells how the designated "poison pen" of the piece, Pete Dotson of the *Blade,* is effectively credited with a key pitching victory when he inspires a pitcher to win.

In T.W. Ford's short story "Golden Boy at First" in *All Sports* for September 1940, overly critical scribe Ben Liggard tries to turn Vic Gamson of the Leopards into a player no one respects and constantly calls the first baseman "Golden Bum." But Gamson wins the day in large part because he helps turn Liggard from awful to admirable in one short story. Liggard's character makes an unexpected but not totally illogical U-turn when the writer himself realizes he has been as unfair as he could be. It's a piece that leaves you feeling good instead of feeling like you need a shower.

26

Baseball on Early Television

Pulp baseball and football stories rarely involved radio personalities, even though radio broadcasts were going full speed during the 1935–1957 era. In contrast, newspaper reporters appeared in many pulp stories, often as central figures. But significant mentions of television merited the least media mention of all, even in the 1950s.

One of the first sports stories to deal with the effects of television on any sport was John Wilson's "Diamond in the Rough," described as "an entertaining novelet" [*sic*] as the cover feature of the first issue of *Popular Baseball* for Spring 1949. In this case, "entertaining" meant tongue-in-cheek.

The prolific Wilson (John Wilson Thorburn) generally wrote serious stories with complex plots, but this little epic contains dozens of malapropisms and other verbal nonsense along with an incredible plot. However, since the vast majority of pulp readers would not yet have seen a television broadcast in 1949, some of them might have taken the story seriously. In retrospect, the story represents the ultimate in quaint writing and reading.

As the story opens, rookie Ringer Rorke has hit two home runs and two doubles in his first three major league games for the Hawks when he is approached on the field—apparently then a pre-game no-no for manager Ben Dolphin—by a dapper guy who turns out to be television announcer "Mushmouth" Hawley, a former major league player and manager.

"Let's get to the point, Ringer," Hawley says. "You've got certain mannerisms that highly displease my television sponsor.... You just can't do the things you do while being televised. For instance, between pitches, you itch and scratch your head something awful. When that itch lessens, you then work over your ears and nose and neck and it is all quite embarrassing to the television audience."

Ringer, a country boy who came out of the coal mines, responds, "I'm unconscious of doing all those things.... Say, I hear a lot of stuff about this television racket. It is really the truth that a fella sittin' in his own house can really see me playing right here in this ball yard?"

This actually might well have been said, since network television was only in its second full season, and then carried a fraction of today's network lineup, without even considering the cable shows and so much else that would begin more than three decades in the future.

Ringer promises to do better, but his manager tells him to itch all he wants. Turns out Dolphin suspects Hawley is after his job. There follow many complications involving Ringer's naïve approach to friends and foes and to his itching, which he just can't seem to stop, much to Hawley's displeasure. Eventually, Hawley tells Ringer, "You are a threat to the whole video industry and the millions of people who enjoy its pictures and my mellow voice."

Ringer soon decides to give himself as much television exposure as possible but so do teammates like catcher Creepy Gatherum and pitcher Bullet Butze. This complicates relationships among teammates and opponents alike. The conservations became hysterical and hilarious, what with verbal malfeasance detailed in what must have been fun for Wilson, even if some of the descriptions of the effects of television on baseball were less than accurate.

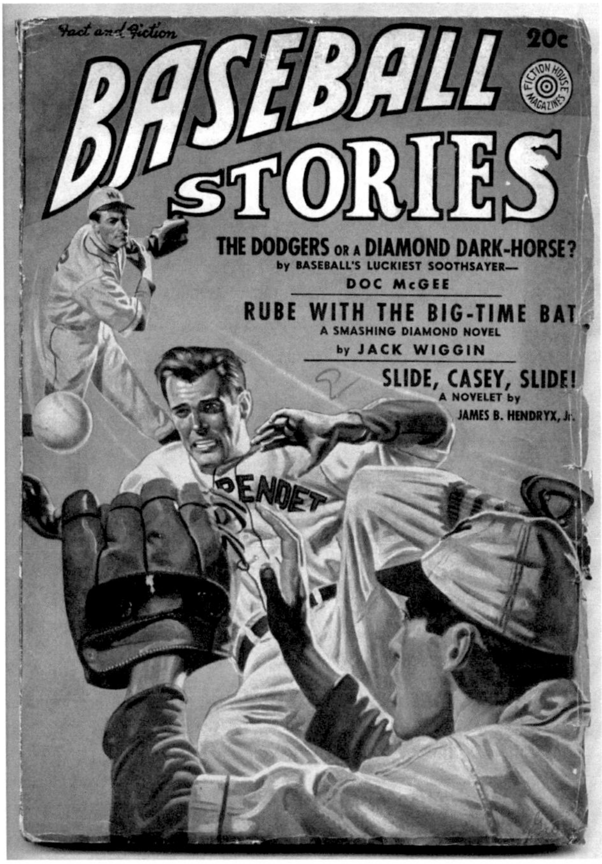

***Baseball Stories*, Summer 1941 (copyright 1941 Flying Stories, Inc.). With his typical clean-line style, George Gross presents a rundown in perspective. He did the vast majority of Fiction House pulp sports covers.**

Adding to the surreal circumstances, someone breaks into Ringer's locker and vandalizes his flea circus! That complicates an already complicated story, even as a depressed Ringer tries to recover as many fleas as possible—you have to read it to believe it.

Here's Wilson's description of the influence of television late in the story:

> Ringer again took down the lion's share of the television honors. He was all over the field, handling both the sphere and the refugee fleas. He suspected, though, that several of the Hawks tried to cut in on his glory. No matter how routine the play, these Hawks seemed intent on making it look hard and thereby [to] hold the television cameras on them....

Somehow, though, manager Dolphin and the players manage to make peace. Oddly and abruptly, Wilson abandons the television theme for the rest of the story as the Hawks climb in the standings. Ringer is vastly relieved to find most of his fleas including their king, a super flea named Joseph, who is located in the ear of an opponent! By the end of this truly unusual epic, Ringer has won the big game with a homer and even made friends with Mushmouth, who fully intends to keep his television gig.

"Ringer, you're all right," Mushmouth says. "You know, I always liked you even though I might have given you a different impression. After all, there is room for you in television and [for] our sponsor, Weedies, too. I predict a great future for all three, including me."

So much for a serious approach to early television in baseball! At the time of this story, many people in the sports and movie industries predicted a dire outcome because of television, but we all know how that turned out.

27

Football's Family Ways

One of the most common themes in pulp football stories is family members competing with and against each other, with all sorts of convoluted plot complications. Such a story is T.W. Ford's "Backfield Brigade" in Columbia's *Super Sports* for January 1950.

It's billed as a lead novel, but it's only 14 pages long. Even so, it's as event-filled as many novels—at least short novels. The protagonist is Flipping Sam Fullen, a passing specialist in the professional ranks with a wife and 7-year-old son. The Flipper—a nickname seemingly derived from "Slingin'" Sammy Baugh, then in the late stages of a brilliant career as a quarterback—is a newcomer to the Red Hawks as the story opens. (Like so many pulp stories, the teams in this tale are identified only by their mascots and not by their cities.) Fullen beats the Titans with one of his typically tricky passes in the final moments, but he isn't celebrating on the field or in the locker room—Sam is concerned because the pass was nearly intercepted. At this point in their season, the Hawks are under suspicion because one of their linemen was caught gambling on games. He was betting on his own team and doing nothing illegal, but it's still against football's rules (just as it was in real life) and got him suspended. What really bothers Fullen is that the title showdown will be with the Cubs, who are led by player-manager Jim "White Flash" Henders—Sam's brother.

Sam is worried that with the newspapers filled with gambling gossip, his widely respected coach, George Murtha, might suspend him for the title game if he knew Henders was his older brother. For now, there is no danger of that—Sam hasn't yet told even his wife, Priscilla, or their son! Considering how long they have been married, that is a true oddity in any sports story plot. Sam is haunted by memories as a youth of getting into bitter battles with Jim, who went with his father when the parents divorced. Sam went with his mother and took her maiden name—another oddity but it shows how emotional the situation is for The Flipper.

Sam finally tells his wife the whole story about Jim, who began the season as Cubs coach after retiring as a player, but returned to action when injuries threatened to ruin his team's chances. Indeed, Jim, sometimes called Benders and sometimes Henders in a case of spectacularly sloppy editing, has shown he is still a great player.

Priscilla urges Sam to tell his coach and team about facing his brother, but Sam feels the team needs him so much that he can't take the chance of a benching to avoid scandal. Jim begins the big game by mocking Sam, and Jim even intercepts one of Sam's passes in the first half. Teammates also have noted a physical resemblance. Then occurs something that may never have occurred in real life, certainly not for many years—a sports editor barges into the locker room at halftime! He tells Coach Murtha that Sam and Jim are brothers, leading Murtha to confront Sam with the question: "Sam, is Jim Henders your brother?" Sam acknowledges the truth and, sure enough, the coach benches him.

But the reader knows Sam won't stay on the bench. After Jim scores a brilliant touchdown on a double reverse for a 14–0 lead, the players insist on the Flipper returning to the game. Captain Parson Miller tells the wise old coach, "Sure,his [Sam's] hands are as clean as can be! We know now. That Henders, his brother, has been taunting us out there, boasting how he'd scared Sam out of the game. How the going was too tough for the kid. And Henders means it, George; we know now." It's interesting that the team captain calls his coach by his first name, while Sam has called him "Mr. Murtha."

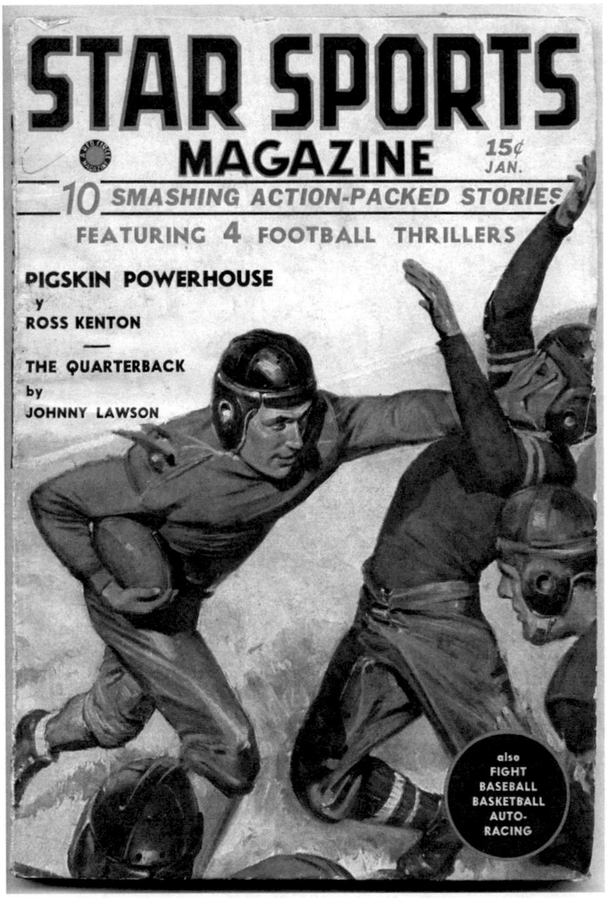

***Star Sports Magazine*, January 1938 (copyright Western Fiction Publishing Co., Inc.). In the leather-helmet era before face masks, J.W. Scott portrays a straight-arm to the face on the cover of this early Red Circle (Marvel) title.**

The Flipper plays the best fourth quarter of his career, of course, and flashes by brother Flash for the winning touchdown in the final minute. That's a purely pulp finish—but there follows something that isn't pulp at all. The White Flash appears in the locker room and shakes hands with the Flipper. "Sonny, I've seen worse football players." To which Sam says, "Thanks. You were a headache yourself more than once today, Jim."

Ford then offers the best lines of the story: "Their hands parted. Henders ducked away. Maybe that was all that would happen between them. Sam didn't know. But he did know he had earned his brother's respect. And there was satisfaction in that." And the coach ends the story by asking, "Anybody here got anything to say about fixed games or gambling players now, huh?"

"Touchdown Reverse"

One of the most unusual college football stories ever presented—and one of the pulpiest—was "Touchdown Reverse" by Harvey Hill in Columbia's *Blue Ribbon Sports* for October 1940. It was the only pulp football (or baseball) story ever credited to Hill.

A college identified as the Denton "U" with the mascot "The Violets" loses its star backfielder to a broken leg in practice. Later, at the training table, inspirational tackle Phil Swiadon notices how well the team's manager, Danny Marlow, wings a loaf of bread to him over a 25-yard space. The next day, Phil notices how well Danny flings a helmet to a player who requests one on the field in practice. Phil notices how much enthusiasm Danny has for his job and asks him if he has ever considered putting his muscular arm to use as a player. Danny tells him "I don't like [actually playing] the game," but Phil convinces him the team need him.

Danny is indeed needed in the next game and shows ability, but Phil notices how mechanically Danny performs. Danny calls it quits, returns as manager, and tells Phil why: His father, Bill "Hurricane" Marlow, is the infamous halfback who cost "the U" a game with a wrong-way run (perhaps inspired by an infamous incident in the Rose Bowl). Danny had told his father he was a substitute on the team when he was actually the manager, but "Hurricane" discovers the truth when he returns to his alma mater and receives recognition from the announcer. The elder Marlow finds Danny in the locker room at halftime and his son decides to play in the second half, after all, in the best pulp tradition.

Danny rallies his team with a touchdown pass but misses the conversion kick (can you imagine, even in fiction, a coach using a kicker who has not practiced all week?). Then, in the final minute when he is trapped behind the line, he decides to run the wrong way in order to have a chance. Then, looking for all the world like his father, he abruptly turns around and fires a 55-yard touchdown pass to a receiver unguarded in the end zone!

It could only happen in the pulps!

"Stand By for Collision"

Stan Hough, another writer credited with only one football story (and no baseball stories) in the pulps, came up with a bit more realistic gambit in "Stand by for Collision" in Fiction House's *All-American Football Magazine* for the First Fall 1946 issue. This time, the key family member is the coach's daughter.

Battle-scarred and temper-plagued Hank Caldwell, a highly athletic combat veteran attending college on the GI Bill at an unnamed university, isn't showing enough football enthusiasm to suit coach Buddha Barnes. Weary after 55 minutes of a hard game, he has trouble getting up after a collision and replies to his coach, "Yeah, I'm all right. Let's get it over with. I need a beer." The coach, offended by the player's wish to break training, immediately removes him.

Later, Hank encounters the coach's daughter, Carol Barnes, in a cocktail lounge. After much discussion about his discomfort with both college and football, she walks away and he decides to leave the unnamed college. But the coach is so desperate to keep Caldwell, he offers him $500 to play two games and gives him an envelope that Caldwell accepts but does not intend to open. Later, the former Marine becomes so violent in his first game back that he nearly kills an opponent who has been kneeing him. Disgusted, the coach tells Caldwell he's off the team, after all.

Realizing he wants to play and stay in school, Caldwell confronts Coach Barnes with the rules of the GI Bill and regains his spot on the team and at the college. But when the coach refuses to play him in the next game, Caldwell threatens to reveal the $500 payment to the college president if he doesn't play him. Hank plays like a star, works well with his teammates and happily sees another player score the winning touchdown.

In the locker room after the game, Caldwell learns that Coach Buddha Barnes had decided to tell the college president about the $500 payment. When the president asks Caldwell if he still has the check, everyone is stunned to learn that no crime has been committed, after all.

Carol, it turns out, had placed a worthless check with one word—OVER—in the envelope. On the back of the check she wrote, "Dear Hank, Sorry to have deceived you but I know as well as you do that you would never cash it anyway. It's just a means of keeping you from running away from your temporary (I pray) dislike of Dad. Love, Carol. P.S. My grand-father was a horse-trader—remember?"

28

Damn Yankees in the South

Many pulp football stories were set in the South and a few had embattled Northern protagonists. Not too many, however, were at least genuine short novels. All too often, pulp sports stories were billed as "novels" when they ran only 30 to 40 columns (15 to 20 pages) and can be read in less than an hour.

One 43-page short novel that takes at least a couple of hours of reading, however, is "Damn Yankee, Quarterback" by Ross Russell in Thrilling Publications' *Popular Football* for Winter 1941, the first issue. This one is fun to read, if only because it's not as far-fetched as many pulp stories of the period. Russell (1909–2000) wrote well over 50 stories of many different sports, plus many more crime tales, in pulps of the 1930s and 1940s, including numerous tales for Street & Smith's *Sport Story Magazine*. But his name was not especially well known because his work was almost entirely confined to the pulps. He is not credited with any paperback novels. For the six publishers spotlighted in this book, Russell wrote only half a dozen football and baseball stories.

"Damn Yankee, Quarterback" (which was featured on the cover without the comma) is a straightforward tale of the hatred between the stars of mythical Dixie College in Georgia—quarterback Bill Sherman, a transfer from College of New England in Massachusetts, and captain/fullback Cracker Roe, a hard-bitten son of the South who is still fighting the War Between the States (as Southerners called it). When reading this now–politically incorrect story, it helps to remember that football fans still lived who remembered the Civil War as children. The other primary figures are Sherman's love interest, Millicent "Milly" Du Raine; the coach, Marine combat sergeant Buck Wever (an odd spelling, to be sure); the overweight center with a squeaky Andy Devine voice, Bubber Sam (his last name is not mentioned); the Old South businessman Dixie's stadium is named after, Colonel Ravanel Du Raine, who is Milly's grandfather; and J.T. Sherman, Bill's father and, like Du Raine, a so-called tycoon in the timber business.

Another major character is Harold "Spec" Claxon, a reporter for the *Statesville Press* who is anything but a sympathetic figure. In fact, early in the story, there is a somewhat shocking scene where Bill Sherman has taken offense to Claxon's dubbing him "General" Sherman, still a name reviled in Georgia for what the real General William Tecumseh Sherman did to Georgia in the Civil War. One paragraph reads: "Bill grabbed him by the lapels. 'Start spreading that General Sherman stuff across your sheet and I'll slap your ears off, you runt.' To which the puny newsman responds, 'I am not a big he-man ... if you want to get tough I suggest picking on somebody your own size—like Cracker Roe, for instance.'"

Bill soon receives a note from Milly, stating she has broken their date, and he soon learns why: Claxon has labeled 1864 and 1940 over pictures of General W.T. Sherman and timber man J.T. Sherman, who is ... "Pictured in a Graphic Depiction of the New Looting of the South by Northern Exploitation!" When Bill confronts Milly, she accuses him unfairly of using her to set up a potential timber deal for slash pine in Georgia between Du Raine and the elder Sherman. Bill eventually convinces Milly that he is on the square, but when the timber men finally meet, an explosion ensues when the elder Sherman refers to the Civil War and the old colonel takes great exception to the term. Having been tipped off to the meeting, Claxon's photographer grabs a photo of the scene and matters hit a new low when that is published.

***Football Action*, First Fall 1943 (copyright 1943 Fiction House, Inc.). With a soldier in the background armed with grenade and rifle, George Gross features a symbolic cover of a quarterback in action. The official is perhaps a bit closer than normal.**

Meanwhile, Dixie has stayed unbeaten with several less-than-impressive performances on the way to a Southeastern Conference title showdown with Major Bob Neyland's Tennessee Vols (many real names are used in this story). Bill makes three horrible mistakes in the first half and is so frustrated by the dislike of so many teammates and by his own poor play that he benches himself. Roe and some other stars on the team, inspired because they have finally driven "General Sherman" to the sideline, rise up in fury and whip the Vols to earn a Sugar Bowl berth. To Dixie's surprise, however, College of New England becomes the Sugar Bowl opponent.

As the story winds down, Coach Wever—who is not prejudiced against Northerners—confronts Bill Sherman and convinces him how and why he can be a better teammate, even though he is no longer the first-string quarterback and despite the bigotry he still faces. Wever, it seems, is a brilliant observer of human nature and psychology as well as football. Both the ever-faithful friend Bubber Sam and Wever tell Sherman that his self-benching turned out to be the team gesture needed to inspire Dixie to victory. Bill volunteers in an ethical way to share what he knows about New England's tactics with Wever and the team while also volunteering to play quarterback on the scout team.

In the end, Sherman sees his replacement sustain a broken leg in workouts during a pileup and impresses his teammates by screaming for help and directing his teammates to prevent the new quarterback from suffering a compound fracture. Wever tells Sherman it's now up to him in the Sugar Bowl. Cracker Roe and Sherman, however, still have not made peace, even though both have worked together in practice because of Wever's impressive discipline. Before the Sugar Bowl, Wever tells Claxon that Sherman will start at quarterback. Claxon responds with a poison-pill question: "But how do the other members of the team feel about playing under a damn Yankee who is just the same as a traitor to his own side?"

Then comes what today would be a shocker and would surely get a coach fired:

> He [Claxon] didn't get any futher. Coach Wever grabbed him by the coat lapels and fairly squeezed him together as he lifted him to his toes. "Listen, you! Another word out of you like that, and I'll tear your head off and make you eat it. I took the trouble to investigate you after all that stuff you spread in the *Statesville Press*, and I know plenty about you and that Wisconsin crowd [Claxon is a transplant] who are trying to queer J.T. Sherman's chances with Colonel Du Raine.... You are the traitor and snake in the grass, Claxon'.... [Wever proceeds to give] "his victim a couple of back-handed slaps with his right hand that loosened a couple of teeth in the reporter's mouth.

It's not long before Wever explains to Du Raine why Bill Sherman is starting the Sugar Bowl ... and the coach tells the old icon everything else he knows, too. During the bowl game, Roe is angry because New England is not using the tactics Stewart described in practice ... until New England does use its infamous "naked reverse" to score against Roe and others to take a 7–6 lead in the third quarter. Roe, realizing for the first time that his hatred for Sherman may have cost his team the game, finally apologizes to Sherman in a long colorful way. Sherman, in the wake of his talk with Wever, has long since decided to accept any apology.

Then it becomes pulpy indeed: In the final minute, Sherman realizes he needs a long run to have a shot at victory and he calls his own number on a risky play. Everyone blocks for him including Roe, but Sherman realizes he must lateral near the goal line and Roe is the man he laterals to. Roe gets the glory of the game-winning touchdown but neither Sherman nor anyone else cares who scores the winner. The team is whole with next year ahead. The two old timber tycoons are going to talk about making everything work in Georgia through modern reforestation, and everyone is invited to share Southern hospitality at a victory party at the Du Raine mansion. Sherman, now a true field general, kisses Milly as the story ends.

"A Coach for Cinderella"

The prolific Joe Archibald tuned in a nifty novelette of Southern football in "A Coach for Cinderella" in *Thrilling Sports* for November 1948. It's the story of ambitious coach Wally Cade, a deeply ethical but non-colorful, by-the-numbers coach of the Durham College Maroons, and his desire to earn the Urbana University job up North.

In the big game between unbeaten teams—scouted by the iconic Urbana coach Pop Walden—the colorful Parson Kinsey coaches his Southern University team to victory over Durham, which has lost its star runner Harry Jorgenson to what Cade realizes from his military experiences could become a life-altering leg injury. Jorgenson begs to go in for a potential winning touchdown from the five-yard line but Cade refuses to risk his health and Durham loses.

When Pop Walden, who has the final say on his successor, enters Durham's locker room, Cade assumes he has told the colorful Parson that he will be the new coach. Instead, Cade is shocked to learn that Walden has chosen him.

> "Things are in the process of a definite change at Urbana. A certain perspective can be lost when men know nothing but success, when victories are taken for granted. A man should taste defeat once in a while to really enjoy the fruits of victory. Out in the business world a man will find he has to learn how to lose, Cade. Oh, we'll have more great teams at Urbana, but we intend to pay more attention to the human equation. We've been looking for a man who considers that angle above his personal triumphs." [Walden tells the astonished Cade,] "I decided on my man when Jorgenson was kept out of that last bid for a touchdown, Cade. I've had you watched all year, Wally, although you weren't aware of it. I've had you scouted and my men reported that you were the best judge of human beings they'd ever seen. An expert on smashing bad complexes and fixations, they said. Cade, will you sign a three-year contract to coach Urbana?"

Those are nice sentiments, perhaps inspired by much talk of how college football was being overemphasized at some schools.

There is a pulpy, unrealistic ending even for a pre-internet era when finding people was sometimes tough. Cade has long carried a photo of Amy Lawrence, whom he met during his military service but has long since lost track of. She calls him and they are soon destined to reunite.

29

The Only Pulp Sports Reprint Title

The only pulp sports title designated for reprints also published one of the most remarkable new stories of the 1950s.

It's likely no coincidence that John Wilson's long and highly unusual novella of high school football, "The Touchdown Way," was apparently a late insert as one of the stories in *Five Sports Classics* for Spring 1951. This was the second issue after Thrilling Publications converted *Exciting Sports* to a quarterly reprint publication. Indeed, this was a bold decision, since no publisher had ever made such a title move regarding sports stories.

Five Sports Classics lasted only four issues, Wilson's fine story notwithstanding, but it's impossible to tell if low circulation or an overall editorial decision about sports pulps caused this unique pulp's demise. In 1951, Thrilling Publications killed its general-interest flagship pulps, *Thrilling Sports* and *Popular Sports*, along with two baseball pulps and two football pulps. The firm's only sports publications after 1951 were the last issue of its *Thrilling Football* annuals in 1952 and the inexplicable appearance of the last issue of *Exciting Baseball* in 1953 after there was no 1952 issue.

Billing the story as a "new football novel by John Wilson," the blurb for "The Touchdown Way" was accurate: "Talk about juvenile delinquents—they don't come any rougher than the kids Howie Arnell had to cope with on the gridiron!" This story is better and timelier than any of the 17 reprints and two other new stories among the 20 that appeared in the four issues. That explains why the reprint credits on the table of contents page for the Spring 1951 issue mistakenly include "By Life or Death," a horse-racing story by Sam Carson from *Popular Sports* for Fall 1942.

Five Sports Classics featured two baseball covers and two football covers during its run from the Winter 1951 issue through Fall 1951. Wilson (the pseudonym of the prolific John "Jay" Thorburn) also had a new football story in the first issue and William Campbell Gault had a new boxing story in the last issue. The selection of reprints followed by pattern of story types in the 1950s—eight baseball, six football, three boxing and one each of crew, wrestling and polo, all highly unusual for that time period. All original sources were cited on the contents page.

As a title, "The Touchdown Way" did not even begin to reflect the theme of the story. Something like "Football Coach Tackles Delinquents" would have been much better. But such a title would have been unique in the annals of sports pulps.

By 1951, there was a lot of talk about juvenile delinquents, though not nearly as much as there would be later in the 1950s and 1960s. A steadily increasing number of novels, movies and television shows dealt with the issue, but sports stories of all types in all media seldom did. Wilson's tale may be the first such sports story, at least in the sense that the first half is about as hard-boiled as any sports story had ever been to that point.

"The Touchdown Way" features at least a dozen major characters: Howie Arnell, high school football coach in his first season at Westfield High in a small city in an unnamed state; four players on his team; two of the small city's businessmen with opposing views; the friend Howie had while growing up in Westfield; one of Howie's athletic directors when Howie coached at a small college; a history teacher/coach at the high school; and the school principal.

Back in his hometown, where he starred in high school, Howie had just been fired after a couple of unsuccessful years at a major college in his early 30s. He didn't realize it yet, but breaking a coaching contract at a smaller college turned out to be a bad move. One of Westfield's leading businessmen, Tom Branston, had done a lot of favors for Howie in his youth and talked Howie into accepted the head coaching job at Westfield, where son Dave Branston was one of the best players but also a troublemaker who followed Pug Steuber, another strong player but also a delinquent bully without a conscience. Dave and Pug were among the many hard-bitten, troubled and trouble-making students at Westfield, both on and off the team.

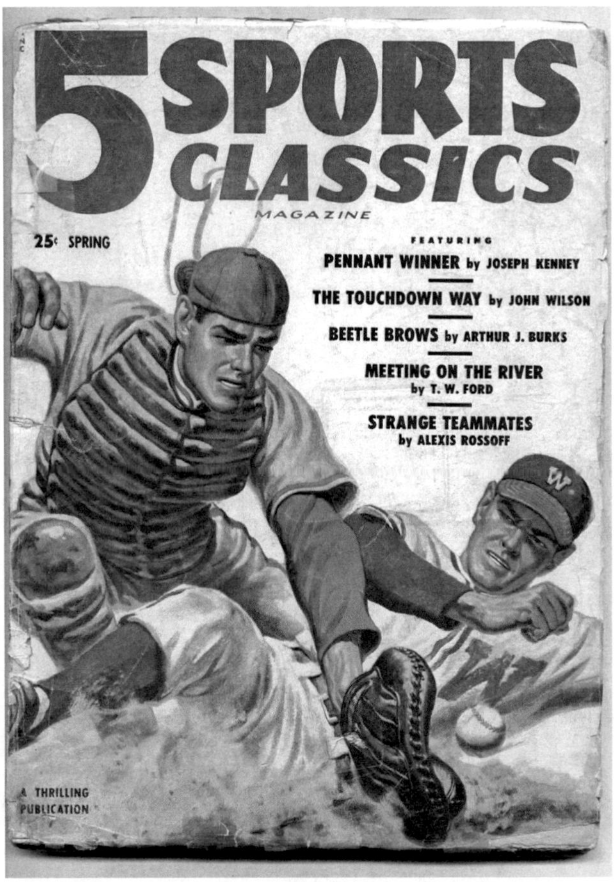

Five Sports Classics, Spring 1951 (copyright 1951 Standard Magazines, Inc.). _Exciting Sports_ was retitled for its final four issues and featured mostly classic reprints, but Thrilling was at the end of its run with sports pulps.

Those who ultimately helped Howie find himself as a person and coach include Paul Terry, the school's principal; Doc Andrews, the teacher/coach; Dan Mixley, the athletic director at Clayton College; Ben Kallen, a holier-than-thou big-time building contractor who comes to realize he had been on the wrong side; and brothers Chick and Billy Kaseta, current and former Westfield players. Howie helps Chick to get over his bitterness over the fact that Howie did not feel Billy was good enough to crack his college football lineup after Billy comes to realize that Howie's evaluation had been correct. Another player, Hank, and Chick emerge as the emotional leaders of Howie's team.

This 30-page story showed how a matter-of-fact, non-emotional but honest and ethical approach was not enough for Howie to succeed with troubled young people and conflicted adults. The story might seem a little corny with the return of Dave and Pug for a significant game after Howie had dropped them from the team, but that only served to show how important it was to give a second chance to troubled young people. Pug returns during halftime of the game, which is a midseason contest rather than a title game or the like. Pug even scores the winning touchdown, but only after he makes his teammates realize he has changed from hard-bitten to hard-driving.

To lend an element of realism, at the end of the story Howie acknowledges that he really still does want to coach in college and accepts Mixley's offer to return to Clayton and its small-college program. This time, Howie realizes he must wait until he is ready to move up to a big-time college program.

Interestingly, the only female in this story makes a cameo appearance as Pug's mother, who is married to the irresponsible man who turned Pug into a football bully. She appears only for a few lines when Howie tries to visit Pug at home to see why he is such a hard-boiled bully.

The football in the story is realistic enough—even the heroic ending, because Pug is indeed the team's best athlete—but it seems odd that nobody on the high school team is willing to stand up to Pug and Dave early on when they are the team's thugs. Indeed, the principal is concerned that the team's dirty play in the earliest games is setting a poor example for students who might be prone to juvenile delinquency like Pug and Howie. It also seems strange that Tom Branston, despite his background as a community leader, feels helpless to prevent his wayward son Dave from constantly seeking out trouble. But then, the real stand-up guy in the story turns out to be Howie, the enlightened coach who is rewarded for not giving up on any of the kids.

It's also intriguing how the two businessmen joined forces at the end, fully realizing that building a town involves creating better schools, parks and opportunities for youth as well as more attractive and valuable buildings, homes and infrastructure.

30

Real-Life Heroes—Eddie Collins and Frank Frisch

Most of the non-fiction accounts and notes in the sports pulps from the six companies covered here are routine and short, although many of them can be fun to read from the standpoint of the era they were written. Street & Smith, not extensively covered in this book, generally had the best and heaviest non-fiction content, all of which is listed by the wonderful FictionMags site on the Internet.

The 1935–1940 sports pulps covered here generally had much more non-fiction content than the ensuing pulps, although fiction always occupied the vast majority of the space. In that pre-war period, many newspaper sports sections had yet to expand the way they would later, and live radio reports were still not as ubiquitous as they would become. In addition, there were far fewer sports books than would be written in the period from the 1940s through the 1970s, from the standpoint of the history of the first half of the 20th century. *Baseball Magazine* was published continuously from 1908 onward and *Baseball Digest* from 1942 on, but general-interest sports content was limited mostly to the slicks such as *Colliers* until the advent of the monthly *Sport Magazine* in 1946 and the weekly *Sports Illustrated* in 1954.

Occasionally, though, a truly worthwhile non-fiction serial would be published, primarily by Popular Publications, to take advantage of the paucity of biographical books. Two such serials appeared from Popular: "Bearing Down in Baseball" by Eddie Collins as told to Arthur Mann, in *Dime Sports* for July, August, September and October 1937 for a total of 55 pages, followed in the next year by "Second Base and Me" by Frank Frisch as told to Arthur Mann in *Dime Sports* for August and October–November 1938 and for December 1938–January 1939 and February–March 1939 for a total of 42 pages. (The Collins epic was referred to as "Bearing Down at Second Base" inside the magazines.)

Arthur Mann was to become a well-known author of books and a huge variety of sports non-fiction and fiction for pulps and slicks, and as a versatile front-office man for the Brooklyn Dodgers. Mann did an entertaining job on what amounts to "short books" on Collins and Frisch, both of whom were enshrined in the Baseball Hall of Fame in Cooperstown, New York, in 1939 and 1947, respectively. At the time these two pieces appeared, Collins had been retired as a player since 1930 and Frisch since 1937, so their adventures were fresh in the minds of most adult readers.

Reading these two pieces provides a vivid "front seat" to much of baseball history, but they also remind the reader how much sports writing has changed in the ensuing eight-plus decades. Beyond events on and off the diamond (such as reactions to trades), there is almost nothing of a personal nature. The wives and families of these athletically amazing stars are barely referred to; in today's magazine features, the personal is often more significant than athletic feats.

Mann has the two infielders refer to their position picks for best in the American League (Collins) and National League (Frisch), but there is nowhere near enough on the statistics amassed by the two during their unusually long careers. (Nor do the serials provide year-by-year career totals, which would have been easy to do.)

There is no mention that by the end of Collins's major league career in 1930, he stood fourth all-time in hits (3,311), second in games played (2,826) and third in stolen bases (743). To leave these accomplishments out may have been an example of humility, but at the very least an editor's note should have been inserted. Likewise, although Frisch played as many as 140 games only seven times in his 19-year career (in seasons of 154 from 1919 through 1937), he still merited mention of his 2,880 hits and 416 stolen bases.

Dime Sports, September 1937 (copyright 1937 Popular Publications, Inc.). Hall of Fame second baseman Eddie Collins (who was elected two years later) and Hall of Fame media wing member Arthur Daley, then a young journalist, are cover-featured as authors along with Judson P. Philips, who became much better known as mystery novelist Hugh Pentecost.

There is also an error of inexplicable proportions when Collins talks about being converted from player to coach by manager Connie Mack "midway through the 1931 season.... I played almost half the season at second base." Collins must have had memories of the 1927 season, his first back with Connie Mack and the Philadelphia A's, when he appeared in 95 games, including 56 at second base. He played in only 36 games in 1928, including 29 as a pinch-hitter and only two at second base, and his nine appearances in 1929 and three in 1930 did not include any fielding appearances.

Collins's touching comment to Mack about his beloved manager's decision goes this way: "Wait a minute! This isn't going to hurt me. I mean it. Look, I'm so happy just being back [with Mack and the Philadelphia Athletics] here with you again, that anywhere you want to put me is all right with me. If I'm more use to you as a coach, just say the word!"

As wonderful and devoted as Collins was, the last paragraph in the third episode is also deceptive: "And that was the way the longest big-league playing career in baseball ended. It began in 1906 at the Fifth Avenue Hotel [New York] when Connie Mack 'invited' me to join his team. It ended 25 years later when he invited me to quit."

Actually, Collins played in only six games in 1906 as "Eddie Sullivan" while a student at Columbia and 14 in 1907. Combined with his infrequent appearances in 1928–1930, the reality is that his 25 years included 20 in a full-time role. In contrast, Ty Cobb played 24 seasons (1905–1928), but his 41 games in 1905 were the only season in which he did not appear at least half time and his total of 3,034 games over 24 years were 208 more than Collins.

Collins notes that when a dean at Columbia discovered he played professional baseball in 1906, he was not allowed to play on the university team in 1907. Collins writes: "It was by no means a disgrace. I had given everything I had to Columbia football and baseball. All I had done was earn enough money to support myself in college. They must have appreciated that because, after taking my captaincy, they promoted me to the job of baseball coach, and I was able to get my diploma without going into debt."

The highlights of Collins's piece include his six World Series appearances, with remarkable high spots under Mack and even more amazing low spots as an honest captain and star of the 1919 Chicago Black Sox. He does a brief but accurate job of recounting the Black Sox scandal, which was exposed near the end of the 1920 season and resulted in a lifetime ban for throwing games received by eight players. He doesn't go into great depth about any one player, but he clearly labels first baseman Chick Gandil as the ringleader. Even though printed 17 years after the scandal broke, memories were too painful for him to do anything but cover the basics in an honest way. One wonders what he would have thought of the film *Eight Men Out*.

Perhaps the most compelling aspect of Collins's story is how he and Mack helped Lefty Grove morph from a temperamental young fireball pitcher to a true teammate. This account alone makes the series well worth reading.

Frank "Frankie" Frisch, the Fordham Flash, was also well worth the four-part series devoted to him, especially because he played for the New York Giants and John McGraw, whom he profiles vividly and accurately as one of the most complex baseball men of the era. Mann much later edited the ground-breaking book *The Real McGraw* by Mrs. John J. McGraw (Blanche), which appeared in 1953 from David McKay and is among the best of the early baseball biographies.

Few players of the 1901–1960 era, encompassing the founding of the American League and the World Series, were involved with as many colorful players as Frisch, who not only played for McGraw's New York Giants in four consecutive World Series (1921–1924) but also played in four more Series with the St. Louis Cardinals including as manager of the 1934 World Series champion "Gas House Gang," which featured Dizzy and Daffy Dean, Pepper Martin, Joe Medwick, Leo Durocher and, of course, Frisch at second and third bases. Frisch played 140 games that year, in which he turned 36.

Frisch goes into great detail about the 1934 World Series, in which the Cardinals clobbered the Tigers in Detroit and the fans responded to Medwick's tough slide into Marv Owen at third base with a seventh-inning barrage of fruit, eggs, bottles and more, forcing Medwick's departure from left field. In 1938, when Frisch wrote this, he didn't touch much on Durocher, who had not yet begun his astoundingly colorful career as manager of the Brooklyn Dodgers and later the New York Giants and Chicago Cubs.

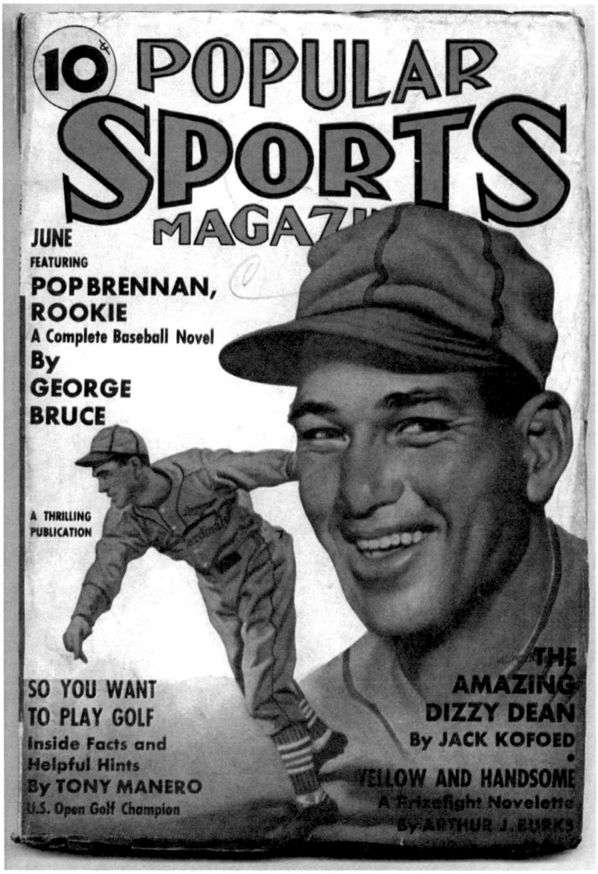

***Popular Sports*, June 1937 (copyright 1937 Better Publications, Inc.). Cardinals pitcher Jay Hanna "Dizzy" Dean is nicely portrayed by Earle Bergey for the first issue of the long-running *Popular Sports*. For the first 11 covers, Bergey painted the period's most popular athletic heroes to go with short biographical features.**

Frisch goes into great detail of how McGraw would mastermind the use of his players—and sometimes send them away before bringing them back—and tells a touching story of how Mrs. McGraw (her given name was not mentioned) reunited Frisch and McGraw at a party after the two had fallen apart for several years after McGraw traded Frisch to the Cardinals.

In the years Collins and Frisch played, the American League had more stars than the National League, primarily because of all the Yankees' stars led by Babe Ruth and Lou Gehrig, along with Detroit's Ty Cobb and Cleveland's Tris Speaker, both of whom finished with Connie Mack and the A's. But Frisch's experiences with McGraw and the Gas House Gang make fascinating reading, too. Mann certainly knew how to pick colorful subjects.

Part II

Catalog of Pulp Baseball and Football from Six Publishers

The following indexes the baseball and football fiction in the sports pulps from Ace, Columbia, Fiction House, Marvel (Red Circle), Popular and Thrilling from their first appearance in 1935 to their last in 1957. It also includes the nine issues of *Athlete* from 1939 to 1940 but does not include Street & Smith's *Sport Story Magazine* (429 issues including two reprint annuals from 1923 to 1943) or Fleischer's *All-American Sport Story Magazine* (45 issues from 1933 to 1938) because those are all included in the FictionMags index on the Internet. The listings below include all the cover themes, as well, since many pulp enthusiasts collect primarily for the covers. I do not list artists because I do not like to guess, but FictionMags does list them when available and confirmed.

This compilation includes all 1,054 sports pulps except for Columbia's *Super Sports* for November 1940, for which I have partial data. If you can supply the complete table of contents, please contact me in care of McFarland. I would also like to be advised of any mistakes or omissions. I do not index non-fiction articles.

Artist credits are taken from sources listed at the end of the index.

Ace Publications

Ace Sports

Vol. 1, No. 1, January 1936. Stories: 7
Cover: Football by Rafael DeSoto
Robert S. Fenton, "Bean Ball" (BB)
Joe Archibald, "Gridiron Grit" (FB)
Ralph Powers, "Frogskin Bait" (FB)

Vol. 1, No. 2, February 1936. Stories: 6
Cover: Hockey by Rafael DeSoto
Joe Archibald, "The Champ Smasher" (FB)

Vol. 1, No. 3, March 1936. Stories: 6
Cover: Boxing by Rafael DeSoto
(No baseball or football)

Vol. 1, No. 4, April 1936. Stories: 7
Cover: Wrestling by Rafael DeSoto
Joe Archibald, "The Fifth Base" (BB)
Herbert E. Smith, "Firebrand" (BB)

Vol. 2, No. 1, May 1936. Stories: 7.
Cover: Baseball by Rafael DeSoto
Archer Jordan, "The Boomerang Bat" (BB)

Vol. 2, No. 2, June 1936. Stories: 7
Cover: Olympic track and field by George Gross
Joe Archibald, "The Blue Grass Slugger" (BB)

Vol. 2, No. 3, July 1936. Stories: 6
Cover: Baseball
Joe Archibald, "The Masked Battery" (BB)
Alexis Rossoff, "The Nut-House Nine" (BB)

Vol. 2, No. 4, August 1936. Stories: 6
Cover: Swimming by Rafael DeSoto
William R. Cox, "Sandlot Slugger" (BB)
Robert S. Fenton, "Hilltop King" (BB)

Vol. 3, No. 1, September 1936. Stories: 7
Cover: Tennis by Rafael DeSoto
Joe Archibald, "Hot Corner Guardian" (BB)

Vol. 3, No. 2, October 1936. Stories: 7
Cover: Baseball by Rafael DeSoto
Joe Archibald, "The Diamond Triangle" (BB)
Glenn Long, "Bat-Shy Ballhawk" (BB)

Vol. 3, No. 3, November 1936. Stories: 6
Cover: Football by Rafael DeSoto
Joe Archibald, "Touchdown Terror" (FB)
Alexis Rossoff, "The Pigskin Prima Donnas" (FB)

Vol. 3, No. 4, December 1936. Stories: 6
Cover: Basketball by Rafael DeSoto
Robert S. Fenton, "Loser's Payoff" (FB)
Bob DeHaven, "Dropkick Martyr" (FB)

Vol. 4, No. 1, January 1937 Stories: 7
Cover: Wrestling by Rafael DeSoto
Robert S. Fenton, "Field Phantom" (FB)

Vol. 4, No. 2, February 1937. Stories: 6
Cover: Hockey by Rafael DeSoto
Charles Marquis Warren, "No-Score Star" (FB)

Vol. 4, No. 3, March 1937. Stories: 7
Cover: Skiing by Rafael DeSoto
(No baseball or football)

Vol. 4, No. 4, April 1937. Stories: 7
Cover: Baseball by Rafael DeSoto
Joe Archibald, "Ballhawk Brood" (BB)

Vol. 5, No. 1, May 1937. Stories: 6
Cover: Track and field by Rafael DeSoto
Robert S. Fenton, "Hurler's Heritage" (BB)

Vol. 5, No. 2, June 1937. Stories: 5
Cover: Baseball by Rafael DeSoto
Joe Archibald, "Diamond Dynamo" (BB)

Vol. 5, No. 3, July 1937. Stories: 5
Cover: Boxing by Rafael DeSoto
Alexis Rossoff, "Slick-Ball Comeback"
Charles Marquis Warren, "Diamond Galahad" (BB)

Vol. 5, No. 4, August 1937. Stories: 5
Cover: Baseball by Rafael DeSoto
Robert S. Fenton, "Fly-Chaser's Code" (BB)
Glenn Long, "Slugger's Legacy" (BB)

Vol. 6, No. 1, September 1937. Stories: 6
Cover: Diving by Rafael DeSoto
Joe Archibald, "Hickory Heritage" (BB)
Alexis Rossoff, "The Bughouse Diamond" (BB)

Vol. 6, No. 2, October 1937. Stories: 5
Cover: Baseball by Norman Saunders
Charles Marquis Warren, "Backstop Nemesis" (BB)
Alexis Rossoff, "Gridiron Goliath" (FB)

Vol. 6, No. 3, November 1937. Stories: 6
Cover: Football by Rafael DeSoto
Joe Archibald, "The Phantom Touchdown" (FB)

Vol. 6, No. 4, December 1937. Stories: 6
Cover: Boxing by Rafael DeSoto

Ralph Powers (Nelson S. Bond), "Bench Warmer Champ" (FB)
Nelson S. Bond, "Gridiron Goal" (FB)
Vol. 7, No. 1, January 1938. Stories: 7
Cover: Hockey by Rafael DeSoto
Don George, "Pigskin Juggernaut" (FB)
Vol. 7, No. 2, February 1938. Stories: 6
Cover: Basketball by Rafael DeSoto
(No baseball or football)
Vol. 7, No. 3, March 1938. Stories: 8
Cover: Hockey by Rafael DeSoto
Charles Marquis Warren, "Glory Bowl" (FB)
Vol. 7, No. 4, April 1938. Stories: 5
Cover: Track and field by Rafael DeSoto
(No baseball or football)
Vol. 8, No. 1, June 1938. Stories: 6
Cover: Baseball
Joe Archibald, "Home Run Heritage" (BB)
Vol. 8, No. 2, August 1938. Stories: 7
Cover: Baseball
Herbert L. McNary, "Backstop for Fate" (BB)
Joe Archibald, "The Mad Mounds Man" (BB)
S. Burdette Inch, "Rookie on a Rampage" (BB)
Vol. 8, No. 3, October 1938. Stories: 7
Cover: Football
Joe Archibald, "Big League Busher" (BB)
Ralph Powers (Nelson S. Bond), "Rough-Cut Diamond" (BB)
Nelson S. Bond, "High-Hat Halfback" (FB)
L.E. Smith, "Pigskin Prejudice" (FB)
Vol. 8, No. 4, December 1938. Stories: 8
Cover: Basketball
G.E. Wallace, "Two-Way Quarterback" (FB)
Lynn Gordon, "Gridder in the Lemon Light" (FB)
Vol. 9, No. 1, February 1939. Stories: 8
Cover: Hockey
Nelson S. Bond, "Bowl Bugaboo" (FB)
Vol. 9, No. 2, April 1939. Stories: 9
Cover: Baseball
E. Newman Eveslade, "Second-Chance Second Baseman" (BB)
Joe Archibald, "Moundsman for a Day" (BB)
Vol. 9, No. 3, June 1939. Stories: 9
Cover: Baseball by Norman Saunders
Nelson S. Bond, "Jack of All Bases" (BB)
Allan Dale, "Trouble Assist" (BB)
Chad Silvay, "Headache Hurler" (BB)
Vol. 9, No. 4, August 1939. Stories: 10
Cover: Baseball
Gene D. Robinson, "Too Much Ball" (BB)
Chad Silvay, "Pitcher by Proxy" (BB)
Nelson S. Bond, "Front Page Backstop" (BB)
Robert M. Kalb, "Balmy Bats" (BB)
Giles A. Lutz, "Diamond Destiny" (BB)
Vol. 10, No. 1, October 1939. Stories: 9
Cover: Baseball
Alexis Rossoff, "The Ten-Man Nine" (BB)
Dean Parker, "Miracle Manager" (BB)
Maurice Phillips, "Double Sacrifice" (BB)
Ron Broom, "Flashback Flop" (BB)
Nelson Hutto, "Skyrocket Scrub" (FB)
Vol. 10, No. 2, December 1939. Stories: 8
Cover: Football by Norman Saunders
Nelson S. Bond, "Mutineers on the Gridiron" (FB)
Steve McNeil, "Million Dollar Gridder" (FB)
Harry Shorten, "Halfback Heritage" (FB)
Vol. 10, No. 3, February 1940. Stories: 9
Cover: Hockey by Norman Saunders
Ralph Powers, "Runaway Kicker" (FB)
Vol. 10, No. 4, April 1940. Stories: 10
Cover: Basketball by Norman Saunders
Gene D. Robinson, "The Fireball Kid" (BB)
Vol. 11, No. 1, June 1940. Stories: 9
Cover: Baseball by Norman Saunders
Alexis Rossoff, "The Jitterbug Hurler" (BB)
Hamilton Craigie, "No Fielder's Choice" (BB)
John Wilson, "Balky Bats" (BB)
Raymond H. Tiffany, "Dead-Arm Fireballer" (BB)
Vol. 11, No. 2, August 1940. Stories: 9
Cover: Baseball by Norman Saunders
Alexis Rossoff, "Million-Buck Batsman" (BB)
Reynolds Phillips, "Horsehide Heritage" (BB)
Dean Parker, "The Payoff Play" (BB)
Vol. 11, No. 3, October 1940. Stories: 8
Cover: Baseball by Norman Saunders
Alexis Rossoff, "Diamond Daredevil" (BB)
Zene Tuttler, "A Pennant on the Prowl" (BB)
C. Paul Jackson, "Horsehide Mutiny" (BB)
John Wilson, "Kick Him for a Goal!" (FB)
Dean Parker, "Pigskin Heritage" (FB)
Vol. 11, No. 4, December 1940. Stories: 7
Cover: Football by Norman Saunders
Alexis Rossoff, "Hot Off the Gridiron" (FB)
Reynolds Phillips, "Iron Men Don't Punt" (FB)
Vol. 12, No. 1, February 1941. Stories: 9
Cover: Hockey by Norman Saunders
(No baseball or football)
Vol. 12, No. 2, April 1941. Stories: 9
Cover: Basketball by Norman Saunders
Nelson S. Bond, "Rookie Mastermind" (BB)
Vol. 12, No. 3, June 1941. Stories: 8
Cover: Baseball by Norman Saunders
John Wilson, "Rookies on the Prod" (BB)
Herbert L. McNary, "Fugitive from the Big League" (BB)
Jackson V. Scholz, "Shortstop Stooge" (BB)
W.H. Temple, "Hurl 'Em and Weep" (BB)
Vol. 12, No. 4, August 1941. Stories: 9
Cover: Baseball by Norman Saunders
John Wilson, "Bush League Reveille" (BB)
Dan Averill, "First Sacker's Fadeout" (BB)
Roe Richmond, "Jinx Rides the Basepath" (BB)
Vol. 13, No. 1, October 1941. Stories: 8
Cover: Baseball by Norman Saunders
John Wilson, "Get That Busher!" (BB)
M.M. Tinney, "Wrong Way Pitcher" (BB)
W.H. Temple, "Southpaw Science" (BB)
Zene Tuttler, "Brass-Knuckled Ballhawk" (BB)
Sam Carson, "Gridiron Heritage" (FB)
Vol. 13, No. 2, December 1941. Stories: 8
Cover: Football
Nelson Hutto, Punt, "Pass—and Pray!" (FB)
Dean Parker, "Pigskin Larceny" (FB)
Harold Norton, "Razzle-Dazzle Dynamite" (FB)

Vol. 13, No. 3, February 1942. Stories: 8
Cover: Hockey by Norman Saunders
(No football or baseball)
Vol. 13, No. 4, April 1942. Stories: 8
Cover: Baseball by Norman Saunders
Duane Yarnell, "Diamond Killer Diller" (BB)
W.H. Temple, "Left-Field Larceny" (BB)
Vol. 14, No. 1, June 1942. Stories: 8
Cover: Baseball by Norman Saunders
John Wilson, "Backstop Firebrand" (BB)
C. Paul Jackson, "Base Blitzkrieg" (BB)
Vol. 14, No. 2, August 1942. Stories: 9
Cover: Baseball by Norman Saunders
Duane Yarnell, Hits, "Runs and Terrors" (BB)
Myles D. Blanchard, "Black Sheep Ballhawk" (BB)
Ned Cady, "Hurlers Handicap" (BB)
Giles A. Lutz, "Two-Time Rookie" (BB)
Vol. 14, No. 3, October 1942. Stories: 8
Cover: Baseball by Norman Saunders
John Wilson, "The SOS Hurler" (BB)
Giles A. Lutz, "Horsehide Outcast" (BB)
W.H. Temple, "Big League Benchwarmer" (BB)
Duane Yarnell, "Pigskin Larceny" (FB)
Bill Heuman, "Gridiron Stumblebum" (FB)
Vol. 14, No. 4, December 1942. Stories: 8
Cover: Football by Norman Saunders
John Wilson, "Babe in the Backfield" (FB)
Theodore J. Roemer, "Pigskin Outlaw" (FB)
Vol. 15, No. 1, February 1943. Stories: 8
Cover: Basketball by Norman Saunders
Ralph Powers, "Forward Pass Misery" (FB)
Vol. 15, No. 2, April 1943. Stories: 8
Cover: Baseball
Duane Yarnell, "Say It with Homers" (BB)
Vol. 15, No. 3, August 1943. Stories: 8
Cover: Baseball
Duane Yarnell, "Dead-Arm Dynamite" (BB)
C. Paul Jackson, "Fireball in the Doghouse" (BB)
W.H. Temple, "Go Back to the Bushes" (BB)
Vol. 15, No. 4, November 1943. Stories: 7
Cover: Baseball by Norman Saunders
Zene Tuttler, "The Thirteenth Inning" (BB)
Theodore J. Roemer, "Beanball Barrage" (BB)
Sam Carson, "Halfback Horseplay" (FB)
Guy Landis, "A Small Slice of Tornado" (FB)
Vol. 15, No. 5 (error; actually Vol. 16, No. 1), November 1947. Stories: 6
Cover: Football by Norman Saunders
Giles A. Lutz, "The Fans Never Forget" (BB)
John Wilson, "The Unhappy Warriors" (FB)
Ted Stratton, "Goal-Line Gold" (FB)
Vol. 16, No. 2, January 1948. Stories: 8
Cover: Hockey by Norman Saunders
M.M. Tinney, "Hypo Hurler's Hurricane Hooks" (BB)
Ted Stratton, "Big Mike's Last TD" (FB)
Gardner Fox, "Johnny No-Name" (FB)
Vol. 16, No. 3, March 1948. Stories: 7
Cover: Hockey by Norman Saunders
Mack Mallory, "McNulty the Great" (BB)
Burgess Leonard, "Stop That Yard Thief" (FB)
Vol. 16, No. 4, May 1948. Stories: 7
Cover: Baseball by Norman Saunders
Gardner F. Fox, "Atomic Fireballer" (BB)
Gordon Farley, "The Boom-Boom Bat" (BB)
Nelson Hutto, "Enigma of the Breakaway Kid" (FB)
Vol. 17, No. 1, July 1948. Stories: 7
Cover: Baseball by Norman Saunders
Gardner F. Fox, "Diamonds in the Rough" (BB)
Reynolds Phillips, "Clutch Chucker" (BB)
Ted Stratton, "The Glory Kicker" (FB)
Vol. 17, No. 2, September 1948. Stories: 6
Cover: Baseball by Norman Saunders
John Wilson, "A Hole in His Mitt" (BB)
Richard Brister, "The Great McGeech" (BB)
Gardner Fox, "Gridiron Goalposts" (FB)
Vol. 17, No. 3, November 1948. Stories: 7
Cover: Football by Norman Saunders
Larry Holden, "The Back of My Spikes to You!" (BB)
John Wilson, "Grid Guts for Sale" (FB)
Duane Yarnell, "Fullback Philosopher" (FB)
Vol. 17, No. 4, January 1949. Stories: 7
Cover: Basketball by Norman Saunders
G.S. Robinson, "The Arm and Me" (BB)
Ted Stratton, "Touchdown Savvy" (FB)

Totals: 68 issues, 494 stories, 93 baseball stories, 51 football stories

Champion Sports

Vol. 1, No. 1, March 1937. Stories: 7
Cover: Boxing champion Jack Dempsey
Jeffry Strictland, "Backfield Feud" (FB)
Vol. 1, No. 2, May 1937. Stories: 9
Cover: Baseball pitcher Carl Hubbell
Alexis Rossoff, "Sermon for a Slugger" (BB)
Ralph Powers, "Hilltop Nemesis" (BB)
Vol. 1, No. 3, July 1937. Stories: 9
Cover: Baseball great Lou Gehrig
Joe Archibald, "Base-Hit Blockade" (BB)
Richard L. Hobart, "Thunder on the Diamond" (BB)
John K. Dughmann and John "Pepper" Martin, "Hill Billy Moundsman" (BB)
Vol. 1, No. 4, September 1937. Stories: 7
Cover: Tennis great Ellsworth Vines
Joe Archibald, "The Black Hawk Sniper" (BB)
Charles Marquis Warren, "Pinch-Hit Destiny" (BB)
Vol. 2, No. 1, November 1937. Stories: 7
Cover: Yale football star Clint Frank
Joe Archibald, "The Diamond Rebel" (BB)
Ben Peter Freeman, "Pigskin Palooka" (FB)
Vol. 2, No. 2, January 1938. Stories: 8
Cover: Hockey star Murray Murdoch
W.H. Temple, "Victory Waterloo" (FB)
Vol. 2, No. 3, March 1938. Stories: 7
Cover: Basketball
(No baseball or football)
Vol. 2, No. 4, May 1938. Stories: 7
Cover: Baseball
Alexis Rossoff, "Umps Are Chumps" (BB)

James Lubitz, "Horsehide Nightmare" (BB)
Dean Heffernan, "Athlete's Finger" (BB)
Vol. 3, No. 1, July 1938. Stories: 9
Cover: Boxing
Joe Archibald, "Horsehide Hurricane" (BB)
W.H. Temple, "Southpaw Hooligan" (BB)
Vol. 3, No. 2, October 1938. Stories: 9
Cover: Baseball
Nelson S. Bond, "Fence-Buster's Waterloo" (BB)
W.H. Temple, "Ball-Hawk Bum" (BB)
Ralph Powers, "Double-Duty Backstop" (BB)
Alexis Rossoff, "The Pigskin Crusader" (FB)
Vol. 3, No. 3, January 1939. Stories: 10
Cover: Football
William R. Cox, "Gridiron Hero Buster" (FB)
Vol. 3, No. 4, March 1939. Stories: 11
Cover: Hockey
(No football or baseball)
Vol. 4, No. 1, May 1939. Stories: 10
Cover: Baseball by Norman Saunders
Alexis Rossoff, "Cream-Puff Slugger" (BB)
Nelson Hutto, "Brainstorm Baseman" (BB)
Gene D. Robinson, "Star-Struck Moundsman" (BB)

Totals: 13 issues, 112 stories, 19 baseball stories, 6 football stories

Variety Sports and 12 Sports Aces

Variety Sports Vol. 1, No. 1, September 1938. Stories: 10
Cover: Medley centered on baseball
William R. Cox, "The Fourth Strike" (BB)
L.K. Peabody, "Double Steal" (BB)
Walter Haefeli, Jr., "Pitcher's Windup" (BB)
12 Sports Aces, Vol. 1, No. 2, December 1938. Stories: 12
Cover: Medley centered on football
Ted Roemer, "Heroes Can't Hit" (BB)
Don George, "Suicide Pass" (FB)
Samuel Taylor, "The Star Bench-Warmer" (FB)
12 Sports Aces, Vol. 1, No. 3, March 1939. Stories: 12
Cover: Medley centered on hockey by Norman Saunders
Nelson Hutto, "No Praise for a Hero" (BB)
Roe Richmond, "Yellow as Sand" (FB)
12 Sports Aces, Vol. 1, No. 4, May–June 1939. Stories: 12
Cover: Medley centered on baseball
Nelson S. Bond, "Three-Strike Comeback" (BB)
Cliff Howe, "The Diamond Ring" (BB)
Howard R. Marsh, "Slugger by Mistake" (BB)
12 Sports Aces, Vol. 2, No. 1, July 1939. Stories: 12
Cover: Medley centered on baseball by Norman Saunders
Alexis Rossoff, "The Magnificent Screwball" (BB)
Ted Roemer, "Lone Wolf on Third" (BB)
Dean Miller, "Slump Medicine" (BB)
Holmes Alexander, "Diamond Dictator" (BB)
12 Sports Aces, Vol. 2, No. 2, September 1939. Stories: 12
Cover: Medley centered on baseball by Norman Saunders
Alexis Rossoff, "Diamond Rebel" (BB)
Frank Money, "Fadeout from Glory" (BB)
W.H. Temple, "Rookie on the Rebound" (BB)
12 Sports Aces, Vol. 2, No. 3, November 1939. Stories: 12
Cover: Medley centered on football by Norman Saunders
Morton Lachman, "Outfield Holdout" (BB)
Alexis Rossoff, "Last-Chance Lineman" (FB)
John Wilson, "No-Letter Man" (FB)
Nelson Hutto, "Touchdown by Mistake" (FB)
12 Sports Aces, Vol. 2, No. 4, January 1940. Stories: 12
Cover: Hockey
Raymond Tiffany, "Retreat from Glory" (FB)
12 Sports Aces, Vol. 3, No. 1, March 1940. Stories: 12
Cover: Medley centered on basketball by Norman Saunders
James Lubitz, "Safety First Rookie" (BB)

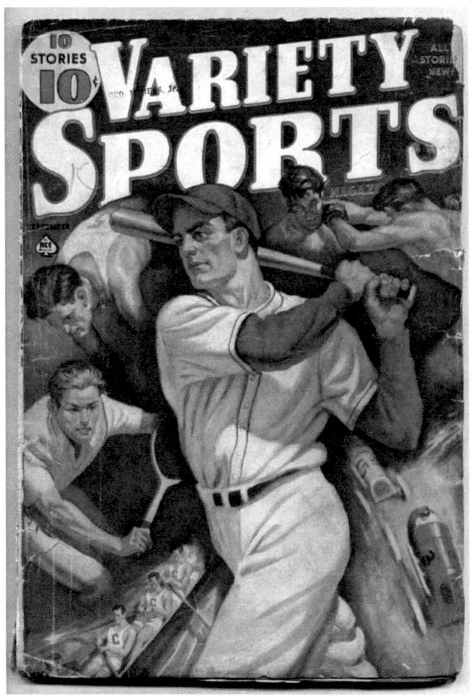

Variety Sports, September 1938 (copyright 1938 Ace Magazines, Inc.). This is actually the first issue of what became _12 Sports Aces_ with the next issue. Ace and Marvel (Red Circle) did a handful of medley covers, with an athlete often surrounded by other sports scenes. Cover by Rafael De Soto.

12 Sports Aces, Vol. 3, No. 2, May 1940.
Stories: 12
Cover: Baseball by Norman Saunders
Alexis Rossoff, "Stars and Strikes" (BB)
William Mayer, "Home Runs Don't Count" (BB)
Giles A. Lutz, "Rookie's Baptism" (BB)

12 Sports Aces, Vol. 3, No. 3, July 1940.
Stories: 12
Cover: Baseball by Norman Saunders
Alexis Rossoff, "The Winning Foul" (BB)
Gene D. Robinson, "Baseball Black Sheep" (BB)
Giles A. Lutz, "Fadeaway Star" (BB)
Zene Tuttler, "Homer by Request" (BB)

12 Sports Aces, Vol. 3, No. 4, September 1940.
Stories: 12
Cover: Baseball by Norman Saunders
Alexis Rossoff, "Hellzapoppin' Hurler" (BB)
Roe Richmond, "Mound Magic" (BB)
M.M. Tinney, "Pigskin Palooka" (FB)

12 Sports Aces, Vol. 4, No. 1, November 1940.
Stories: 12
Cover: Football by Norman Saunders
Lew Ort, "Big League Baldy" (BB)
Alexis Rossoff, "Pigskin Plunger" (FB)
Ron Broom, "Pro from the Panhandle" (FB)
John Wilson, "Born to the Gridiron" (FB)

12 Sports Aces, Vol. 4, No. 2, January 1941.
Stories: 10
Cover: Football
John Wilson, "Gridiron Snakehips" (FB)
Harrison Hendryx, "Hell-Sent Heritage" (FB)

12 Sports Aces, Vol. 4, No. 3, March 1941.
Stories: 12
Cover: Hockey
Zene Tuttler, "Diamond Duel" (BB)

12 Sports Aces, Vol. 4, No.4, May 1941.
Stories: 12
Cover: Baseball by Norman Saunders
John Wilson, "Hot Corner Hi-Jinks" (BB)
Rick Bailey, "Horsehide Duel" (BB)

12 Sports Aces, Vol. 5, No. 1, July 1941.
Stories: 12
Cover: Baseball
Herbert L. McNary, "Horsehide Hellions" (BB)
Zene Tuttler, "Diamond Double Cross" (BB)
Theodore J. Roemer, "Boomerang on the Basepath" (BB)
Gene D. Robinson, "Ballhawk Paradise" (BB)
Giles A. Lutz, "Hell's Fire Mentor" (BB)

12 Sports Aces, Vol. 5, No. 2 September 1941.
Stories: 11
Cover: Baseball
Herbert L. McNary, "Big League Bum's Rush" (BB)
Mac Davis, "Horsehide Miracle Man" (BB)
John Wilson, "The Basepath Bugaboo" (BB)
Zene Tuttler, "Not for the Grandstand" (BB)
Giles A. Lutz, "Diamond Blitzkrieg" (BB)
Theodore J. Roemer, "Lone Wolf on the Gridiron" (FB)
Jay Thorburn (John Wilson's real name), "Last-Chance Lineman" (FB)

12 Sports Aces, Vol. 5, No. 3, November 1941.
Stories: 10
Cover: Football
John Wilson, "The Fourth Strike" (BB)
M.M. Tinney, "Base Hits by Request" (BB)
Mac Davis, "Miracle Moundsman" (BB)
Duane Yarnell, "Gridiron Graveyard" (FB)
Theodore J. Roemer, "Blocking Spot Blues" (FB)
Jay Thorburn (John Wilson's real name), "Pigskin Chopping Block" (FB)

12 Sports Aces, Vol. 5, No. 4, January 1942.
Stories: 11
Cover: Hockey
Johnston McCulley, "Gridiron Renegade" (FB)
Duane Yarnell, "Hipper-Dipper Dynamite" (FB)
W.H. Temple, "Pigskin Morning Glory" (FB)

12 Sports Aces, Vol. 6, No. 1, March 1942.
Stories: 12
Cover: Basketball
(No baseball or football)

12 Sports Aces, Vol. 6, No. 2, May 1942.
Stories: 12
Cover: Baseball
Duane Yarnell, "No Strikes and Out!" (BB)
M.M. Tinney, "Soup Bone Miracle Man" (BB)
C. Paul Jackson, "Jinx for a Horsehide Hero" (BB)

12 Sports Aces, Vol. 6, No. 3, July 1942.
Stories: 11
Cover: Baseball by Norman Saunders
Zene Tuttler, "Diamond Daffydills" (BB)
C.K. Bopp, "When Inside Is Out" (BB)
Jay Thorburn (John Wilson's real name), "Moundsman's Handicap" (BB)

12 Sports Aces, Vol. 6, No. 4, September 1942.
Stories: 11
Cover: Baseball by Norman Saunders
John Wilson, "Thumbs Down on a Fireballer" (BB)
W.H. Temple, "Brushoff for a Backstop" (BB)
Sam Carson, "Basepath Hellion" (BB)
Sidney Renthal, "Horsehide Sense" (BB)

12 Sports Aces, Vol. 7, No. 1, November 1942.
Stories: 10
Cover: Football by Norman Saunders
W.H. Temple, "World Series Goat" (BB)
Ralph Powers, "Hitter's Folly" (BB)
Hank Willard, "Grandstand Stooge" (FB)
John Wilson, "Say It with Touchdowns" (FB)
Cliff Howe, "Destiny's Gridster" (FB)
Jay Thorburn (John Wilson's real name), "Pigskin Squeeze Play" (FB)

12 Sports Aces, Vol. 7, No. 2, January 1943.
Stories: 13
Cover: Hockey by Norman Saunders
M.M. Tinney, "Bench Warmer's Grid Grudge" (FB)
Dale Cochrane, "The Touchdown Fool" (FB)
W.H. Temple, "Pigskin Paydirt" (FB)

12 Sports Aces, Vol. 7, No. 3, March 1943.
Stories: 12
Cover: Basketball
(No baseball or football)

12 Sports Aces, Vol. 7, No. 4, May 1943. Stories: 9
Cover: Baseball by Norman Saunders
Joe Archibald, "Spike That Man Out!" (BB)
W.H. Temple, "Pop-Off Rookie" (BB)
George Richmond, "Meet Me Under the Grandstand" (BB)
12 Sports Aces, Vol. 8, No. 1, September 1943. Stories: 8
Cover: Baseball by Norman Saunders
Theodore J. Roemer, "Sabotage on the Pennant Trail" (BB)
Zene Tuttler, "There Goes the Series!" (BB)
L.C. Levin, "Squeeze Play for a Busher" (BB)
W.H. Temple, "Twister Vengeance" (BB)
12 Sports Aces, Vol. 8, No. 2, December 1943. Stories: 9
Cover: Football
Zene Tuttler, "Boom Town Slugger" (BB)
Duane Yarnell, "Blitz Buster on the Gridiron" (FB)
Gene Normandy, "Pigskin Grandstander" (FB)

Totals: 30 issues, 339 stories, 63 baseball stories, 30 football stories

Ace Publications totals: 111 issues, 945 stories, 175 baseball stories, 87 football stories

Columbia Publications

All-American Sports

Vol. 1, No. 1, December 1940. Stories: 9
Cover: Football
Eric Rober, "World Series Sap" (BB)
T.W. Ford, "Suicide in the Stadium" (FB)
Joe Blair, "Hoosegow Halfback" (FB)
Vol. 1, No. 2, February 1941. Stories: 9
Cover: Boxing
Tom Grover, "Yellow" (BB)
T.W. Ford, "Rose Bowl Tonsils" (FB)
Harry Shorten, "Grudge Gridder" (FB)
William O'Sullivan, "It's Only a Game" (FB)

Totals: 2 issues, 18 stories, 2 baseball stories, 5 football stories

All Sports

Vol. 1, No. 1, September 1939. Stories: 7
Cover: Boxing
T.W. Ford, "Battery for Rent" (BB)
James W. Egan, "Twenty Grand for a Bench Warmer" (BB)
Noel Loomis, "Touchdown Stooge" (FB)
Eric Rober, "Shackled Backs" (FB)
Vol. 1, No. 2, February 1940. Stories: 8
Cover: Hockey
C. Paul Jackson, "Tackles Take Plenty" (FB)
William Cullen Fay, "Spot Passer" (FB)
Vol. 1, No. 3, September 1940. Stories: 9
Cover: Baseball
T.W. Ford, "Golden Boy at First" (BB)
Curtis Bishop, "Blood on the Bases" (BB)
Bud Nelson, "Bean Ball Smoke" (BB)
Robert D. Price, "Soft Stuff" (BB)
Zene Tuttler, "Good Field, No Hit" (BB)
Vol. 1, No. 4, January 1941. Stories: 8
Cover: Football
Bud Nelson, "Baseball Batty" (BB)
T.W. Ford, "Pigskin Bomber" (FB)
Richard Brister, "The Glory Dodger" (FB)
Harry Lash, "Rebel of the Backfield" (FB)
Vol. 1 No. 5, July 1941. Stories: 8
Cover: Baseball
Eric Rober, "Dugout Duellist" (BB)
T.W. Ford, "Fireman Save My Ball Game" (BB)
Herbert E. Smith, "Road Trip" (BB)
Tom Grover, "Homicide Hitter" (BB)
Vol. 1, No. 6, October 1941. Stories: 10
Cover: Baseball
C. Paul Jackson, "Guts Are Enough" (BB)
Mat Rand, "Stooge of the Battery" (BB)
Zene Tuttler, "Texas Star" (BB)
T.W. Ford, "The Star Must Shine" (FB)
T.J. Roemer, "This Way to Glory" (FB)
Vol. 2, No. 1, December 1941. Stories: 10
Cover: Football by J.W. Scott
Fred Steelman, "Sleep Shutout" (BB)
T.W. Ford, "Pigskin Pantywaist" (FB)
Richard Brister, "Half a Halfback" (FB)
Eric Rober, "Idols Die Hard" (FB)
Cliff Campbell, "Grid Tornado" (FB)
Vol. 2, No. 2, March 1942. Stories: 9
Cover: Hockey

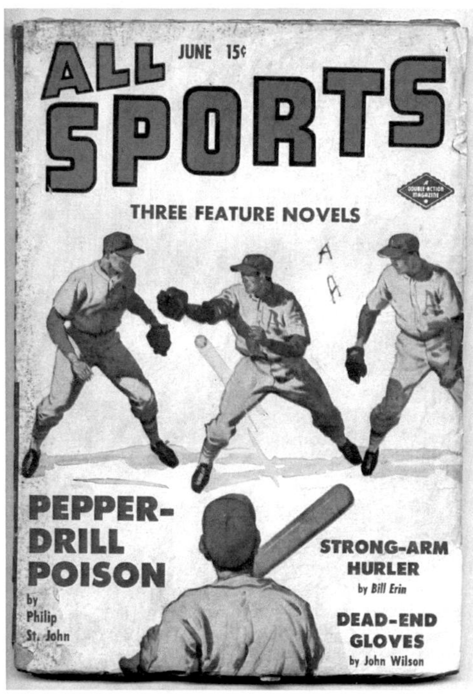

***All Sports*, June 1949 (no copyright indicated). This cover features a clever Columbia "pepper drill."**

A.R. Thurman (Arthur Mann), "A Ghost at First" (BB)
William Heuman, "The Eyes Have It" (BB)
Dan Thomas, "No Rest for a Pigskin Warrior" (FB)

Vol. 2, No. 3, May 1942. Stories: 9
Cover: Baseball
T.W. Ford, "Spikes for a Sandlotter" (BB)
Tom Grover, "Headache Over the Hot Corner" (BB)
Eric Rober, "Diamond Discard" (BB)
Zene Tuttler, "Little Sir Echo" (FB)

Vol. 2, No. 4, July 1942. Stories: 6
Cover: Baseball
T.W. Ford, "The Pilot Prodigy" (BB)
Zene Tuttler, "The Phantom Pitcher" (BB)
Will Loyd, "Gridiron Galahad" (FB)

Vol. 2, No. 5, September 1942. Stories: 9
Cover: Baseball
T.W. Ford, "The Meal Ticket" (BB)
Eric Rober, "Beauty in the Bullpen" (BB)
Lionel Grover, "The Catcher Is a Thief" (BB)
Cliff Campbell, "Bogus Baseman" (BB)
Herb Roemer, "The Best Laid Plans" (BB)

Vol. 2, No. 6, November 1942. Stories: 9
Cover: Baseball
Theodore Roemer, "Ball-Hawk Playboy" (BB)
Harlowe Jukes, "It's America's Pastime" (BB)
T.W. Ford, "Black Sheep of the Stadium" (FB)
Dave Goodis, "For Gold or Glory" (FB)
Russell Gray (Bruno Fischer), "Eleven Goliaths" (FB)
Joseph Lomas, "Ballyhooed Pigskinner" (FB)
Bill Heuman, "Ground Hog" (FB)

Vol. 3, No. 1, March 1943. Stories: 6
Cover: Boxing
William Heuman, "World Series Goat" (BB)
Tom Thursday, "Flip Van Winkle" (BB)
Roe Richmond, "Football Feud" (FB)
Sam Carson, "Ramparts of Courage" (FB)

Vol. 3, No. 2, May 1943. Stories: 9
Cover: Baseball
A.R. Thurman (Arthur Mann), "Service Stripe" (BB)
T.W. Ford, "The Blowhard Backstop" (BB)
Zene Tuttler, "A Glove and a Prayer" (BB)
Richard Brister, "Big League Bust" (BB)
Russell Gray (Bruno Fischer), "No Brains Allowed" (FB)

Vol. 3, No. 3, Summer 1943. Stories: 8
Cover: Baseball
T.W. Ford, "Slacker on the Mound" (BB)
Roe Richmond, "Morale Buster" (BB)
Zene Tuttler, "Keystone Klucks" (BB)
E.E. Halleran, "Straight Football" (FB)

Vol. 3, No. 4, Fall 1943. Stories: 9
Cover: Football
Ted Douglas, "Bullpen Protégé" (BB)
Tom Thursday, "Screwballoney" (BB)
Eric Rober, "Bantam Cock" (BB)
T.W. Ford, "They Also Serve" (FB)
William Heuman, "Line Coach" (FB)

Vol. 3, No. 5, Winter 1943–1944. Stories: 7
John J. Wallace, Winning Pitcher, "Dodson" (BB)
A.R. Thurman (Arthur Mann), "Baseball Prodigy" (BB)
Zene Tuttler, "Goal Posts in the Sky" (FB)

Vol. 3, No. 6, Spring 1944. Stories: 8
Cover: Baseball
Cliff Campbell, "Swing from the Spikes" (BB)
Arthur Mann, "International Pastime" (BB)
T.W. Ford, "4F and Flashy" (BB)
William Campbell, "Bleacher Shy" (BB)
Dean Parker, "Line Smasher" (FB)

Vol. 4, No. 1, Summer 1944. Stories: 7
Cover: Baseball
Cliff Campbell, "Murderer's Mound" (BB)
C. Paul Jackson, "The Veteran Rookie" (BB)
Roe Richmond, "Comeback for Corben" (BB)

Vol. 4, No. 2, Winter 1944–1945. Stories: 7
Cover: Football
Arthur Mann, "Team of Symbols" (BB)
William H. Bragan, "Stop—Thieves!" (BB)
T.W. Ford, "The Broken Back" (FB)

Vol. 4, No. 3, November 1948 (after long hiatus). Stories: 7
Cover: Baseball
T.W. Ford, "Gimme That Ball" (BB)
Larry Holden, "Spike the Man Down!" (BB)
W.T. Ballard, "A Bird in the Bush League" (BB)
John Wilson, "Brother Blocker" (FB)

Vol. 4, No. 4, February 1949. Stories: 7
Cover: Boxing
T.W. Ford, "Horsehide Has-Been" (BB)
Raymond Dreyfack, "Moron on the Mound" (BB)
Wadsworth Nealey, "A Rackety Rax for the Bears" (FB)

Vol. 4, No. 5, April 1949. Stories: 6
Cover: Baseball
Norman Ober, "Hell on the Mound" (BB)
W.P. Brothers, "Infield Prima Donna" (BB)
Tom Dowling, Jr., "Beanballs for the Kid" (BB)

Vol. 4, No. 6, June 1949. Stories: 6
Cover: Baseball
Zene Tuttler, "Steal That Signal" (BB)
Bill Erin, "Strong-Arm Hurler" (BB)
Philip St. John (Lester del Rey), "Pepper-Drill Poison" (BB)
Gardner F. Fox, "Football Letters" (FB)

Vol. 5, No. 1, August 1949. Stories: 7
Cover: Baseball
Jackson Barrow, "One More Fireball" (BB)
Jack Farley, "Hell on Dirt Oval" (BB)
William O'Sullivan, "Manage Them Busher!" (BB)

Vol. 5, No. 2, October 1949. Stories: 7
Cover: Baseball
Philip St. John (Lester del Rey), "They're All Tough, Rookie!" (BB)
William O'Sullivan, "Soft Streak" (BB)
Mal Kent, "No-Hit Trial" (BB)

Vol. 5, No. 3, December 1949. Stories: 8 (all-football issue)
Cover: Football
T.W. Ford, "Gridiron Double-Cross"
Roe Richmond, "Win with Deadwood"
Cliff Campbell, "Fighting Chance"

David C. Cooke, "Cyclone on Cleats"
William O'Sullivan, "Ex-Substitute"
Jim Duncan, "Corn with a Heart"
Mat Rand, "Don't Let Them Down!"
Eric Rober, "The Old Timer"
Vol. 5, No. 4, February 1950. Stories: 6
Zene Tuttler, "Fatball Phenom" (BB)
Van McNair, Jr., "Big Angle Guy" (BB)
Roe Richmond, "The Big One" (BB)
Wadsworth Nealey, "Peel One for Spud" (FB)
Lee Floren, "Fullback for Today" (FB)
William O'Sullivan, "Front Man" (FB)
Vol. 5, No. 5, April 1950. Stories: 6
Cover: Baseball
Roe Richmond, "Bonus Baby" (BB)
Philip St. John (Lester del Rey), "Hate That Horsehide!" (BB)
Cliff Campbell, Look Alive, "Busher!" (BB)
V.K. Emden (James Blish), "Big-Time Rookie" (BB)
Vol. 5, No. 6, June 1950. Stories: 6
Cover: Baseball
Roe Richmond, "The Quick Pennant Bums" (BB)
Bill Erin, "Rabbit-Head Radcliffe" (BB)
John Wilson, "Heads-Up Hurler" (BB)
Vol. 6, No. 1, August 1950. Stories: 6
Cover: Baseball
Bill Erin, "Bury Him in Texas!" (BB)
David C. Cooke, "A Pitch in Time" (BB)
T.W. Ford, "Diamond Discipline" (BB)
James L. Harte, "Gridiron Revenge" (FB)
Vol. 6, No. 2, October 1950. Stories: 5
Cover: Baseball
Roe Richmond, "Fireball Fireman" (BB)
Theodore Roemer, "Baseball Is My Business" (BB)
Milton Lesser, "Hot Corner Clown" (BB)
Vol. 6, No. 3, December 1950. Stories: 7
Louis Trimble, "Doctor Shortstop" (BB)
Norman Ober, "Half a Catcher" (BB)
Roe Richmond, "Go Down Fighting" (FB)
Mar Rand, "Decoy Man" (FB)
Vol. 6, No. 4, February 1951. Stories: 6
Cover: Boxing
Louis Trimble, "Last Ball Game" (BB)
Norman Ober, "Lightweight Eleven" (FB)
Richard Brister, "Piggy-Back" (FB)
Vol. 6, No. 5, April 1951. Stories: 8
Cover: Baseball
Wadsworth Nealey, "Rebirth of the Blues" (BB)
Norman Ober, "Grounder Shy" (BB)
Humphrey Jones, "Halfway Hitter" (BB)
Mat Rand, "The Diamond Serf" (BB)
Richard Brister, "The Big Tank" (FB)
Vol. 6, No. 6, June 1951. Stories: 7
Cover: Baseball
George Kilrain, "Big House Bambino" (BB)
J.J. Mathews, "Gold Brick Fireballer" (BB)
Louis Trimble, "Blowhard Ballhawk" (BB)
T.W. Ford, "Too Big for the Game" (FB)
James L. Harte, "Touchdown Twins" (FB)
Vol. 7, No. 1, September 1951. Stories: 8
Cover: Baseball
Robert Sidney Bowen, "Money Pitcher" (BB)
Jim Moore, "The Eatin' Kid" (BB)
Wallace McKinley, "Saffron-Streak Catcher" (BB)
Bill Erin, "Reverse That Decision!" (BB)
Edwin Johnson, "Burn the Bats Down" (BB)

Totals: 37 issues, 275 stories, 101 baseball stories, 52 football stories

Blue Ribbon Sports

Vol. 1, No. 1, December 1937. Stories: 7
Cover: Football
Bob DeHaven, "Beethoven's Fifth" (BB)
A.R. Thurman (Arthur Mann), "The Talking Pitcher" (BB)
Glenn Long, "Sentimental Quarterback" (FB)
Vol. 1, No. 2, January 1938. Stories: 7
Cover: Boxing
Thomas R. Thomson, "Skip the Cheers" (BB)
Walter Roeber Schmidt, "Double Victory" (FB)
Vol. 1, No. 3, March 1938. Stories: 8
Cover: Basketball
William O'Sullivan, "Twist Pitcher" (BB)
A.R. Thurman (Arthur Mann), "Screwball" (BB)
Vol. 1, No. 4, May 1938. Stories: 8
Cover: Boxing

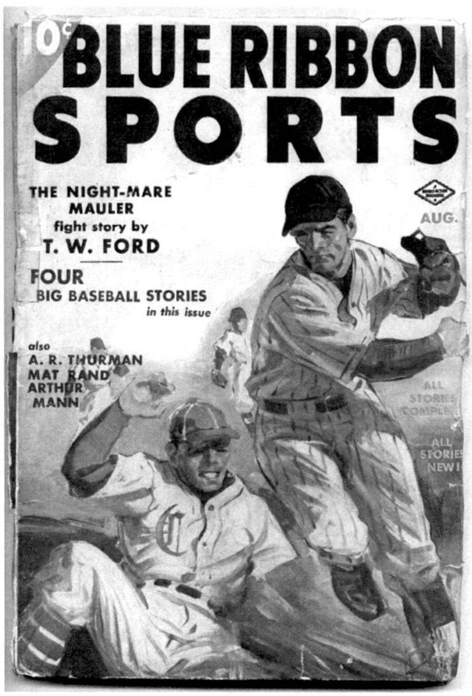

Blue Ribbon Sports, August 1938 (copyright 1938 Blue Ribbon Sports). The fielder tries to complete a double play on this Columbia cover, despite a rather awkward slide by the base runner.

Curtis Bishop, "Winning Streak" (BB)
A.R. Thurman (Arthur Mann), "Bats in the Dugout" (BB)
Vol. 1, No. 5 (August 1938). Stories: 11
Cover: Baseball
A.R. Thurman (Arthur Mann), "The Umpire State" (BB)
James Rourke, "Head Work" (BB)
Mat Rand, "Over the Fence" (BB)
Cliff Campbell, "Star-Bound Rookie" (BB)
Ernie Phillips, "Softball Is for Sissies" (Softball)
Brady Black, "Hillbilly Football" (FB)
Vol. 1, No. 6, November 1938. Stories: 9
Cover: Boxing
Walter Roeber Schmitt, "Ball Shy" (BB)
Mat Rand, "Danger—Lowdown Curves" (BB)
W.H. Temple, "Win or Get Out" (BB)
James Rourke, "Double Play" (BB)
T.W. Ford, "Gridiron Vendetta" (FB)
Vol. 2, No. 1, February 1939. Stories: 11
Cover: Boxing
J.R. Marion, "Diamond Feud" (BB)
Arthur Mann, "Winter Baseball" (BB)
James Rourke, "Double Play" (BB)
T.W. Ford, "Gridiron Outcasts" (FB)
Herbert L. McNary, "A Pass to Glory" (FB)
Tom Grover, "The Bonus Bucking Tackle" (FB)
Vol. 2, No. 2, April 1939. Stories: 11
Cover: Boxing
Eric Rober, "Sideline Scorer" (FB)
Vol. 2, No. 3, July 1939. Stories: 9
Cover: Baseball
E. Newman Eveslade, "Kill the Ump" (BB)
Sam White, "Trick Ball Artist" (BB)
J.R. Marion, "Native Ivory" (BB)
Vol. 2, No. 4, September 1939. Stories: 9
Cover: Baseball
Curtis Bishop, "Waiver Route for a Vet" (BB)
Zene Tuttler, "Diamond Engineer" (BB)
Roe Richmond, "Joke Ball" (BB)
W.H. Temple, "Price Tag Rookie" (BB)
Vol. 2, No. 5, December 1939. Stories: 9
Cover: Football
Herbert L. McNary, "King of the Bullpen" (BB)
T.W. Ford, "The Touchdown Tornado" (FB)
Zene Tuttler, "Grudge Gridder" (FB)
T.J. Roemer, "The Big Four Bucker" (FB)
Nelson Hutto, "Pass Catcher's Decoy" (FB)
Vol. 2, No. 6, April 1940. Stories: 7
Cover: Baseball
T.W. Ford, "Feud at First" (BB)
John Wilson, "Crippled Pitchers" (BB)
Richard Brister, "Baseball Brat" (BB)
Vol. 3, No. 1, October 1940. Stories: 8
Cover: Baseball
Harry Shorten, "Round Trip for a Rookie" (BB)
Bud Nelson, "Pennant Pilot" (BB)
Norman L. Paul, "Diamond Courage" (BB)
Harvey Hill, "Touchdown Reverse" (FB)

Totals: 13 issues, 114 stories, 33 baseball stories, 13 football stories.

Sports Fiction

Vol. 1, No. 4 (first issue, perhaps continued from a non-sports title), April 1938. Stories: 9
Cover: Baseball
William R. Cox, "You Gotta Be Tough" (BB)
Ernie Phillips, "Fool for Luck" (BB)
Glenn Long, Flynn and Son, "Big Leaguers" (BB)
Nelson S. Bond, "The Kid Brother" (FB)
Vol. 1, No. 5, July 1938. Stories: 10
Cover: Baseball
E. Newman Eveslade, "The Last Laugh" (BB)
Mat Rand, "Opening Game" (BB)
Arthur Mann, "Science at Third" (BB)
W.H. Temple, "Pull Hitter" (BB)
Vol. 1, No. 6, November 1938. Stories: 9
Cover: Baseball
Arthur Mann, "Color Bearer" (BB)
Cliff Campbell, "Pennant Pirates" (BB)
James Rourke, "Fight Is Right" (BB)
Wilcey Earle, "Jinx Batter" (BB)
Vol. 2, No. 1, February 1939. Stories: 10
Cover: Football
James Roarke, "Thunder Over Second" (BB)
J.R. Marion, "Wench in the Machinery" (BB)
T.W. Ford, "Rose Bowl Road Bum" (FB)
Curtis Bishop, "To Hell with Glory" (FB)
Ted Roemer, "Gridiron Feud" (FB)
Vol. 2, No. 2, July 1939. Stories: 11
Cover: Baseball
E. Newman Eveslade, "The Bonehead on First" (BB)
Mat Rand, "Cocksure" (BB)
Bud Nelson, "Brother Eight Ball" (BB)
A.R. Thurman (Arthur Mann), "The Hunch Player" (BB)
James Roarke, "Pigskin Pygmy" (FB)
Vol. 2, No. 3, September 1939. Stories: 11
Cover: Baseball
Eric Rober, "Keystone Captive" (BB)
Bud Nelson, "Sold to the Cellar" (BB)
Arthur Mann, "Ivory Hunter's Headache" (BB)
Frank E. Carson, "The Best Man at Second" (BB)
A.R. Thurman (Arthur Mann), "Switch-Hitter Frame-Up" (BB)
Vol. 2, No. 4, November 1939. Stories: 10
Cover: Football
Gene D. Robinson, "Good Time Moundsman" (BB)
Roe Richmond, "The Diamond Rabbit" (BB)
Jack Tanner, "Born to Slug" (BB)
T.W. Ford, "The Gridiron Goats Revolt" (FB)
Eric Rober, "The Lost Star" (FB)
Vol. 2, No. 5, February 1940. Stories: 9
Cover: Football
Nelson Hutto, "Five Inning Wonder" (BB)
Harry Shorten, "Touchdown Tornado" (FB)
Gene D. Robinson, "Bargain in the Backfield" (FB)
Edward B. Reynolds, "Touchdown Stooge" (FB)
John Wilson, "No Gridiron Tramps Allowed" (FB)

Vol. 2, No. 6, June 1940. Stories: 9
Cover: Baseball
T.W. Ford, "Burglar on the Basepath" (BB)
James Lubitz, "Wildflower Windup" (BB)
C.S. Montanye, "The Cloud Bumper" (BB)
William Mayer, "Star on the Bench" (BB)
Vol. 3, No. 1, October 1940. Stories: 8
Cover: Baseball
T.W. Ford, "Dynamite Soupbone" (BB)
Bud Nelson, "Storm Cellar" (BB)
Brian Loomis, "The Hell Helmet" (FB)
Harry Shorten, "Toy Quarterback" (FB)
Vol. 3, No. 2, Spring 1941. Stories: 9
Cover: Baseball
T.W. Ford, "Ghost on the Mound" (BB)
Marvin Ryerson, "Diamond in the Rough" (BB)
Jack Tanner, "Major Midget" (BB)
Eric Rober, "Homicide at the Hot Corner" (BB)
Reynolds Phillips, "Nitro Blocker" (BB)
Vol. 3, No. 3, Summer 1941. Stories: 9
Cover: Baseball
Tom Grover, "Spikes for the Busher" (BB)
H.E. Smith, "The Greater Game" (BB)
Eric Rober, "Goofy Like a Fox" (BB)
Mat Rand, "Shadow Over the Diamond" (BB)
Nick Zura, "Diamond Outcast" (BB)
Vol. 3, No. 4, Winter 1941–1942. Stories: 10
Cover: Boxing
Zene Tuttler, "Super Gloom Guy" (BB)
T.W. Ford, "Headguard for a Ghost" (FB)
Bill Heuman, "Pay Dirt" (FB)
Richard Brister, "Fullback's Fadeout" (FB)
Vol. 3, No. 5, Spring 1942. Stories: 8
Cover: Baseball
Robert H. Bryan, "World Series War" (BB)
T.W. Ford, "Screwball Wanted" (BB)
William Heuman, "Star Dust" (BB)
Cliff Campbell, "Dynamite Catcher" (BB)
Joseph Lomas, "Let Him Eat Mud" (FB)
Mat Rand, "The Zero Hour" (FB)
Vol. 3, No. 6, Summer 1942. Stories: 9
Cover: Baseball
Marvin Ryerson, "Diamond Cut Diamond" (BB)
Zachary Strong, Home, "Steal Home!" (BB)
Zene Tuttler, "Schnozzola Shortstop" (BB)
Joe Brennan, "Won't Be Bitter" (BB)
Bill Heuman, "Kid Rat" (BB)
Vol. 4, No. 1, Fall 1942. Stories: 9
Cover: Football
Eric Rober, "A Mite of Smite" (BB)
Marvin Ryerson, "Castoff Ballhawk" (BB)
T.W. Ford, "Backfield Bombshell" (FB)
Roe Richmond, "Shipwreck Shane" (FB)
Sam Carson, "Touchdown by Proxy" (FB)
Robert Leslie Bellem, "Army Game" (FB)
Vol. 4, No. 2, Winter 1942–1943. Stories: 9
Cover: Football
Robert Leslie Bellem, "Jackpot Hero" (FB)
Zene Tuttler, "Gridiron Rip Van Winkle" (FB)
Sam Carson, "Glory Gridiron" (FB)
Vol. 4, No. 3, Spring 1943. Stories: 8
Cover: Baseball
Eric Rober, "Mr. Whacko Comes Through" (BB)
T.W. Ford, "The Spike-Slamming Fool" (BB)
Arthur Mann, "Northern Exposure" (BB)
A.R. Thurman (Arthur Mann), "Diamond Dust" (BB)
Theodore Roemer, "Kid Catcher" (BB)
Zene Tuttler, "One Man Gang" (FB)
Vol. 4, No. 4, Summer 1943. Stories: 8
Cover: Baseball
Zene Tuttler, "Sun Field Slugger" (BB)
Eric Rober, "A Jinx Never Dies" (BB)
Tom Grover, "Benchwarmer's Comeback" (BB)
Lee Floren, "Sawed Off Backstop" (BB)
Robert W. Nealy (Wadsworth Nealey), "The Boys Played Rough" (FB)
Vol. 4, No. 5, Fall 1943. Stories: 9
Cover: Boxing
Zene Tuttler, "Fireball Feud" (BB)
William A. Jones, "Touchdown Fever" (FB)
Eric Rober, "The Snapback" (FB)
William Heuman, "End Trouble" (FB)
Cliff Campbell, "Nightmare Backfield" (FB)
Vol. 4, No. 6, Winter 1943–1944. Stories: 8
Cover: Basketball
Eric Rober, "Crucial Game for Pop" (BB)
T.W. Ford, "Touchdown at Tobruk" (FB)
Eugene Pawley, "Tin Ears" (FB)
Vol. 5, No. 2 (no Vol. 5, No. 1 issued), Summer 1944. Stories: 8
Cover: Boxing
C. Paul Jackson, "Bargain Basement Ballhawk (advertised for never-issued Spring issue)" (BB)
Marvin Ryerson, "Cloud Over Short" (BB)
Tom Thursday, "I'm Very Smart" (BB)
Richard Brister, "Hippity Hop" (BB)
Michael Fleming, "Baseball Heart" (BB)
Vol. 5, No. 3, June 1947 (after hiatus). Stories: 7
Cover: Baseball
Tom Thursday, "The Moore the Merrier" (BB)
Richard Brister, Run, Rookie, "Run!" (BB)
T.W. Ford, "Candidate for the Boneyard" (BB)
Lee Floren, "There's a Place for Razzle-Dazzle" (FB)
Vol. 5, No. 4, September 1947. Stories: 6
Cover: Baseball
T.W. Ford, "Star Struck" (BB)
John Wilson, "No Strikes and Out" (BB)
Arthur Mann, "The Surgeon" (BB)
Vol. 5, No. 5, December 1947. Stories: 5
Cover: Football
James Blish, "Bats for Brains" (BB)
Eric Rober, "From Sideline to Goal Line" (FB)
Ted Stratton, "Red for Courage" (FB)
C. Paul Jackson, "Campus Payoff" (FB)
Vol. 5, No. 5 (error, duplicates the previous issue), April 1948. Stories: 8
Cover: Baseball
John Wilson, "Make Way for a Fireball" (BB)
T.W. Ford, "The Hurson Hurricane" (BB)
Giles A. Lutz, "I Need a Pennant" (BB)
Si Farrell, "Woe Is Me" (BB)
Vol. 5, No. 6 (above error never corrected), July 1948. Stories: 6
Cover: Baseball

T.W. Ford, "Meal Ticket on the Mound" (BB)
Herbert L. McNary, "Shadows on the Diamond" (BB)
Larry Holden, "Build-Up" (BB)
Rae Dragonette-Dye, "Right Off the Bat" (BB)
Vol. 6, No. 1, October 1948. Stories: 7
Cover: Baseball
Joe Brennan, "I Can't Be Hit" (BB)
James Blish, "Double-Clutch Danger" (BB)
Rae Dragonette, "Low and Wild" (BB)
M.M. Tinney, "One-Man Gang" (FB)
Vol. 6, No. 2, January 1949. Stories: 7
Cover: Football
David A. Kyle, "Beanball Bugaboo" (BB)
John Wilson, "Backfield Bombshell" (FB)
James Blish, "Gridiron Workhorse" (FB)
Vol. 6, No. 3, March 1949. Stories: 8
Cover: Baseball
Walt Brown, "Rah-Rah Busher" (BB)
Norman Ober, Biff, "Sock and Whammy" (BB)
T.W. Ford, "The Diamond Bum" (BB)
Tom Dowling, Jr., "Control" (BB)
Zene Tuttler, "Goal-Line Gamble" (FB)
Vol. 6, No. 4, May 1949. Stories: 7
Cover: Baseball
Roe Richmond, "The $75,000 Lemon" (BB)
Zene Tuttler, "Star Bust" (BB)
Robert Sidney Bowen, "If at First" (BB)
Vol. 6, No. 5, September 1949. Stories: 8 (all-baseball issue)
Cover: Baseball
John Wilson, "Diamond Kingpin"
Zene Tuttler, "Cheese Clouter"
David C. Cooke, "The Has-Been Hurler"
M.M. Tinney, "Grease That Flipper!"
Mal Kent, "The Stand-Off Kid"
Walt Brown, "Gentleman's Gentleman"
E.E. Clement (R.W. Lowndes), "Lose for the Payoff"
Willard Crandall, "Call That Pitch!"
Vol. 6, No. 6, November 1949. Stories: 6 (all-baseball issue)
Cover: Baseball
Roe Richmond, "The Uphill Fight"
John Wilson, "Love That Busher!"
Bill Erin, "Strong Arm Crybaby"
Mat Rand, "Red Hair, Raw Temper"
John Van Praag, "Leadfoot Wonder"
Cliff Campbell, "No-Credit Guy"
Vol. 7, No. 1, January 1950. Stories: 6
Cover: Football
Philip St. John (Lester del Rey), Play Ball, "Morning Glories" (BB)
Roe Richmond, "Black Sheep Halfback" (FB)
Cliff Campbell, "Touchdown Tornado" (FB)
T.W. Ford, "Grassroots Gridiron Game" (FB)
Mar Rand, "Grudge Gridder" (FB)
Vol. 7, No. 2, March 1950. Stories: 7
Cover: Boxing
Roe Richmond, "Diamond Rebel" (BB)
T.W. Ford, "Pilot on the Spot" (BB)
Vol. 7, No. 3, June 1950. Stories: 8
Cover: Baseball
Humphrey Jones, Play Ball, "Busher" (BB)
T.W. Ford, "The Grand-Larceny Kid" (BB)
John Wilson, "Base Hits and Blood" (BB)
Jack Rogers, "Lady's Day" (BB)
James L. Harte, "A Time to Play—A Time to Coach" (FB)
Vol. 7, No. 4, August 1950. Stories: 6
Cover: Baseball
Zene Tuttler, "Tag That Man" (BB)
T.W. Ford, "Baseball Blood" (BB)
Norman Ober, "The Nifty Nine" (BB)
Jackson Barrow, "Man-Sized Catcher" (BB)
William Fitzwald, "Coach on Trial" (FB)
Vol. 7, No. 5, October 1950. Stories: 7
Cover: Baseball
Bill Erin, "The Rube Runs Wild" (BB)
Richard Brister, "Mister Pitch" (BB)
John Wilson, "Pigskin Magic" (FB)
Cliff Campbell, "Reluctant Touchdowns" (FB)
Vol. 7, No. 6, December 1950. Stories: 6
Cover: Boxing
Mat Rand, "Wench at Shortstop" (women's BB)
Bill Erin, "All-American Loafer" (FB)
Cliff Campbell, "The Money-Back Tackle" (FB)
Vol. 8, No. 1, February 1951. Stories: 6
Cover: Boxing
James L. Harte, "Case of the Red-Headed Shortstop" (BB)
Richard Brister, "I Play for Dough" (FB)
Vol. 8, No. 2, April 1951. Stories: 8
Cover: Baseball
T.W. Ford, "The Star Hater" (BB)
Bill Erin, "The Prodigal Pitcher" (BB)
Louis Trimble, "Hot-Corner Hotshot" (BB)
Cliff Campbell, "Break That Pilot!" (BB)
James L. Harte, Cast Your Own Shadow, "Kid" (FB)
Lester del Rey, "Solitaire for Two" (FB)
Vol. 8, No. 3, June 1951. Stories: 7
Cover: Baseball
George Kilrain, "Grandstand Guy" (BB)
T.W. Ford, "Bullpen Bellhop" (BB)
David C. Cooke, "Red-Hot Rookie!" (BB)
Norman Ober, "Smoky Sluggers" (BB)
Vol. 8, No. 4, September 1951. Stories: 11
Cover: Baseball
Eric Rober, "The Never-Has-Been" (BB)
T.W. Ford, "Picture Player" (BB)
Cosmo Bennett, "Comeback Slugging" (BB)
Bill Erin, "Big Brother" (BB)
Norman Ober, "Too Many Pilots" (BB)
J.J. Mathews, "Ears for Justice" (FB)

Totals: 43 issues, 347 stories, 136 baseball stories, 57 football stories.

Sports Winners

Vol. 1, No. 2 (first issue; continued from Real Northwest), February 1938. Stories: 10
Cover: Hockey
Brian Loomis, "Pitcher's Courage" (BB)
Nelson S. Bond, "Pigskin Payoff" (FB)
Vol. 1, No. 3, April 1938. Stories: 9
Cover: Basketball

Nelson Bond, "Glass Arm Gardiner" (BB)
Glenn Long, "Payment in Pigskin" (FB)
Vol. 1, No. 4, June 1938. Stories: 8
Cover: Boxing
Herbert L. McNary, "High and Inside" (BB)
J.J. Meany, "Little Dynamite" (BB)
Charles Pifer, "Time Out" (FB)
Vol. 1, No. 5, October 1938. Stories: 10
Cover: Baseball
James Rourke, "Too Much Fight" (BB)
A.R. Thurman (Arthur Mann), "Umpires Can't Win" (BB)
Mat Rand, "A Hit Is an Out" (BB)
Arthur Mann, "The Guess Hitter" (BB)
Vol. 1, No. 6, January 1939. Stories: 9
Mat Rand, "Pitcher's Payoff" (BB)
James Rourke, "Diamond Goat" (BB)
J.R. Marion, "Master Mind" (BB)
Ross Russell, "Pigskin Pariah" (FB)
T.W. Ford, "Backfield Bookkeeper" (FB)
A.R. Thurman (Arthur Mann), "The One-Man Backfield" (FB)
Vol. 2, No. 1, March 1939. Stories: 10
Cover: Boxing
Mat Rand, "High Hard One" (BB)
Eric Rober, "Monday Morning Quarterback" (FB)
Vol. 2, No. 2, July 1939. Stories: 8
Cover: Boxing
Arthur Mann, "Keystone Cousins" (BB)
Bud Nelson, "Baseball Is Business" (BB)
Vol. 2, No. 3, September 1939. Stories: 9
Cover: Baseball
Arthur Mann, "Charged Battery" (BB)
Bud Nelson, "Base Stealer's Handicap" (BB)
Eric Rober, "First Sacker for Sale" (BB)
William Mayer, "Two Fingers and a Prayer" (BB)
T.W. Ford, "Marko the Magnificent" (BB)
Vol. 2, No. 4, November 1939. Stories: 9
Cover: Football
Bud Nelson, "The Slump Breaker" (BB)
T.W. Ford, "Tackle to Kill!" (FB)
Forrest Kleinman, "Gravy-Train Gridder" (FB)
Eric Rober, "The Four Flying Bombers" (FB)
Vol. 2, No. 5, March 1940. Stories: 8
Cover: Boxing
Mat Rand, "Diamond Destiny" (BB)
Dougal McDougal, "Block That Jinx" (FB)
Vol. 2, No. 6, June 1940. Stories: 8
Cover: Baseball
T.W. Ford, "Big Noise of the Bullpen" (BB)
W.H. Temple, "You Gotta Slug" (BB)
Bud Nelson, "The Put-Out Kid" (BB)
Vol. 3, No. 1, January 1941. Stories: 9
Cover: Football
Earl Campbell, "Contract Backfire" (BB)
Eric Rober, "Wild Bull of the Bases" (BB)
T.W. Ford, "Kill the Coach" (FB)
Bud Nelson, "Pygmy in the Grid Top" (FB)
Edward B. Reynolds, "The Phantom Blocker" (FB)
Vol. 3, No. 2, July 1941. Stories: 8
Cover: Baseball by J.W. Scott
T.W. Ford, "Misfit on the Mound" (BB)
Eric Rober, "Tamer of the Diamond Devils" (BB)
Wayne Pool, "Falling Star" (BB)
Tom Grover, "Diamond Doomed" (BB)
David Goodis, "Diamond Doctor" (BB)
Vol. 3, No. 3, November 1941. Stories: 7
Cover: Medley centered by football
William Heuman, "No-Hitter" (BB)
Eric Rober, "The Swap Backs" (FB)
T.W. Ford, "The Star Pays Off" (FB)
Cliff Campbell, "Pigskin Dictator" (FB)
Vol. 3, No. 4, January 1942. Stories: 9
Cover: Football
Marvin Ryerson, "A Hero Is Born" (BB)
Eric Rober, "Torpedo Tailback" (FB)
Richard Brister, "A Dozen for Dallas" (FB)
Zachary Strong, "Quarterback Scoop" (FB)
Bill Heuman, "Football Fantasy" (FB)
Vol. 3, No. 5, April 1942. Stories: 8
Cover: Baseball
T.W. Ford, "Bogus Ball-Buster" (BB)
A.R. Thurman (Arthur Mann), "Southern Exposure" (BB)
Eric Rober, "Good Field, No. Hit" (BB)
Cliff Campbell, "Money Player" (FB)
Vol. 3, No. 6, June 1942. Stories: 8
Cover: Boxing
T.W. Ford, "The Eight-Ball Backstop" (BB)
Mat Rand, "Taps for a Slugger" (BB)
Cliff Campbell, "Angle Guy" (BB)
Richard Brister, "Hay Fever Hitter" (BB)
Charles Coombs, "Tackle Treachery" (FB)
Vol. 4, No. 1, August 1942. Stories: 7
Cover: Baseball
T.W. Ford, "Bribed Behind the Bat" (BB)
Willard Crandall, "Slide Shy" (BB)
Cliff Campbell, "Baseball Bred" (BB)
Vol. 4, No. 2, November 1942. Stories: 8
Cover: Football
Eric Rober, "Bring on the Goat" (BB)
Cliff Campbell, "Bullpen Bum" (BB)
Edward L. Moynahan, "Hired Hand" (FB)
Bill Heuman, "The Proving of Breezy Smith" (FB)
Zene Tuttler, "Gridiron Plodder" (FB)
Vol. 4, No. 3, January 1943. Stories: 8
Cover: Football
Tom Thursday, "Home Runyan" (BB)
T.W. Ford, "The 22 Coaches" (FB)
Robert N. Bryan, "The Masked Halfback" (FB)
Harrison Hendryx, "Football Brains" (FB)
Vol. 4, No. 4, Summer 1943. Stories: 8
Cover: Baseball
T.W. Ford, "Frame That Bum!" (BB)
A.R. Thurman (Arthur Mann), "The Umpire State" (BB)
Tom Thursday, "Fountain of Ruth" (BB)
Vol. 4, No. 5, Fall 1943. Stories: 9
Cover: Football
T.W. Ford, "The Glory Hunter" (BB)
Zene Tuttler, "Strikeout Sweetheart" (BB)
William A. Jones, "The Tornado Twins" (FB)
Eric Rober, "Football Sucker" (FB)
C. Paul Jackson, "The Tackle Takes It" (FB)

Vol. 4, No. 6, Spring 1944. Stories: 7
Cover: Football
Eric Rober, "The No-Clutch Kid" (BB)
Tom Thursday, "Base on Bolds" (BB)
Roe Richmond, "Cash Rawl Comes Back" (FB)
Sam Carson, "No Crowd, No Glory, But Passes!" (FB)
Vol. 5, No. 1, October 1950 (long hiatus). Stories: 9
Cover: Baseball
Robert Turner, "Has-Been's Comeback" (BB)
Bill Erin, "Guts at the Plate" (BB)
Richard Brister, "Devil in the Dugout" (BB)
Vin Paradis, "Matter of Guts" (BB)
David C. Cooke, "While the Crowd Cheers" (FB)
D.A. Kyle, "Touchdown Tyrant" (FB)
Vol. 5, No. 2, January 1951. Stories: 7
Cover: Football
George O. Smith, "Wreck That Rookie!" (BB)
Bill Erin, "Mayhem for Practice" (FB)
H.C. Butler, "Pigskin Playboy" (FB)
T.W. Ford, "It Takes Two" (FB)
Eric Rober, "Half a Back" (FB)
Vol. 5, No. 3, April 1951. Stories: 9
Cover: Baseball
T.W. Ford, "No Hit, No Run, No Field!" (BB)
John Wilson, "Big League Busher" (BB)
Eric Rober, "The Vengeance Hurler" (BB)
Cliff Campbell, "Rough on Redheads" (BB)
James L. Harte, "Right on the Bean" (BB)
Vol. 5, No. 4, July 1951. Stories: 9
Cover: Baseball
T.W. Ford, "The Blasted Bomber"
J.J. Mathews, "Eager-Beaver Busher"
H.C. Eaton, "You Gotta Be Fast!" (BB)
Eric Rober, "The Comedy Kid" (BB)
Cliff Walters, "Here Comes the Pitch" (BB)
James L. Harte, "No Feud Like an Old Feud" (FB)
J.H. Loring, "No Substitute for Honor" (FB)
Vol. 5, No. 5, October 1951. Stories: 10
Cover: Baseball
George Lewis, "World Series Heart" (BB)
Mal Kent, "The Last Stand Kid" (BB)
Norman Ober, "New-Fangled Baseball" (BB)
James L. Harte, "Mysterious Catcher" (BB)
Edwin Johnson, "Fire in His Arm" (BB)
J.H. Loving, "Long Trip to the Top" (BB)
Vol. 5, No. 6, January 1952. Stories: 8
Cover: Football
Jim Moore, "It's All in the Record Books" (BB)
James L. Harte, "No Time to Retire" (BB)
Roe Richmond, "Goal to Go" (FB)
George Kilrain, Goodbye, "Uncle Jim!" (FB)
H.C. Butler, "Gridiron Ghost" (FB)
Cosmo Bennett, "Get That Combination" (FB)
Vol. 6, No. 1, April 1952. Stories: 10
Cover: Baseball
Roe Richmond, Get Mad, "Busher!" (BB)
J.J. Mathews, "Smokeball Loafer" (BB)
Jim Moore, "Six-Gun Playoff" (BB)
Hal K. Wells, "The Lady and the Umpire" (BB)
Wadsworth Nealey, "Inspiration Guy" (BB)
James L. Harte, "The Assassin and the Keystone Sack" (BB)
King McCord, "The Mighty Minaham" (FB)
(Continued as Ten Story Sports, Second Series)

Totals: 30 issues, 256 stories, 82 baseball stories, 47 football stories

Super Sports

Vol. 1, No. 6 (first issue, continued from another title), September 1938. Stories: 12
Cover: Baseball
Cliff Campbell, "Down the Hot Corner" (BB)
W.H. Temple, "Bantam Backstop" (BB)
Mar Rand, "Double Play" (BB)
James Rourke, "The Indian Sign" (BB)
Wilcey Earle, "Slugger's Limbo" (BB)
Vol. 2, No. 1, December 1938. Stories: 11
Cover: Football
A.R. Thurman (Arthur Mann), "Stormy Knight" (BB)
Arthur Mann, "Circus Baseball" (BB)
James Rourke, "They Never Come Back" (BB)
T.W. Ford, "The Sound Proof Slash-Back" (FB)
Ron Broom, "Wing Wizard" (FB)
Curtis Bishop, "Fumble Threat" (FB)
Duane Yarnell, "Gridiron Bruiser" (FB)
Vol. 2, No. 2, March 1939. Stories: 11
Cover: Hockey
Jesse Albert, "The Ivory Hunter" (BB)
William O'Sullivan, "Forgotten Man of the Backfield" (FB)
Vol. 2, No. 3, June 1939. Stories: 11
Cover: Baseball
Robert Sidney Bowen, "Infield Fury" (BB)
Bud Nelson, "Ivory Trouble" (BB)
Gene D. Robinson, "Nobody Loves a Home Run King" (BB)
J.R. Marion, "The Big Bluff" (BB)
Robert D. Price, "Great Grange's Ghost" (FB)
Vol. 2, No. 4, August 1939. Stories: 12
Cover: Baseball
T.W. Ford, "Doughboy of the Diamond" (BB)
Bud Nelson, "Pitcher's Heart" (BB)
Jackson Sprague, "Sparkling Backstop" (BB)
James Rourke, "College Dude" (BB)
Harmon Bellamy, "Squeeze Play" (BB)
Earl Campbell, "Diamond Mayhem" (BB)
Mat Rand, "Pigskin Baby" (FB)
Vol. 2, No. 5, October 1939. Stories: 10
Cover: Boxing
Eric Rober, "The Iron Man in the Mask" (BB)
Bud Nelson, "To Help a Rookie" (BB)
Mat Rand, "The Spike Dodger" (BB)
Giles A. Lutz, "Mound Exile" (BB)
Joe Holland, "Touchdown Tramp" (FB)
Vol. 2, No. 6, March 1940. Stories: 9
Cover: Football
Joe Gregg, "Tiger Stripes" (FB)
Steve McNeal, "The Ghost of Frankenstein" (FB)
Bud Nelson, "Quadruple Threat" (FB)
Vol. 3, No. 1, July 1940. Stories: 10
Cover: Baseball

Bud Nelson, "Diamond Dazzler" (BB)
Mat Rand, "Big-League Busher" (BB)
Earl Campbell, "Keystone Double Cross" (BB)
James Roarke, "Smokeball Wizard" (BB)
Robert N. Bryan, "The Eighty Grand Jinx" (BB)
Dougal McDougal, "Mound Courage" (BB)
Vol. 3, No. 2, November 1940. Stories: 9 (estimated)
(Issue not seen, so likely may be more baseball or football stories.)
Cover: Baseball
T.W. Ford, "Touchdown Taunted" (FB)
Vol. 3, No. 3, March 1941. Stories: 9
Cover: Boxing
T.W. Ford, "Pitch, Clown, Pitch" (BB)
Bud Nelson, "Pitchers Need Guts" (BB)
Nick Zura, "Backfire Backstop" (BB)
Harry Shorten, "The Great Man Jones" (FB)
John Wilson, "Gold Plated Touchdowns" (FB)
C. Paul Jackson, Grid War, "Navy Style" (FB)
Tom Grover, "Pay to Play Gridster" (FB)
Vol. 3, No. 4, June 1941. Stories: 9
Cover: Baseball
T.W. Ford, "Belt It Busher" (BB)
Jack Tanner, "Man ... Baseball Brand" (BB)
H.E. Smith, "Big League Timber" (BB)
Eric Rober, "Soupbone for Sale" (BB)
Harry Shorten, "Losers Take All" (BB)
Mat Rand, "Touchdown Tourists" (FB)
Vol. 3, No. 5, October 1941. Stories: 10
Cover: Baseball
Eric Rober, "Orphans in the Outfield" (BB)
Marvin Ryerson, "Old Dynamite" (BB)
W. Crandall, "Miracle Arm Screwball" (BB)
Tom Grover, "The Saffron Streak Star" (FB)
T.W. Ford, "The Triple Threat Juggler" (FB)
Vol. 3, No. 6, December 1941. Stories: 10
Cover: Boxing
Marvin Ryerson, "No Place for Sentiment" (BB)
T.W. Ford, "More Passes" (FB)
Eric Rober, "Break That Back" (FB)
William Heuman,"The Outsider" (FB)
Edgar D. Kramer, "Pigskin Even-Stephens" (FB)
Vol. 4, No. 1, February 1942. Stories: 8
Cover: Football
Cliff Campbell, "All-American Fraud Back" (FB)
Eric Rober, "The Cleat Clown" (FB)
Mat Rand, Bye, "Bye Ivy League" (FB)
Vol. 4 , No. 2, May 1942. Stories: 10
Cover: Baseball
T.W. Ford, "The Magnificent Screwball" (BB)
A.R. Thurman (Arthur Mann), "Siamese Infielders" (BB)
Cliff Campbell, "I'm a Bum" (BB)
Mat Rand, "Big Brother Boss" (BB)
T.J. Roemer, "Varsity Clan" (FB)
Vol. 4, No. 3, July 1942. Stories: 9
Cover: Baseball by A. Leslie Ross
Tom Grover, "Two O'Clock Pitcher" (BB)
T.W. Ford, "Run, Thief, Run" (BB)
Cliff Campbell, "Hit 'Em Where They Ain't" (BB)
William Heuman, "Beef 'N Bones" (BB)
Vol. 4, No. 4, October 1942. Stories: 8
Cover: Baseball
T.W. Ford, "Frame That Star" (BB)
Tom Grover, "Johnny in the Clutch" (BB)
Myles D. Blanchard, "Stars as Beautiful" (BB)
William Heuman, "V Is for Five Spot" (BB)
Zene Tuttler, "The Nine Old Men (left out of table of contents)" (BB)
Roe Richmond, "Slugging Slacker" (BB)
Vol. 4, No. 4 (error), December 1942. Stories: 7
Cover: Football
William Heuman, "It's a Gift" (BB)
T.W. Ford, "The Cleat Traitor" (FB)
Mat Rand, "Suicide in the Stadium" (FB)
Eric Rober, "Gridiron Renegade" (FB)
Tom Grover, "Pinch Kicker" (FB)
Vol. 4, No. 4 (error; third such listing in a row), February 1943. Stories: 9
Cover: Football
Richard Brister, "Bonus for Hogan" (BB)
William A. Rutledge III, "Diamond Blackout" (BB)
A.R. Thurman (Arthur Mann), "Gridiron Heat" (FB)
Tom Grover, "Make for the Goat" (FB)
T.W. Ford, "Gridiron Lone Wolf" (FB)
Vol. 4, No. 5 (error never corrected), May 1943. Stories: 9
Cover: Baseball (infinity cover)
T.W. Ford, "Trouble Guy" (BB)
Richard Brister, "Jonah" (BB)
Bill Heuman, "The Devil Is an Angel" (BB)
Cliff Campbell, "It's a Long Way Home" (BB)
Zene Tuttler, "Blast Furnace Fullback" (FB)
Vol. 4, No. 6, July 1943. Stories: 8
T.W. Ford, "The Gambling Goons" (BB)
Zene Tuttler, "Soldier's Last Strike" (BB)
Theodore Roemer, "The Shortstop Twist" (BB)
Sam Carson, "Payoff Passes" (FB)
Vol. 5, No. 1, October 1943. Stories: 8
Cover: Baseball
T.W. Ford, "From Foxhole to Dugout" (BB)
A.R. Thurman (Arthur Mann), "Balata Baloney" (BB)
Tom Thursday, "Truth Is Stranger Than Fiction" (BB)
Robert W. Nealey (Wadsworth Nealey), "Sailors Take Warning" (FB)
Vol. 5, No. 2, January 1944. Stories: 7
Zene Tuttler, "Twilight of a Mound Star" (BB)
T.W. Ford, "The Hunger Back" (FB)
Paul Aurandt (Paul Harvey), "Pigskin in the Sky" (FB)
Vol. 5, No. 3, April 1944. Stories: 7
Cover: Boxing
T.W. Ford, "Sandlot Phenom" (BB)
Sam Carson, "Base Hits on Blong Blong" (BB)
Dave Goodis, "The Big Boy from Belmont" (FB)
Vol. 5, No. 4, July 1946 (after hiatus). Stories: 6
Cover: Baseball
T.W. Ford, "Million Dollar Washout" (BB)
Richard Brister, "Mad Dog in the Dugout" (BB)
Arthur Mann, "One of a Series" (BB)

A.R. Thurman (Arthur Mann), "Diamond Cutter" (BB)
Vol. 5, No. 5, September 1946. Stories: 8
Cover: Baseball
T.W. Ford, "Mite Behind the Mask" (BB)
Seymour Irving Pichin, "Sharp Like an Eagle" (BB)
Ted Stratton, "Who's Got That Football?" (FB)
Cliff Campbell, "In Fake Cleats" (FB)
Vol. 5, No. 6, December 1946. Stories: 7
Cover: Baseball
Roe Richmond, "World Series" (BB)
Willard Crandall, "Gridiron Baseball" (BB)
T.W. Ford, For Sale, "One Screwball Back" (FB)
Vol. 6, No. 1, February 1947. Stories: 8
Cover: Football
Arthur Mann, "Roscoe and the Magic Bat" (BB)
Cliff Campbell, "The Promoter" (BB)
T.W. Ford, "The Killer Coach" (FB)
Vol. 6, No. 2, June 1947. Stories: 7
Cover: Baseball
Duane Yarnell, Give It a Ride, "Rookie" (BB)
Cliff Campbell, "Big League Stage Fright" (BB)
T.W. Ford, "Showdown at Shortstop" (BB)
Vol. 6, No. 3, September 1947. Stories: 5
Cover: Baseball
T.W. Ford, Swing, Ya Bum, "Swing!" (BB)
John Wilson, "Hot Corne Hi-Jinx" (BB)
Roe Richmond, "The Man Who Beat Merriwell" (BB,FB)
Arthur Mann, "Ambidexterity Unlimited" (BB)
Vol. 6, No. 4, December 1947. Stories: 5
Cover: Baseball
John Wilson, "Keep Hollering Busher!" (BB)
Gardner Fox, "Basement Backstop" (BB)
Roe Richmond, "The Swede" (FB)
Vol. 6, No. 5, April 1948. Stories: 6
Cover: Baseball
William Tenn (Philip Klass), "Sawed Off and Scrappy" (BB)
T.J. Roemer, "Shortstop Slugger" (BB)
T.W. Ford, "Big Muscles on Cleats" (FB)
Vol. 6, No. 6, July 1948. Stories: 7
Cover: Baseball
T.W. Ford, "Bat Magic" (BB)
Norman Ober, "The Bull Story" (BB)
John Wilson, "Spike Him Out!" (BB)
Tom Thursday, "The Tapeworm Turns" (BB)
Vol. 7, No. 1, October 1948. Stories: 7
Cover: Baseball
Zene Tuttler, "Smash That Apple!" (BB)
Curt Brannon, "Storm at Second" (BB)
James Blish, "The Hustler" (BB)
Vol. 7, No. 2, January 1949. Stories: 8
Cover: Boxing
Rae Dragonette-Dye, "The Stray Genius" (BB)
James Blish, "The Touchdown Tenderfoot" (FB)
David A. Kyle, "Too Many Heroes" (FB)
William Fitzgerald, "The Third Stringer" (FB)
Sam Merwin, Jr., "Blocking Blues" (BB)
Vol. 7, No. 3, April 1949. Stories: 7
Cover: Boxing
David C. Cooke, "The Stardust Kid" (BB)
Robert Sidney Bowen, "Pennant Pacer" (BB)
Dean Owen, "The Clown" (BB)
Larry Holden, "Pigskin Punk" (FB)
Vol. 7, No. 4, July 1949. Stories: 8
Cover: Baseball
Roe Richmond, "The Goat Turns" (BB)
Norman Ober, "The Pinch Pilot" (BB)
Robert Sidney Bowen, "Big Moment" (BB)
Zene Tuttler, "Horsehide Doctor" (BB)
David C. Cooke, "Mr. Pigskin Comes Back" (FB)
Vol. 7, No. 5, October 1949. Stories: 6
Cover: Baseball
Zene Tuttler, "Big League Brat" (BB)
Philip St. John (Lester del Rey), "Detour to the Majors" (BB)
J.W. Benjamin, "Hitting Is My Business" (BB)
Vol. 7, No. 6, January 1950. Stories: 8
Cover: Football
D.A. Kyle, "Halfway Hurler" (BB)
T.W. Ford, "Backfield Brigade" (FB)
Mat Rand, "Buck the Big Four" (FB)
Cliff Campbell, "Gridiron Outcast" (FB)
Vol. 8, No. 1, March 1950. Stories: 7
Cover: Baseball
Roe Richmond, "Slugger's Revenge" (BB)
Philip St. John (Lester del Rey), "Train That Bum!" (BB)
Cliff Campbell, "Bull-Pen Star" (BB)
John Wilson, Play Rough, "Gridder" (FB)
Vol. 8, No. 2, June 1950. Stories: 7
Cover: Baseball
Bill Erin, "The Know-How Slugger" (BB)
T.W. Ford, "Glamor Strikes" (BB)
Robert Turner, "The Mad Moundsman" (BB)
Vol. 8, No. 3, September 1950. Stories: 10
Cover: Baseball
John Wilson, "Rookie of the Year" (BB)
Jackson Barrow, "Occupational Hazard" (BB)
T.W. Ford, "Blackmailer Behind the Bat" (BB)
Cliff Campbell, "Little Guy" (BB)
James L. Harte, "Barnaby Goes South" (BB)
Vol. 8, No. 4, December 1950. Stories: 10
Cover: Football
Joe Brennan, "Too Good a Ball Player" (BB)
James Harte, "Double-Exposure" (BB)
Bill Erin, "The Reluctant Gridder" (FB)
Cosmo Bennett, "Ride 'Em Cowboy!" (FB)
Cliff Campbell, "Scandal Passes" (FB)
T.W. Ford, "Sunday Showdown" (FB)
Richard Brister, "The Ground Gainer" (FB)
Vol. 8, No. 5, March 1951. Stories: 8
Cover: Roller derby
James Harte, "Duster's Second Chance" (BB)
H.C. Eaton, "Menace in the Field" (BB)
Mat Rand, Johnny Argyle, "Shortstop" (BB)
John Wilson, "Dead-End Touchdowns" (FB)
J.H. Loring, "The Magnificent Arm" (FB)
Vol. 8, No. 6, June 1951. Stories: 9
Cover: Baseball
T.W. Ford, "Two Strikes on Him!" (BB)
George Lewis, "Hungry Man" (BB)
Jim Moore, "Rockets (Rigby) and the Old-Timers" (BB)
Richard Brister, "Has-Been on the Hill" (BB)

Vol. 9, No. 1, September 1951. Stories: 11
Cover: Baseball
T.W. Ford, "Shadow Over the Dugout" (BB)
Ernie Johnson, "Left-Hander's Local" (BB)
J.J. Mathews, "Talent Scout's Luck" (BB)
Jim Moore, "Stretch-Drive Secret" (BB)
James L. Harte, "The Famous Quadruple Play" (BB)
H.C. Eaton, "The Run-Around Guy" (BB)
J.H. Loring, Like Father, "Like Son" (FB)
Vol. 9, No. 2, December 1951. Stories: 7 (all-baseball issue)
Cover: Baseball
Hunt Collins (Evan Hunter), "Fury on First"
Wadsworth Nealey, "Mangled Moundsman"
T.E. Haggerty, "Catching Is Murder"
J.H. Loring, "The King-Sized Series"
Seven Anderton, "Grand Finale"
James L. Harte, "No Place for a Gentleman"
Mat Rand, "Haunted Hitter"
Vol. 9, No. 3, March 1952. Stories: 8
Cover: Boxing
Wadsworth Nealey, "The Way to Win" (BB)
Jim Moore, "Rockets (Rigby) and the Romans" (BB)
Seven Anderton, "Battlers All" (BB)
William F. Schwartz, "Never Too Old" (BB)
George Kilrain, "Offensive End" (FB)
Vol. 9, No. 4, June 1952. Stories: 8
Cover: Baseball
Seven Anderton, "Clouting Clowns" (BB)
H.C. Butler, "Keystone Coward" (BB)
Wadsworth Nealey, "That Guy, High" (BB)
Jim Moore, "Block That Revolution" (FB)
Cliff Campbell, "Boos for the Braves" (FB)
Vol. 9, No. 5, September 1952. Stories: 7
Cover: Baseball
Wadsworth Nealey, "Old Three Hundred" (BB)
Robert Sidney Bowen, "Rookie on the Hook" (BB)
H. Wieand Bowman, "No String to Pull" (BB)
George Kramer, "Pennants and Petticoats" (BB)
Seven Anderton, "Sixty-Minute Guy" (FB)
Vol. 9, No. 6, December 1952. Stories: 8
Cover: Baseball
Robert Turner, "Those Pennant Bums" (BB)
Roe Richmond, "Farewell Performance" (BB)
William F. Schwartz, "Hot-Corner Handicap" (BB)
Christopher Fleming, "Catching Is Brutal" (BB)
James L. Harte, "By Act of Congress" (BB)
Vol. 10, No. 1, March 1953. Stories: 8
Cover: Boxing
William F. Schwartz, "That Old Gray Mare" (BB)
Norman Ober, "Bluenose's Hairy Gridder" (FB)
Jim Moore, "The Good News Days (Rockets Rigby)" (FB)
Vol. 10, No. 2, June 1953. Stories: 9
Cover: Baseball
Seven Anderton, "A Wing and a Prayer" (BB)
Roe Richmond, "Castoff Champs" (BB)
William F. Schwartz, "Bye, Bye, Rookie!" (BB)
Richard Brister, "Baby at the Plate" (BB)
Vol. 10, No. 3, September 1953. Stories: 9
Cover: Horse racing
Roe Richmond, "E for Error" (BB)
J.J. Mathews, "Base Knock Rhythm" (BB)
Cliff Campbell, "Pennant Flight" (BB)
David James, "The Snowman Playeth" (BB)
Vol. 10, No. 4, December 1953. Stories: 6
Cover: Baseball
Seven Anderton, "Pixilated Pinch-Hitter" (BB)
David James, "I Am Not Blind!" (BB)
Roe Richmond, "Classic Comeback" (BB)
Dan Valentine, "Southpaws Should Stay Single" (BB)
Vol. 10, No. 5, March 1954. Stories: 4
Wadsworth Nealey, "You're Out, "Mister Manager!" (BB)
Gene Rodgers, "Has Anyone Seen Jones?" (BB)
Richard Brister, "The Americanization of Eddie Buck" (FB)
Vol. 10, No. 6, June 1954. Stories: 8
Cover: Baseball
Mel Colton, "King of the Hill" (BB)
Gene Rodgers, "The Unexpected Champs" (BB)
William F. Schwartz, "Too Many Homers" (BB)
Dan Valentine, "The Night-Time Kid" (BB)
David James, "Tommy the Toe" (FB)
Vol. 11, No. 1, September 1954. Stories: 5
Cover: Baseball
Seven Anderton, "Break Up the Moguls" (BB)
Jim Moore, "Rockets (Rigby) On the Mound" (BB)
Francis Hamilton, "The Big Leaguer" (BB)
1955 annual. Stories: 4
Cover: Baseball
Richard Brister, "Just Pitch to Me, Kid" (BB)
Seven Anderton, "Golden Calf" (BB)
1956 annual. Stories: 7
Cover: Baseball
Bill Erin, "Guts and a Prayer" (BB)
Robert Silverberg, "Beanball Hurler" (BB)
Milton Lesser, "Grits for the Slugger" (BB)
Michael Avallone, "Last Place Clubs Don't Die" (BB)
1957 annual. Stories: 9
Cover: Baseball
Robert Silverberg, "Egghead on the Mound" (BB)
Calvin M. Knox (Robert Silverberg), "Outfield Outlaw" (BB)
Robert A. Madle, "Moment of Glory" (BB)
William F. Schwartz, "Cupid Takes the Series" (BB)
Michael Avallone, "Power the Ball Plateward" (BB)
Robert L. Teague, "Secret Weapon" (BB)
Louis Trimble, "One-Time Pitcher" (BB)

Totals: 61 issues, 500 stories, 196 baseball stories, 73 football stories.

Ten Story Sports

Vol. 4, No. 6 (continued from Real Northwest Adventures), July 1937. Stories: 9
Cover: Baseball

Arthur Mann, "Rifle Arm" (BB)
Walter Roeber, "Schmidt Guts" (BB)
William R. Cox, "The Ramblin' Wildcats" (FB)
Vol. 5, No. 1, October 1937. Stories: 10
Cover: Baseball
Arthur Mann, "Flash in the Pan" (BB)
Terry Turner, "Dizzy Daffydills" (BB)
Samuel Taylor, "A Trap for Lady Luck" (FB)
Vol. 5, No. 2, December 1937. Stories: 9
Cover: Football
Cliff Campbell, "Diamond Dust" (BB)
Charles E. Pifer, "Soft" (Softball)
Arthur Mann, "Last Year's Hero" (FB)
Vol. 5, No. 3, February 1938. Stories: 9
Cover: Hockey
Ernie Phillips, "Keystone Feud" (BB)
William R. Cox, "All-American Backfield" (FB)
Curtis Bishop, "Touchdown Twins" (FB)
Vol. 5, No. 4, April 1938. Stories: 9
Cover: Boxing
Arthur Mann, "Unsafe at Second" (BB)
William R. Cox, "Unlike Father" (BB)
Mat Rand (William R. Cox using house name), "Rose Bowl" (FB)

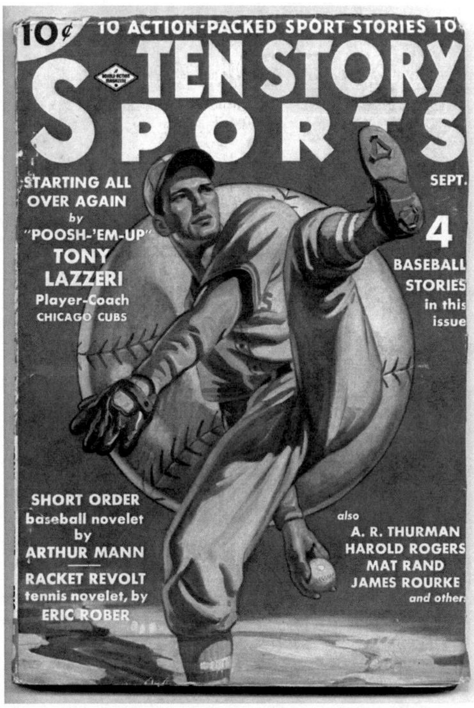

***Ten Story Sports*, September 1938 (copyright 1938 Blue Ribbon Magazines Inc.). Columbia was not known for symbolic covers, but this unsigned, uncredited beauty for *Ten Story Sports* was a vivid exception. Former Yankees great Tony Lazzeri, then in his only year as a player-coach for the Cubs, contributes a non-fiction piece.**

Vol. 5, No. 5, June 1938. Stories: 9
Cover: Baseball
Arthur Mann, "The Gay Receiver" (BB)
Ernie Phillips, "Hearts and Diamonds" (BB)
Bob DeHaven, "A Switch in Nine" (BB)
Vol. 5, No. 6, September 1938. Stories: 9
James Rourke, "Nine Assists and Two Errors" (BB)
Arthur Mann, "Short Order" (BB)
Nelson Bond, "The Horseshoe Kid" (BB)
Mat Rand, "A Switch in Time" (BB)
Vol. 6, No. 1, December 1938. Stories: 9
Cover: Football
James Rourke, "Outfield Glory" (BB)
Mat Rand, "Three and Two" (BB)
T.W. Ford, "Touchdowns from Heaven" (FB)
Arthur Mann, "Grid Leak" (FB)
William R. Cox, "Goal-Line Comeback" (FB)
Vol. 6, No. 2, February 1939. Stories: 9
Cover: Boxing
A.R. Thurman (Arthur Mann), Feld's Angels (Softball)
T.W. Kick, "Block That Kick!" (BB)
Tom Grover, "Thunderbolt Back" (FB)
Vernon James, "Stadium Sage" (FB)
Vol. 6, No. 3, April 1939. Stories: 10
Cover: Baseball
J.R. Marion, "The Baseball Nut" (BB)
James Rourke, "Undergraduate Baseball" (BB)
Tom Grover, "Namesake Poison" (FB)
Vol. 6, No. 4, June 1939. Stories: 10
Cover: Baseball
Arthur Mann, "Too Many Strikes" (BB)
E. Newman Eveslade, "Backstop's Nemesis" (BB)
Ernie Phillips, "Rabbit Ears" (BB)
T.W. Ford, "No Rookies Wanted" (BB)
Vol. 6, No. 5, August 1939. Stories: 9
Cover: Baseball by J.W. Scott
Curtis Bishop, "The Nothing Pitcher" (BB)
Giles A. Lutz, "There's Always Next Year" (BB)
Zene Tuttler, "Rowdy" (BB)
Vol. 6, No. 6, October 1939. Stories: 8
Cover: Motor-scooter racing
James W. Egan, "Wrong-Arm Battery" (BB)
Eric Rober, "The Diamond Doctor" (BB)
Tom Grover, "Gridiron Nurse-Maid" (BB)
Vol. 7, No. 1, February 1940. Stories: 8
Cover: Football
Harry Shorten, "Pigskin Payoff" (FB)
James Roarke, "Headlines Halfback" (FB)
Vol. 7, No. 2, July 1940. Stories: 9
Cover: Baseball
T.W. Ford, "The Schoolboy Screwball" (BB)
Zene Tuttler, "Pennant Fever" (BB)
Mat Rand, "Dizzy Daffydills" (BB)
Eric Rober, "The Pay-Off Platter" (BB)
Vol. 7, No. 3, November 1940. Stories: 8
Cover: Boxing
Robert N. Bryan, "The Bench Warmer" (BB)
Marvin Ryerson, "Home Run at Midnight" (BB)
William O'Sullivan, "The King Is Dead" (FB)
T.W. Ford, "Papa Comes to Alma Mater" (FB)

Vol. 7, No. 4, March 1941. Stories: 6
Cover: Boxing
T.W. Ford, "Clubhouse Crybabies" (BB)
Eric Rober, "Hotshot for Shortstop" (BB)
Tom Grover, "High Spikes for the Heller Guy" (BB)
Mar Rand, "Master Mind" (BB)
Vol. 7, No. 5, June 1941. Stories: 9
Cover: Baseball
T.W. Ford, "The Keystone Comic" (BB)
Eric Rober, "Double Play Duellist" (BB)
Herbert E. Smith, "Ballplayer-Soldier" (BB)

Ten Story Sports (Second Series, Continued from Sports Winners)

Vol. 6, No. 2, July 1952. Stories: 10
Cover: Baseball
Seven Anderton, "The Spoiler" (BB)
William F. Schwartz, "The Bonus Kid" (BB)
Lionel J. Eastermann, "Southpaw" (BB)
Richard Brister, "Itch in the Outfield" (BB)
Vol. 6, No. 3, October 1952
Cover: Baseball
Seven Anderton, "The Big Win" (BB)
Roe Richmond, "Durk on the Diamond" (BB)
Robert Sidney Bowen, "Carbon Copy" (BB)
George Kramer, "The Magic Number" (BB)
Glen Monroe, "The Bonus Bust" (BB)
William F. Schwartz, "The Four-Handed Passer" (FB)
Vol. 6, No. 4, January 1953. Stories: 9
Cover: Football
James L. Harte, "Traded Into Trouble" (BB)
Jim Moore, "Ringer Round the Ozark" (BB)
Seven Anderton, "Gridiron Worry-Wort" (FB)
William F. Schwartz, "The Transformation of Big Brute Klein" (FB)
Norman Ober, "Blue Streak Guy" (FB)
Louis Trimble, "Hillbilly Hotshot" (FB)
Vol. 6, No. 5, April 1953. Stories: 8
Cover: Boxing
Wadsworth Nealey, "Mr. Dipsy-Do" (BB)
William F. Schwartz, "The Fading Fireman" (BB)
J.W. Benjamin, "Terror at Short" (BB)
Jim Moore, "Drums Over the Diamond" (BB)
David James, "The Odds Are on Bodkin" (FB)
Vol. 6, No. 6, July 1953. Stories: 8
Cover: Baseball
Seven Anderton, "Nize Bonus Baby" (BB)
David James, "Lucky the Terror" (BB)
Roe Richmond, "The Weakest Link" (BB)
William F. Schwartz, "Twilight on the Hill" (BB)
Richard Gunn, "The Passer Who Couldn't Miss" (FB)
Vol. 7, No. 1, October 1953. Stories: 8
Cover: Baseball
Roe Richmond, "Handy Andy" (BB)
David James, "Nine Short Men" (BB)
Christopher Fleming, "The Bonus Bust" (BB)
William F. Schwartz, "The Big Stick" (BB)
Richard Brister, "Iron Man Out" (FB)
Vol. 7, No. 2, January 1954. Stories: 7
Cover: Football
Christopher Fleming, "Clutch Hitter" (BB)
Gene Rodgers, Brush Him Back, "Busher!" (BB)
H.C. Butler, "Pass Your Way to Glory" (FB)
Richard Brister, "Backfield Brat" (FB)
Lee Floren, "With Adhesive Tape and Guts" (FB)
Vol. 7, No. 3, April 1954. Stories: 7
Cover: Baseball
Roe Richmond, "Comeback Champs" (BB)
William F. Schwartz, "The Last Out" (BB)
Mat Rand, "The No-Hit Hurler" (BB)
Gene Rodgers, "The Rookie and the Pro" (BB)
Vol. 7, No. 4, July 1954. Stories: 6
Cover: Baseball
Jim Moore, "The Fizzling Fireman" (BB)
Gene Rodgers, "Part-Time Guy" (BB)
Frank Smith, "Dig In, Busher!" (BB)
William F. Schwartz, "Moaner on the Mound" (BB)
Vol. 7, No. 5, October 1954. Stories: 7
Cover: Baseball
Gene Rodgers, "Hit for Me, Busher!" (BB)
D.S. Halacy, Jr., "The Easy Out" (BB)
Norman Ober, "So Sayeth the Commish" (BB)
William F. Schwartz, "Extra Compensation" Guy" (BB)
Vol. 7, No. 6, January 1955. Stories: 9
Cover: Football
Ford Clark, "Repeat Performance" (BB)
Jay Tyler (R.W. Lowndes), "The Last Walk" (BB)
Gene Rodgers, "The Sixty-Minute Grind" (FB)
Leonard Jackson, "Jawbone" (FB)
Bern Sharfman, "School Spirit" (FB)
Vol. 8, No. 1, April 1955. Stories: 7
Cover: Baseball
Mark Carrel, "The Blues Come Back" (BB)
William F. Schwartz, "Sabotage Swinger" (BB)
H.C. Butler, "Play Ball, Playboy!" (BB)
J.J. Mathews, "Patience at the Plate" (BB)
Vol. 8, No. 2, July 1955. Stories: 8
Cover: Baseball
William F. Schwartz, "The Big Hit" (BB)
Mel Colton, "In Relief from Yesterday" (BB)
E. Lee Allen, "Last Ditch Series" (BB)
Wadsworth Nealey, "Farewell Performance" (BB)
Jack Ritchie, "The Saints Go Stumbling On" (FB)
Vol. 8, No. 3, October 1955. Stories: 7
Cover: Baseball
Michael Avallone, "Headache Hurler" (BB)
Wadsworth Nealey, "Diamond Thinker" (BB)
E. Lee Allen, "Pinch Hit!" (BB)
J.J. Mathews, "Excess Baggage" (BB)
Vol. 8, No. 4, January 1956. Stories: 6
Cover: Football
Tom Thursday, "Explanation to the Press" (BB)

Richard Brister, "All-American Cleat Clowns" (FB)
Bill Erin, "Kill the Punter" (FB)
Vol. 8, No. 5, April 1956. Stories: 7
Cover: Baseball
William F. Schwartz, "Rookie on the Spot" (BB)
Robert Silverberg, "This Isn't Last Year" (BB)
Mark Carrell, "Fielder's Choice" (BB)
Sidney Offit, "Serious Southpaw" (BB)
Jim Moore, "Toreador Tailback" (FB)
Vol. 8, No. 6, July 1956. Stories: 8
Cover: Baseball
William F. Schwartz, "The Diamond Miracle" (BB)
Robert Silverberg, "Bat-Shy" (BB)
Sidney Offit, "Ice-Water" (BB)
Harlan Clay, "The Extra Fix" (BB)
Bill Erin, "Lefty's Greatest" (BB)
Vol. 9, No. 1, October 1956. Stories: 8
Cover: Baseball
Robert Silverberg, "Stretch Drive" (BB)
Bill Erin, "Last Start" (BB)
Sidney Offit, "Veteran Benchwarmer" (BB)
Jack Ritchie, "Popular Guy" (BB)
Kenneth Buckley, "No Phony Hero" (FB)
Vol. 9, No. 2, January 1957. Stories: 7
Michael Avallone, "Breadwinners Don't Loaf" (BB)
Edgar Daniel Kramer, "Hell's Acre Hurler" (BB)
H.C. Butler, "Brute in the Backfield" (FB)
Saul Anthony, "Second String Carrier" (FB)
William F. Schwartz, "Emergency Man" (FB)

Totals: 37 issues, 303 stories, 110 baseball stories, 40 football stories.

Columbia totals: 223 issues, 1,813 stories, 660 baseball stories, 287 football stories.

Fiction House

All American Football Magazine

Vol. 1, No. 1, Fall 1938. Stories: 6
Cover: George Gross?
William Heyliger (ghosted by William R. Cox), "Gangway for the Iron Horse!"
Lee Bond (Nelson S. Bond), "The Destiny Backfield"
Harold M. Sherman, "Touchdown Tornado"
William R. Cox, "Wise-Guy Wingman"
Stewart Hoskins, "The Money Kicker"
Stephen Walmsley, "Sparkplug"
Vol. 1. No. 2, Fall 1939. Stories: 6
Cover: George Gross?
Curtis Bishop, "The Four Wild Horsemen"
Jack Wiggin, "Fool for Glory"
Herbert L. McNary, "The Touchdown Twister"
William R. Cox, "Tramp Athlete"
Roe Richmond, "Mr. Rabbit-Heart"
Andrew I. "Albert, Get That Guy!"
Vol. 1, No. 3, Fall 1940. Stories: 8
Cover: Norman Saunders
Curtis Bishop, "The Galloping Ghost"
Tom O'Neill, "Grudge Guys"
Moran Tudory, "The Pigskin Soldier"
Jack Wiggin, "Duke of the Scrubs"
Roe Richmond, "Ringer!"
Linton Davies, "Snapper-Backer"
Stewart Sterling (Prentice Winchell), "Goal to Go!"
Bill Cook, "Climax Runner"
Vol. 1, No. 4, Fall 1941. Stories: 7
Cover: Norman Saunders
Curtis Bishop, "Army Jeep"
Joe Finlay, "Glory Back"
Harrison Hendryx (James B. Hendryx, Jr.), "The Fourth Quarter Flyer"
Nelson Bond, "'Plow 'Em Farmer'"
William Campbell Gault, "A Pass and a Prayer"
Gene D. Robinson, "Miss All-American"
Roe Richmond, "Grid Blood"
Vol. 1, No. 5, First Fall 1942. Stories: 5
Cover: George Gross
Stewart Sterling (Prentice Winchell), "Big-Shot Rookie"
Jackson V. Scholz, "Front Page Tailback"
Cosmo Bennett, "Galloping Goon"
Bill Heuman, "Bohunk's Pay Streak"
Jack Kofoed, "Pigskin Bombardiers"
Vol. 1, No. 6, Second Fall 1942. Stories: 7
Cover: Norman Saunders
Nelson S. Bond, "March of the Pigskin Robots"
Herbert L. McNary, "Guardhouse Champs"
Stewart Sterling (Prentice Winchell), "Santa Claus at Center"
Bill Heuman, "Freeze-Out"
Roe Richmond, "Ten Grand Buck"
J.B. Thornton, "Win or Else"
Gene D. Robinson, "All the Queen's Men"
Vol. 1, No. 7, First Fall 1943. Stories: 6
Cover: George Gross
William Heuman, "Point-a-Minute Powerhouse"
J.B. Thornton, "Greenbacks on the Goalpost"
Duane Yarnell, "The Star-Spangled Spinback"
Joe Archibald, "Bronco Rides the Gridiron"
Nelson S. Bond, "Between the Halves"
Jackson V. Scholz, "Commando in the Backfield"
Vol. 1, No. 8, Second Fall 1943. Stories: 6
Cover: George Gross
William Heuman, "A Punt and a Prayer"
Jackson V. Scholz, "Here Comes Hogan!"
David Brandt, "Runback Rodeo"
Curtis Bishop, "Refugee from a Touchdown"
Matt Quinlan, "Lash and Carry"
Vol. 1, No. 9, First Fall 1944. Stories: 5
Cover: George Gross
Curtis Bishop, "'Pass Me to Glory'"
William Heuman, "Pride of the Whiz Kids"
Tom O'Neill, "Sideline Svengali"
C. Paul Jackson, "Six-Point Sucker"
Nelson Hutto, "Blocking Bum"
Vol. 1, No. 10, Second Fall 1944. Stories: 6
Cover: George Gross
William Heuman, "Gangway for a Touchdown Thief"
Ted Roemer, "Paydirt Pariah"

Jackson V. Scholz, "Bombshell on the Bench"
David Brandt, "The Cleat Masher"
Eugene Pawley, "The Point Pirate"
J.B. Thornton, "Blockers for Sale!"
Vol. 1, No. 11, First Fall 1945. Stories: 5
Cover: George Gross
Bill Heuman, "Juggernaut on Cleats"
Bill Cox, "The Dixie Driver"
Curtis Bishop, "Blockers Aweigh!"
Foy Evans and Jack Rogers, "You Gotta Have Guts"
Richard Brister, "The Pulverizer"
Vol. 1, No. 12, Second Fall 1945. Stories: 5
Cover: George Gross
Bill Cox, "Six-Point Rebel"
Nelson Hutto, "Downfield Bombshell"
Curtis Bishop, "The Kid from Hard-Knocks U."
Robert S. Kelley, "The Crimson Sweater"
Wilton Hazzard, "Backfield Backwash"
Vol. 2, No. 1, First Fall 1946. Stories: 6
Cover: George Gross
Bill Heuman, "The Devil's at Quarter"
C. Paul Jackson, "Tailspin Tailback"
William R. Cox, "Air Express to Coffin Corner"
Stan Hough, "'Stand By for Collision'"
Burgess Leonard, "The Big Bluff"
Richard Brister, "Magic at Tackle"
Vol. 2, No. 2, Second Fall 1946. Stories: 5
Cover: George Gross
Stewart Sterling (Prentice Winchell), "The Saga of Payoff Pete"
Harold Rogers, "Double Cross on the Bench"
Burgess Leonard, "The Pigskin Plunderers"
Jack Goldstein, "Grid Gal"
Richard Brister, "'Pitch Me a Pass'"
Vol. 2, No. 3, First Fall 1947. Stories: 5
Cover: George Gross
Harold Rogers, "Pigskins Ain't for Ladies"
Fred Malina, "No Ivy for a Bum!"
Duane Yarnell, "'Make with the Six-Point Magic, Faker'"
Ted Stratton, "Money-Arm"
Joe Brennan, "Rose Bowl Boomerang"
Vol. 2, No. 4, Second Fall 1947. Stories: 5
Cover: George Gross
Stewart Sterling (Prentice Winchell), "Texas Likes 'Em Cleat-Loco"
H. Gordon Lewis, "Featherweight Thunderer"
Duane Yarnell, "The Six-Point Crusader"
C. Paul Jackson, "Carry the Coach"
Harold Helfer, "Tip-Toe Traipskowitz"
Vol. 2, No. 5, First Fall 1948. Stories: 5
Cover: George Gross
Paul Porter, "Joe the Toe"
Add Aretz, "Pride of the Whiz-Kids"
Burgess Leonard, "March of the Gridiron Goons"
Dick Friendlich, "The Saga of Malcolm O'Shanter"
Ted Roemer, "Power Guy"
Vol. 2, No. 6, Second Fall 1948. Stories: 6
Cover: George Gross
Joe Alfreds, "'Pass Me a Headline'"
Duane Yarnell, "The Lost Eleven"
Burgess Leonard, "Six Prayers for Midget O'Hara"
Roy B. Frentz, "The Bench Bum"
Ted Stratton, "Old Number Nine"
Don Lawson, "The Big Game"
Vol. 2, No. 7, First Fall 1949. Stories: 5
Cover: George Gross
Ted Stratton, "A Plunge and a Prayer"
John Starr, "Fumbler Bum"
L.R. Robinson, "Curtains for Cooler"
Burgess Leonard, "Six-Point Atom from Hard Knocks U."
Tom O'Neill, "'And the Band Played Dixie'"
Vol. 2, No. 8, Second Fall 1949. Stories: 5
Cover: George Gross (reprinted from First Fall 1942)
Bart Cassidy, "Blockers Aweigh!"
Oliver Shank, "The Pigskin Butcher"
William R. Cox, "The Revolt of the Red Vikings"
Jim Goodrich, "Half-Time Hellion"
Joe Brennan, "'Go Get Me Six'"
Vol. 2, No. 9, Fall 1950. Stories: 5
Cover: George Gross
Eugene Pawley, "Beware the End Zone Ghost"
Wilton Hazzard, "Million Dollar Toe" (reprinted from A-A Football, 1940, as by Nelson Bond)
Burgess Leonard, "The Flying Saucer Kid"
William R. Cox, "Golden Boy at the Flank"
Gardner F. Fox, "The Pigskin Pirate"
Vol. 2, No. 10, Fall 1951. Stories: 7
Cover: George Gross (reprinted from First Fall 1943)
Bill Cox, "Goal-Line Ghost of the Dixie Rebels"
Anson Slaughter (William R. Cox), "They Played for Glory" (reprinted from *Bull's-Eye Sports*, Winter 1938–1939, as by Bill Arcy)
Dean Owen, "Refugee from a Touchdown"
John Starr, "A Punt, a Pass—and a Powerhouse" (reprinted from *Bull's-Eye Sports*, Summer 1939, as by Nelson Bond)
Tom O'Neill, "Tailspin Tailback"
Don Kingery, "Yesterday's Warrior"
Walter H. Boyce, "The Case of Mrs. Pigskin"
Vol. 2, No. 11, Fall 1952. Stories: 5
Cover: George Gross (reprinted from First Fall 1944)
Curtis Bishop, "'Pass Me to Glory'" (reprinted from A-A Football, First Fall 1944)
Bill Heuman, "Pride of the Whiz-Kids" (reprinted from A-A Football, First Fall 1944)
Melvin Sturgis, "The Grid-Irony Touch"
Ralph Ackerman, "Queen at Quarterback"
Wilton Hazzard, "A Punt and a Prayer" (reprinted from A-A Football, Second Fall 1943, as by William Heuman)
Vol. 2, No. 12, Fall 1953. Stories: 3
Cover: George Gross (reprinted from Second Fall 1944)
Burgess Leonard, "Mr. Quarterback!"
William Heuman, "Gangway for a

Touchdown-Thief!" (reprinted from A-A Football, Second Fall 1944)
Jackson V. Scholz, "Bombshell on the Bench (reprinted from A-A Football, Second Fall 1944)

Totals: 24 issues, 134 stories

Baseball Stories

Vol. 1, No. 1, Spring 1938. Stories: 8
Cover: George H. Gross
William Heyliger, "Sand-Lot Champ"
Linton Davies, "Smart Money Ball"
Harold M. Sherman, "Miss Pinch Hitter"
William R. Cox, "Three Strikes Is Out!"
John Wiggin, "Hard-Luck Guy"
William A. Davenport, "The Sing-Sing Southpaw"
Ted Fox, "Bench Beauty"
Frank T. Blair, "Mr. Big Mouth from the Minors"

Vol. 1, No. 2, Summer 1938. Stories: 8
Cover: George H. Gross
Linton Davies, "Miss Hollywood's Nine"
Ted Winslow, "Gambler's Game"
Harold M. Sherman, "Slugger!"
Joe Finley, "Money Player"
Frank T. Blair, "Bleacher Bait"
Tarleton Collier, "Traded Down the River"
Edward L. Leamon, "Kill That Guy!"
Mark Adam, "Ex-Big League"

Vol. 1, No. 3, Spring 1939. Stories: 8
Cover: George H. Gross
Herbert L. McNary, "The Pennant Pushers"
William R. Cox, "Big Shot from the Bush League"
Harold M. Sherman, "Crooked Ball"
Linton Davies, "Smoke Slinger"
Bud Tuttle, "The Arkansas Rabbit"
Mark Adam, "I Wuz Robbed"
Stewart Sterling (Prentice Winchell), "'The Dust-Off Kid'"
James B. Hendryx, "Pinch-Hitter!"

Vol. 1, No. 4, Summer 1939. Stories: 8
Cover: George H. Gross
Curtis Bishop, "The Last Mile"
DeWitt Shank, "Pitcher Poison"
Herbert L. McNary, "The Man Behind the Mask"
Linton Davies, "Dynamite Nine"
John Wiggin, "Clancy the 'Cleaner-Upper'"
William R. Cox, "The Fifth Infielder"
Joe Finley, "Screwball"
E. Newman Eveslade, "Hey, Mr. Hard Case!"

Vol. 1, No. 5, Spring 1940. Stories: 10
Cover: George H. Gross
Linton Davies, "Hard-Luck Hurler"
Curtis Bishop, "The Big Run"
DeWitt Shank, "Slugger from Iowa"
Joe Finley, "The Fence Buster"
Tom O'Neill, "'Take Him Out!'"
Gene D. Robinson, "Grandstander"
Albert I. Albert, "Pitcher's Choice"
Douglas Oliver, "Soldier at the Bat"
Jack Wiggin, "Jeeper's Jinx"
Jack Kofoed, "Spikes for Spite"

Vol. 1, No. 6, Summer 1940. Stories: 9
Cover: George H. Gross
Linton Davies, "Million Dollar Bat-Boy"
William R. Cox, "Hit and Run"
Nelson S. Bond, "The Basepath Burglar"
Mark Adam, "Comes the Revolution"
DeWitt Shank, "Mound-Fever"
Falls Maury, "Howdy, Mr. Cat!"
Sidney Renthal, "Mr. Bird Brain from the Bush League"
Nelson Hutto, "Block That Plate!"
Jack Wiggin, "Ol' Rubber Arm"

Vol. 1, No. 7, Spring 1941. Stories: 9
Cover: George H. Gross
Curtis Bishop, "Double Trouble"
James B. Hendryx, "Swatter's Mite"
William R. Cox, "The First Base Fireman"
Fred G. Steelman, "Bad Boy from the Bush League"
Joe Finley, "Series Fever"
Roe Richmond, "The 3-and-2 Clutch"
Jack Wiggin, "Slide, Sailor, Slide!"
DeWitt Shank, "Holler Guy"
Linton Davies, "The Pitcher with Only a Prayer"

Vol. 1, No. 8, Summer 1941. Stories: 9
Cover: George H. Gross
Jack Wiggin, "Rube with the Big Time Bat"
James B. Hendryx, Jr., "Slide, Casey, Slide!"
William R. Cox, "Rookie in the Clutch"
Pete Drummond, "Mr. Mura Strikes Out"
Fred G. Steelman, "Prima Donna Poison"
Gene Juda, "No Admittance"
Ed Leamon, "Oh, You Cousin!"
Gene D. Robinson, "She Swung and Missed"
DeWitt Shank, "Diamond Draft"

Vol. 1, No. 9, Spring 1942. Stories: 7
Cover: George H. Gross
Curtis Bishop, "Killer Diller"
Jack Wiggin, "Odds on the Rabbit"
Stewart Sterling (Prentice Winchell), "Don't Crowd a Clouter"
Felix Mendelsohn, Jr., "Two O'Clock Hitter"
Gene D. Robinson, "The Bullpen Blonde"
Moran Tudory, "Squeeze Play"
Jack Kofoed, "Holder-Outer"

Vol. 1, No. 10, Summer 1942. Stories: 7
Cover: George H. Gross
Curtis Bishop, "The .400 Firecracker"
William R. Cox, "The Ash-Can Gang"
Cosmo Bennett, "Ol' Dead Arm"
Nelson S. Bond, "'Baseball Is a Business'"
DeWitt Shank, "Bench Jockey"
James B. Hendryx, Jr., "'Now Pitching for Mabel!'"
Roe Richmond, "Iron Man"

Vol. 1, No. 11, Spring 1943. Stories: 7
Cover: George H. Gross
William Heuman, "Pride of the Bullpen"
Nelson S. Bond, "Slugger with a Strikeout Bat"
Dan Cheyenne, "Big-League Bonanza"
J.B. Thornton, "Pennant Madness"

William R. Cox, "Ride 'Em, Rookie"
Duane Yarnell, "Diamond Dupe"
Edward Howey, "Misery on the Mound"
Vol. 1, No. 12, Summer 1943. Stories: 7
Cover: George H. Gross
Duane Yarnell, "Eight Bums and a Batboy"
William Heuman, "Busher in the Gravy League"
J.B. Thornton, "Double-Cross Dugout"
Nelson S. Bond, "Taming of the Screwball"
Tom O'Neill, "Bullpen Bonanza"
Nelson A. Hutto, "Big League Local"
Frederick H. Chase, "The Sourdough Sluggers"
Vol. 2, No. 1, Spring 1944. Stories: 8
Cover:
William Heuman, "Fan That Fence-Buster!"
Duane Yarnell, "Speedboy with the Devil Spikes"
Curtis Bishop, "The Pennant Pilot"
Tom O'Neill, "Cupid's Clouters"
Richard Brister, "The Zero Pitch"
Hal K. Wells, "Southpaw Svengali"
J.B. Thornton, "The Twilight Twirler"
Bill Gorman, "Chance for Glory"
Vol. 2, No. 2, Summer 1944. Stories: 8
Cover: George H. Gross (reprinted from Spring 1938)
Curtis Bishop, "The Pennant Punk"
William Heuman, "Nine Sluggers and a Clown"
C. Paul Jackson, "Phantom at Short"
J.B. Thornton, "Dugout Dracula"
W.R.O. Gwinn, "Pretty Pitcher"
Peter Young, "Brat and the Big Bat"
Tom O'Neill, "'Bench Thar Bum'"
Vol. 2, No. 3, Spring 1945. Stories: 8
Cover: George H. Gross (reprinted from Spring 1939)
William Heuman, "Bushers Are Dynamite!"
Theodore Roemer, "Caliph of the Hill"
John Starr, "'Clout 'Em, Clancy!'"
Arthur Mann, "Double-Cross Battery"
Thomas Thursday, "Oliver Twisted"
William D. Gorman, "Diamond Devil"
Richard Brister, "Rookies Are Human"
John C. Ropke, "Bean-Ball Burke"
Vol. 2, No. 4, Summer 1945. Stories: 6
Cover: George H. Gross
Bill Heuman, "Wonder Boy"
Richard Brister, "Rollickin' Rookie"
Tom O'Neill, "Jinx Inning"
C. Paul Jackson, "Keystone Carnage"
Curtis Bishop, "Three Strikes for G.I. Joe"
Harry Quinn, "The Kid Takes Over"
Vol. 2, No. 5, Spring 1946. Stories: 6
Cover: George H. Gross
Curtis Bishop, "Base-Hit Blues"
C. Paul Jackson, "The Flag Chaser"
Jackson V. Scholz, "The Big Rhubarb"
Larry Schulenberg, "Demise of an Arm"
Nelson A. Hutto, "Cellar Trouble"
John C. Ropke, "Bottle Bait"
Vol. 2, No. 6, Summer 1946. Stories: 6
Cover: George H. Gross
Curtis Bishop, "Plumber at the Plate"
Bill Heuman, "'Goodbye, Pennant'"
Harold Rogers, "The Last Pitch"
J.B. Thornton, "Sluggers Gold"
Tom Sayres, "Mound Angel"
Paul R. McCully, "Ol' Knucklehead"
Vol. 2, No. 7, Spring 1947. Stories: 6
Cover: George H. Gross
Harold Rogers, "Crusaders from the Dugout"
Duane Yarnell, "The Hot Tamale Kid"
Zene Tuttler, "Showdown Pitch"
Larry Schulenberg, "Prescription for Mariotti"
John T. Sullivan, "Vitamins Make Pennants"
John Ropke, "Seniorita Beanball"
Vol. 2, No. 8, Summer 1947. Stories: 9
Cover: George H. Gross
Harold Rogers, "Hit and Run for Red Hot Mama"
Zene Tuttler, "Doctor, Save My Soup Bone!"
Tom O'Neill, "Say It with Strikeouts!"
Lloyd Derrickson, "Tinker's Target"
John Starr, "Sandlot Flash"
H.C. Butler, "Kid from Kokomo"
Harold Helfer, "The 3-Score Backstop"
Burt Sims, "High and Inside"
A.N. Borno, "Flinch-Hitter"
Vol. 2, No. 9, Spring 1948. Stories: 6
Cover: George H. Gross
Duane Yarnell, "'You Asked for It, Busher'"
Burgess Leonard, "Throw the High, Hard One"
Ed Howey, "Move Back the Fence"
John Starr, "Payoff at the Plate"
Chas. M. Rose, "The Seventh Game"
Norman Ober, "Cupid Throws a Curve"
Vol. 2, No. 10, Summer 1948. Stories: 7
Cover: George H. Gross
Curtis Bishop, "Horsehide Magician of the Graveyard Nine"
Tom O'Neill, "Showdown at Short"
Robert J. McCully, "The Bonus Blues"
Burgess Leonard, "'Toss Me a Fat One, Busher'"
Lloyd Derrickson, "Love That Curve"
Frank Muffin, "'They Called Him "Hands"'"
Gardner F. Fox, "Cinderella Glove"
Vol. 2, No. 11, Spring 1949. Stories: 8
Cover: George H. Gross
Duane Yarnell, "Angel in the Dugout"
William O'Sullivan, "Hot-Corner Howler"
Bill Erin, "The Ladies Day Kid"
Paul Porter, "Behind the Bat"
Raymond Dreyfack, "It Shouldn't Happen to a Dodger Fan"
Joe Brennan, "Catcher's Last Stand"
Eddie English, "Sermon on the Mound"
John Starr, "Stop-Gap Hurler"
Vol. 2, No. 12, Summer 1949. Stories: 6
Cover: George H. Gross
Ted Stratton, "Taming of the Screwballs"
Burgess Leonard, "The Last Pitch of Hap Andrews"
Paul Porter, "A Wing and a Prayer"
O.D. Shank, "Pitcher Poison"
Joe Brennan, "Don't Bait a Scout"
M.P. Schehrer, "Tiger Fox and the Little Red Hat"

Vol. 3, No. 1, Spring 1950. Stories: 7
Cover: George H. Gross
Burgess Leonard, "When Gallagher Took the Mound!"
Wilton Hazzard, "Slugger's Wild!"
J.J. Cliff, "Accordin' to the Book"
Russell Gray (Bruno Fischer), "The Girl in Box 15"
Luke Torley (James Blish), "The Big Hate"
Vin Paradis, "'McCrory—Shortstop'"
Russ Davis, "Horsehide Homicide"
Vol. 3, No. 2, Summer 1950. Stories: 6
Cover: George H. Gross
Burgess Leonard, "Bonus Brat with the Golden Flipper"
Add Aretz, "Poison Behind the Plate"
Zene Tuttler, "The Two O'Clock Terror"
Joe Brennan, "The Rookie Tamer"
Gardner F. Fox, "Hot Corner Has-Been"
Michael Avallone, "'Aw, Let the Kid Hit'"
Vol. 3, No. 3, Spring 1951. Stories: 6
Cover: George H. Gross (reprinted from Spring 1942)
Burgess Leonard, "Busher with the Big League Heart"
Bill Erin, "The Bonus Beauty"
Add Aretz, "Make Mine Strikeouts"
J.J. Cliff, "Foul Ball!"
O.J. Lester, "The Pitch That Ruined a Conway"
Roy Lopez, "Hot Corner Blues"
Vol. 3, No. 4, Summer 1951. Stories: 6
Cover: George H. Gross
A.N. Borno, "Southpaws Aren't Sane"
Add Aretz, "Slow Ball 'Em to Death"
Bill Erin, "Bonanza!"
Giles A. Lutz, "The Foul Ball Kid"
Harold Rogers, "Backstop Bombardier"
Willard Crandall, "Coach Jitters"
Vol. 3, No. 5, Spring 1952. Stories: 4
Cover: George H. Gross
Burgess Leonard, "A Fool for Cheers"
Joseph Finley, "The Last Nine"
Michael Avallone, "One More Miracle!"
Joe Brennan, "Horsehide Homicide"
Vol. 3, No. 6, Summer 1952. Stories: 5
Cover: George H. Gross
Burgess Leonard, "The Rhubarb Kid"
George Karger, "The 1000–1 Shot!"
Norman Ober, "Pennant Palsy"
Zene Tuttler, "A Glove and a Prayer"
E.J. Bowman, "Con with the Curve"
Vol. 3, No. 7, Spring 1953. Stories: 6
Cover: George H. Gross (reprinted from Spring 1944)
Burgess Leonard, "The Slugger from Heaven"
Zene Tuttler, "Bye, Bye Bushers!"
Joe Brennan, "Sizzler from the Sandlot"
George Johnson, "Johnny Crutch"
Gene Olson, "Doldrums in the Dugout"
Dick Friendlich, "The Face at First"
Vol. 3, No. 8, Summer 1953. Stories: 5
Cover: George H. Gross (reprinted from Spring 1953)
Burgess Leonard, "Herman, the Hot-Stick Kid"
William R. Cox, "Ride 'Em, Rookie"
Dan T. Kelliher, "Long Live Spike Hendricks"
Scott Thurber, "Mound Miser"
Gene Olson, "The Strikeout Salesman"
Vol. 3, No. 9, Spring 1954. Stories: 4
Cover: George H. Gross (reprinted from Summer 1945)
Burgess Leonard, "The Whiz-Kid"
Dan T. Kelliher, "Keystone Killer"
George Johnson, "Utility Guy"
Michael Walters, "That Lady Was an Ump"

Totals: 33 issues, 229 stories.

Bull's-Eye Sports

Vol. 1, No. 1, Winter 1938–1939. Stories: 11
Cover: Football
Linton Davies, "Hot Corner Hellion" (BB)
Bill Arcy (William R. Cox), "They Played for Glory" (FB)
Kurt Engstrom, "The Six-Point Shuttle" (FB)
William R. Cox, "Front-Page Backfield" (FB)
Don Newall (Nelson S. Bond), "Scooter!" (FB)
Nelson S. Bond, "Born to the Gridiron" (FB)

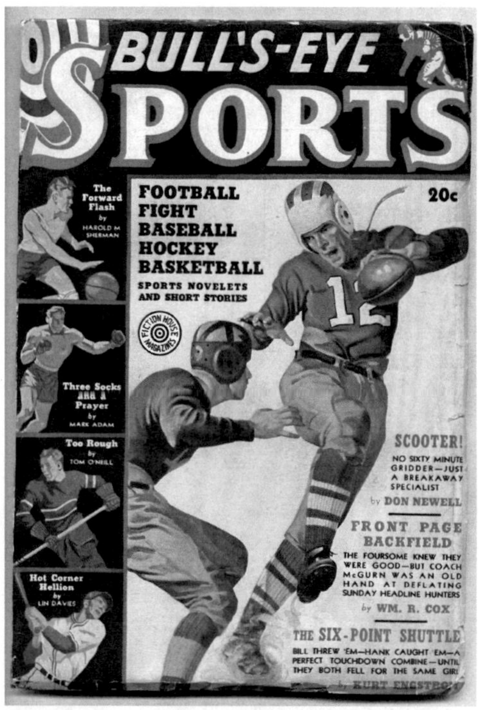

***Bull's-Eye Sports*, Winter 1938–1939 (copyright 1938 Real Adventures Publishing Co., Inc.). George Gross does the honors for the first of a three-issue run for Fiction House's only attempt at an anthology sports pulp. Fiction House operated under numerous sub-publishers for business purposes, but the target symbol was featured on its covers.**

Vol. 1, No. 2, Spring 1939. Stories: 10
Cover: Baseball
Tom O'Neill, "The Texas Teaser" (BB)
Gene D. Robinson, "Miss Mrs. Manager" (BB)
Linton Davies, "Big-Time Rookie" (BB)
Albert L. Albert, "Diamond Dupe" (BB)
William R. Cox, "Murderers' Row" (BB)
Vol. 1, No. 3, Summer 1939. Stories: 10
Cover: Baseball
Linton Davies, "The Diamond Horse-Shoe" (BB)
Albert A. Jayne, "The Great Rube" (BB)
Stewart Sterling (Prentice Winchell), "Half-Pint Hellion" (FB)
DeWitt Shank, "The Door-Mat Eleven" (FB)
William R. Cox, "Line Buckaroo" (FB)
Nelson S. Bond, "A Punt, a Pass—and a Powerhouse" (FB)

Totals: 3 issues, 31 stories, 8 baseball stories, 9 football stories.

Football Action

Vol. 1, No. 1, Fall 1939. Stories: 9
Cover: George Gross?
Mark Adam, "Swivel-Hipped Yokel"
Gilbert K. Griffith, "The Triple-Threat Phoney"
Herbert L. McNary, "Anchors Aweigh"
Tom O'Neill, "Grandstand Hero"
Richard Sale, "Mudder"
William R. Cox, "Work-Horse Glory"
Wilton R. Holm, "Money Player"
Lin Davies, "The Celluloid Champs"
Gene D. Robinson, "The All-America Dumb-Cluck"
Vol. 1, No. 2, Fall 1940. Stories: 7
Cover: C. Reed
Herbert L. McNary, "Navy's Ball!"
Linton Davies, "Touchdown Famine"
Duane Yarnell, "Touchdown Express"
Curtis Bishop, "Ten Men and a Glory Grabber"
William R. Cox, "End Around"
Mark Adam, "Razzle-Dazzler"
Reynolds Phillips, "Fumble Fingers"
Vol. 1, No. 3, Fall 1941. Stories: 7
Cover: George Gross
Curtis Bishop, "The Unholy Grailers"
Herbert L. McNary, "Coffin Corner Kaydet"
Stewart Sterling (Prentice Winchell), "Block That Kick!"
Jack Wiggin, "'They Shall Not Pass'"
William R. Cox, "Rose Bowl Express"
Moran Tudory, "Dixie Dynamite"
Jeff Dunn, "Glory Road"
Vol. 1, No. 4, First Fall 1942. Stories: 8
Cover: Norman Saunders
Nelson S. Bond, "Power-Man"
William R. Cox, "Ten Dopes and a Hero"
Bill Heuman, "The Farmer Takes the Ball"
Curtis Bishop, "One for the Coach"
Roe Richmond, "To the Last White Stripe"
Jackson V. Scholz (ghosted by William R. Cox), "Hoodoo Mascot"
Tom O'Neill, "Touchdowns for Hire"
Moran Tudory, "The Iron Brigade"
Vol. 1, No. 5, Second Fall 1942. Stories: 7
Cover: George Gross
Jack Wiggin, "Hayseed at Center"
Jackson Scholz (ghosted by William R. Cox), "Ten-Yard Tornado"
William R. Cox and William Fay, "The Touchdown Commandos"
William Heuman, "Ol' Has-Been"
Herbert L. McNary, "Johnny Comes Marching Home"
J.B. Thornton, "The All-American Pantywaist"
Wilburn Peacock, "Trophy Game"
Vol. 1, No. 6, First Fall 1943. Stories: 8
Cover: George Gross
Jackson V. Scholz (ghosted by William R. Cox), "Ghost on the Goal-Line"
Bill Heuman, "Hepcat in the Huddle"
William R. Cox, "The Hurry-Up Eleven"
Nelson A. Hutto, "Tank-Torn Tornado"
Ted Stratton, "Time Out for Glory"
Jay Karth, "Fourth-Down Flareback"
John Starr, "Handyman"
Craig Rankin, "Wings for a Gridiron Gob"
Vol. 1, No. 7, Second Fall 1943. Stories: 7
Cover: George Gross

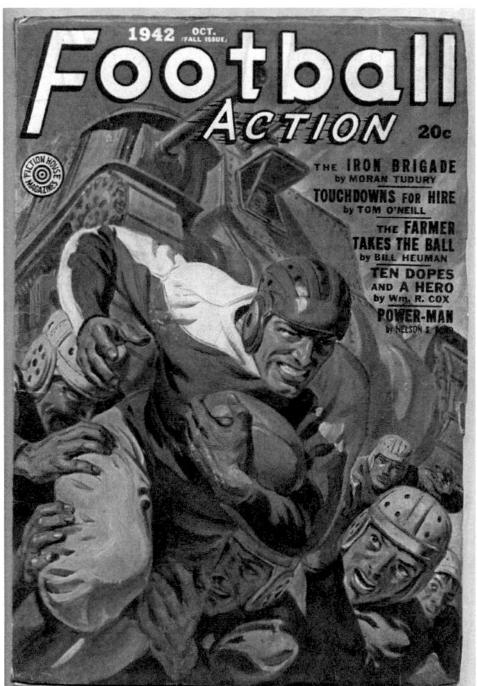

***Football Action*, First Fall 1942 (copyright 1942 Fiction House, Inc.). Seemingly escorted by a tank, an intense ball-carrier tries to cross the goal line as envisioned by Norman Saunders.**

William Heuman, "Pass Their Pants Off"
Roy R. Grady, "King of the Gridiron"
Wilburn Peacock, "The Pigskin Profiteer"
William R. Cox, "The Big Blond Goon"
Nelson S. Bond, "Wrong Way Wingback"
Peter Hamilton, "The Griping Gridmaster"
Ted Stratton, "Killer with Cleats"

Vol. 1, No. 8, First Fall 1944. Stories: 6
Cover: George Gross
William Heuman, "Your Ball, Smart Guy"
Herbert L. McNary, "Gob on the Goal Line"
Carl G. Hodges, "Dynamite with Cleats"
Jackson V. Scholz (ghosted by William R. Cox), "Backfield Bazooka"
William R. Cox, "Sixty Minute Sorehead"
Reynolds Phillips, "Half-Pint"

Vol. 1, No. 9, Second Fall 1944. Stories: 5
Cover: George Gross
Jackson Scholz (ghosted by William R. Cox), "Battle Stations, Navy"
C. Paul Jackson, "Phantom in the Tailback Slot"
William R. Cox, "The Pigskin Cavalier"
Larry McLane, "Hothead in the Huddle"
Harold Rogers, "Rocket Bomb Rookie"

Vol. 1, No. 10, Second Fall 1944. Stories: 6
Cover: George Gross
Curtis Bishop, "The Prayer-Pass Kid"
Jackson Scholz, "Mr. Goat of the Navy"
Ted Stratton, "Locker Room Lemon"
Ted Roemer, "Front-Line Fullback"
Richard Brister, "End Zone Zero"
Tom O'Neill, "Ol' Mister Sure Feet"

Vol. 1, No. 11, Second Fall 1945. Stories: 5
Cover: George Gross
Curtis Bishop, "West Point Whirlwind"
Bill Heuman, "Pigskin Paradise"
Bill Cox, "Winged Cleats"
Richard Brister, "Pass-Master"
J.B. Bannon, "The Banner Bearer"

Vol. 1, No. 12, First Fall 1946. Stories: 7
Cover: George Gross
C. Paul Jackson, "The Dypsy-Do Boys"
Harold Rogers, "'Say It with Yards'"
Curtis Bishop, "'Blockers Ain't So Dumb'"
Bill Heuman, "Phantom in the Flat Zone"
Tom O'Neill, "Gold to Go!"
Brad King, "Tough Tomato"
Richard Brister, "Pigskin Purge"

Vol. 2, No. 3 (error), Second Fall 1946. Stories: 7
Cover: George Gross
Tom O'Neill, "Six-Point Blockade Runner"
Herbert L. McNary, "Paydirt Prima Donna"
Burgess Leonard, "Gangway for the Cleat Clowns!"
Theodore J. Roemer, "Old Tackles Never Die"
Bill Heuman, Signed, "Sealed and Double-Crossed"
Richard Brister, "Touchdown Tease"
Stewart Sterling (Prentice Winchell), "The Goon Is Terrific!"

Vol. 2, No. 4 (error never corrected), First Fall 1947. Stories: 6
Cover: George Gross
Zene Tuttler, "Little Mister Zero—Paydirt Bound!"
Gardner Fox, "Quitter at Quarter"
Duane Yarnell, "Gangway for the Grid Bums!"
Nelson Hutto, "Six-Point Bombardier"
C. Paul Jackson, "Scrubs Eat Dirt"
Linton Davies, "The Juggling Fool"

Vol. 2, No. 5, Second Fall 1947. Stories: 5
Cover: George Gross
Stewart Sterling (Prentice Winchell), "The Dipsy-Do Dazzler"
Tom O'Neill, "Fullback Fury"
Duane Yarnell, "Mr. Fix-It, the Touchdown Tout"
Les Etter, "Double Trouble at Safety"
Zene Tuttler, "Kick a Point—and Die!"

Vol. 2, No. 6, First Fall 1948. Stories: 7
Cover: George Gross
Bill Erin, "Give 'Em the Axe, Hayseed!"
Jackson Scholz, "Block, You Soreheads!"
William R. Cox, "Kid Twinkletoes"
Joe Alfreds, "Six-Point Savage"
John Northway, "Glory on the Bench"
E.B. Hamilton, "Mousetrap Madman"
Ted Stratton, "Iron Man"

Vol. 2, No. 7, Second Fall 1948. Stories: 5
Cover: George Gross
Duane Yarnell, "March of the Iron Helmets"
Sterling Stewart (Prentice Winchell), "Six-Point Bombshell"
William R. Cox, "Weepin' Willy, the Touchback Kid"
Bill Erin, "Wing-Ding Waterboy"
Ted Stratton, "Big Boss of the Backfield"

Vol. 2, No. 8, First Fall 1949. Stories: 6
Cover: George Gross
Bill Heuman, "Captain Zany Calls the Plays"
William R. Cox, "'Pass, You Touchdown Chumps'"
Add Aretz, "The Gold Cleat Kid"
Paul Porter, "Six Point Swindle"
Ted Roemer, "Destiny Back"
Les Etter, "A Blueblood Won't Block"

Vol. 2, No. 9, Second Fall 1949. Stories: 5
Cover: Norman Saunders
Curtis Bishop, "The Lost Eleven" (reprinted from A-A Football, First Fall 1942)
Giles A. Lutz, "Ghost on the Goal Line"
Wilton Hazzard, "Moleskin Misfit"
Bill Heuman, "Quitter at Quarter"
William R. Cox, "Front-Page Backfield" (reprinted from *Bull's-Eye Sports*, Winter 1938–1939)

Vol. 2, No. 10, Fall 1950. Stories: 6
Cover: George Gross
Ted Stratton, "Gangway for Hot-Rod Bogan!"
Wendell Chapin, "Fourth-Quarter Hellion"
Wilton Hazzard, "Quick-Kicking Hick" (reprinted from Second Fall 1943, as by Nelson Bond)
Ben Mobley, "Touchdown Clown"
Larry Holden, "Battle Stations, Varsity!"
Tom O'Neill, "Goalpost Glory"

Vol. 2, No. 11, Fall 1951. Stories: 7
Cover: George Gross
William R. Cox, "The Phantom Four"
Tom O'Neill, "Wise-Guy Wingman" (reprinted from A-A Football, 1938, as by William R. Cox)
John Starr, "Call of the Cleats"
Joe Brennan, "A Pass—and a Prayer"
Wilton Hazzard (Nelson Bond), "Scooter!" (reprinted from *Bull's-Eye Sports,* Winter 1938, as by Don Newall)
Don Kingery, "The Sub"
Aaron Slaughter, "Line Buckaroo" (reprinted from *Bull's-Eye Sports,* Fall 1939, as by William R. Cox)
Vol. 2, No. 12, Fall 1952. Stories: 4
Cover: George Gross
Burgess Leonard, "The Mad Dogs of Doane"
Wilton Hazzard, "Paydirt Pariah" (reprinted from Second Fall 1944, as by Ted Roemer)
George Johnson, "The Coach at Seneca"
Lloyd Derrickson, "Love by the Yard"
Vol. 3, No. 1, Fall 1953. Stories: 5
Cover: George Gross (reprinted from Second Fall 1943)
William R. Cox, "The Big Blond Goon" (reprinted from Second Fall 1943)
William Heuman, "Pass Their Pants Off" (reprinted from Second Fall 1943)
Nelson S. Bond, "Wrong Way Wingback" (reprinted from Second Fall 1943)
Burgess Leonard, "A Pro Is Born"
Gene Olson, "T Is for Tornado"

Totals: 23 issues, 145 stories (counting reprints twice)

Football Stories

Vol. 1, No. 1, Fall 1937. Stories: 7
Cover: George Gross
Oliver Shank, "Stumble, Fumble"
T.W. Ford, "The All-American Show-Off"
William Heyliger, "He Could Take It!"
Quentin Reynolds, "Don't Bet on Glory"
Roger Daniels, "Fourth-Down Dynamite"
T. Morris Longstreth, "The Pigskin Napoleon"
Jack Cochran, "Iron Man"
Vol. 1, No. 2, Fall 1938. Stories: 8
Cover: George Gross
William R. Cox, "Mr. All-America"
Linton Davies, "First-Half Hero"
Herbert L. McNary, "Fight On—Army!"
Tarleton Collier, "Triple Threat"
Steve Sorensen, "Delayed Dynamite"
John Wiggin, "No Guts—No Glory!"
Bernard Penrose, "One Minute to Go!"
Clarence Barr Thomas, "Ace of the Scrubs"
Vol. 1, No. 3, Fall 1939. Stories: 7
Cover: George Gross
William R Cox, "The End-Zone Express"
Lin Davies, "The Four Forgotten Crusaders"
Stewart Sterling (Prentice Winchell), "All-America Holdout"
Curtis Bishop, "Interference"
Mark Adam, "Hold That Line!"
John Wiggin, "Sideline Strategist"
John Wilson, "Fame Is No Fool"
Vol. 1, No. 4, Fall 1940. Stories: 8
Cover: George Gross
Jack Wiggin, "The Ashcan Eleven"
William R. Cox, "The Pigskin Cowboy"
DeWitt Shank, "The All-America Prima Donna"
Nelson S. Bond, "The Lad with the Million Dollar Toe"
Duane Yarnell, "The Freshwater Flash"
James B. Hendryx, Jr., "Touchdown Slinger"
Roy Gannon, "Master-Minder"
Jeff Dunn, "...And the Band Played Dixie!"
Vol. 1, No. 5, Fall 1941. Stories: 6
Cover: George Gross
DeWitt Shank, "The Deacon from Dixie"
William R. Cox, "Hold That Line!"
Nelson S. Bond, "Touchdown Twister"
Forrest Kleinman, "The All-America Stooge"
Cosmo Bennett, "Sergeant Six Points"
Moran Tudory, "A Pass to Papa"
Vol. 1, No. 6, First Fall 1942. Stories: 7
Cover: Allen Anderson
Bill Heuman, "Mutiny on the Bench"

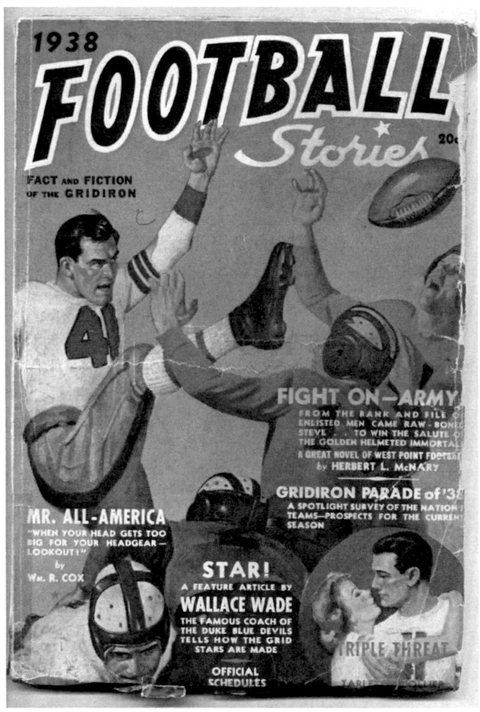

Football Stories, Fall 1938 (copyright 1938 Fiction House, Inc.). On the second issue, George Gross mixes a punt rush with a kiss in the right corner to illustrate the rewards of college life for a football hero.

James B. Hendryx, Jr., "Cupid Wears Cleats"
Herbert L. McNary, "All-American Sub"
Bill Fay, "The Pigskin Palookas"
Gene D. Robinson, "Comin' Round the Mountain"
Jackson V. Scholz, "Backfield Bomb"
Roe Richmond, "Touchdown Terrors"

Vol. 1, No. 7, Second Fall 1942. Stories: 7
Cover: Allen Anderson
Bill Heuman, "Two Yards from Glory"
William R. Cox, "Run, Rabbit, Run!"
Gene D. Robinson, "Pigskin Paradise"
J.B. Thornton, "The Hard-Luck Kid"
Nelson S. Bond, "Sorehead"
Jackson V. Scholz (ghosted by William R. Cox), "Svengali QB"
Curtis Bishop, "The Blocking Brothers"

Vol. 1, No. 8, First Fall 1943. Stories: 7
Cover: George Gross
Stewart Sterling (Prentice Winchell), "The Fumbling Phantom"
William R. Cox, "Revolt of the Red Vikings"
C. Paul Jackson, "Power Guy"
Curtis Bishop, "Mr. Great from Georgia"
Daniel Winters, "Five-Minute Flash"
Bill Heuman, "Coffin Corner Crazy"
Ted Stratton, "Elmer the Groundhog"

Vol. 1, No. 9, Second Fall 1943. Stories: 8
Cover: George Gross
Stewart Sterling (Prentice Winchell), "Pour on the Power!"
J.B. Thornton, "The Coach Runs Wild"
Bill Heuman, "Crazylegs Carries the Mail"
Ted Stratton, "Pigskin Barrage"
Don Rainey, "Son of the Ripper"
C. Paul Jackson, "Leatherneck Lateral"
Tom O'Neill, "Bull of the Backfield"
Nelson S. Bond, "The Quick-Kicking Hick"

Vol. 1, No. 10, First Fall 1944. Stories: 6
Cover: George Gross
Curtis Bishop, "Give a Halfback Wings"
Ted Roemer, "The Pigskin Privateer"
Tom O'Neill, "Fourth-Quarter Miracle"
Jackson V. Scholz, "The Gorgeous Goon"
William Heuman, "The Phantom Blocker"
Roy C. Rainey, "Fumble-Bum"

Vol. 1, No. 11, Second Fall 1944. Stories: 6
Cover: George Gross
Jackson Scholz (ghosted by William R. Cox), "Sixty Minute Skyrocket"
Jack Volney (Jackson V. Scholz), "Pigskin Puppet!"
Ted Stratton, "Erin Go Brawl!"
Curtis Bishop, "Stack 'Em, Line!"
C. Paul Jackson, "Three Minute Hotshot"
William R. Cox, "The Dixie Dreadnaught"

Vol. 1, No. 12, First Fall 1945. Stories: 6
Cover: George Gross
Curtis Bishop, "Texas TNT"
C. Paul Jackson, "Pop-Off from Paducah"
William Heuman, "Swivel Hips"
Ted Stratton, "The Great Brain"
Richard Brister, "Bench Back"
Brad King, "The Million-Dollar Sub"

Vol. 2, No. 1, Second Fall 1945. Stories: 5
Cover: George Gross
Jackson V. Scholz, "The Great Frosh Fizzle"
Curtis Bishop, "All-America Robot"
Wilton Hazzard, "The Touchdown Pirates"
Tom O'Neill, "Gridiron Gravy"
Jack Volney (Jackson V. Scholz), "The Mighty Blocker"

Vol. 2, No. 2, First Fall 1946. Stories: 6
Cover: George Gross
Harold Rogers, "Six-Point Mutineers"
Brad King, "The Fumble Threat"
Curtis Bishop, "Never Let Tackles Think"
John K. Northway, "Touchdown Tramp"
C. Paul Jackson, "Hold That Headline!"
Richard Brister, "Backfield Playboy"

Vol. 2, No. 3, Second Fall 1946. Stories: 8
Cover: George Gross
Burgess Leonard, "Cinderella Scatback"
Curtis Bishop, "The Big Wind from Texas"
Brad King, "You Can't Fumble Forever"
Duane Yarnell, "The Mad Manhattans"
Ted Stratton, "The Interferin' Kid"
Joe Brennan, "Plunderer's Game"
Lloyd Derrickson, "Goalpost Gamble"
Willie Graham, "The Old Fighting Spirit"

Vol. 2, No. 4, First Fall 1947. Stories: 7
Cover: George Gross
Bill Erin, "Wolfpack in Moleskin"
Zene Tuttler, "To Hell with the Scrubs"
Curtis Bishop, "Big Brain at QB"
Gardner Fox, "Somebody's Gotta Lose"
Richard Brister, "Part-Time Star"
Ted Stratton, "Blocking Blonde"
Richard K. Tapscott, "Cold Cleats"

Vol. 2, No. 5, Second Fall 1947. Stories: 4
Cover: George Gross
John Wiggin, "The Hep-Cat Backs"
Curtis Bishop, "Six-Point Slave Gang"
Harold Rogers, "'Give Him a Basket!'"
Ted Stratton, "Rabbits Can't Pass"

Vol. 2, No. 6, First Fall 1948. Stories: 5
Cover: George Gross
Burgess Leonard, "Bury Me Not in Coffin Corner"
Joe Alfreds, "Shanty Town Express"
Duane Yarnell, "Scared Scatback"
Ted Stratton, "Tackle-Shy Terror"
E.B. Hamilton, Jr., "'What's the Score, Musclehead?'"

Vol. 2, No. 7, Second Fall 1948. Stories: 5
Cover: Norman Saunders
William O'Sullivan, "Revolt of the Cleat Happy Clowns"
Stewart Sterling (Prentice Winchell), "No Points for Jughead"
Bill Erin, "A Ticket to Paydirt"
E.B. Hamilton, Jr., "Call Me 'Fling Fingers'"
William R. Cox, "The Derelicts from Dixie"

Vol. 2, No. 8, First Fall 1949. Stories: 5
Cover: George Gross (reprinted from First Fall 1943)
Curtis Bishop, "Mr. Great from Georgia!" (reprinted from First Fall 1943)

William R. Cox, "Holo at Fullback"
Stewart Sterling (Prentice Winchell), "The Fumbling Phantom" (reprinted from First Fall 1943)
Ted Roemer, "Kick for the Double-Cross"
Reynolds Phillips, "Money-Arm"
Vol. 2, No. 9, Second Fall 1949. Stories: 5
Cover: Allen Anderson (reprinted from Second Fall 1942)
John Starr, "Two Yards from Glory" (reprinted from Second Fall 1942 as by William Heuman)
Curtis Bishop, "The Blocking Brothers" (reprinted from Second Fall 1942)
DeWitt Shank, "The Door-Mat Eleven"
Gardner F. Fox, "One Play McKay"
Ted Stratton, "Six-Point Famine"
Vol. 2, No. 10, Fall 1950. Stories: 7
Cover: George Gross (reprinted from Second Fall 1943)
Ted Stratton, "Boss of the Backfield Mutineers"
Linton Davies, "First-Half Hero" (reprinted from the 1938 issue)
J.B. Thornton, "Pigskin Payoff"
O.D. Shank, "'Brother, Can You Spare a Block?'"
Wayne D. Mote, "Touchdown Thunder"
Von McNair, Jr., "Break-a-Way Guy"
Harold Helfer, "The Ghost of Barney McNutt"
Vol. 2, No. 11, Fall 1951. Stories: 6
Cover: George Gross (reprinted from First Fall 1944)
Burgess Leonard, "Pigskin Privateer"
Don Kingery, "Revolt of the Robot Eleven"
Tom O'Neill, "Half-Pint Hellion" (reprinted from *Bull's-Eye Sports*, Fall 1939, as by Stewart Sterling)
Wilton Hazzard, "The Fourth-Quarter Flyer" (reprinted from A-A Football, Fall 1941, as by Harrison Hendryx)
March Lacy, "Samson and His Dilemma"
Giles A. Lutz, "Cold Cleats"
Vol. 2, No. 12, Fall 1952. Stories: 5
Cover: George Gross (reprinted from Second Fall 1944)
Burgess Leonard, "The Rose Bowl Raider"
Nelson A. Hutto, "The All-American Sub"
Gene Olson, "The Ground Eaters"
Add Aretz, "A Chip Off the Old 66"
J.B. Thornton, "Blockers for Sale!" (reprinted from A-A Football, Second Fall 1944)
Vol. 3, No. 1, Fall 1953. Stories: 5
Cover: Reprinted from First Fall 1945
Jack Rogers, "The Triple Threat Tramp"
Charles Freeman, "Cleats of Treachery"
William Heuman, "Swivel Hips" (reprinted from First Fall 1945)
Curtis Bishop, "Texas TNT" (reprinted from First Fall 1945)
Gene Olson, "Coswell Calls 'Em Crazy"

Totals: 25 issues, 156 stories (counting reprints twice)

Marvel (Red Circle) Publications

All Baseball Stories

Vol. 1, No. 1 (one shot), October 1947. Stories: 7
Cover: Allen Anderson
Roe Richmond, "Hit Away, Has-Been!"
C. Paul Jackson, "Don't Brand a Busher Yellow"
Giles A. Lutz, "The Pitching Machine"
John Wilson, "The Greatest Ball Team in the World"
Theodore Roemer, "Iron Man in the Mask"
Gene D. Robinson, "Curves Crazy"
Richard Brister, "Pariah Pitcher"

All Football Stories

Vol. 1, No. 1 (one shot), December 1947. Stories: 7
Cover:
C. Paul Jackson, "Tiger on the Team"
Theodore J. Roemer, "Money Player—Paydirt Bound!"
J. Phillip List, "Triple-Threat Blockers"
George Kilrain, "Bull at Full"
Henry Bela Bachrach, "Touchdown Temper"
Ted Stratton, "Touchdown Medicine Man"
James Blish, "Backfield Business"

Best Sports

Vol. 1, No. 1, January 1937. Stories: 7
Cover: Football
Arthur Mann, "Pigskin Parade" (FB)
Ernest Hamilton, "The Ringer" (FB)
Samuel Taylor, "Gridiron Fury" (FB)
Vol. 1, No. 2, March 1937. Stories: 8
Cover: Hockey by Stockton Mulford
Jonesy Taylor, "He Can Take It" (BB)
Charlie Lewis, "No Alibi" (FB)
Vol. 1, No. 3, June 1937. Stories: 9
Cover: Baseball star Bob Feller by H.W. Scott
William Edward Hayes, "The Diamond Murders" (BB)
Charlie Lewis, "Second Chance" (BB)
Jerry Tolan, "The Nine Old Men" (BB)
Jonesy Taylor, "The Double Play Kids" (BB)
Johnny Lawson, "Pigskin Pusher" (FB)
Vol. 1, No. 4, November 1937. Stories: 10
Cover: Boxing by J.W. Scott
Jerry Tolan, "Borderland Baseball" (BB)
Charlie Lewis, "Up from the Sticks" (BB)
Clint Stewart, All-Around Athlete (part BB)
Jonesy Taylor, "Sluggers All" (BB)
Johnny Lawson, "Ring Bone" (FB)
Vol. 1, No. 5, February 1938. Stories: 10
Cover: Basketball by H.W. Scott
William Edward Hayes, "Diamond Tornado" (BB)
William H. Pears, "Fence-Busters" (BB)
Coy Williams, "Touchdown for a Lady" (FB)
Walt Clark, "While 80,000 Watched" (FB)
E. Newman Eveslade "One Minute Left"(FB)
Vol. 1, No. 6, May 1938. Stories: 10
Cover: Baseball

Dale Cole, "Practice Pitcher" (BB)
Ross Kenton, "Hoodoo Diamond" (BB)
Falls Maury, "The Dancing Southpaw" (BB)
William R. Cox, "Pitchers Can't Hit" (BB)
Vol. 2, No. 1, August 1938. Stories: 10
Cover: Boxing
Arthur Mann, "Trouble at First" (BB)
Gary Sheene, "Big Shot Rookie" (BB)
Johnny Lawson, "The Ghost Pitcher" (BB)
Hal Lee, "Fighting Blood" (BB)
Bart Victor, "Eddie the Flash" (BB)
James W. Egan, "A Fool for Glory" (FB)
Vol. 2, No. 2, December 1938. Stories: 10
Cover: Football by H.W. Scott
Jonesy Taylor, "The Everlasting Jinx" (BB)
C. Paul Jackson, "The Kid Can Take It" (BB)
Don Partney, "Smashing Through" (FB)
Dale Cole, "Anything Goes" (FB)
Cosmo Bennett, "Back to Back" (FB)
Vol. 2, No. 3, March 1939. Stories: 10
Cover: Boxing by H.W. Scott
Johnny Lawson, "Pitchers and Ponies" (BB)
J.J. Meany, "Horsehide Harmony" (BB)
Richard L. Hobart, "Hard—Like Steel" (BB)
Lawrence Perry, "Pigskin Fury" (FB)
Vol. 2, No. 4, June 1939. Stories: 10
Cover: Baseball
Jack Daley, "The Hot Corner Kid" (BB)
Paul Carney, "Clouting Fool" (BB)
Walt Clark, "Big League Graveyard" (BB)
W.H. Temple, "Fielder's Folly" (BB)
Vol. 2, No. 5, December 1939. Stories: 10
Cover: Football by J.W. Scott
Giles A. Lutz, "Twin Trouble" (BB)
Cyril Plunkett, "Steel Heart—Steel Arm" (BB)
Jack Daly, "Blood Will Tell" (FB)
Curtis Bishop, "Touchdown Fever" (FB)
Roe Richmond, "Interference Be Damned" (FB)
R. DeWitt Miller, "Flying Cleats" (FB)
Vol. 2, No. 1, October 1947 (after hiatus). Stories: 9
Cover: Baseball
C. Paul Jackson, "One-Man Team from Texas" (BB)
Theodore J. Roemer, "Base-Hits Mean Bullets!" (BB)
Orbe Bosick, "The Big-League Busher" (BB)
E.E. Halleran, "Quarterback on the Mound" (BB-FB)
J.J. Meany, "Pennant Politician" (BB)
Giles A. Lutz, "The Touchdown Marvels" (FB)
Vol. 2, No. 2, January 1948. Stories: 9
Cover: Football
Theodore J. Roemer, "Halfback from Hades" (FB)
John Wilson, "Tackles Come Tough!" (FB)
Richard Brister, "The Clown Wore Cleats" (FB)
Vol. 2, No. 3, May 1948. Stories: 7
Cover: Baseball
Roe Richmond, "Big Leaguers Never Quit!" (BB)
T.W. Ford, "Riot at the Hot Corner" (BB)
Arnold Hano, "Pigskin Purgatory" (FB)
Vol. 2, No. 4, September 1948. Stories: 6
Cover: Boxing
John Wilson, "Buggy Whip" Hurler's Pennant Fever" (BB)
Jay Thorburn (John Wilson's real name), "Pressure Pilot" (BB)
Vol. 2, No. 5, February 1950 (after hiatus). Stories: 10
Cover: Football by Norman Saunders
Bill Erin, "Substitute for a Diamond King" (BB)
Nelson Hutto, "All Signs Off!" (BB)
Harrison Hendryx, "Pivot, Feint, Take It Over!"
Johnny Lawson, "Hellion at Half" (FB)
Vol. 2, No. 6, November 1950. Stories: 11
Cover: Baseball by Norman Saunders
John Wilson, "Diamond in the Rough" (BB)
Norman Ober, "The Pitching Fool" (BB)
C. Paul Jackson, "Brother Battery" (BB)
Bill Erin, "Hate on the Mound" (BB)
Robert Turner, "Hot Corner Hotshot" (BB)
Milton Lesser, "Quadruple Threat Man" (FB)
Vol. 2, No. 7, February 1951. Stories: 10
Cover: Football by Norman Saunders
Ted Stratton, "Satan in Center" (BB)
Don Kingery, "Last Chance for Glory" (BB)
C. Paul Jackson, "The King of Swap" (BB)
Martin Madancy, "Where There's Smokey, There's a Fireball" (BB)
Bill Erin, "Pass 'Em Blind!" (FB)
Joe Brennan, "Big League Pigskinner" (FB)
Vol. 2, No. 8, May 1951. Stories: 9 (only digest issue)
Cover: Baseball by Norman Saunders
Duane Yarnell, "Pitch for Your Life" (BB)
Roe Richmond, "Backstop from the Bench" (BB)
Zene Tuttler, "Brains in His Bat" (BB)
Philip St. John (Lester del Rey), "A Pennant to Remember" (BB)
Vol. 2, No. 9, August 1951. Stories: 10
Cover: Baseball by Norman Saunders
H.C. Butler, "OK, You Want Home Runs?" (BB)
Bill Erin, "Hot Corner—Cool Head" (BB)
Jack Rodgers, "Homicide Hurler" (BB)
Humphrey Jones, "Fastball Fox" (BB)
Vol. 2, No. 10, December 1951. Stories: 9
Cover: Boxing by Norman Saunders
Duane Yarnell, "The Rookie Wanted Revenge" (BB)
C. Paul Jackson, "Fast Pitch" (BB)
Don Kingery, "Mound War" (BB)
Gardner F. Fox, "The Tackle No Team Could Tame" (FB)
Johanas L. Bouma, "Last Quarter Means No Quarter!" (FB)

Totals: 21 issues, 194 stories, 62 baseball stories, 30 football stories.

Big Baseball Stories

Vol. 1, No. 1, May 1948. Stories: 5
Cover: Allen Anderson
Duane Decker, "Home Runs Don't Count" (Johnny Madigan)
Robert Turner, "Mutiny on the Mound"
George Kilrain, "Ride That Rookie!"

Richard Brister, "Joe Harvard, Giant Killer"
Roe Richmond, "Kid Brother to a Big Leaguer"
Vol. 1, No. 2, August 1948. Stories: 5
Cover: Allen Anderson?
Philip St. John (Lester del Rey), "Fastballs for Sale"
John Wilson, "Cinderella at Second"
C. Paul Jackson, "Sixty Grand Bum"
James Blish, "Slide, Sucker, Slide"
Wesley Peter Bryan, "Back to the Bushes"
Vol. 1, No. 3, November 1948. Stories: 5
Cover: Allen Anderson?
Robert Turner, "Fighting Fool on First"
Zene Tuttler, "Mystery on the Mound"
John Wilson, "Hit the Dirt, Busher!"
Wesley Peter Bryan, "Dig My Grave in Centerfield!"
Duane Decker, "Ninth-Inning Blues"

Totals: 3 issues, 15 stories

Big Book Sports

Vol. 1, No. 1, November 1947. Stories: 7
Cover: Football
Robert Turner, "Hurler from Hades" (BB)
Herbert L. McNary, "Killer in the Backfield" (FB)
Richard Brister, "Huddle Trouble" (FB)
Damon Knight, "Touchdown Torment" (FB)
Vol. 1, No. 2, Winter 1947–1948. Stories: 7
Cover: Basketball
George Kilrain, "Grid Kid from Hell's Kitchen" (FB)
Totals for Big Sports Magazine and Big Book Sports: 6 issues, 47 stories, 11 baseball stories, 8 football stories.

Big Sports Magazine

Vol. 1, No. 1, May 1948. Stories: 8
Cover: Baseball, football, track, and boxing
John Wilson, "Infield Inferno" (BB)
James Blish, "Ten Yards to Glory" (FB)
Vol. 1, No. 2, July 1948. Stories: 8
Cover: Baseball
M.M. Tinney, "Infield Outlaw" (BB)
Roe Richmond, "Diamond Destiny" (BB)
Bart Victor, "Hollow Guy" (BB)
Bill Longgood, "Screwball Chucker" (BB)
Vol. 1, No. 3, September 1948. Stories: 8
Cover: Baseball by Allen Anderson
Bill Erin, "Centerfield Is a Rookie's Cemetery" (BB)
Roe Richmond, "Pennant-Maker" (BB)
John Van Praag, "Vocal Boy" (BB)
John Wilson, "All-American Guy" (FB)
Vol. 1, No. 4, November 1948. Stories: 9
Cover: Football by Norman Saunders
Giles A. Lutz, "Play Ball or Else!" (BB)
Jerry Tolan, "First Baseman for Sale" (BB)
Robert Turner, "Paydirt Is My Destination" (FB)
Humphrey Jones, "Pigskin Heart" (FB)

Complete Sports

Vol. 1, No. 1, March 1937. Stories: 10
Cover: Boxing by H.W. Scott
William Edward Hayes, "The Diamond Dud" (BB)
T.K. Hawley, "Jinxed!" (BB)
Carmony Gove, "Touchdown Gift" (FB)
Vol. 1, No. 2, June 1937. Stories: 11
Cover: Baseball by H.W. Scott
Arthur Mann, "Smoke Ball!" (BB)
Charlie Lewis, "Pitch with Your Brains" (BB)
Jonesy Taylor, "The Troublemaker" (BB)
Ross Kenton, "The Tango Kid" (BB)
Paul Kenny, "The Running Fool" (FB)
Vol. 1, No. 2 (error), September 1937. Stories: 10
Cover: Baseball by J.W. Scott
Charlie Lewis, "Swing That Stick" (BB)
John T. McIntyre, "First Base Medicine" (BB)
Jerry Tolan, "Squeeze Play" (BB)
Herbert McNary, "Prize Rookie"
Johnny Lawson, "Pigskin Musketeers" (FB)
Vol. 1, No. 4, January 1938. Stories: 10
Cover: Football by H.W. Scott
Bart Victor, "Steady in the Clutch" (BB)
James Hall, "The Winning Soup Bone" (BB)
Johnny Lawson, "The Old Man Comes Back" (BB)
C. Paul Jackson, "Names Don't Count" (FB)
Sam Carson, "The Pigskin Fool" (FB)
Ron Broom, "Running Wild" (FB)
Vol. 1, No. 5, April 1938. Stories: 11
Cover: Boxing by J.W. Scott
Theodore Roemer, "Tough Guy" (BB)
Mel Carson, "Left-handed Violet" (BB)
R. DeWitt Miller, "In the Shadow of the Goal" (FB)
Vol. 1, No. 6, July 1938. Stories: 10
Cover: Baseball by J.W. Scott
William Edward Hayes, "The Stars That Shine" (BB)
Bart Victor, "The Hustler" (BB)
Hal Lee, "The Grouch" (BB)
Johnny Lawson, "Bush League Demon" (BB)
Fred McIsaac, "The Zulus Go to Town" (BB)
Ernie Phillips, "Gridiron Feud" (FB, not in table of contents)
Vol. 1, No. 6, October 1938 (error: should be Vol. 2, No. 1). Stories: 10
Cover: Boxing by J.W. Scott
Clint Warner, "Pitcher's Payoff" (BB)
Ross Kenton, "Hooks and Crooks" (BB)
Jonesy Taylor, "Prize Hitter" (BB)
Bart Victor, "The Diamond Mug" (BB)
Herbert E. Smith, "Signal's On" (FB)
Vol. 2, No. 2, January 1939. Stories: 10
Cover: Football by J.W. Scott
William Edward Hayes, "Major League Sandlotter" (BB)
Frank Spain, "Pigskin Poison" (FB)
William Culver, "Coming Through!" (FB)
Herbert Dalmas, "It's a Fake" (FB)
Vol. 2, No. 3, MayJune 1939. Stories: 10
Cover: Baseball

Johnny Lawson, "When Southpaws Meet" (BB)
C. Paul Jackson, "Rookies Have to Be Tough" (BB)
Jack Daley, "Simple Simon Slugger" (BB)
Will James, "Spikes for a Scrapper" (BB)
Roe Richmond, "Coach's Backfield Dream" (FB)

Vol. 2, No. 4, November 1939. Stories: 10
Cover: Football
James W. Egan, "The Dazzler" (BB)
Bart Victor, "The Curve's the Things" (BB)
Falls Maury, "The Champs Are Coming" (BB)
E.W. Hoskins, "Glory and Gold" (FB)

Vol. 2, No. 5, April 1940. Stories: 8
Cover: Boxing by J.W. Scott
Ted Roemer, "Infield Streak" (BB)
Duane Yarnell, "Smash That Line" (FB)

Vol. 2, No. 6, August 1940. Stories: 9
Cover: Baseball by J.W. Scott
Arthur K. Barnes, "A Fool for Base Hits" (BB)
Ronald Oliphant, "Million-Dollar Trio" (BB)
Cosmo Bennett, "A Great Man Bats" (BB)
W.K. Perdue, "Sub for a Ball-Slammer" (BB)
Fred Merrick, "Chicken Wing" (BB)

Vol. 3, No. 1, January 1941. Stories: 8
Cover: Football by J.W. Scott
Roe Richmond, "The Big League Bushers" (BB)
Harold Rogers, "The Fighting Fullback" (FB)
David Brandt, "A Fool for Touchdowns" (FB)
Johnny Lawson, "The Kid Who Could Kick" (FB)
Wil Keefe, "Hit That Line!" (FB)
Cosmo Bennett, "Substitute for an All-America" (FB)

Vol. 3, No. 2, June 1941. Stories: 8
Cover: Baseball by J.W. Scott
Duane Yarnell, "Iron Man on the Mound" (BB)
Cosmo Bennett, "World Series Wrecker" (BB)
Nelson Hutto, "Murderers' Row—for Rookies Only!" (BB)
Johnny Lawson, "Diamond Laughs" (BB)

Vol. 3, No. 3, September 1941. Stories: 9
Cover: Baseball by J.W. Scott
Zene Tuttler, "Baseball in His Blood" (BB)
Roe Richmond, "Fire 'Em Thar Fireball!" (BB)
Herbert L. McNary, "The Battling Busher" (BB)
J.J. Meany, "Miracle Man on the Mound" (BB)
Richard Brister, "Rookie on a Rampage" (BB)

Vol. 3, No. 4, November 1941. Stories: 8
Cover: Football by Norman Saunders
C. Paul Jackson, "Pitch Your Heart Out!" (BB)
Nelson Hutto, "Pigskin Payoff" (FB)
Cosmo Bennett, "Straight-Arm Steam Roller" (FB)
Duane Yarnell, "Eleven-Man Wrecking Crew" (FB)
John Wilson, "High-Scoring Hellion" (FB)

Vol. 3, No. 5, January 1942. Stories: 7
Cover: Football by H.W. Scott
James W. Egan, "When a Ball-Murderer Gets Mad" (BB)
Giles A. Lutz, "Pressure Proof" (BB)
C. Paul Jackson, "Headline Halfback" (FB)
Duane Yarnell, "Line-Smashing Lunatic" (FB)

Vol. 3, No. 6, April 1942. Stories: 8
Cover: Boxing by J.W. Scott
C. Paul Jackson, "Fifty Grand Means Fan Em" (BB)
Henry Bela Bachrach, "Fireball Fever" (BB)

Vol. 4, No. 1, July 1942. Stories: 6
Cover: Baseball by Norman Saunders
Duane Yarnell, "Baseball's for Blood, Busher!" (BB)
Cosmo Bennett, "Southpaw Sabotage" (BB)
Giles A. Lutz, "Fence-Buster Boomerang" (BB)

Vol. 4, No. 2, September 1942. Stories: 7
Cover: Baseball
C. Paul Jackson, "Bush-League Boy-Wonder" (BB)
Nelson Hutto, "Home Run King for Hire!" (BB)
Norman L. Paul, "Baseball Plus" (BB)

Vol. 4, No. 3, November 1942. Stories: 6
Cover: Football by Norman Saunders
C. Paul Jackson, "Pigskin Piledriver" (FB)
Theodore J. Roemer, "Tough Team" (FB)
Ronald Oliphant, "Take It Over, USA!" (FB)
Roe Richmond, "The Rebel Halfback" (FB)

Vol. 4, No. 4, January 1943. Stories: 7
Cover: Football by Norman Saunders
Mac Davis, "Formula for Base Hits" (BB)
Duane Yarnell, "All-American Means Fight!" (FB)
C. Paul Jackson, "A Demon for First Downs" (FB)
J.J. Meany, "Pigskin Paradise" (FB)
Giles A. Lutz, "Hothead Halfback" (FB)
Roe Richmond, With Line Smashes, "Long Passes and Luck!" (FB)

Vol. 4, No. 5, April 1943. Stories: 7
Cover: Basketball
J.J. Meany, "I'll Take Pay-Off Pitchers" (BB)
Duane Yarnell, "The Touchdown Twins" (FB)

Vol. 5, No. 1 (no Vol. 4, No. 6 issued, September–October 1946, after hiatus). Stories: 7
Cover: Baseball
Theodore Roemer, "Fighter in the Bullpen" (BB)
Johnny Lawson, "Hate, Heroes and Base Hits" (BB)
W.H. Temple, "Grid King Who Never Played Football" (FB)

Vol. 5, No. 2, January 1947. Stories: 6
Cover: Football
Duane Yarnell, "The Million-Dollar Line-Smasher" (FB)

Vol. 5, No. 3, March 1947. Stories: 9
Cover: Basketball
W.H. Temple, "Tough Team" (BB)
Jerry Tolan, "The Touchdown Terrors" (FB)
Richard Brister, "All-American Means All Out!"

Vol. 5, No. 4, June 1947. Stories: 9
Cover: Baseball
Giles A. Lutz, "Rookie Rebel" (BB)
Bart Victor, "Accent on Base Hits" (BB)
Ralph Yergen, "Coward at the Plate" (BB)
Herbert L. McNary, "Dude of the Diamond" (BB)
Cosmo Bennett, "Watch Heffernan" (FB)

Vol. 5, No. 4 (error), September 1947. Stories: 9
Cover: Baseball
C. Paul Jackson, "Pennant Fever" (BB)
H.C. Butler, "Coward in the Clutch" (BB)
Duane Decker, First Inning's, "Worst Inning" (BB)
E.E. Halleran, "Quiet—Pitcher at Work!" (BB)
J.B. DuVall, "Diamond King's Kid" (BB)
Theodore J. Roemer, "Touchdowns for Sale!"
Vol. 5, No. 6 (error corrected), December 1947. Stories: 8
Cover: Football
Roe Richmond, "Wanted: A Halfback Hero!" (FB)
Richard Brister, "Pigskin Pirates" (FB)
Zene Tuttler, "Backfield Battering Ram" (FB)
C. Paul Jackson, "Scarecrow in the T-Slot" (FB)
Vol. 6, No. 1, April 1948. Stories: 9
Cover: Basketball
H.C. Butler, "The Razzle-Dazzle Kid!" (FB)
Richard Brister, "Triple Threat Backfield" (FB)
Vol. 6, No. 2, July 1948. Stories: 11
Cover: Baseball
T.W. Ford, "Hit Away, Holler Guy!" (BB)
T.K. Hawley, "Stranger in the Infield" (BB)
W.H. Temple, "Busher on the Mound" (BB)
Paul Carney, "The Series Wrecker" (BB)
Johnny Lewis, "Glory Be Damned!" (FB)
Vol. 6, No. 3, October 1948. Stories: 10
Cover: Baseball
Duane Decker, "Base-Thief to Mound Marvel (Eddie Lasky)" (BB)
Zene Tuttler, "Dynamite in His Bat" (BB)
W.H. Temple, "Pitcher-Ears" (BB)
Louis Trimble, "Pennant for Sale!" (BB)
Roger Johnson, "Pitch Your Heart Out!" (BB)
Les Etter, "Wild Man on the Gridiron" (FB)
Vol. 6, No. 4, January 1949. Stories: 10
Cover: Football
Robert Turner, "Eat Dirt, Busher!" (BB)
T.J. Roemer, "Kid Brother to a Big League" (BB)
Bill Erin, "Brothers Under the Pigskin" (FB)
John Wilson, "Pay-Off for the Glory Boy!" (FB)
Richard Brister, "The All-American Scrub" (FB)
Jerry Tolan, "Lug Leather for Your Life!" (FB)
Vol. 6, No. 5, April 1949. Stories: 11
Cover: Baseball
David C. Cooke, "The Home Run That Wasn't" (BB)
Jim Duncan, "That Baseball Instinct" (BB)
Zene Tuttler, "Tiger on the Ten Stripe" (FB)
Richard Brister, "Pardon My Cleats!" (FB)
Vol. 6, No. 6, July 1949. Stories: 9
Cover: Baseball
Giles A. Lutz, "Bear Down, Busher!" (BB)
Norman Ober, "Base Hits in His Blood" (BB)
Duane Yarnell, "Ballhawk" (BB)
John Wilson, "Touchdowns Come Tough!" (FB)
Vol. 7, No. 1, October 1949. Stories: 11
Cover: Baseball, football, and boxing
Giles A. Lutz, "Tough Rookie" (BB)
H.C. Butler, "Spike Shy Means Yellow!" (BB)
Richard Brister, "Diamond King for a Day" (BB)
Robert Turner, "Home Runs Will Be My Revenge!" (BB)
Ray Morrison, "Fifty Touchdowns to Go!" (FB)
Vol. 7, No. 2, January 1950. Stories: 10
Cover: Football
Bill Erin, "World Series Wrecker" (BB)
J.W. Benjamin, "Horsehides, Horseshoes and Horselaughs" (BB)
Chick Coombs, "Diamond Dilemma" (BB)
Roe Richmond, "King of the Golden Horde" (FB)
Jack Rogers, "Get That Little Guy!" (FB)
Philo St. John (Lester del Rey), "Razzle-Dazzle Redemption" (FB)
Vol. 7, No. 3, April 1950. Stories: 10
Cover: Baseball by Norman Saunders
Zene Tuttler, "Pitch for a Pennant!" (BB)
Ralph Berard, "Bat-Boy's Homer" (BB)
John Wilson, "The Touchdown Machine" (FB)
Leonard Keller, "Hell-Bound Halfback" (FB)
Vol. 7, No. 4, July 1950. Stories: 10
Cover: Baseball by Norman Saunders
Ted Stratton, "Second Sacker, Deluxe!" (BB)
Robert Turner, "Hurling Dervish" (BB)
Zene Tuttler, "Hot Corner Houdini" (BB)
Vol. 7, No. 5, October 1950. Stories: 10
Cover: Baseball by Norman Saunders
Roe Richmond, "Keystone Killer" (BB)
Lee Q. Evans, "Fence-Buster—or Fake?" (BB)
Ted Stratton, "Hit Away!" (BB)
Zene Tuttler, "The Big-League Way" (BB)
Johnny Lawson, "The No-Good Nine" (BB)
Vol. 7, No. 6, December 1950. Stories: 10
Cover: Football and baseball by Norman Saunders
Norman Ober, "One-Man Infield" (BB)
Roy Lopez, "Sandlot Savvy" (BB)
Charlie Lewis, "Horsehide—or Horseplay?" (BB)
C. Paul Jackson, "Pull a Touchdown Out of the Sky" (FB)
Duane Yarnell, "Rose Bowl to Go!" (FB)
Robert Hammond, "Play-for-Pay Steam Roller" (FB)
Vol. 7, No. 7, February 1951. Stories: 10
Cover: Football by Norman Saunders
Roe Richmond, "A Hitter's Got to Hate!" (BB)
Zene Tuttler, "Phantom Fireballer" (BB)
Thomas L. Cavanaugh, "Rookie Riot" (BB)
Chas. M. Rose, "Okay, All-American, 'Show Us!'" (FB)
Bill Erin, "The Tackle Who Talked Tough" (FB)
Rich Kendrick, "Fifty Grand Football" (FB)
Vol. 7, No. 8, May 1951. Stories: 6
Cover: Baseball by Norman Saunders (only digest issue of *Complete Sports*)
Bill Erin, "High, Hard One to Glory" (BB)
Norman Ober, "Sissy at Second" (BB)
Zene Tuttler, "Carry a Big Stick" (BB)
Vol. 7, No. 9, August 1951. Stories: 10
Cover: Baseball by Norman Saunders
Norman Ober, "G.I. on the Mound" (BB)
Thomas Cavanaugh, "Play Ball, Playboy!" (BB)

Bob Bernat, "Speak Softly" (BB)
Brent North, "Great Field—No Hit" (BB)
Vol. 7, No. 10, November 1951. Stories: 9
Cover: Baseball by Norman Saunders
Duane Yarnell, "Belligerent Busher" (BB)
Milton Lesser, "Fence Buster" (BB)
Thad Kowalski, "The Rookie and the Has-Been" (BB)
Ted Stratton, "The Scrub Who Called Himself Terrible Terrill" (FB)
Vol. 7, No. 11, February 1952. Stories: 9
Cover: Football by Norman Saunders
Giles A. Lutz, "Smart Rookie" (BB)
Charlie Lewis, "The Magnificent Arm" (BB)
Bill Erin, "Fugitive from a Gridiron" (FB)
Chas. M. Rose, "The Big Try" (FB)
Vol. 7, No. 12, July 1952. Stories: 7
Cover: Baseball by Norman Saunders
Joe Brennan, "The Mound King and the Rookie" (BB)
Theodore Roemer, "A Guy to Win Games" (BB)
Johnny Lawson, "Varsity Fodder" (FB)
Vol. 8, No. 1, September 1952. Stories: 8
Cover: Baseball by Norman Saunders
Bill Erin, "This Is the Big One!" (BB)
Giles A. Lutz, "The Great Arm" (BB)
John Suiter, "Hit-and-Run!" (BB)
Brent North, "Wanted, Winning Teams Only" (FB)
Vol. 8, No. 2, November 1952. Stories: 7
Cover: Baseball by Norman Saunders
Duane Decker, "Miracle at the Plate" (BB)
Bill Erin, "The Sell-Out" (BB)
Duane Yarnell, "Last Year's Hero" (FB)
Vol. 8, No. 3, January 1953. Stories: 9
Cover: Five different sports scenes by Norman Saunders
Burgess Leonard, "You Mow 'Em Down" (BB)
Wadworth Nealey, "The King of What?" (BB)
Duane Yarnell, "Operation Goal-Line" (FB)
William R. Cox, "A Dream for Football Freddy" (FB)
Vol. 8, No. 4, March 1953. Stories: 10
Cover: Baseball by Norman Saunders
Bill Erin, "The Busher Had a Fastball" (BB)
Nelson Hutto, "Look Who Calls Himself a Ballplayer!" (BB)
Bryce Walton, "Great Heart" (BB)
William F. Schwartz, "The Broken Bat" (BB)
Don Kingery, "Get the Big Guy!" (FB)
Vol. 8, No. 5, May 1953. Stories: 14
Cover: Baseball
Bill Erin, "Mean Man with a Bat" (BB)
James L. Harte, "Hall of Fame" (BB)
Bob Dywer, "While Ignatius Slept in Left Field" (BB)
Vince McKeough, "Lucky Handout" (BB)
Ted Stratton, "Anything for a Pal" (FB)
Vol. 8, No. 6, December 1953. Stories: 7
Cover: Baseball by Norman Saunders
Giles A. Lutz, "And the Rookie Got Mad" (BB)
H.C. Butler, "A Pennant for Tommy" (BB)
Bill Erin, "Great Player" (FB)
Vol. 9, No. 1, March 1954. Stories: 13
Cover: Baseball by Norman Saunders
Jim Egan, "Low and Outside" (BB)
Al Cooper, "A Perfect Game" (BB)
James L. Harte, "Batty" (BB)
J. Eugene Chrisman, "Without Pitching a Single Ball" (BB)
Nelson A. Hutto, "The Smart Play" (FB)
Vol. 9, No. 2, July 1954. Stories: 14
Cover: Outdoors and sports scenes by Norman Saunders
Bill Erin, "The Rookie Who Never Laughed" (BB)
Thomas Cavanaugh, "Send In Your Secret Weapon" (BB)
Norman Ober, "Full Count" (BB)
Lloyd Derrickson, "What It Took" (FB)
Vol. 9, No. 3, October 1954. Stories: 8
Cover: Outdoor and sports scenes by Norman Saunders
Roe Richmond, "Hot Corner" (BB)
H.C. Butler, "Bonus Baby" (BB)
Milton Lesser, "Close One" (BB)
Chick Coombs, "The Biggest Game" (FB)
Vol. 9, No. 4, January 1955. Stories: 8
Cover: Football by Norman Saunders
Johnny Lawson, "Instead of a Pinch Hitter" (BB)
Roe Richmond, "The Blazer's Year" (FB)
Vol. 9, No. 5, April 1955. Stories: 7
Cover: Baseball by Norman Saunders
John Wilson, "The Worst Player on the Team" (BB)
Giles A. Lutz, "The Kid Who Loved to Hit" (BB)
Theodore J. Roemer, "Between Halves" (FB)
Vol. 9, No. 6, July 1955. Stories: 8
Cover: Outdoor and baseball by Norman Saunders
Russell Gray (Bruno Fischer), "Slaughter in the Afternoon" (BB)
William Cox, "The Home Run King" (BB)
Johnny Lawson, "One Two-Bit Hit" (BB)
William Heuman, "Million Dollar Touchdown" (FB)
Vol. 10, No. 1, October 1955. Stories: 5
Cover: Outdoor scenes by Norman Saunders
Ted Stratton, "Just the Catcher" (BB)
Ken Jason, "Yesterday's Hero" (FB)

Totals: 60 issues, 540 stories, 162 baseball stories, 87 football stories.

Real Sports

Vol. 1, No. 2 (first issue), February 1938. Stories: 10
Cover: Boxing by J.W. Scott
Lawrence Perry, "The Great God Maydock" (BB)
William Jerome, "Mr. Ghost Goes to Town" (FB)
Nelson S. Bond, "The Mighty Atom" (FB)
Dale Cole, "When a Man's a Man" (FB)
E.J. Lalley, "Glass-Jaw Fullback" (FB)

Vol. 1, No. 3, June 1938. Stories: 12
Cover: Baseball
Curtis Bishop, "Twenty Straight for a Rookie" (BB)
Johnny Lawson, "Over the Fence" (BB)
Clint Warner, "Remote Control" (BB)
Fred G. Steelman, "The Spectacular Center" (BB)
T.K. Hawley, "Mr. Hayseed Goes to Town" (BB)
Herbert L. McNary, "The Marshmallow Line" (FB)

Vol. 1, No. 4, September 1938. Stories: 10
Cover: Baseball by J.W. Scott?
William Edward Hayes, "Hot Corner Headache" (BB)
William Culver, "Lost Control" (BB)
Johnny Lawson, "Up from the Bushes" (BB)
Clint Warner, "One-Man Ball Club" (BB)
Jonesy Taylor, "A Has-Been Scores" (BB)

Vol. 1, No. 5, January 1939. Stories: 10
Cover: Football by H.W. Scott
W.H. Temple, "Bullpen Pitcher" (BB)
Ross Kenton, "Lose to Win" (BB)
Johnny Lawson, "Big League Busher" (BB)
Omar Gwinn, "Trouble Comes Double" (FB)
Colbert Lewis, "No Bowl of Roses" (FB)
Nelson S. Bond, "The Phantom Blocker" (FB)

Vol. 1, No. 6, April 1939. Stories: 10
Cover: Boxing by J.W. Scott?
Walter Hartman, "Peter's Pan" (BB)
James W. Egan, "For the Good of the Team" (BB)
Omar Gwinn, "The Million Dollar Halfback" (FB)

Vol. 1, No. 7, October 1947 (after hiatus). Stories: 9
Cover: Baseball by Allen Anderson
Theodore Roemer, "The Fabulous Fence Buster" (BB)
Roe Richmond, "Big-League Bum" (BB)
Duane Decker, "Foot in the Bucket" (BB)
Will Keefe, "Born to the Big Leagues" (BB)
Richard Brister, "Hero at Halfback" (FB)

Vol. 1, No. 8, January 1948. Stories: 7
Cover: Basketball, signed Mat
Richard Brister, "Heavy Hitter" (BB)
George Kilrain, "Dream Backfield, Nightmare Team" (FB)

Vol. 1, No. 9, April 1948. Stories: 8
Cover: Scenes of four sports, signed Mat
Zene Tuttler, "Dead-Arm Dynamite" (BB)
Wayne Pool, "If You Can't Pitch—Fight!" (BB)
James Blish, "Touchdown Destiny" (FB)

Vol. 1, No. 10, June 1948. Stories: 8
Cover: Baseball by Allen Anderson
T.W. Ford, "Calamity Hurler" (BB)
Duane Decker, "Shadow Over Shortstop" (BB)
H.C. Butler, "Only Bushers Are Yellow" (BB)
Willard Crandall, "The Great Screwball" (BB)

Vol. 1, No. 11, August 1948. Stories: 7
Cover: Baseball by Allen Anderson
Robert Turner, "Bushers Don't Come Back!" (BB)
Gardner Fox, "The Magnificent Mute" (BB)
Ray Morrison, "Glass-Arm Guy" (BB)
Wesley Peter Bryan, "Quarterback in the Sky" (FB)

Vol. 1, No. 12, November 1948. Stories: 9
Cover: Baseball by Allen Anderson
Robert Turner, "Hot-Corner Kid from Hell's Kitchen" (BB)
John Wilson, "Three Strikes—You're In!" (BB)
Zene Tuttler, "Last Chance Rookie" (BB)
Duane Decker, "The Batboy Who Won a Pennant" (BB)
David C. Cooke, "White-Line Warrior" (FB)

Totals: 11 issues, 100 stories, 34 baseball stories, 14 football stories.

Sports Action

Vol. 1, No. 1, December 1937. Stories: 12
Cover: Football by H.W. Scott
W.F. Sturm and J.F. McCann, "Hill-Billy Pitcher" (BB)
Lewis Y. Hagy, "In and Outer" (BB)
J.J. Meany, "The Cry of the Wolves" (BB)
John F. Maury (Falls Maury), "Off Side" (FB)
James Binney, "Stars and Spinners" (FB)
Duane Yarnell, "The Touchdown Kid" (FB)

Vol. 1, No. 2, March 1938. Stories: 10
Cover: Boxing by H.W. Scott
Oswald Tufte, "The Roughneck" (BB)
William R. Cox, "Foxy Grandpa" (BB)
Harvey Jackson, "The Cheers Rang Out" (FB)
John Leslie, "Ticket to Glory" (FB)

Vol. 1, No. 3, June 1938. Stories: 10
Cover: Baseball by J.W. Scott
Glenn Long, "Big Feller" (BB)
William Hartley, "New Blood" (BB)
Johnny Lawson, "Once a Screwball" (BB)
Bart Victor, "What's in a Name" (BB)
William R. Cox, "Old Guard and New" (FB)

Vol. 1, No. 4, September 1938. Stories: 10
Cover: Baseball by Norman Saunders
Jerry Tolan, "The Home Run Quitter" (BB)
Bart Victor, "Jinxed!" (BB)
Johnny Lawson, "Million Dollar Arm" (BB)
Clint Warner, "Nine Roughnecks" (BB)
Walt Morey, "The Touchdown Fool" (FB)

Vol. 1, No. 5, December 1938. Stories: 10
Cover: Football by J.W. Scott
Jonesy Taylor, "All Balled Up" (BB)
James W. Egan, "Double Feature Bill" (BB)
Harmon Bellamy, "Marked for Slaughter" (FB)
Sam Carson, "The Three Musketeers" (FB)
Omar Gwinn, "Pigskin Prey" (FB)

Vol. 1, No. 6, February 1939. Stories: 10
Cover: Boxing by H.W. Scott
Walt James, "The Diamond Nitwit" (BB)
Carl Shepherd, "Rah Rah Bonehead" (BB)
Herbert Dalmas, "Smash That Line" (FB)
Curtis Bishop, "The Will to Win" (FB)

Vol. 2, No. 1, April–May 1939. Stories: 10
Cover: Baseball by H.W. Scott
Johnny Lawson, "Baseball and Blue Blood" (BB)
Walt Clark, "Southern Beauty" (BB)

James W. Egan, "Luck o' the Irish" (BB)
Omar Gwinn, "Pro-Ball Pass Master" (FB)
Vol. 2, No. 2, September 1940 (after hiatus). Stories: 9
Cover: Baseball by J.W. Scott
Duane Yarnell, "Diamond Destiny" (BB)
W.H. Temple, "A Batter Is Born" (BB)
Roe Richmond, "Dead-Arm Dynamite" (BB)
Colbert Lewis, "Mound Ghost" (BB)
Herbert McNary, "Hit-and-Run Holiday" (BB)
Vol. 2, No. 3, January 1941. Stories: 9
Cover: Football by J.W. Scott
Duane Yarnell, "Back to the Bushes, Rookie!" (BB)
Harold Rogers, "All-American Cannonball" (FB)
John Murray Reynolds, "The Touchdown Tornado" (FB)
Gene D. Robinson, "Pigskin Steam-Roller" (FB)
Herbert L. McNary, "Rose Bowl or Bust" (FB)
Cosmo Bennett, "Go Out There and Play Football" (FB)
Vol. 2, No. 4, May 1941. Stories: 9
Cover: Baseball by J.W. Scott
Roe Richmond, "Diamond Duel" (BB)
Harold de Polo, "Home-Run Hurricane" (BB)
J.J. Meany, "The Pennant Pirate" (BB)
Johnny Lawson, "Umpire with a Heart" (BB)
Vol. 2, No. 5, July 1941. Stories: 9
Cover: Baseball by J.W. Scott (says five baseball thrillers, but really six)
Roe Richmond, "Strike-Out King or Coward" (BB)
C. Paul Jackson, "One-Man Ball Club" (BB)
Zene Tuttler, "Diamond Dynamite" (BB)
J.J. Meany, "Paste It Out of the Park!" (BB)
Will Keefe, "Five-Inning Fireballer" (BB)
Carl Shephard, "Black-Sheep Moundsman" (BB)
Vol. 2, No. 6, October 1941. Stories: 8
Cover: Football by J.W. Scott
Harold Rogers, "Diamond Demon" (BB)
C. Paul Jackson, "Hot-Corner Hurricane" (BB)
Jackson V. Scholz, "Fighting Fool in the Backfield" (FB)
Ronald Oliphant, "Coward Who Made All-America" (FB)
Johnny Lawson, "Too Many Touchdowns" (FB)
Vol. 3, No. 1, December 1941. Stories: 9
Cover: Football by H.W. Scott
Harrison Hendryx, "Once a Slugger" (BB)
Richard Brister, "Fireball Fury" (BB)
C. Paul Jackson, "The Triple-Threat Terror" (FB)
Zene Tuttler, "Backfield Bomber" (FB)
Theodore J. Roemer, "Touchdowns for Sale" (FB)
Vol. 3, No. 2, February 1942. Stories: 8
Cover: Boxing by H.W. Scott
Johnny Lawson, "Bullpen Pitcher" (BB)
Duane Yarnell, "Behind Ten Pigskin Pile-Drivers!" (FB)
Zene Tuttler, "Touchdown Trouble" (FB)
Harold Rogers, "Broken-Field Butcher" (FB)
Roe Richmond, "Hammer and Smash Don't Make a Halfback!" (FB)
Vol. 3, No. 3, May 1942. Stories: 9
Cover: Baseball by J.W. Scott
W.H. Temple, "Power Hitter" (BB)
Duane Yarnell, "Diamond King Draftee" (BB)
C. Paul Jackson, "Horsehide Hellion" (BB)
Theodore J. Roemer, "The Pigskin Express" (FB)
Vol. 3, No. 4, August 1942. Stories: 6
Cover: Baseball
Duane Yarnell, "Give It a Ride, Rookie!" (BB)
Nelson Hutto, "Army-Bound Fireballer" (BB)
C. Paul Jackson, "When a Busher Goes Big League" (BB)
Vol. 3, No. 5, October 1942. Stories: 6
Cover: Baseball
Duane Yarnell, "Power That Secret Pitch!" (BB)
Jack Tanner, "Extra-Base Barrage" (BB)
Giles A. Lutz, "Second-String Grid King" (FB)
Ron Broom, "Pigskin Powerhouse" (FB)
Vol. 4, No. 1, August 1947 (after hiatus; no Vol. 3, No. 6, issued). Stories: 9
Cover: Baseball
Roe Richmond, "Fielder's Fury" (BB)
E.E. Halleran, "Pitch Like You Fight!" (BB)
John Wilson, "Horsehide Houdini" (BB)
Duane Yarnell, "The Fireballing Fool" (BB)
Giles A. Lutz, Big, "Touch and Smart" (FB)
Vol. 4, No. 2, November 1947. Stories: 8
Cover: Football
Johnny Lawson, "Diamond Fool" (BB)
Roe Richmond, "The Pigskin Pariah" (FB)
Theodore J. Roemer, "Iron-Man Lanyard" (FB)
Sam Carson, "Varsity Vengeance" (FB)
Lee Floren, "Football Crazy" (FB)
Vol. 4, No. 3, March 1948. Stories: 9
Cover: Basketball
Ernest Hamilton, "Line-Smashing Butcher" (FB)
Jerry Tolan, "Spectacular Quarterback" (FB)
Herbert L. McNary, "The Mighty Midget" (FB)
Vol. 4, No. 4, June 1948. Stories: 9
Cover: Baseball
Jack Rogers, "Special Delivery on the Mound" (BB)
Zene Tuttler, "Diamond Guts" (BB)
Kenneth Putnam (William Tenn), "Bean-Ball Boomerang" (BB)
W.H. Temple, "Haywire Hitter" (BB)
Cordner Nelson, "Three Cheers for Clarence" (FB)
Vol. 4, No. 5, December 1948. Stories: 9
Cover: Football
Paul Carney, "Special Delivery" (BB)
Philip St. John (Lester del Rey), "Killer on Cleats" (FB)
Jerry Tolan, "Six Points from Salvation" (FB)
Theodore Roemer, "Pariah of the Gridiron" (FB)
Louis Trimble, "The Guy from Yesterday" (FB)

Totals: 22 issues, 207 stories, 59 baseball stories, 44 football stories.

Sports Leaders

Vol. 1, No. 1, April 1948. Stories: 8
Cover: Boxing
H.C. Butler, "Base Hits Are Big Business" (BB)
James Blish, "Fullback Frankenstein" (FB)
Vol. 1, No. 2, July 1948. Stories: 9
Cover: Baseball
Norman Ober, "Born to the Big Leagues" (BB)
Jack L. Norman, "Bushers Don't Come Back!" (BB)
Clyde A. Richards, "Smoke Ball Hurler" (BB)
Wayne Pool, "Tough Enough, Short Enough!" (BB)
William Heuman, "Butcher in the Backfield" (FB)
Vol. 1, No. 3, October 1948. Stories: 8
Cover: Baseball
Bill Erin, "Powerhouse at the Plate" (BB)
Roe Richmond, "Big Leaguers Are Born" (BB)
Giles A. Lutz, "Catcher Killer" (BB)
Orlando Rigoni, "Touchdown Treachery" (FB)

Sports Short Stories

December 1947. Stories: 10
Cover: Football
Bart Victor, "Sandlot Sensation" (BB)
Jim Jones, "Don't Throw Your Arm Away!" (BB)

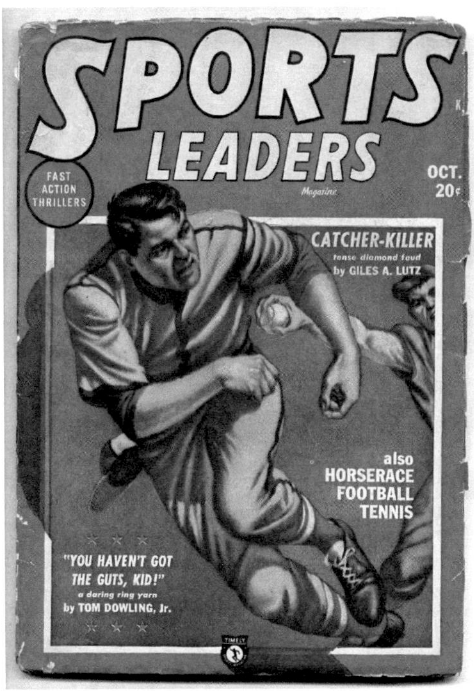

Sports Leaders, October 1948 (copyright 1948 Stadium Publishing Corporation). Here's a rundown play in perspective for this short-lived Marvel title.

Herbert L. McNary, "Born to the Backfield" (FB)
Richard Brister, "Moose on the Loose" (FB)
Tom Storme, "Professor IQ—Quarterback" (FB)
Cosmo Bennett, "Ball-Toting Bulldozer" (FB)
March 1938. Stories: 10
Cover: Baseball by Norman Saunders
Zene Tuttler, "Dean Man on the Mound" (BB)
Richard Brister, "Fourth Down, Four Hundred to Go" (FB)
Henry Bela Bachrach, "Backfield Badman" (FB)
July 1948. Stories: 10
Cover: Boxing
Bill Heuman, "Gashouse Galahad" (BB)
Theodore Roemer, "The Kid Who Owned a Ball Team" (BB)
John Van Praag (Scott Meredith), "The Magic Bat" (BB)
Gene D. Robinson, "The Everlasting Scrub" (FB)
Ted Stratton, "Paydirt Payoff" (FB)
November 1948. Stories: 10
Cover: Baseball
Bill Erin, "Steal Home, Slugger!" (BB)
John Wilson, "Home Run Fever" (BB)
Richard Brister, "Eight Men—and Trouble!" (BB)
Louis Trimble, "Backfield Braintruster" (FB)
Jerry Tolan, "The Rambling Wreckers" (FB)

Totals for Sports Leaders and Sports Short Stories: 7 issues, 65 stories, 17 baseball stories, 13 football stories.

Star Sports Magazine

Vol. 1, No. 1, October 1936. Stories: 9
Cover: Boxing by J.W. Scott
William Edward Hayes, "Take Him Out!" (BB)
Murray Hoyt, "All-Star Sissy" (BB)
Ted Collier, "Gift Horsehide" (BB)
Vol. 1, No. 2, December 1936. Stories: 10
Cover: Football by H.W. Scott
Samuel Taylor, "The Kid Comes Back" (BB)
Charles Woodford, "Special Delivery" (BB)
John Carlisle, "Death Strikes the Gridiron" (BB)
James Hall, "Crack That Line" (FB)
Vol. 1, No. 3, February 1937. Stories: 10
Cover: Boxing by J.W. Scott
Randolph Preston, "Sleepy Slams Them" (BB)
Samuel Taylor, "Perfect Pete" (FB)
Vol. 1, No. 4, April 1937. Stories: 10
Cover: Wrestling
Charlie Lewis, "No. One Pitcher" (BB)
Jonesy Taylor, "Diamond Feud" (BB)
Vol. 1, No. 5, July 1937. Stories: 10
Cover: Baseball by H.W. Scott
William Edward Hayes, "Ball Hawk" (BB)
Ross Kenton, "Keeper of the Pennant" (BB)
Charlie Lewis, "Perfect Game" (BB)
Miller Borden, "Wise Guy" (BB)
Jonesy Taylor, "Bushers Not Allowed" (BB)

A.L. Thurman (Arthur Mann), "Inspiration Pitcher" (BB)
Johnny Lawson, "Play It Safe"
Vol. 1, No. 6, October 1937. Stories: 10
Cover: Baseball by H.W. Scott
William Edward Hayes, "A Glove and a Prayer" (BB)
Jerry Tolan, "Bean Ball Buster" (BB)
Rex Evans, "The Pennant Kid" (BB)
Jonesy Taylor, "Hot Corner Grouch" (BB)
James Lassiter, "Pitchers' Duel" (BB)
Johnny Lawson, "Gridiron Ghost" (FB)
Vol. 2, No. 1, January 1938. Stories: 10
Cover: Football by J.W. Scott
Hal Lee, "The Pennant Homer" (BB)
T.K. Hawley, "Triple Action" (BB)
Ross Kenton, "Pigskin Powerhouse" (FB)
Walt Clark, "Johnny One-Point" (FB)
Johnny Lawson, "The Quarterback" (FB)
Jay Gregg, "Between Halves" (FB)
Vol. 2, No. 2, April 1938. Stories: 10
Cover: Basketball
Robert S. Bowen, "Lightning at Second" (BB)
Jerry Tolan, "Behind the Plate" (BB)
Harry Butman, "Brothers Under the Pigskin" (FB)
Vol. 2, No. 3, July 1938. Stories: 9
Cover: Baseball by J.W. Scott
Jonathan Brooks (Lowell Mellett), "Diamond Cut Diamond" (BB)
Hal Lee, "Baseball Brain" (BB)
Johnny Lawson, "Nor So Dumb" (BB)
T.K. Hawley, "A Pitcher Named Smith" (BB)
C. Paul Jackson, "Pigskin Phantom" (FB)
Vol. 2, No. 4, November 1938. Stories: 11
Cover: Football by J.W. Scott
T.K. Hawley, "Diamond Dictator" (BB)
Clint Warren, "The Screwball Slinger" (BB)
Johnny Lawson, "Mind Over Batter" (BB)
Hal Lee, "High, Wide and Handsome" (BB)
Jonesy Taylor, "Flying Cleats" (FB)
James W. Egan, "Iron Man Maple" (FB)

Totals: 10 issues, 99 stories, 31 baseball stories, 13 football stories.

Marvel/Red Circle totals: 143 issues, 1,289 stories, 398 baseball stories, 216 football stories.

Popular Publications

Dime Sports

Vol. 1, No. 1, July 1935. Stories: 8
Cover: Baseball by Hubert Rogers
Glenn Long, "The Emperor of Errors" (BB)
William Chamberlain, "Big League Showman" (BB)
Vol. 1, No. 2, August 1935. Stories: 7
Cover: Swimming
Glenn Long, "Two Strikes on Big Bo" (BB)
Bill Dexter, "Poison for Southpaws" (BB)
Vol. 1, No. 3, September 1935. Stories: 7
Cover: Baseball
Alden H. Norton, "The Busher from Broken Twig" (BB)
Henry A. Sutherland, "The Boomerang Ball" (BB)
Vol. 1, No. 4, October 1935. Stories: 8
Cover: Football
Palmer Hoyt, "The Bloomer Battery" (BB)
Glenn Long, "Kicker's Courage" (FB)
Harry Shaftel, "The Brother Act" (FB)
Vol. 1, No. 5, November 1935. Stories: 6
Cover: Football
Moran Tudury, "The Great Garrity" (FB)
Jack Kofoed, "The Outside" (FB)
Ramon Kennicott, "Blocking Back" (FB)
Vol. 1, No. 6, December 1935. Stories: 7
Cover: Football
Moran Tudury, "Glory Road" (FB)
Townsend Evans, "The Bigger They Come" (FB)
Vol. 2, No. 1, January 1936. Stories: 7
Cover: Hockey
Clarence Dicks, "The Grand Old Man" (FB)
Vol. 2, No. 2, February 1936. Stories: 6
Cover: Basketball
Vol. 2, No. 3, March 1936. Stories: 7
Cover: Boxing
J.J. Meany, "The Patent Medicine Kid" (BB)
Vol. 2, No. 4, April 1936. Stories: 6
Cover: Baseball
Judson P. Philips, "Grapefruit League Feud" (BB)
Vol. 2, No. 5, May 1936. Stories: 6
Cover: Baseball
Judson P. Philips, "He Could Take It!" (BB)
Alden H. Norton, "Battery Trouble" (BB)
Vol. 2, No. 6, June 1936. Stories: 7
Cover: Baseball
Ernie Phillips, "Crab Clawson" (BB)
Arthur G. Kenney, "Two Errors at Second" (BB)
Vol. 3, No. 1, July 1936. Stories: 6
Cover: Track
Judson P. Phillips, "The Five-Dollar Wonder" (BB)
Vol. 3, No. 2, August 1936. Stories: 7
Cover: Baseball
O.B. Myers, "Fly Paper Sticks" (BB)
Ron Broom, "Supercharger" (FB)
Vol. 3, No. 3, September 1936. Stories: 6
Cover: Baseball
Judson P. Philips, "Pinch Rooter" (BB)
Vol. 3, No. 4, October 1936. Stories: 6
Cover: Football
Judson P. Philips, "Old Rubber Arm" (BB)
Ben Peter Freeman, "The Pigskin Puzzle" (FB)
Vol. 3, No. 5, November 1936. Stories: 7
Cover: Football
Arthur Mann, "Umpires Are Poison" (BB)
Judson P. Philips, "Touchdown!" (FB)
David Crewe, "A Day for Camden" (FB)
O.B. Myers, "Gold Bowl or Bust" (FB)
Vol. 3, No. 6, December 1936. Stories: 7
Cover: Football
Judson P. Philips, "Goal to Go!" (FB)
Bob DeHaven, "Halfback Heritage" (FB)

Vol. 4, No. 1, January 1937. Stories: 6
Cover: Hockey
Judson P. Philips, "All-American's Shoes" (FB)
Moran Tudury, "Triple Threat" (FB)
Vol. 4, No. 2, February 1937. Stories: 6
Cover: Basketball
Arthur Mann, "Hold 'Em, Line!" (FB)
Vol. 4, No. 3, March 1937. Stories: 5
Cover: Boxing
Vol. 4, No. 4, April 1937. Stories: 6
Cover: Baseball
Judson P. Phillips, "Ball Hawk" (BB)
Vol. 4, No. 5, May 1937. Stories: 5
Cover: Baseball
Judson P. Philips, "Star Tamer" (BB)
William Jerome, "It's a Tough League" (BB)
Vol. 4, No. 6, June 1937. Stories: 6
Cover: Baseball
Judson P. Philips, "The Clean-Up Spot" (BB)
William O'Sullivan, "Hot Corner" (BB)
Vol. 5, No. 1, July 1937. Stories: 7
Cover: Baseball
William R. Cox, "Holler Guy" (BB)
Vol. 5, No. 2, August 1937. Stories: 5
Cover: Track
Judson P. Philips, "After the Big Guy" (BB)
A.R. Thurman (Arthur Mann), "Spot Pitcher" (BB)
Vol. 5, No. 3, September 1937. Stories: 5
Cover: Baseball
Lewis Y. Hagy, "Mound Master" (BB)
William R. Cox, "Bric-a-Brac Guy" (FB)
Vol. 5, No. 4, October 1937. Stories: 7
Cover: Football
Judson P. Philips, "Three on the Sacks" (BB)
William O'Sullivan, "Grandstander" (FB)
Clark Boley, "Saturday's Sub" (FB)
Vol. 5, No. 5, November 1937. Stories: 7
Cover: Football
William R. Cox, "Big League Brain" (BB)
Judson P. Philips, "The Phantom of Coffin Corner" (FB)
Nelson S. Bond, "Balloon Head" (FB)
Vol. 5, No. 6, December 1937. Stories: 6
Cover: Football
Judson P. Philips, "Army's Ball!" (FB)
William R. Cox, "The Climax Kid" (FB)
Vol. 6, No. 1, January 1938. Stories: 6
Cover: Hockey
David Crewe, "Touchdown Fever" (FB)
Vol. 6, No. 2, February 1938. Stories: 7
Cover: Basketball
William R. Cox, "The Lame-Brain Kid" (BB)
C. Paul Jackson, "Rose Bowl Rebel" (FB)
William Hartley, "Thrill Merchant" (FB)
Vol. 6, No. 3, March 1938. Stories: 6
Cover: Boxing
Ben Peter Freeman, "Big Rube" (BB)
William R. Cox, "Little Poison" (FB)
Vol. 6, No. 4, April 1938. Stories: 7
Cover: Baseball
William R. Cox, "Dynamite on the Sacks" (BB)
Judson P. Philips, "The Nothing Ball" (BB)
Vol. 6, No. 5, May 1938. Stories: 6
Cover: Baseball
Judson P. Philips, "Million Dollar Arm" (BB)
William R. Cox, "Big Shot" (BB)
Vol. 6, No. 6, June 1938. Stories: 7
Cover: Baseball
Judson P. Philips, "Million Dollar Arm" (BB)
W.H. Temple, "You Gotta Stretch" (BB)
Vol. 7, No. 1, August 1938. Stories: 7
Cover: Track
Judson P. Philips, "Sandlotter" (BB)
William R. Cox, "Dugout Clown" (BB)
W.H. Temple, "Swap Trouble" (BB)
Nelson S. Bond, "Touchdown Medicine" (FB)
Vol. 7, No. 2, October–November 1938. Stories: 7
Cover: Baseball
Judson P. Philips, "Pennant Trouble" (BB)
W.H. Temple, "Place Hitter" (BB)
William R. Cox, "College Try" (FB)
Vol. 7, No. 3, December 1939–January 1940. Stories: 6
Cover: Football
William R. Cox, "The Powerhouse Battery" (BB)
Clark Boley, "Line Crusher" (FB)
Vol. 7, No. 4, February–March 1939. Stories: 6
Cover: Basketball
William O'Sullivan, "Play for Home" (BB)
William R. Cox, "Sixty Minute Thunderbolt" (FB)
Roger G. Spellman (William R. Cox), "Punt, Pass and Pray" (FB)
Vol. 7, No. 5, April–May 1939. Stories: 7
Cover: Baseball
William R. Cox, "Fence Buster" (BB)
David Crewe, "Bushers Fight Hardest" (BB)
Vol. 7, No. 6, June–July 1939. Stories: 6
Cover: Baseball
William R. Cox, "Clutch Chucker" (BB)
David Crewe, "Holler Guy" (BB)
Vol. 8, No. 1, August–September 1939. Stories: 7
Cover: Baseball
William R. Cox, "World Series Blues" (BB)
W.H. Temple, "Cannonball Kid" (BB)
Robert Sidney Bowen, "Son of the Mound" (BB)
Roger G. Spellman (William R. Cox), "Glory Spot" (FB)
Vol. 8, No. 2, October 1939. Stories: 7
Cover: Football
William R. Cox, "The Bombers Are Coming" (BB)
W.H. Temple, "Half-Pint Halfback" (FB)
Roger G. Spellman (William R. Cox), "Pigskin Payoff" (FB)
Vol. 8, No. 3, November 1939. Stories: 6
Cover: Football
Roger G. Spellman (William R. Cox), "Money on the Sacks" (BB)
William R. Cox, "The Team from Coffin Corner" (FB)
Moran Tudury, "Rose Bowl Goat" (BB)
Vol. 8, No. 4, December 1939. Stories: 6
Cover: Football

David Crewe, "Relief Chucker" (BB)
Joe Archibald, "Sandlot Dynamite" (BB)
William R. Cox, "The One-Way Kid" (FB)
William Hartley, "You Gotta Be Tough" (FB)
Vol. 8, No. 5, January 1940. Stories: 7
Cover: Football
Roger G. Spellman (William R. Cox) (BB)
William Hartley, "The Bloody Yards" (FB)
David Goodis, "Knock 'Em Down Guy" (FB)
Vol. 8, No. 6, February 1940. Stories: 6
Cover: Basketball
David Crewe, "Pennant Trouble" (BB)
William Heuman, "Punt, Pass and Pray" (FB)
Moran Tudury, "Rose Bowl Outcast" (FB)
Vol. 9, No. 1, March 1940. Stories: 6
Cover: Boxing
David Crewe, "A Run for the Mick" (BB)
William Hartley, "Pass Crazy" (FB)
Vol. 9, No. 2, April 1940. Stories: 7
Cover: Baseball
William R. Cox, "Base Hits for Baby" (BB)
William O'Sullivan, "The Heel" (BB)
Sam Carson, "Pop-Off Cast-Off" (BB)
Vol. 9, No. 3, May 1940. Stories: 7
Cover: Baseball
William R. Cox, "Hit 'Em Where They Ain't" (BB)
W.H. Temple, "Outfield Outcast" (BB)
Vol. 9, No. 4, June 1940. Stories: 7
Cover: Baseball
Roger G. Spellman (William R. Cox), "The Glass Arm Kid" (BB)
Vol. 9, No. 5, July 1940. Stories: 7
Cover: Baseball
William R. Cox, "Storm Over Third Base" (BB)
David Crewe (William R. Cox using house name), "Double-Header Blues" (BB)
Vol. 9, No. 6, August 1940. Stories: 7
Cover: Baseball
Norman L. Paul, "Jinx Buster" (BB)
Daniel Winters, "Keystone Kid" (BB)
Vol. 10, No. 1, September 1940. Stories: 7
Cover: Baseball
Jackson V. Scholz (ghosted by William R. Cox), "Diamond Doctor" (BB)
William R. Cox, "The Kid from Touchdown Street" (FB)
Moran Tudury, "Million Dollar Quarterback" (FB)
Vol. 10, No. 2, October 1940. Stories: 6
Cover: Football
Robert S. Bowen, "Ball Shy" (BB)
Daniel Winters, "Six Points for Patsy" (FB)
Burgess Leonard, "Breakaway Kid (Enemy's Ball on cover)" (FB)
Moran Tudury, "Line of Battle" (FB)
Vol. 10, No. 3, November 1940. Stories: 5
Cover: Football
Daniel Winters, "The Glass-Arm Kid" (BB)
David Crewe, "Texas Leaguer" (BB)
David Goodis, "Lug That Leather!" (FB)
Vol. 10, No. 4, December 1940. Stories: 6
Cover: Football
William R. Cox, "A Spot for a Slugger" (BB)
James W. Egan, "Old Picklepaw" (BB)
Norman Paul, "Rose Bowl Road" (FB)
Clark Bodey, "Line Wrecker" (FB)
Vol. 10, No. 5, January 1941. Stories: 7
Cover: Basketball
Holmes Alexander, "Bear Down, Busher!" (BB)
William R. Cox, "Steamroller Kid" (FB)
Walton M. Smith, "Old College Try" (FB)
Vol. 10, No. 6, February 1941. Stories: 6
Cover: Boxing
Robert Sidney Bowen, "Poison to Rookies" (BB)
William R. Cox, "Goal to Go!" (FB)
John Bender, "Strictly for Suckers" (FB)
Vol. 11, No. 1, March 1941. Stories: 7
Cover: Baseball
David Crewe, "Half-Pint Holler Guy" (BB)
Robert Sidney Bowen, "Sacrifice at Second" (BB)
Nelson A. Hutto, "Suicide Spot" (FB)
Vol. 11, No. 2, April 1941. Stories: 7
Cover: Baseball
Daniel Winters, "Get Me a Slugger!" (BB)
Ward Redfield, Jr., "The Man Behind the Mask" (BB)
Vol. 11, No. 3, June 1941. Stories: 8
Cover: Baseball
William R. Cox, "The Wrong-Way Kid" (BB)
William Heuman, "Alibi Al" (BB)
W.H. Temple, "Utility Man" (BB)
Vol. 11, No. 4, August 1941. Stories: 7
Cover: Baseball
W.H. Temple, "Cellar Champions" (BB)
Daniel Winters, "Pivot Spot Blues" (BB)
Vol. 11, No. 5, October 1941. Stories: 5
Cover: Football
David Crewe, "Glass Arm Kid" (BB)
W.H. Temple, "Trouble at Second" (BB)
Daniel Winters, "The Last, Long Yard" (FB)
Vol. 11, No. 6, December 1941. Stories: 6
Cover: Football
Jack Tanner, "Spikes Up!" (BB)
Norman L. Paul, "Get Those Goals!" (FB)
Vol. 12, No. 1, February 1942. Stories: 6
Cover: Basketball
W.H. Temple, "Price Tag Rookie" (BB)
Burgess Leonard, "Football, Farewell" (FB)
Vol. 12, No. 2, April 1942. Stories: 7
Cover: Baseball
David Crewe, "The Powerhouse Kid Comes Home" (BB)
William R. Cox, "Slow Bunt to Third" (BB)
Ray P. Shotwell, "Keystone Hitters" (BB)
William Campbell Gault, "Suicide Schedule" (FB)
Vol. 12, No. 3, June 1942. Stories: 7
Cover: Baseball
James B. Hendryx, "Go Down Swinging, Bums!" (BB)
Ray P. Shotwell, "Relief Chucker" (BB)
Vol. 12, No. 4, August 1942. Stories: 7
Cover: Baseball
Norman L. Paul, "The Heart of a Busher" (BB)
A.R. Thurman (Arthur Mann), "Another Feller" (BB)

Ray P. Shotwell, "He Runs Alone" (FB)
William Heuman, "The Duke Comes Home" (FB)
Vol. 12, No. 5, October 1942. Stories: 6
Cover: Football
David Crewe, "Busher at Shortstop" (BB)
Daniel Winters, "You Gotta Get Hits!" (BB)
William R. Cox, "Special Delivery Kid" (FB)
Vol. 12, No. 6, December 1942. Stories: 7
Cover: Football
David Crewe, "A Letter for Boom-Boom" (BB)
William Heuman, "The Hot Spot" (BB)
Burgess Leonard, "Pull Out and Block, Bums!" (FB)
Norman L. Paul, "Tell It to the Marines" (FB)
Vol. 13, No. 1, February 1943. Stories: 5
Cover: Basketball
Daniel Winters, "Throw 'Em with Your Heart" (BB)
David Crewe, "Holler Guy" (BB)
Vol. 13, No. 2, April 1943. Stories: 6
Cover: Baseball
William Heuman, "Three on the Sacks" (BB)
Norman L. Paul, "The American Way" (FB)
Vol. 13, No. 3, June 1943. Stories: 6
Cover: Baseball
William R. Cox, "Slug One for the Navy!" (BB)
David Crewe, "Trouble at Short" (BB)
Vol. 13, No. 4, August 1943. Stories: 7
Cover: Baseball
Theodore Roemer, "The Four for Four Kid" (BB)
Ray P. Shotwell, "Relief Chucker" (BB)
Lance Kermit, "Touchdown Tornado" (FB)
Vol. 13, No. 5, October 1943. Stories: 5
Cover: Football by Sam Cherry
Ray P. Shotwell, "Bear Down, Busher!" (BB)
W.H. Temple, "Eleven Men and a Prayer" (FB)
Vol. 13, No. 6, December 1943. Stories: 7
Cover: Football by Sam Cherry
David Crewe, "Ball Hawk" (BB)
Theodore J. Roemer, "Flying Quarter" (FB)
Vol. 14, No. 1, February 1944. Stories: 8
Cover: Basketball by Sam Cherry
Daniel Winters, "Bushers Don't Win" (BB)
David Crewe, "Breakaway Guy" (FB)
Vol. 14, No. 2, April 1944. Stories: 7
Cover: Baseball by Sam Cherry
Roy C. Rainey, "The Way of the Mighty" (BB)
David Crewe, "Keep on Swinging" (BB)
Ray P. Shotwell, "Series Goat" (BB)
Ben Peter Freeman, "Pigskin Powerhouse" (FB)
Vol. 14, No. 3, June 1944. Stories: 7
Cover: Baseball by Sam Cherry
William Heuman, "Boy Wonder" (BB)
Roy C. Rainey, "The Last Trojan" (BB)
David Crewe, "Bric-a-Brac Kid" (FB)

NOTE: Many covers by Charles De Feo

Totals: 81 issues, 523 stories, 120 baseball stories, 75 football stories.

Fifteen Sports Stories

Vol. 1, No. 1, February 1948. Stories: 12
Cover: Boxing
Judson Philips, "Mow the Guy Down!" (BB)
Nelson Hutto, "Hit the Dirt, Busher!" (BB)
David Crewe, "Spike Shy" (BB)
Theodore J. Roemer, "Fight, Scrub, Fight!" (FB)
Vol. 1, No. 2, March 1948. Stories: 11
Cover: Baseball
Ray P. Shotwell, "Bench Warmer" (BB)
Nelson Hutto, "Belt One, Busher!" (BB)
Roy Hilligoss, "Scatterball Kid" (BB)
David Crewe, "Slide, Alfred, Slide!" (BB)
W.H. Temple, "Pro Ball Palooka" (FB)
Vol. 1, No. 3, April 1948. Stories: 10
Cover: Baseball
Judson Philips, "Win or Else Guy" (BB)
Zene Tuttler, "Rowdy" (BB)
Vol. 1, No. 4, May 1948. Stories: 10
Cover: Boxer
Judson Philips, "Hot on Spikes" (BB)
Zene Tuttler, "Chatter Guy" (BB)
David Crewe, "Star Bust" (BB)
Vol. 2, No. 1, June 1948. Stories: 9
Cover: Baseball
William Heuman, "Mr. Shortstop" (BB)
Nelson Hutto, "Rookie from Nowhere" (BB)
Robert Shankland, "The Reluctant Southpaw" (BB)
Vol. 2, No. 2, July 1948. Stories: 10
Cover: Baseball
Theodore J. Roemer, "Mow 'Em Down Kid" (BB)
W.H. Temple, "The Busher from Hell's Acres" (BB)
Way C. Lee, "Hot Corner Jitters" (BB)
Vol. 2, No. 3, August 1948. Stories: 9
Cover: Boxing
William R. Cox, "Slug Away Kid" (BB)
William Heuman, "Thunder Over Third" (BB)
Vol. 2, No. 4, September 1948. Stories: 11
Cover: Baseball
Judson P. Philips, "Scrapiron Kid" (BB)
William R. Cox, "Hitter Jitters" (BB)
William Jerome, "Once Upon a Nine" (BB)
Jimmie Jamieson, "Once a Busher" (BB)
Roy C. Rainey, "Crazy Cleats" (BB)
Vol. 3, No. 1, October 1948. Stories: 9
William Heuman, "No Hits, No Runs, No Terrors" (BB)
Zene Tuttler, "Big Meet Cyclone" (BB)
Ted Stratton, "Plunder Guy" (FB)
Vol. 3, No. 2, November 1948. Stories: 10
Cover: Boxing
William Heuman, "Rubber Wing" (BB)
Roney Scott (William Campbell Gault), "Touchdown Tornado" (FB)
Vol. 3, No. 3, January 1949. Stories: 9
Cover: Basketball
T.W. Blood, "One Pitch for Blood" (BB)
John D. MacDonald, "Take the Bum Out!" (BB)
Judson Philips, "Goal or Bust Guy" (FB)
Daniel Winters, "Bustaway Cleats" (FB)

Vol. 3, No. 4, March 1949. Stories: 10
Cover: Basketball
Judson P. Philips, "No Quarter Kid" (FB)
Daniel Winters, "Glory Passer" (FB)
Vol. 4, No. 1, May 1949. Stories: 12
Cover: Baseball
William Heuman, "No Man's Sacks" (BB)
Ray P. Shotwell, "Hell on the Hill" (BB)
William R. Cox, "Glory Runner" (FB)
Vol. 4, No. 2, July 1949. Stories: 11
Cover: Baseball
William R. Cox, "Way of the Mighty" (BB)
Bill Erin, "Four-for-Four Guy" (BB)
W.H. Temple, "Wrong Way Rookie" (BB)
Nelson Hutto, "Suicide Chucker" (BB)
John Wade Farrell (John D. MacDonald), "Bye, Bye, Backfield" (FB)
Vol. 4, No. 3, September 1949. Stories: 10
Cover: Baseball
Daniel Winters, "Belt It Out, Busher!" (BB)
William Heuman, "Outlaw Arm" (BB)
William R. Cox, "Ride 'Em Down, Rookie!" (BB)
John D. MacDonald, "Six Points to Remember" (FB)
Reynolds Phillips, "T-and-T Back" (FB)
Vol. 4, No. 4, November 1949. Stories: 9
Cover: Football
Lance Kermit, "Say It with Spikes" (BB)
William Heuman, "Wrong-Way Back" (FB)
John D. MacDonald, "Run the Man Down" (FB)
Vol. 5, No. 1, January 1950. Stories: 10
Cover: Basketball
Lance Kermit, "Trouble Play" (BB)
William Campbell Gault, "White Line Raider" (FB)
David Crewe, "Six-Point Heart" (FB)
William R. Cox, "Last Yard Guy" (FB)
Vol. 5, No. 2, March 1950. Stories: 9
Cover: Track
David Crewe, "Mister Four-for-Four" (BB)
William Campbell Gault, "Calamity Back" (FB)
Vol. 5, No. 3, May 1950. Stories: 10
Cover: Baseball
William Heuman, "Keystone Spoiler" (BB)
William R. Cox, "Get Two Guy" (BB)
Lance Kermit, "The Last Big Six" (FB)
Vol. 5, No. 4, July 1950. Stories: 9
Cover: Baseball
Judson Philips, "Belt One, Rook!" (BB)
Edward Carlson, "The Big Hit" (BB)
Johanas L. Bouma, "One More Hill" (BB)
Vol. 6, No. 1, September 1950. Stories: 10
Cover: Baseball
Judson Philips, "Rookie Wrecker" (BB)
Van McNair, Jr., "Heartbreak Hill" (BB)
Jackson V. Scholz, "Grandstander" (BB)
David Crewe, "Glass Arm Kid" (BB)
William Campbell Gault, "Tinsel Tailback" (FB)
Vol. 6, No. 2, November 1950. Stories: 9
William Heuman, "Two-Away Terror" (BB)
Bob Reed, "White Line Wrecker" (FB)
Vol. 6, No. 3, January 1951. Stories: 9
Cover: Football
Nelson Hutto, "Poison on the Mound" (BB)
Bob Reed, "Scatter Back" (FB)
Roy C. Rainey, "Six Point Pirate" (FB)
Vol. 6, No. 4, April 1951. Stories: 10
Cover: Track
Daniel Winters, "Second Chance Chucker" (BB)
David Crewe (William R. Cox using house name), "The Last Out" (BB)
William Hartley, "Thrill Merchant" (FB)
Vol. 7, No. 1, June 1951. Stories: 9
Cover: Baseball
William Hartley, "Sunday Pitcher" (BB)
Daniel Winters, "Catch Hell, Rook!" (BB)
William R. Cox, "The Thunder Yard" (FB)
Vol. 7, No. 2, August 1951. Stories: 11
Cover: Baseball
Daniel Winters, "Clutch Guy!" (BB)
David Crewe, "Trouble at Third" (BB)
Bob Reed, "Spikes Over Short" (BB)
Van McNair, Jr., "Murder at Bat" (BB)
Lance Kermit, "The Big Six" (FB)
Vol. 7, No. 3, October 1951. Stories: 10
Daniel Winters, "The Big Mouth Kid" (BB)
David Crewe, "Infield Outlaw" (BB)
William Heuman, "Calamity Spikes" (BB)
T.W. Ford, "All-or-Nothing Back" (FB)
Vol. 7, No. 4, December 1951. Stories: 9
Cover: Boxing
Daniel Winters, "The Big Bad Bruins" (BB)
David Crewe, "Touchdown Fever" (FB)
Johanas L. Bouma, "That Long "Last Down" (FB)
Vol. 8, No. 1, February 1952. Stories: 10
Cover: Basketball
William R. Cox, "Spikes Over Short" (BB)
John Wilson, "Big Out" (BB)
Daniel Winters, "Sixty Minute Guy" (FB)
Vol. 8, No. 2, April 1952. Stories: 9
Cover: Baseball
William Heuman, "Two-or-Nothing Kid" (BB)
William R. Cox, "Nobody's Nine" (BB)

NOTE: Some stories are reprints, under the same or different titles.

Totals: 30 issues, 296 stories, 69 baseball stories, 32 football stories.

New Sports

Vol. 1, No. 1, January 1947. Stories: 8
Cover: Boxing
William R. Cox, "The Dipsy-Do Kid" (BB)
David Crewe, "Blitz Around Second" (BB)
Roy C. Rainey, "Ghost of the White Lines" (FB)
Ted Stratton, "Fade-Out" (FB)
Vol. 1, No. 2, March 1947. Stories: 8
Cover: Boxing
Roy C. Rainey, "Siege Gun" (BB)
Daniel Winters, "Lift One for Lew!" (BB)
W.H. Temple, "Pigskin Prima Donnas" (FB)
David Crewe, "Holler Guy" (FB)
Vol. 1, No. 3, May 1947. Stories: 7
Cover: Baseball

Daniel Winters, "Second Base Blues" (BB)
Nelson Hutto, "Once a Busher" (BB)
William R. Cox, "Punt, Pass—and Pray" (FB)

Vol. 1, No. 4, July 1947. Stories: 7
Cover: Baseball
William Heuman, "Gashouse Guy" (BB)
Ray P. Shotwell, "Hell on Spikes" (BB)
Roy C. Rainey, "Jumping Joe from Idaho" (FB)

Vol. 2, No. 1, September 1947. Stories: 6
Cover: Baseball
William Heuman, "Four-Four-Four Guy" (BB)
Theodore J. Roemer, "Dugout Danny" (BB)
Curtis Bishop, "The Pass-Happy Kid" (FB)

Vol. 2, No. 2, November 1947. Stories: 8
Cover: Football
Roy C. Rainey, "Sudden Death Kid" (BB)
W.H. Temple, "Suicide at Second" (BB)
Daniel Winters, "The Touchdown Kid" (FB)

Vol. 2, No. 3, December 1947. Stories: 8
Cover: Football
Roy C. Rainey, "The Tarrytown Terror" (BB)
Theodore J. Roemer, "A Pitch for Your Money" (BB)
William Heuman, "Glory Road" (FB)
Richard Brister, "Breakaway Guy" (FB)
Ted Stratton, "White Line Raider" (FB)

Vol. 2, No. 4, January 1948. Stories: 9
Cover: Football by Norman Saunders
William Heuman, "Junk Ball Chucker" (BB)
Lance Kermit, "Right Left Arm" (BB)
T.W. Ford, "Larceny Guy" (BB)
Nelson Hutto, "Bench the Bum!" (BB)
William R. Cox, "Razzle-Dazzle Kid" (FB)

Vol. 3, No. 1, February 1948. Stories: 6
Cover: Basketball
William Heuman, "The Busher" (BB)
Roy C. Rainey, "Crazy Legs" (FB)

Vol. 3, No. 2, March 1948. Stories: 7
Cover: Boxing
David Crewe, "Series Goat" (BB)
Ray P. Shotwell, "Spikes Over Second" (BB)

Vol. 3, No. 3, April 1948. Stories: 6
Cover: Baseball
Nelson Hutto, "High, Hard and Dynamite!" (BB)
Daniel Winters, "You Pay for Your Dollar" (FB)

Vol. 3, No. 4, May 1948. Stories: 6
Cover: Baseball
Ted Stratton, "Fancy Dan the Cleanup Man" (BB)
William Heuman, "Big League Busher" (BB)

Vol. 4, No. 1, June 1948. Stories: 7
Cover: Baseball
Bill Erin, "Slug One for Rocky!" (BB)
William Heuman, "Pay-Off Chucker" (BB)

Vol. 4, No. 2, July 1948. Stories: 7
Cover: Track
Roe Richmond, "Knock 'Em Down Kid" (BB)
William Heuman, "Belt One, Busher!" (BB)
Burgess Leonard, "The Big Shoes" (FB)

Vol. 4, No. 3, August 1948. Stories: 7
Cover: Baseball
William Heuman, "Three and Two Guy" (BB)
Lance Kermit, "Groove One for Lefty!" (BB)
John Wells, "Tough Time Kid" (FB)

Vol. 4, No. 4, September 1948. Stories: 7
Cover: Baseball by Norman Saunders
Nelson Hutto, "Death on the Sacks" (BB)
Daniel Winters, "Glass Arm Groove Baller" (BB)
Reynolds Phillips, "Rough on Rookies" (BB)
John Wells, "Goal-Line Tornado" (FB)

Vol. 5, No. 1, October 1948. Stories: 7
Cover: Football
Daniel Winters, "Double Kill Guy" (BB)
William R. Cox, "Thunder Over Second" (BB)
William Heuman, "The Kid from Coffin Corner" (FB)

Vol. 5, No. 2, November 1948. Stories: 7
Cover: Football
Theodore J. Roemer, "Hellcatcher" (BB)
William R. Cox, "Belt One, Busher!" (BB)
Les Etter, "Goal Crazy" (FB)

Vol. 5, No. 3, December 1948. Stories: 6
Cover: Football
Daniel Winters, "Dust 'Em, Busher!" (BB)
William Heuman, "Sock, Block—and Pray!" (FB)
Ted Stratton, "Goal Line Raider" (FB)

Vol. 5, No. 4, February 1949. Stories: 6
Cover: Boxing
Bob Reed, "Double or Nothing Guy" (BB)
John D. MacDonald, "Fight, Scrub, Fight!" (FB)

Vol. 6, No. 1, April 1949. Stories: 7
Cover: Baseball
(No baseball stories, despite the cover theme)
Nelson A. Hutto, "Cleats of the Mighty" (FB)

Vol. 6, No. 2, June 1949. Stories: 8
Cover: Baseball
Reynolds Phillips, "Run Wrecker" (BB)
William R. Cox, "Hit-and-Hurry Guy" (BB)
Roy Lopez, "Wrong Way Ace" (BB)

Vol. 6, No. 3, August 1949. Stories: 8
Cover: Baseball
Daniel Winters, "Drag 'Em Down Kid" (BB)
W.H. Temple, "Catch Hell, Rookie!" (BB)
Guy Guilford, "Eleven Unbreakables" (FB)

Vol. 6, No. 4, October 1949. Stories: 7
Cover: Baseball
Daniel Winters, "Hit-Away Kid" (BB)
William R. Cox, "Second-Chance Nine" (BB)
Reynolds Phillips, "Fight, Scrub, Fight!" (FB)

Vol. 7, No. 1, December 1949. Stories: 6
Cover: Football
John Wilson, "Last Chance Sacks" (BB)
Ted Stratton, "No Quarter Dynamite" (FB)
William R. Cox, "Razzle-Dazzle Kid" (FB) (different from January 1948)
Nelson Hutto, "Halfway Back" (FB)

Vol. 7, No. 2, February 1950. Stories: 7
Cover: Basketball
Lance Kermit, "Money Pitch" (BB)
Theodore J. Roemer, "Suicide Back" (FB)

Vol. 7, No. 3, April 1950. Stories: 7
Cover: Baseball
Russell Gray (Bruno Fischer), "Suicide Spikes" (BB)
Van McNair, Jr., "The Big Fix" (FB)

Vol. 7, No. 4, June 1950. Stories: 9
Cover: Baseball

William Heuman, "Catch Hell, Busher!" (BB)
William R. Cox, "Run Wrecker" (BB)
Bill Erin, "Spikes of the Mighty" (BB)
David Crewe, "Razzle-Dazzle Guy" (FB)
Vol. 8, No. 1, August 1950. Stories: 10
Cover: Baseball
William R. Cox, "Win or Else, Guy" (BB)
Sam Merwin, Jr., "Hoodoo Spikes" (BB)
David Crewe, "The Master Mind" (BB)
Johanas L. Bouma, "The Long Yard" (FB)
Vol. 8, No. 2, October 1950. Stories: 7
Cover: Baseball
Burgess Leonard, "Sudden Death Sacks" (BB)
David Crewe, "Good Field, No Hit" (BB)
William Heuman, "Fire Around Short" (BB)
Theodore J. Roemer, "The Graveyard Nine" (BB)
Vol. 8, No. 3, December 1950. Stories: 9
Cover: Football
Don Kingery, "Thunder Wood" (BB)
George Kilrain, "Cash and Carry Guy" (FB)
Duane Yarnell, "Blitz Buster" (FB)
William Heuman, "Hit-and-Hurry Back" (FB)
Vol. 8, No. 4, February 1951. Stories: 8
Roy C. Rainey, "The Busher from Broken Twig" (BB)
Louis Trimble, "Hell on the Hill" (BB)
Vol. 9, No. 1, May 1951. Stories: 7
Cover: Baseball
Daniel Winters, "Say It with Base Hits!" (BB)
Ted Stratton, "Suicide Chucker" (BB)
Vol. 9, No. 2, July 1951. Stories: 6
Cover: Baseball
Daniel Winters, "Bye-Bye Blaster" (BB)
William Heuman, "Thunder Wood" (BB)
David Crewe (William R. Cox using house name), "Buzz Saw Back" (FB)

NOTE: Numerous stories have the same titles or are reprints.

Totals: 34 issues, 246 stories, 67 baseball stories, 36 football stories.

Sports Novels

Vol. 1, No. 1, April–May 1937. Stories: 5
Cover: Baseball by Charles DeFeo
Joe Gregg, "Horsehide Destiny" (BB)
O.B. Myers, "The Quarter That Kills" (FB-Crew)
Vol. 1, No. 2, June–July 1937. Stories: 6
Cover: Baseball
William O'Sullivan, "Diamond Dust" (BB)
Tom Runyon, "Base Hits and Blood" (BB)
Toby Hertz, "Umpire" (BB)
Vol. 1, No. 3, August–September 1937. Stories: 6
Cover: Boxing
Ben Peter Freeman, "Clutch Pitcher" (BB)
Walter J. Higgins, "Cleats and Cinders" (FB-Track)
Vol. 1, No. 4, October–November 1937. Stories: 6
Cover: Football
A.R. Thurman (Arthur Mann), "If at First" (BB)
Alden H. Norton, "The Flying Dutchman" (BB)
William Hartley, "Touchdown Twins" (FB)
Larry Jones (William R. Cox), "Legs" (FB)
Vol. 2, No. 1, December 1937–January 1938. Stories: 5
Cover: Football
Ben Peter Freeman, "Blood on the Bases" (BB)
Walter J. Higgins, "Trouble for Tony" (FB)
Vol. 2, No. 2, February–March 1938. Stories: 5
Cover: Hockey
Tom Runyon, "Fence Buster" (BB)
Vol. 2, No. 3, April–May 1938. Stories: 7
Cover: Baseball
Walter J. Higgins, "Once a Busher" (BB)
William O'Sullivan, "Hell on the Bases" (BB)
Vol. 2, No. 4, June–July 1938. Stories: 6
Cover: Baseball
William O'Sullivan, "Play Ball!" (BB)
William Hartley, "Smoke Ball" (BB)
Vol. 3, No. 1, August–September 1938. Stories: 7
Cover: Baseball
William R. Cox, "Big League Guy" (BB)
William O'Sullivan, "Too Old to Fight" (BB)
William Jerome, "Six Points for Glory" (FB-Boxing)
Roger G. Spellman (William R. Cox), "Pigskin Magic" (FB)
Vol. 3, No. 2, October–November 1938. Stories: 5
Cover: Football

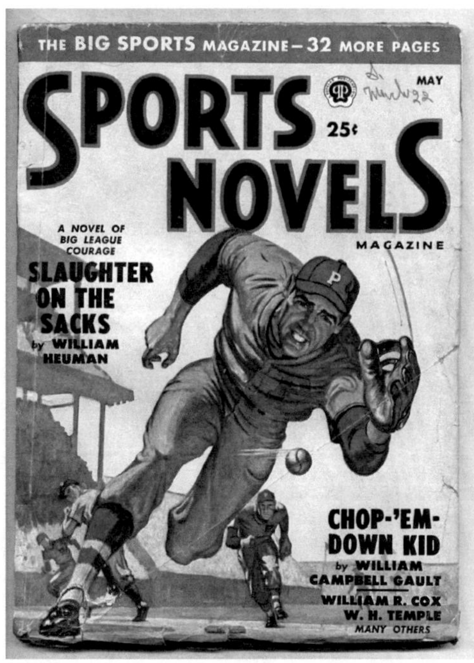

***Sports Novels*, May 1950 (copyright 1950 Popular Publications, Inc.). Even at 132 pages (counting covers), "The BIG SPORTS Magazine" almost never ran a legitimate novel. There are nine stories in this issue.**

Ben Peter Freeman, "Bleachers Bum" (BB)
William Jerome, "The Little Giant" (FB)
Alden H. Norton, "Cleats and Glory" (FB)
Vol. 3, No. 3, December 1938–January 1939. Stories: 5
Cover: Football
William R. Cox, "Big League Boots" (BB)
William Hartley, "Bring Home the Leather!" (FB)
Vol. 3, No. 4, February–March 1939. Stories: 6
Cover: Boxing
George Franklin, "Back to the Bushes" (BB)
William R. Cox, "Blocking Back" (FB)
Vol. 4, No. 1, April–May 1939. Stories: 6
Cover: Baseball
William Jerome, "Big Time Guy" (BB)
William Hartley, "Rules for Rookies" (BB)
Vol. 4, No. 2, June–July 1939. Stories: 6
Cover: Baseball
William R. Cox, "Base Hits for a Busher" (BB)
Roger G. Spellman (Cox), "The Hard Way" (BB)
Vol. 4, No. 3, August–September 1939. Stories: 5
Cover: Baseball
Ben Peter Freeman, "Sunday Pitcher" (BB)
Roger G. Spellman (William R. Cox), "Sixty Minutes of Murder" (FB)
Vol. 4, No. 4, October–November 1939. Stories: 6
Cover: Football
William R. Cox, "The Bum Can't Hit!" (BB)
William Hartley, "Thunder from the Stands" (FB)
Vol. 5, No. 1, January–February 1940. Stories: 6
Cover: Basketball
William Hartley, "Those Bums Can Be Beaten!" (BB)
George Franklin, "Leather Lugger" (FB)
Vol. 5, No. 2, April 1940. Stories: 6
Cover: Basketball
Alden H. Norton, "Throw the Bum Out!" (BB)
Daniel Winters, "A Ball Game for Bronco" (FB)
Vol. 5, No. 3, June 1940. Stories: 6
Cover: Baseball
William Hartley, "The Kid with the Golden Arm" (BB)
Nelson Hutto, "Money Game" (BB)
Vol. 5, No. 4, August 1940. Stories: 6
Cover: Baseball
Alden H. Norton, "The Kid in the Iron Mask" (BB)
David Crewe, "The Busher from Dugan's Bluff" (BB)
Moran Tudury, "Here Comes the Army!" (FB)
Vol. 6, No. 1, October 1940. Stories: 7
Cover: Baseball
William R. Cox, "A Man with a Mitt" (BB)
Daniel Winters, "The Last Bloody Yard" (FB)
Vol. 6, No. 2, December 1940. Stories: 5
Cover: Football
Alden H. Norton, "Clean-Up Guy" (BB)
William R. Cox, "Six Yards for Sweeney" (FB)
Moran Tudury, "Mule Team" (FB)
Vol. 6, No. 3, February 1941. Stories: 7
Cover: Hockey
Ross Russell, "Huddle Trouble" (FB)
Moran Tudury, "Old Army Team" (FB-Track)
Vol. 6, No. 4, April 1941. Stories: 7
Cover: Baseball
Tim Cohane, "Man in Blue" (BB)
Ray P. Shotwell, "Nothing on the Ball" (BB)
W.H. Temple, "Hit the Dirt, Busher!" (BB)
Ross Russell, "Farewell Appearance" (FB)
Vol. 7, No. 1, June 1941. Stories: 7
Cover: Baseball
William R. Cox, "Hit Away, Busher!" (BB)
Robert Sidney Bowen, "Spike Shy" (BB)
W.H. Temple, "Second-Division Heart" (BB)
Walter C. Higgins, "Get in There and Block" (FB)
Vol. 7, No. 2, August 1941. Stories: 7
Cover: Baseball
Norman L. Paul, "Back to the Bushes, Bum!" (BB)
Lance Kermit, "Ten-Year Man" (BB)
Ray P. Shotwell, "Win One for Willy" (FB)
Vol. 7, No. 3, October 1941. Stories: 7
Cover: Baseball
Norman L. Paul, "Get Me Some Runs!" (BB)
David Crewe, "Fifty Grand Flop" (BB)
Daniel Winters, "Leather Lugger" (FB)
Robert S. Kelly, Farewell, "Mr. Football" (FB)
Vol. 7, No. 4, December 1941. Stories: 6
Cover: Football
T.W. Ford, "Dust 'Em Off, Busher!" (BB)
W.H. Temple, "Bleachers Bum" (BB)
Stewart Sterling (Prentice Winchell), "Touchdown Tornado" (FB)
Daniel Winters, "The One Quarter Kid" (FB)
Vol. 8, No. 1, February 1942. Stories: 5
Cover: Basketball
W.H. Temple, "Good Field—No Hit" (BB)
Ross Russell, "Backfield Bum" (FB)
Vol. 8, No. 2, April 1942. Stories: 7
Cover: Boxing
Daniel Winters, "Razzle-Dazzle Kid" (BB)
W.H. Temple, "Hot Spot Hot-Shot" (BB)
William Heuman, "Kick That Point!" (FB)
Vol. 8, No. 3, June 1942. Stories: 6
Cover: Baseball
C. Paul Jackson, "Clutch Hitter" (BB)
W.H. Temple, "Bush League Pilot" (BB)
Vol. 8, No. 4, August 1942. Stories: 8
Cover: Baseball
W.H. Temple, "The Big League Way" (BB)
William Heuman, "Spot Pitcher" (BB)
Ray P. Shotwell, "The Law of the Gridiron" (FB)
Vol. 9, No. 1, October 1942. Stories: 7
Cover: Football
William R. Cox, "The Keystone Kid" (BB)
David Crewe, "Cash-and-Carry Ball Hawk" (BB)
Daniel Winters, "Get That Goal!" (FB)
Vol. 9, No. 2, December 1942. Stories: 5
Cover: Football
Daniel Winters, "Dust Off the Duke!" (BB)

David Crewe, "Touchdowns Are My Business" (FB)
Burgess Leonard, "Ivy League Invader" (FB)
Vol. 9, No. 3, February 1943. Stories: 6
Cover: Basketball
William Heuman, "For Sale—One Pennant" (BB)
Burgess Leonard, "Hold 'Em, Soldier!" (FB)
Jackson V. Scholz, "Wrong Way Wing Back" (FB)
Vol. 9, No. 4, April 1943. Stories: 8
Cover: Baseball
Bill Heuman, "Bush League Backstopper" (BB)
David Crewe, "Trouble at Third" (BB)
Lance Kermit, "The Babe Comes Back" (BB)
Vol. 10, No. 1, July 1943. Stories: 5
Cover: Baseball
William R. Cox, "Double Play Guy" (BB)
Nelson A. Hutto, "Bear Down, Rookie!" (BB)
Vol. 10, No. 2, October 1943. Stories: 6
Cover: Track
William Heuman, "Play Ball, Busher!" (BB)
W.H. Temple, "Mutiny on the Diamond" (BB)
Daniel Winters, "The Buck-a-Yard Kid" (FB)
R.C. Rainey, "Gridiron Tyrant" (FB)
Vol. 10, No. 3, January 1944. Stories: 6
Cover: Basketball
David Crewe, "Clean-Up Guy" (BB)
Daniel Winters, "The Last White Line" (FB)
Robert S. Kelley, "Goodbye to Glory" (FB)
William R. Cox, "The Timid Tailback" (FB)
Vol. 10, No. 4, April 1944. Stories: 8
Cover: Baseball
David Crewe, "Good Field, No Hit" (BB)
Ron Broom, "Nothing Ball" (BB)
Lance Kermit, "Fifty Grand Flop" (BB)
Theodore J. Roemer, "Ace of the Uprights" (FB)
Vol. 11, No. 1, July 1944. Stories: 8
Cover: Baseball
Daniel Winters, "Say It with Base Hits!" (BB)
Joel Reeve (William R. Cox), "One Hoss Team" (BB)
Ray P. Shotwell, "A Present for Pop" (FB)
Roy C. Rainey, "Scatback" (FB)
Vol. 11, No. 2, February 1946 (after hiatus). Stories: 9
Cover: Baseball
Roy C. Rainey, "Bear Down, Busher!" (BB)
David Crewe, "Clean-Up Guy" (BB)
Daniel Winter, "Fence Buster" (BB)
Lance Kermit, "The Last White Line" (FB)
Vol. 11, No. 3, April 1946. Stories: 8
Cover: Baseball
David Crewe, "Champ!" (BB)
William Heuman, "Holler Guy" (BB)
William Jerome, "Carry That Mail!" (FB)
Vol. 11, No. 4, June 1946. Stories: 8
Cover: Baseball
W.H. Temple, "Spikes at the Hot Corner" (BB)
William R. Cox, "Go Down Swinging!" (BB)
Roy C. Rainey, "Tough Guy" (FB)
Vol. 12, No. 1, August 1946. Stories: 9
Cover: Baseball
Burgess Leonard, "Pennant Buster" (BB)
Roy C. Rainey, "Gashouse Guy" (BB)
David Crewe, "Special Delivery Kid" (FB)
Ted Stratton, "The Last White Line" (FB)
Vol. 12, No. 2, October 1946. Stories: 8
Cover: Baseball
William Heuman, "Unlucky Seventh" (BB)
Roy C. Rainey, "Slam 'Em, Busher" (BB)
Daniel Winters, "Six Points for Patsy" (BB) (reprinted from *Dime Sports*, August 1940)
Vol. 12, No. 3, December 1946. Stories: 10
Cover: Football
Roy C. Rainey, "Fence Buster" (BB)
David Crewe, "Bushers Don't Belong" (BB)
William Heuman, "Glory Road" (FB)
Curtis Bishop, "The Ghost of Coffin Corner" (FB)
Lance Kermit, "Goal to Go!" (FB)
Vol. 12, No. 4, February 1947. Stories: 8
Cover: Basketball
Curtis Bishop, "Spikes Around Second" (BB)
Davis Crewe, "Million Buck Castoff" (BB)
William R. Cox, "Halfway Back" (FB)
Roy C. Rainey, "Goal to Go!" (FB)
Vol. 13, No. 1, April 1947. Stories: 8
Cover: Baseball
Daniel Winters, "Two Strikes on Steve" (BB)
Roy C. Rainey, "The Knock 'Em Down Kid" (BB)
William Heuman, "Halfback Hellion" (BB)
David Crewe, "The Ghost of Coffin Corner" (FB)
Vol. 13, No. 2, June 1947. Stories: 8
Cover: Baseball
Daniel Winters, "Trouble at Short" (BB)
William Heuman, "Good Hit, No Field" (BB)
W.H. Temple, "Hit the Dirt, Busher!" (BB)
John Wilson, "Clamor Boy" (BB)
Roy C. Rainey, "Buck-a-Yard Guy" (FB)
Vol. 13, No. 3, August 1947. Stories: 8
Cover: Boxing
John Wells (William Holder), "Glass-Arm Guy" (BB)
John Wilson, "King of the Keystone" (BB)
David Crewe, "Hell on the Hot Corner" (BB)
Roy C. Rainey, "The Last White Line" (FB)
Richard Brister, "Glory Road" (FB)
Vol. 13, No. 4, October 1947. Stories: 8
Cover: Football
William Heuman, "Hit One for Freddie!" (BB)
Roy C. Rainey, "Spikes Over Second" (BB)
Daniel Winters, "Knock 'Em Down Guy" (FB)
David Crewe, "End on a Spot" (FB)
Vol. 14, No. 1, November 1947. Stories: 8
Cover: Football by Norman Saunders
Theodore J. Roemer, "Nine Men from Hunger" (BB)
Roy C. Rainey, "Call Me Lefty" (BB)
Zene Tuttler, "Goal to Go!" (FB)
Nelson A. Hutto, "Line Buster" (FB)
Vol. 14, No. 2, December 1947. Stories: 7
Cover: Football
Roy C. Rainey, "Second Hand Champ" (BB)
W.H. Temple, "Eight Men and a Busher" (BB)

David Crewe, "Busher Pilot" (BB)
Nelson A. Hutto, "Back Field Wrecker" (FB)
Vol. 14, No. 3, January 1948. Stories: 7
Cover: Boxing
William Heuman, "No Hit, No Run" (BB)
David Crewe, "Slump Buster" (BB)
Ron Broom, "Glory Maker" (FB)
William Campbell Gault, "The Heart Guy" (FB)
Vol. 14, No. 4, February 1948. Stories: 8
Cover: Baseball
Curtis Bishop, "Hit Away Guy" (BB)
W.H. Temple, "Double or Nothing Kid" (BB)
William R. Cox, "Last Minute Back" (FB)
Vol. 15, No. 1, March 1948. Stories: 8
Cover: Boxing
William Heuman, "Put the Wood to It, Busher!" (BB)
Giles A. Lutz, "Trail's End" (BB)
Vol. 15, No. 2, April 1943. Stories: 7
Cover: Baseball
Burgess Leonard, "Star Maker" (BB)
Daniel Winters, "Three-Alarm Kid" (BB)
Vol. 15, No. 3, May 1948. Stories: 7
Cover: Track
Daniel Winters, "Ball Hawk" (BB)
William Heuman, "Bear Down, Busher!" (BB)
William R. Cox, "Roll to the Bowl" (FB)
Vol. 15, No. 4, June 1948. Stories: 8
Cover: Baseball
David Crewe, "Run, Busher, Run!" (BB)
Theodore J. Roemer, "Clean-Up Chucker" (BB)
Zene Tuttler, "Take the Bum Out!" (BB)
Vol. 16, No. 1, July 1948. Stories: 8
Cover: Baseball
Lance Kermit, "Boy Wonder" (BB)
Roy C. Rainey, "No Hit Guy" (BB)
Nelson Hutto, "The Tookerville Terror" (BB)
John Wells (William Holder), "Glass-Arm Kid" (BB)
Vol. 16, No. 2, August 1948. Stories: 9
Cover: Baseball
Roe Richmond, "Slump Buster" (BB)
Daniel Winters, "Rough on the Sacks" (BB)
Lance Kermit, "Busher on a Spot" (BB)
William R. Cox, "Breakaway Guy" (FB)
Vol. 16, No. 3, September 1948. Stories: 9
Cover: Boxing
Burgess Leonard, "The Big Wood" (BB)
H.W. Bowman, "High Spike Guy" (BB)
Bill Erin, "Blaze 'Em Down, Busher!" (BB)
John D. MacDonald, "Runaway Cleats" (FB)
Vol. 16, No. 4, October 1948. Stories: 9
Cover: Football
Larry Holden, "Murder at Bat!" (BB)
John Randolph Phillips, "Bleader Blaster" (BB)
William Jerome, "Thunder Cleats!" (FB)
Les Etter, "Last Down Dynamite" (FB)
Vol. 17, No. 1, November 1948. Stories: 8
Cover: Football
Burgess Leonard, "The Bomber from Murderers' Row" (BB)
Duane Decker, "Last Chance Chucker (Eddie Lasky)" (BB)
William Heuman, "Last Down Guy" (FB)
William R. Cox, "Slap That Tackle Down" (FB)
Bob Reed, "Last-Minute Lightning" (FB)
Vol. 17, No. 2, January 1949. Stories: 9
Cover: Football
William Heuman, "Runaway Spikes" (BB)
Sam Merwin, Jr., "Reckoning at Second" (BB)
Theodore J. Roemer, "Smash Back" (FB)
William R. Cox, "Wrong-Way Cleats" (FB)
Daniel Winters, "Goal Line Raider" (FB)
Vol. 17, No. 3, March 1949. Stories: 10
Cover: Basketball
Daniel Winters, "Pour 'Em in Guy" (BB)
Jimmie Jamieson, "Play Ball!" (BB)
John D. MacDonald, "Last Chance Cleats" (FB)
Vol. 17, No. 4, May 1949. Stories: 9
Cover: Baseball
Wallace Umphrey, "Last Chance Chucker" (BB)
William R. Cox, "Second Hand Star" (FB)
Vol. 18, No. 1, July 1949. Stories: 10
Cover: Baseball
Daniel Winters, "A Pitch and a Prayer" (BB)
Roe Richmond, "Hoodoo Hitter" (BB)
William R. Cox, "Blast Em, Busher!" (BB)
Wallace Umphrey, "Crash and Carry" (FB)
Vol. 18, No. 2, September 1949. Stories: 9
Cover: Baseball
William Heuman, "Over-the-Wall Guy" (BB)
Ted Stratton, "Hurlaway Arm" (BB)
William R. Cox, "Spikes Over Second" (BB)
Theodore J. Roemer, "Glory Goal" (FB)
Vol. 18, No. 3, November 1949. Stories: 9
Cover: Boxing
Lance Kermit, "Calamity Wing" (BB)
T.W. Ford, "Pennant Buster" (BB)
William Heuman, "Six Points or Bust" (FB)
William R. Cox, "Buck-a-Yard Kid" (FB)
Theodore J. Roemer, "Glory to Go" (FB)
Vol. 18, No. 4, January 1950. Stories: 10
Cover: Football
William R. Cox, "Jinx Buster" (BB)
Lance Kermit, "All the Way Guy" (BB)
Daniel Winters, "Cleats of the Mighty" (FB)
William Heuman, "Tearaway Terror" (FB)
Larry Holden, "Glory Runner" (FB)
Vol. 19, No. 1, March 1950. Stories: 8
Cover: Boxing
Roy C. Rainey, "Slug One for Mike!" (BB)
William R. Cox, "Trouble Goal" (FB)
Vol. 19, No. 2, May 1950. Stories: 9
Cover: Baseball
Daniel Winters, "Danger in Left" (BB)
William Heuman, "Slaughter on the Sacks" (BB)
William R. Cox, "Last-Yard Cleats" (FB)
Vol. 19, No. 3, July 1950. Stories: 9
Cover: Baseball
Daniel Winters, "Put the Wood to It, Busher!" (BB)
William Heuman, "One Run for Glory!" (BB)
William R. Cox, "Steelaway Spikes" (BB)
Theodore J. Roemer, "Second Chance" (BB)
David Crewe (William R. Cox using a house name), "Sixty Minute Guy" (FB)

Vol. 19, No. 4, September 1950. Stories: 10
Cover: Baseball
Daniel Winters, "Whammy Buster" (BB)
William R. Cox, "Last Chance Spikes" (BB)
David Crewe, "Clean-Up Guy" (BB) (reprinted from February 1946)
Herbert L. McNary, "That Last, Long Yard" (FB)
Vol. 20, No. 1, November 1950. Stories: 8
Cover: Football
William R. Cox, "Pennant Buster" (BB)
William Heuman, "Six or Nothing Guy" (FB)
Vol. 20, No. 2, January 1951. Stories: 7
Cover: Football
William Heuman, "Rally Rebel" (BB)
Daniel Winters, "The Buck-a-Yard Kid" (FB)
Vol. 20, No. 3, April 1951. Stories: 7
Cover: Basketball
Daniel Winters, "Terror at Second" (BB)
William Campbell Gault, "Star Bust" (FB)
Vol. 20, No. 4, June 1951. Stories: 8
Cover: Baseball
Daniel Winters, "Suicide Hill" (BB)
David Crewe (William R. Cox using a house name), "Gangway Cleats" (FB)
Vol. 21, No. 1, August 1951. Stories: 8
Daniel Winters, "High, Hard and Dynamite" (BB)
Roy C. Rainey, "The Way of the Mighty" (BB) (reprinted from *Dime Sports*, April 1944)
William Heuman, "Suicide Sacker" (BB)
David Crewe (William R. Cox using a house name), "Crash Back" (FB)
Vol. 21, No. 2, October 1951. Stories: 8
Cover: Baseball
Daniel Winters, "Poison on the Sacks" (BB)
Bob Reed, "The Last Out" (BB)
William Heuman, "Slump Buster" (BB)
Lance Kermit, "The Moose Comes Home" (BB)
Vol. 21, No. 3, December 1951. Stories: 7
Cover: Football
David Crewe, "Second Chance Hill" (BB)
Roy C. Rainey, "Fifty Grand Flop" (reprinted from April 1944) (BB)
William Campbell Gault, "The Last Big Yard" (FB)
William Heuman, "Plunder Cleats" (FB)
Vol. 21, No. 4, February 1952. Stories: 8
Cover: Boxing
Roy C. Rainey, "The Kid in the Iron Mask" (BB) (reprinted from August 1940, as by Alden Norton)
William R. Cox, "No-Hitter" (BB)
Roney Scott (William Campbell Gault), "Fury Yard" (FB)
Vol. 22, No. 1, April 1952. Stories: 9
Cover: Baseball
Daniel Winters, "Poison Arm" (BB)
William Heuman, "Tough—As in Diamond" (BB)
Lance Kermit, "Perfect Game" (BB)

NOTE: Many stories have the same titles or are reprints.

Totals: 85 issues, 621 stories, 170 baseball stories, 100 football stories.

Totals for Popular Publications: 230 issues, 1,686 stories, 426 baseball stories, 243 football stories.

Street & Smith

Athlete

Vol. 1, No. 1, August 1939. Stories: 4
Cover: Boston Red Sox baseball star Jimmie Foxx in photo
Arthur Mann, "Trial and Error" (BB)
Vol. 1, No. 2, September 1939. Stories: 4
Cover: New York Yankees baseball star Red Ruffing in photo
Richard McCann, "Everything's Fixed" (BB)
Jesa Carver, "Strike! Called!" (BB)
Vol. 1, No. 3, October 1939. Stories: 4
Cover: Fordham football star John Kuzman in photo
Jack Kofoed, "Big League Stuff" (BB)
Bob Considine, "Football Bum" (FB)
Stanley Woodward, "To Hell with Glory" (FB—Part I of III)
Vol. 1, No. 4, November 1939. Stories: 5
Cover: Marquette football star Ward Cuff in photo
Richard McCann, "The Holdout" (BB)
Phil R. Sheridan, "Jericho Jones" (FB)
Stanley Woodward, "To Hell with Glory" (FB—Part II of III)
Vol. 1, No. 5, December 1939. Stories: 4
Cover: USC football star Grenville Lansdell in photo
Jack Kofoed, "The Anderson Boys" (FB)
John F. McJennett, "A Job on the Block" (FB)
Timothy Cohane, "The Hound of Autumn" (FB)
Stanley Woodward, "To Hell with Glory" (FB—Part III of III)
Vol. 1, No. 6, January 1940. Stories: 6
Cover: Boston Bruins hockey star Roy Conacher in photo
Arthur Mann, "Buck and the New Deal" (BB)
Vol. 2, No. 1, February 1940. Stories: 5
Cover: Boxing by Paul D'ome
Rainey Abbot, "Who's a Screwball?" (BB)
Vol. 2, No. 2, March 1940. Stories: 6
Cover: Basketball by Paul D'ome
Royal Hall (Jackson V. Scholz), Lowe, "the Poor Indian" (BB)
Vol. 2, No. 3, April 1940. Stories: 5
Cover: Baseball by Paul D'ome
Mack Donlan, "Kidnapped Star" (BB)
Edward L. Leamon, "He Couldn't Take It" (BB)

Totals: 9 issues, 43 stories, 10 baseball stories.

Thrilling Publications

Best Football Novels

Vol. 1, No. 1 (one shot), December 1942. Stories: 4

Sam Merwin, Jr., "Ten Men and a Brain"
Herbert L. , "The Flying Fortress"
Harold Rogers, "Hipper-Dipper"
L. P. Holmes, "The Longest Yard"

Exciting Baseball

Vol. 1, No. 1, Spring 1949. Stories: 10
Cover: Earle Bergey? (unsigned, uncredited)
John Wilson, "Utility Star"
Harrison Hendryx, "Rowdy Dow"
William O'Sullivan, "The Fabulous Greene"
Jack Terry, "For the Old Guy"
Bill Erin, "Sunday Pitcher"
Don Sobol, "Six to Make Ready"
T.W. Ford, "Buttercup Ball"
Kenny Kenmare (Will F. Jenkins), "Viva Beisbol!"
H.C. Butler, "Midget on the Mound"
Hal K. Wells, "Another Day for Truck"
Vol. 1, No. 2, Fall 1949. Stories: 9
Cover: Earle Bergey
T.W. Ford, "The Diamond Imposter"
John Wilson, "Right Field for Sale"

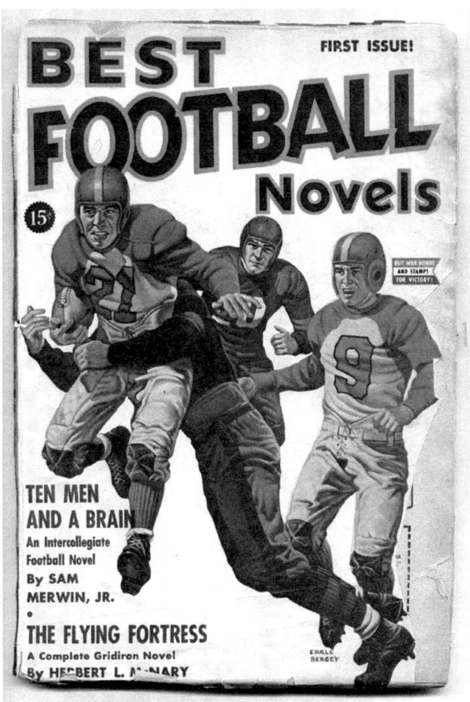

Best Football Novels, December 1942 (copyright 1942 Nedor Publishing Company). Earle Bergey portrays a runner trying to slip a tackler as a would-be blocker avoids a holding penalty. This title began as a quarterly but this was the only issue published, perhaps because wartime paper rationing began to take effect.

Tom Tucker (Don Tracy), "The Rookie Is a Veteran"
Robert S. Fenton, "The End of the Season"
Joe Archibald, "Behind the Box Scores"
William O'Sullivan, "Just Like Eating Pie"
Roy Lopez, "Set 'Em on Fire!"
Hal K. Wells, "One Error-Named Papa"
Jack Terry, "Crazy Horse of the Diamond"
Vol. 1, No. 3, 1950 issue. Stories: 9
Cover: Unsigned, uncredited
John Wilson, "Lesson from a Rookie"
Herbert L. McNary, "Say It with Curves"
Tom Tucker (Don Tracy), "The Man Behind the Bat"
William Heuman, "The Saga of Boone McCloud"
William O'Sullivan, "One of the Gang"
Robert Sidney Bowen, "A Lot to Learn"
Jack Kofoed, "The Pitching Archeologist"
Bob Wilton, "Hot Corner Blues"
Joe Gregg, "A Pitcher to Suit"
Vol. 1, No. 4, 1951 issue. Stories: 8
Cover: Unsigned, uncredited
John Wilson, "The Hitting Fool"
Robert Sidney Bowen, "Bunt Crazy"
Sam Merwin, Jr., "Safe All Around"
Add Aretz, "Horsehide Heart"
Theodore J. Roemer, "Flash on the Diamond"
Sid Wilton, "In the Clutch"
Cosmo Bennett, "Plate Shy"
Seven Anderton, "Ball Four"
Vol. 2, No. 1, Spring 1953. Stories: 9
Cover: Unsigned, uncredited
Giles A. Lutz, "Nice Guys Don't Win Pennants"
T.W. Ford, "The Diamond Spot"
Charles Molyneaux Brown, "Rookie from the Big House"
Sid Wilton, "Like a Million Bucks"
Seven Anderton, "The Feminine Touch"
Robert Sidney Bowen, "Pennant for a Lady"
Hal K. Wells, "Press-Box Manager"
Cosmo Bennett, "Ducks on the Pond"
Sam Brant, "Inspiration for Freddie"

Totals: 45 baseball stories.

Exciting Football

Vol. 1, No. 1 (only one issue in Vol. 1), Winter 1942. Stories: 5
Cover: Earle Bergey
Duane Yarnell, "Army Man"
Nelson Hutto, "Goal-Line Express"
Joe Archibald, "Like Father—Like Fun!"
Henry Bela Bachrach, "Fullbacks Can't Have Fingers"
John A. Thompson, "Left-Handed Runner"
Vol. 2, No. 1, Winter 1943. Stories: 6
Cover: Earle Bergey
Herbert L. McNary, "West Point Bombardier"
Will Bruce, "Awkward Squad"
Carter Sprague (Sam Merwin, Jr.), "With the Greatest of Ease"
Nelson A. Hutto, "Line Buster"

Sam Merwin, Jr., "Boots Across the Sea"
Harold Rogers, "Cleated Tribute"
Vol. 2, No. 2, Winter 1944. Stories: 8
Cover: Earle Bergey
Duane Yarnell, "A Pass and a Prayer"
Arthur K. Barnes, "A 4F Can Fight, Too"
Matt Lee (Sam Merwin, Jr.), "The Protein Test"
Robert S. Fenton, "Dooley's Leopards"
Sam Merwin, Jr., "The Football Legacy"
Vance Porter, "Not to the Fleet"
Joe Archibald, "The Idol Worshipper"
Theodore J. Roemer, "The Blocking Bum"
Vol. 2, No. 3, Winter 1945. Stories: 7
Cover: Earle Bergey
T.W. Ford, "Under False Colors"
Joe Archibald, "Tackled by Gunnison"
C. Paul Jackson, "Pigskin Comeback"
Nelson A. Hutto, "Goal Line Gunner"
John Gartner, "Last Game"
Ted Stratton, "The Smith, a Mighty Shrimp Was He"
Johnston McCulley, "Touchdown in the Fog"
Vol. 3, No. 1, Winter 1946. Stories: 7
Cover: Rudolph Belarski
Will Bruce, "Purple Heart Passer"

***Exciting Football,* Winter 1945 (copyright 1944 Better Publications, Inc.). Earle Bergey's classic image of a hero's arm encircling the goalpost when they were on the goal line. The famed pulp historian John Gunnison likes the featured story "Tackled by Gunnison" by Joe Archibald.**

C. Paul Jackson, "The Crucial Game"
Richard Brister, "Caution Corner"
Sam Merwin, Jr., "The 'T' Server"
Jack Kofoed, "Double Cross Block"
Robert S. Gordon, "Proxy Quarterback"
Carter Sprague (Sam Merwin, Jr.), "The Champion"
Vol. 3, No. 2, Fall 1946. Stories: 6
Cover: Earle Bergey
William J. O'Sullivan, "Million Dollar Baby"
Roger Fuller (Don Tracy), "My Friend—the Rat"
Jack Kofoed, "Baldy and the Mamma's Boy"
Joe Gregg, "Sometimes They Come Back"
Carter Sprague (Sam Merwin, Jr.), "Fight Talk"
Sam Merwin, Jr., "Beanpole"
Vol. 3, No. 3, Winter 1948. Stories: 7
Cover: Earle Bergey
Theodore J. Roemer, "Scourge of the Gridiron"
William O'Sullivan, "Grand Old Man"
Tracy Mason (Don Tracy), "Football Bum"
Richard Brister, "On Top of the Game"
Matt Lee (Sam Merwin, Jr.), "Chance for Glory"
Joe Archibald, "Touchdown Testimonial"
Ted Stratton, "One Hard-Boiled Egg"
Vol. 4, No. 1, Fall 1948. Stories: 11
Cover: Sam Cherry
Herbert L. McNary, "Power of West Point"
William O'Sullivan, "Twenty-Two Orphans"
T.W. Ford, "Scatback's Comeback"
Richard Brister, "Twinkle, Twinkle Little Tackle"
Sam Merwin, Jr., "Three-Play Charlie"
C. Paul Jackson, "Tailback Trouble"
Johnston Carroll, "No Substitute for Valor"
V.A. Saluda, "Trigger Man"
Joe Gregg, "No Box Office"
Kenny Kenmare (Will F. Jenkins), "Lug That Leather"
Duane Yarnell, "Blocking Back Bum"
Vol. 4, No. 2, Fall 1949. Stories: 9
Cover: Earle Bergey
William O'Sullivan, "Navy on Parade"
M.M. Tinney, "The Last White Stripe"
Sam Merwin, Jr., "The Varsity Road"
Will Urbanna, "Sauce for the Goose"
John Gartner, "Football Man"
Stewart Sterling (Prentice Winchell), "Hard-Way Harrigan"
Joe Gregg, "Block That Gremlin"
Kenny Kenmare (Will F. Jenkins), "Carry Your Own Mail"
V.A. Saluda, "The Twister Gets It Straight"
Vol. 4, No. 3, Fall 1950. Stories: 8
Cover: Unsigned, uncredited
Robert Sidney Bowen, "The Hard-Boiled Coach"
Sam Merwin, Jr., "Touchdown Chorus"
William O'Sullivan, "The Glory Road"
Richard Brister, "My Future Just Passed"
Herbert L. McNary, "A Goal to Gain"
W.C. Tuttle, "Buckshot in the Backfield"

Edward Howey, "Six-Point Engineer"
Kenny Kenmare (Will F. Jenkins), "Lucky Stiff"
Vol. 5, No. 1, Fall 1951. Stories: 6
Cover: Unsigned, uncredited
John Wilson, "Thunder Back"
William Campbell Gault, "Glory Guy"
Rod Grane, "Hit 'Em Where They Live!"
William O'Sullivan, "Relax, Junior"
T.W. Ford, "Saturday's Has-Been" (reprinted from *Exciting Sports*, Winter 1944)
Roe Richmond, "Gridiron Glory" (reprinted from *Popular Sports*, December 1938)

Totals: 11 issues, 80 football stories.

Exciting Sports

Vol. 1, No. 1, Winter 1941. Stories: 5
Cover: Football by Earle Bergey
M.D. Sullivan, "Blind Man's Bluff" (BB)
Herbert L. McNary, "Army, Goal to Go" (FB)
Nelson A. Hutto, "Cleats of Courage" (FB)
Vol. 1, No. 2, Spring 1941. Stories: 4 (all-baseball issue)
Cover: Earle Bergey
Jack Terry, "Behind the Plate"
T.W. Ford, "Hot Rock Heaver"
J.J. Meany, "The Blimp Flies High"
Harold dePolo, "Celebrity Chaser"
Vol. 1, No. 3, Summer 1941. Stories: 6 (all-baseball issue)
Cover: Earle Bergey
Alexis Rossoff, "Strange Teammates"
Bob DeHaven, "There'll Be Some Changes Made"
Allen Jayne, "Yes, Mr. Harmon"
C. Paul Jackson, "The Glass Arm"
John Easterly, "The Foul Ball"
Ford Smith, "Keystone Play"
Vol. 2, No. 1, Fall 1941. Stories: 6 (all-football issue)
Cover: Earle Bergey
Don Tracy, "Gridiron Grenadiers"
Joe Archibald, "California—or Bust"
Duane Yarnell, "Pigskin Ghost"
Harold Rogers, "Blocking Back"
W.H. Temple, "A Halfback Has to Take It"
Robert Sidney Bowen, "Little Man, What Next?"
Vol. 2, No. 2, Winter 1942. Stories: 7 (all-football issue)
Cover: Earle Bergey
T.W. Ford, "The Key-Man Kid"
Don Tracy, "The Money Player"
Walt Bruce (Ballard), "The Dope"
Jack B. Creamer, "Single-Threat Man"
Jackson Cole (house name), "Back to Back"
William Heuman, "Football Fantasy"
Sam Merwin, Jr., "Running Background"
Vol. 2, No. 3, Spring 1942. Stories: 7 (all-baseball issue)
Cover: Earle Bergey
William O'Sullivan, "Homers for Sale"
Sam Carson, "Beanball Payoff"
Alexis Rossoff, "Spike Shy"
Nelson A. Hutto, "Take the Bum Out"
Robert Sidney Bowen," And I Mean Bunt!"
Ross Russell, "Four-Inning Flipper"
Don Tracy, "Batteries for Today"
Vol. 3, No. 1, Summer 1942. Stories: 6 (all-baseball issue)
Cover: Earle Bergey
Arthur Mann, "The Cracked Pitcher"
Will Bruce, The Final Out"
Don Tracy, "You Can't Steal First"
William Heuman, "Sandlot Sweethearts"
A.R. Thurman (Arthur Mann), "Hunger at the Plate"
W.H. Temple, "World Series Walkout"
Vol. 3, No. 2, Fall 1942. Stories: 5 (all-football issue)
Cover: Earle Bergey
Herbert L. McNary, "Shadow of the Goal"
C. Paul Jackson, "Navy Team"
Cosmo Bennett, "Boot 'Em Cowboy"
Johnston McCulley, "Woes Bowl"
Jackson V. Scholz, "Gridiron Scoop"
Vol. 3, No. 3, Winter 1943. Stories: 5 (all-football stories)
Cover: Earle Bergey
T.W. Ford, "Pigskin Topkick"
C. Paul Jackson, "Touchdown Taboo"
Johnston McCulley, "Squad Clown"
Henry Bela Bachrach, "Gilt Edge Halfback"
Sam Merwin, Jr., "Block That Back"
Vol. 4, No. 1, Spring 1943. Stories: 6 (all-baseball issue)
Cover: Earle Bergey
Duane Yarnell, "Hit and Run"
Herbert L. McNary, "The Millionaire Kid"
Nelson Hutto, "Play It Safe!"
Carter Sprague (Sam Merwin, Jr.), "The Luck of the Bengals"
A.R. Thurman (Arthur Mann), "Fresh Heir"
William Heuman, "War Horse"
Vol. 4, No. 2, Summer 1943. Stories: 6 (all-baseball issue)
Cover: Earle Bergey
Tracy Mason (Don Tracy), "Fallen Hero"
Sam Merwin, Jr., "Starstruck Southpaw"
Theodore J. Roemer, "Diamond Palooka"
Richard Brister, "First Base Flop"
Ronald Oliphant, "Baseball Ghost"
Harold dePolo, "The Woodsman from Vermont"
Vol. 4, No. 3, Fall 1943. Stories: 6 (all-football issue)
Cover: Earle Bergey
Sam Merwin, Jr., "Touchdown in Tunisia"
Tracy Mason (Don Mason), "Little Tin Whistle"
Ted Stratton, "Blame It on the War"
Vance Porter, "It Has to Be Football"
Jack O'Brien, "Tanglefoot's Place"
Carter Sprague (Sam Merwin, Jr.), "Four-F Charley"
Vol. 5, No. 1, Winter 1944. Stories: 7 (all-football issue)
Cover: Earle Bergey

C. Paul Jackson, "Backfield Bomber"
Sam Merwin, Jr., "The Running Back"
Jack O'Brien, "The Eleventh Sucker"
Johnston McCulley, "The Ghost of Danny Frayne"
Willis S. Graham, "Gridiron Softie"
Paley Brien (Johnston McCulley)
Jack Terry, "Touchdown for the Army"
Vol. 5, No. 2, Spring 1944. Stories: 6 (all-baseball issue)
Cover: Earle Bergey
William O'Sullivan, "The Rookie Shortstop"
Sam Merwin, Jr., "The Nothing Ball"
A.R. Thurman (Arthur Mann), "What a Relief"
Carter Sprague (Sam Merwin, Jr.), "Double or Anything"
Don Tracy, "Most Valuable Player"
W.H. Temple, "Big League Busher"
Vol. 5, No. 3, Fall 1944 (no Summer issue). Stories: 7 (all-baseball issue)
Cover: Earle Bergey
Herbert L. McNary, "First Place or Bust!"
Robert Sidney Bowen, "Diamond Dynamite"
Jackson Cole (house name), "Say It with Curves"
Carter Sprague (Sam Merwin, Jr.), "Jughead Jonah"
Don Tracy, "For the Good of the Game"
Jack O'Brien, "Sometimes You Gamble"
Richard Brister, "First Base Blues"
Vol. 6, No. 1, Winter 1945. Stories: 6 (all-football issue)
Cover: Earle Bergey
T.W. Ford, "Saturday's Has-Been"
Ted Stratton, "The Big Rush"
Sam Merwin, Jr., "The Turtle-Back"
Richard Brister, "Sing a Song of Six Points"
Johnston McCulley, "Fumblefist Plays the Game"
William D. Gorman, "Jailbird Formation"
Vol. 6, No. 2, Spring 1945. Stories: 7 (all-baseball issue)
Cover: Earle Bergey
Herbert L. McNary, "Come Out Batting"
T.W. Ford, "Big League Fluke"
Max Carey, "Baseball Doctor"
Matt Lee (Sam Merwin, Jr.), "Spotty Performance"
Richard Brister, "Get Me Two Games"
Cliff Watters, "Pitch 'Em, Pete"
W.H. Temple, "The Comeback Trail"
Vol. 6, No. 3, Fall 1945 (No Summer issue). Stories: 8
Cover: Football by Earle Bergey
W.H. Temple, "Suicide at Second" (BB)
Robert Sidney Bowen, "Big Moment" (BB)
Richard Brister, "Prince Hit" (BB)
Will Bruce, "Ticket to Booneville" (BB)
William Heuman, "Gridiron Gamble" (FB)
Sam Merwin, Jr., "Pile Driver" (FB)
Vol. 7, No. 1, Spring 1946 (No Winter issue). Stories: 7
Cover: Baseball by Earle Bergey
Joseph Kenney, "Pennant Winner" (BB)
Joe Archibald, "Football Fuehrer" (FB)
Vol. 7, No. 2, Summer 1946. Stories: 5
Cover: Baseball by Rudolph Belarksi
T.W. Ford, "Spikes in the Spotlight" (BB)
Vol. 7, No. 3, Fall 1946. Stories: 8
Cover: Football by Rudolph Belarski
Will Lloyd, "Front-Running Chucker" (BB)
Ernie Hartwell, "Star on Paper" (BB)
Will Bruce, "A Fortune on First" (BB)
William O'Sullivan, "It's Only a Game" (FB)
Tracy Mason (Don Tracy), "Settled in Full" (FB)
Vol. 8, No. 1, Winter 1947. Stories: 9
Cover: Basketball by Earle Bergey
Robert Sidney Bowen, "Pinch Pitcher" (BB)
T.W. Ford, "They Do Come Back" (FB)
Robert S. Fenton, "Pigskin Patten" (FB)
Vol. 8, No. 2, Spring 1947. Stories: 10
Cover: Baseball by Earle Bergey
John Wilson, "Base Hit Blues" (BB)
Roger Fuller (Don Tracy), "The Glass Head" (BB)
T.W. Ford, "The Big Try" (BB)
J. Lane Linklater, "It Ain't Soft, Chum" (Softball)
Marvin Ryerson, "Hot Corner Headache" (BB)
Vol. 8, No. 3, Summer 1947. Stories: 8
Cover: Baseball by Earle Bergey
Roger Fuller (Don Tracy), "Hitchy-Coo Hitter" (BB)
Harrison Hendryx, "The Queen of Diamonds" (BB)
Vol. 9, No. 1, Fall 1947. Stories: 8
Cover: Football by Earle Bergey
T.W. Ford, "The Spot Pitcher" (BB)
Joseph Kenney, "The Bubble Bath King" (FB)
Roger Fuller (Don Tracy), "Feud in the Backfield" (FB)
C. Paul Jackson, "Goal Line Payoff" (FB)
Vol. 9, No. 2, December 1947. Stories: 6
Cover: Football
T.W. Ford, "Wings Over the Diamond" (BB)
Bill Erin, "Bench Captain" (FB)
Vol. 9, No. 3, February 1948. Stories: 7
Cover: Hockey
Perry Dixon (Joe Archibald), "The Hard Way" (FB)
Willis Graham, "Ghost on the Gridiron" (FB)
Vol. 10, No. 1, April 1948. Stories: 7
Cover: Baseball by Earle Bergey
William O'Sullivan, "Play Ball" (BB)
Ted Stratton, "Champ" (BB)
T.W. Ford, "Backstop on the Spot" (BB)
Tracy Mason (Don Tracy), "Football Rediscovered" (FB; set in 3493 ad)
Vol. 10, No. 2, June 1948. Stories: 8
Cover: Baseball by Earle Bergey
Don Keene, "Big League Miracle" (BB)
Joe Gregg, "What Price Shanty?" (BB)
Jack Kofoed, "The Frame" (FB)
Vol. 10, No. 3, August 1948. Stories: 8
Cover: Baseball by Earle Bergey
Bill Erin, "The Veteran and the Rookie" (BB)
W.C. Tuttle, "The Investment of Christy Jones" (BB)

Robert Sidney Bowen, "Big Time Boy" (BB)
Walter Roeber Schmidt, "In Tribute Only" (FB)
Vol. 11, No. 1, October 1948. Stories: 8
Cover: Football by Earle Bergey
Roy Lopez, "Born for the Big Leagues" (BB)
Cosmo Bennett, "Bullpen Busher" (BB)
Tom Tucker (Don Tracy), "Gambler's Gold" (FB)
Vol. 11, No. 2, December 1948. Stories: 7
Cover: Football by Sam Cherry
Robert Sidney Bowen, "You Never Know" (BB)
Herbert L. McNary, One Down, "Ten to Go" (FB)
Roger Fuller (Don Tracy), "Old Million Bucks" (FB)
Vol. 11, No. 3, February 1949. Stories: 6
Cover: Baseball by Earle Bergey
Don Keene, "The Understudy" (BB)
T.J. Roemer, "Foul Over First" (BB)
Day Keene, "The Understudy" (FB)
Richard Brister, "Pigskin Pressure" (FB)
Vol. 12, No. 1, Summer 1949. Stories: 7
Cover: Baseball by Earle Bergey
William O'Sullivan, "The Veteran Catcher" (BB)
Joe Gregg, "That's Different" (FB)
Vol. 12, No. 2, Fall 1949. Stories: 6
Cover: Baseball by Earle Bergey
John Wilson, "The Cardboard Coach" (BB)
William O'Sullivan, "Pigskin in the Spring" (FB)
Vol. 12, No. 3, Winter 1950. Stories: 6
Cover: Football by Earle Bergey
Hal K. Wells, "Luck Is No Lady" (BB)
John Wilson, "Chalk Line Champions" (FB)
Vol. 13, No. 1, Spring 1950. Stories: 7
Cover: Baseball
Joe Gregg, "Most Valuable Player" (BB)
T.W. Ford, "The Third Stringer" (FB)
Vol. 13, No. 2, Summer 1950. Stories: 5
Cover: Baseball
William O'Sullivan, "The Red-Headed Latin" (BB)

Totals: 38 issues, 253 stories, 102 baseball stories, 68 football stories.

Five Sports Classics (formerly *Exciting Sports*)

Vol. 13, No. 3, Fall 1950. Stories: 7
Cover: Football (unsigned, uncredited)
William O'Sullivan, "Bigger Than Baseball" (BB) (reprinted from *Popular Sports*, October 1938, as "Bigger Than the Game")
Sam Merwin, Jr., "Starstruck Southpaw" (BB) (reprinted from *Exciting Sports*, Summer 1943)
T.W. Ford, "Under False Colors" (FB) (reprinted from *Exciting Football*, Winter 1945)
Nelson S. Bond, "Rose Bowl Fever" (FB) (reprinted from *Popular Sports*, December 1939)
Vol. 14, No. 1, Winter 1951. Stories: 5
Cover: Football (unsigned, uncredited)
John Wilson, "The Fielder from Nowhere" (BB) (reprinted from *Popular Sports*, June 1939)
Alexis Rossoff, "Gridiron Shortstop" (BB) (reprinted from *Thrilling Sports*, Winter 1943)
John Wilson, "The Key Block" (FB) (new story)
Arthur Mann, "Hellion in the Backfield" (FB) (reprinted from *Popular Sports*, February 1938)
Vol. 14, No. 2, Spring 1951. Stories: 6
Cover: Baseball (unsigned, uncredited)
Joseph Kenney, "Pennant Winner" (BB) (reprinted from *Exciting Sports*, Spring 1946)
Alexis Rossoff, "Strange Teammates" (BB) (reprinted from *Exciting Sports*, Summer 1941)
John Wilson, "The Touchdown Way" (FB) (new story)
Vol. 14, No. 3, Summer 1951. Stories: 8
Cover: Baseball (unsigned, uncredited)
Richard Brister, "Potentially Great" (BB)
T.W. Ford, "The Millionaire Kid" (BB) (reprinted from *Exciting Sports*, Spring 1943, as by Herbert L. McNary)
Will Bruce, "Purple Heart Passer" (FB) (reprinted from *Exciting Football*, Winter 1946)
Hal K. Wells, "Not Enough Psychology" (new story)

Totals: 4 issues, 26 stories, 8 baseball stories, 7 football stories.

Popular Baseball

Vol. 1, No. 1, Spring 1949. Stories: 11
Cover: Earl Bergey
John Wilson, "Diamond in the Rough"
Roy Lopez, "Suffering Cats"
Kenny Kenmare (Will F. Jenkins), "The Gilded Lily"
T.W. Ford, "Payoff at the Hot Corner"
Matt Lee (Sam Merwin, Jr.), "You Never Can Tell"
Robert Sidney Bowen, "One Man's Loss"
Scott Morgan (house name), "Rocks in His Head"
Joe Gregg, "What's in a Record?"
Joe Archibald, "Campus Ivory"
Arthur William Rickard, "Boot One, Bully!"
William O'Sullivan, "The Long Throw"
Vol. 1, No. 2, Spring 1950. Stories: 9
Cover: Earle Bergey
William O'Sullivan, "Wearer of the Purple"
Roe Richmond, "Slugger's Last Stand"
John Wilson, "No Chaos for a Busher"
Larry Holden, "Pitchers Get Lonely"
Carter Sprague (Sam Merwin, Jr.), "Home Run No. 716"
Orlando Rigoni, "Three Strikes You're In!"
Jackson V. Scholz, "Umpire Bait"

Roy Lopez, "Fight It Out, Busher"
Tom Tucker (Don Tracy), "Boy Wonder"
Vol. 1, No. 3, Summer 1950. Stories: 8
Cover: Unsigned, uncredited
John Wilson, "The Bush League Road"
M.M. Tinney, "Too Hot to Handle"
Sam Merwin, Jr., "A Sportsman in Center"
Robert Sidney Bowen, "The Ghost Pitcher"
T.W. Ford, "Brains Behind the Bat"
Richard Brister, "The Lou Embree Blues"
Roy Lopez, "Storm Over Second"
William R. Cox, "The Tired Third Baseman"
Vol. 1, No. 3 (error), Spring 1951. Stories: 8
Cover: Unsigned, uncredited
Add Aretz, "The Pitch-and-Pray Guy"
Zene Tuttler, "Second Sack Stooge"
Hal K. Wells, "Oil for the Hot Corner"
Richard Brister, "The Very Foul Ball"
T.W. Ford, "Verdict from the Bullpen"
James W. Egan, "In the Clutch"
C. Paul Jackson, "The Glass Arm" (reprinted from *Exciting Sports*, Summer 1941)
Robert Sidney Bowen, "Batteries for Today" (reprinted from *Popular Sports*, Spring 1944)

Totals: 4 issues, 36 baseball stories.

Popular Football

Vol. 1, No. 1, Winter 1941. Stories: 6
Cover: Earle Bergey
Ross Russell, "Damn Yankee, Quarterback"
Duane Yarnell, "The Flop from Flatbush"
Nelson A. Hutto, "Gridiron Gamble"
Sam Carson, "The Team Is the Thing"
Johnston McCulley, "Pinch Kicker"
William Campbell Gault, "Political Halfback"
Vol. 2, No. 1, Winter 1942. Stories: 6
Cover: Earle Bergey
T.W. Ford, "Headline Halfback"
Don Tracy, "Ailsworth the Fourth"
William Heuman, "The Law of the Gridiron"
Johnston McCulley, "Dugan Gets His Letter"
John A. Thompson, "Goal to Go"
Sam Merwin, Jr., "Grid Amateurs"
Vol. 3, No. 1, Winter 1943. Stories: 6
Cover: Earle Bergey
Duane Yarnell, "The Swamp Fox"
Tracy Mason (Don Tracy), "The Army Coach"
Jack Kofoed, "Buy Me That Team"
Don Keene, "Little Pepper"
Cosmo Bennett, "Football Is for Sissies"
Carter Sprague (Sam Merwin, Jr.), "Pivot Man"
Vol. 4, No. 1, Winter 1944. Stories: 8
Cover: Earl Bergey
C. Paul Jackson, "Pigskin Ranger"
Sam Carson, "The Freshmen Take Over"
Herbert L. McNary, "The Lion's Roar"
Ron Broom, "The Rangeland Rioter"
Sam Merwin, Jr., "The Unbeaten Trail"
John L. Benton (house name), "The Kicking Fool"
Joe Archibald, "Chalk, Stripes and Gold"
Vance Porter, "The Hard Way"
Vol. 4, No. 2, Winter 1945. Stories: 8
Cover: Earl Bergey
Theodore Roemer, "The Last Ten Yards"
Herb Kamm, "An Apple for Butch"
Sam Merwin, Jr., "An Apple for Buck"
Matt Lee (Sam Merwin, Jr.), "Ignoblest Roman"
Ted Stratton, "Stars Over the Gridiron"
William D. Gorman, "Centers Earn No Glory"
Richard Brister, "Touchdown Production"
G. Wayman Jones (house name), "The Scrappler"
Vol. 4, No. 3, Winter 1946. Stories: 7
Cover: Rudolph Belarski
Herbert L. McNary, "Army, Goal to Go"
Jackson Cole (house name), "Divided Glory"
Michael O'Brien, "Block Buster"
John X. Brown, "The Off Tackle"
Richard Brister, "Varsity Venom"
Jack Kofoed, "The Leopard's Spots"
Sam Merwin, Jr., "The Big Win"
Vol. 5, No. 1, Winter 1947. Stories: 7
Cover: Earle Bergey
T.W. Ford, "The One-Quarter Ace"
Will Bruce, "Target for Saturday"
C. Paul Jackson, "Press Box Quarterback"
William J. O'Sullivan, "What's It to Me?"
Kenny Kenmare (Will F. Jenkins), "Glory at a Price"
Louis L'Amour, "Backfield Battering Ram"
Burgess Leonard, "The Glory Road"
Vol. 5, No. 2, Fall 1947. Stories: 9
Cover: Earle Bergey
William O'Sullivan, "Pivot Man"
Sam Merwin, Jr., "The Head Coach"
Roger Fuller (Don Tracy), "The Top-Kick"
Joe Gregg, "Of These We Sing"
Robert Sidney Bowen, "The Human Side"
Willis Graham, "Play, Clown, Play"
Walter Roeber Schmidt, "Yesterday's Hero"
C. Paul Jackson, "Autograph on a Pigskin"
Carter Sprague (Sam Merwin, Jr.), "The Chiseler"
Vol. 5, No. 3, Winter 1949. Stories: 10
Cover: Unsigned, uncredited
Roger Fuller (Don Tracy), "Mister Dumbjohn"
Robert Sidney Bowen, "Next Year's Has-Been"
Joseph Kenney, "The Blocker"
Richard Brister, "All-American Mess"
John Wilson, "A Touchdown for Willy"
Nelson A. Hutto, "Good-Bye to Glory"
Sam Merwin, Jr., "His Ears Had Heard the Glory"
Perry Dixon (Richard Brister), "Supernatural Athlete"
Matt Lee (Sam Merwin, Jr.), "Payoff on Panic"
Robert S. Fenton, "Letter Man"
Vol. 6, No. 1, Fall 1949. Stories: 9
Cover: Unsigned, uncredited
T.W. Ford, "The Comeback Halfback"
Roger Fuller (Don Tracy), "The Two Jimpsons"
William O'Sullivan, "Friday's Children"
Richard Brister, "Varsity Million"
Jack Terry, "Johnny on the Spot"
Kenny Kenmare (Will F. Jenkins), "Team Man"

Tom Parsons, "Pigskin Santa Claus"
Joe Gregg, "The Devil You Know"
Sam Merwin, Jr., "Fuze Under Fullback"
Vol. 6, No. 2, Fall 1950. Stories: 8
Cover: Unsigned, uncredited
Add Aretz, "Gridiron Giant Killers"
Robert Sidney Bowen, "One Last Throw"
John Wilson, "Third-String Center"
Sam Merwin, Jr., "Cleats in the Mud"
Giles A. Lutz, "Last Game"
William Campbell Gault, "Blocking Brother"
H.C. Butler, "Chumps Can't Be Champs"
Harrison Hendryx, "The Great Moment"
Vol. 6, No. 3, Fall 1951. Stories: 8
Cover: Unsigned, uncredited
Bill Erin, "Rough Road to Glory"
Richard Brister, "The Old Master Fainter"
William O'Sullivan, "The Saint and the Sinner"
Sam Merwin, Jr., "Ten Men and a Brain" (reprinted from *Best Football Novels*, December 1942)
Harrison Hendryx, "Clown" (reprinted from *Liberty Magazine*, 1944)
Robert McGrath, "Fifty-Fifty"
Johanas L. Bouma, "Touchdown Glory"
Joseph Kenney, "The Bubble Bath King" (reprinted from *Exciting Sports*, Fall 1947)

Popular Sports

Vol. 1, No. 1, June 1937. Stories: 7
Cover: St. Louis Cardinals baseball star Dizzy Dean by Earle Bergey
George Bruce, "Pop Brennan, Rookie" (BB)
Vol. 1, No. 2, August 1937. Stories: 6
Cover: Boxing star James J. Braddock by Earle Bergey
Arthur Mann, "Front Office Baseball" (BB)
Vol. 1, No. 3, October 1937. Stories: 5
Cover: New York Yankees baseball star Lou Gehrig by Earle Bergey
Joe Archibald, "Bats and Stripes" (BB)
Vol. 2, No. 1, December 1937. Stories: 5
Cover: Yale football star Larry Kelley by Earle Bergey
Lt. R.G. Emery, "Curtis of Central" (BB)
George Bruce, "Time Out for Glory" (FB)
Vol. 2, No. 2, February 1938. Stories: 5
Cover: Hockey star Eddie Shore by Earle Bergey
Arthur Mann, "Hellion in the Backfield" (FB)
Vol. 2, No. 3, April 1938. Stories: 5
Cover: Boxer Barney Ross by Earle Bergey
Robert Sidney Bowen, "Ghost Letter" (BB)
Burt L. Shurtleff, "One More Season" (FB)
Vol. 3, No. 1, June 1938. Stories: 5
Cover: St. Louis Cardinals star Joe Medwick
Charles Marquis Warren, "The Diamond Star" (BB)
Vol. 3, No. 2, August 1938. Stories: 6
Cover: Tennis star Don Budge by Earle Bergey
Sam Merwin, Jr., "Play for Home" (BB)
Gunnison Steele (Ben Gardner), "Heap Fine Ball" (BB)
Vol. 3, No. 3, October 1938. Stories: 5
Cover: Cleveland Indians star Bob Feller by Earle Bergey
Arthur Mann, "The Desert League" (BB)
Vol. 4, No. 1, December 1938. Stories: 5
Cover: Football star Sammy Baugh by Earle Bergey
W.H. Temple, "The Boneyard Ballplayer" (BB)
Roe Richmond, "Gridiron Glory" (FB)
Vol. 4, No. 2, February 1939. Stories: 5
Cover: Stanford basketball star Hank Luisetti by Earle Bergey
Spencer Towne, "The Pigskin Buccaneer" (FB)
Vol. 4, No. 2 (error), April 1939. Stories: 7
Cover: Boxing by Earle Bergey
Frederick C. Painton, "One Thousand Percent" (BB)
Vol. 4, No. 3 (error not corrected), June 1939. Stories: 6
Cover: Baseball by Earle Bergey
Jack Weaver, "The Fielder from Nowhere" (BB)
Don Tracy, "A Team for the General" (BB)
Vol. 5, No. 1, August 1939. Stories: 8
Cover: Horse racing by Earle Bergey
Nelson S. Bond, "Back to the Bushes" (BB)
John Easterly, "Windmill Willie" (Softball)
Vol. 5, No. 2, October 1939. Stories: 5
Cover: Football by Earle Bergey
William O'Sullivan, "Bigger Than the Game" (BB)
Jack Weaver, "Big Noise" (FB)
Vol. 5, No. 3, December 1939. Stories: 8
Football by Earle Bergey
Harold de Polo, "No Ball Player" (BB)
Nelson S. Bond, "Rose Bowl Fever" (FB)
Vol. 6, No. 1, February 1940. Stories: 4
Cover: Football by Earle Bergey
Harold de Polo, "Parachute Pete" (BB)
Jackson V. Scholz, "Head Coach (Coach Brick Haley)" (FB)
Vol. 6, No. 2, April 1940. Stories: 3
Cover: Baseball by Earle Bergey
Nelson S. Bond, "Million Dollar Infield" (BB)
Vol. 6, No. 3, Summer 1940. Stories: 3
Cover: Horse racing by Earle Bergey
Victor Spencer, "Pitchout" (BB)
Vol. 7, No. 1, Fall 1940. Stories: 3
Cover: Baseball by Earle Bergey
Robert Sidney Bowen, "Diamond Destiny" (BB)
William Mayer, "Feud on Cleats" (FB)
Vol. 7, No. 2, Winter 1941. Stories: 3
Cover: Football by Earle Bergey
Jackson V. Scholz, "The Falcon Squadron" (FB)
Vol. 7, No. 3, Spring 1941. Stories: 2
Cover: Boxing by Earle Bergey
Vol. 8, No. 1, Summer 1941. Stories: 2
Cover: Baseball by Earle Bergey
T.W. Ford, "Big League Busher" (BB)
Vol. 8, No. 2, Fall 1941. Stories: 4
Cover: Baseball by Earle Bergey
Robert Sidney Bowen, "Bench Manager" (BB)
Vol. 8, No. 3, November 1941. Stories: 4
Cover: Football by Earle Bergey
Duane Yarnell, "Goal Line Glory" (FB)

Vol. 9, No. 1, Winter 1942. Stories: 3
Cover: Football by Earle Bergey
T.W. Ford, "Pigskin Renegades" (FB)
Vol. 9, No. 2, Spring 1942. Stories: 4
Cover: Baseball by Earle Bergey
Jackson V. Scholz, "Soldiers at Bat" (BB)
Joe Archibald, "Fallen Star" (FB)
Vol. 9, No. 3, Summer 1942. Stories: 6
Cover: Baseball by Earle Bergey
Robert Sidney Bowen, "Fielder's Choice" (BB)
W.H. Temple, "Pitcher in a Jam" (BB)
Vol. 10, No. 1, Fall 1942. Stories: 5
Cover: Football by Earle Bergey
Sam Merwin, Jr., "Get That Kid" (BB)
T.W. Ford, "Hold That Stadium" (FB)
Vol. 10, No. 2, Winter 1943. Stories: 5
Cover: Football by Earle Bergey
Bob DeHaven, "To B1 or Not to Be One" (BB)
Jack Kofoed, "Lucky Kid" (BB)
Jack Terry, "War Babies" (FB)
Vol. 10, No. 3, Spring 1943. Stories: 5
Cover: Baseball by Earle Bergey
Robert Sidney Bowen, "The Major Comes Back" (BB)
T.W. Ford, "Tell It to the Tackle" (FB)
Vol. 11, No. 1, Summer 1943. Stories: 4
Cover: Baseball by Earle Bergey
Herbert L. McNary, "Shortstop Scrapper" (BB)
Vol. 11, No. 2, Fall 1943. Stories: 6
Cover: Football by Earle Bergey
Vance Porter, "Foul Balls" (BB)
Jack Terry, "The Last White Line" (FB)
Vol. 11, No. 3, Winter 1943–1944. Stories: 5
Cover: Football by Earle Bergey
Sam Merwin, Jr., "It's All in the Game" (BB)
Duane Yarnell, "Pass to Glory" (FB)
Vol. 12, No. 1, Spring 1944. Stories: 5
Cover: Baseball by Earle Bergey
Robert Sidney Bowen, "Batteries for Today" (BB)
Duane Yarnell, "Spring Training Blues" (BB)
A.P. Cooke, "Ice Water Pitcher" (BB)
Vol. 12, No. 2, Summer 1944. Stories: 6
Cover: Baseball by Earle Bergey
Joe Archibald, "The Tokyo Express" (BB)
Arthur K. Barnes, "Busher" (BB)
Vol. 12, No. 3, Fall 1944. Stories: 5
Cover: Football by Earle Bergey
Robert S. Fenton, "First Down America" (FB)
Ted Stratton, "One-Way Street" (FB)
Vol. 13, No. 1, Winter 1945. Stories: 6
Cover: Football by Rudolph Belarski
Herbert L. McNary, "The Glory Grabber" (FB)
Vol. 13, No. 2, Spring 1945. Stories: 5
Cover: Baseball by Earle Bergey
Robert Sidney Bowen, "Hot Corner" (BB)
Sam Merwin, Jr., "Triple Kill" (BB)
Matt Lee (Sam Mervin, Jr.), "The Smaller They Are" (FB)
Ted Stratton, "Football Is That Way" (FB)
Vol. 13, No. 3, Fall 1945 (no Summer issue). Stories: 6
Cover: Football by Earle Bergey
Jackson V. Scholz, "Apple Buster" (BB)
Ron Broom, "Clarkson's Pasture" (BB)
T.W. Ford, "Borrowed Spotlight" (FB)
Vol. 14, No. 1, Spring 1946 (no Winter issue). Stories: 7
Cover: Baseball by Earle Bergey
William O'Sullivan, "The Kid Catcher" (BB)
Cliff Walters, "The Owl and the Foul" (BB)
Robert S. Fenton, "War and Football" (FB)
Vol. 14, No. 2, Summer 1946. Stories: 7
Cover: Baseball by Earle Bergey
John Pershing McAllister, "Putout, Unassisted" (BB)
Sam Merwin, Jr., "The Imperfectionist" (BB)
Vol. 14, No. 3, Fall 1946. Stories: 8
Cover: Football by Earle Bergey
Roger Fuller (Don Tracy), "Dear Old Exover" (FB)
William O'Sullivan, Lots of Mustard, "Please" (FB)
Joe Gregg, "Five-Star Boomerang" (FB)
Vol. 15, No. 1, Winter 1947. Stories: 7
Cover: Boxing by Earle Bergey
William C. Fay, "The Drip" (BB)
Joe Archibald, Watch That Play, "Little Man" (FB)
Richard Brister, "The Line Looked Bad" (FB)
Vol. 15, No. 2, Spring 1947. Stories: 9
Cover: Baseball by Earle Bergey
T.W. Ford, "The Red Neck" (BB)
Art Shapiro, "Records Don't Count" (BB)
Vol. 15, No. 3, Summer 1947. Stories: 9
Cover: Baseball by Earle Bergey
Roger Fuller (Don Tracy), Third Strike, "Called" (BB)
Sam Merwin, Jr., "The Long Ball" (BB)
Vol. 17, No. 1 (Vol. 16 skipped entirely), Fall 1947. Stories: 9
Cover: Football by Earle Bergey
T.W. Ford, "Dead Legs at Shortstop" (BB)
Robert Sidney Bowen, "Never Too Old" (BB)
Richard Brister, "Manager's Madness" (BB)
Joe Archibald, "Mirror on His Shoulder" (FB)
Willis Graham, "Substitute Halfback" (FB)
Vol. 17, No. 2, December 1947. Stories: 7
Cover: Football (unsigned, uncredited)
John Wilson, "Too Many Base Hits" (BB)
A.N. Borno, "No-Hitter" (BB)
William O'Sullivan, "Conference Coach" (FB)
Vol. 17, No. 3, February 1948. Stories: 7
Cover: Basketball (unsigned, uncredited)
Roger Fuller (Don Tracy), "Between the Halves" (FB)
Sam Merwin, Jr., "The Post-College Try" (FB)
Vol. 18, No. 1, April 1948. Stories: 7
Cover: Baseball by Earle Bergey
Robert Sidney Bowen, "Danger—Spikes at Work" (BB)
Bill Erin, "The Cypher Slugger" (BB)
Matt Lee (Sam Merwin, Jr.), "Duster" (BB)
Roger Fuller (Don Tracy), "Young Man's Fancy" (FB)
William O'Sullivan, "Country Boy" (FB)
Vol. 18, No. 2, June 1948. Stories: 7
Cover: Baseball by Sam Cherry

Roy Lopez, "The Greatest Hitter in the World" (BB)
Burt Armstrong, "Jose Plays the Base" (BB)
Lew Martin, "The Hipper-Dipper Play" (FB)

Vol. 18, No. 3, August 1948. Stories: 9
Cover: Baseball by Sam Cherry
Tom Tucker (Don Tracy), "The Relief Hurler" (BB)
Herbert L. McNary, "Fireballing Ace" (BB)
H.C. Butler, "Jinx Pitcher" (BB)
Carter Sprague (Sam Merwin, Jr.), "Autumn Lunacy" (FB)

Vol. 19, No. 1, October 1948. Stories: 7
Cover: Football by Earle Bergey
Joe Archibald, Fireman, "Save My Ball Game" (BB)
Robert Sidney Bowen, "By Hook or by Crook" (BB)
William O'Sullivan, "The Touchdown Trail" (FB)

Vol. 19, No. 2, December 1948. Stories: 7
Cover: Football by Earle Bergey
Edward Howey, "Sing a Song of Base Hits" (BB)
Joe Archibald, "Sideline Ghost" (FB)
Burgess Leonard, "Born Football" (FB)

Vol. 19, No. 3, February 1949. Stories: 6
Cover: Football
Ivan March, "A Hundred Pounds of Heart" (BB)
John Wilson, "Old Man in the Backfield" (FB)

Vol. 20, No. 1, Spring 1949. Stories: 6
Cover: Baseball by Earle Bergey
William O'Sullivan, "Bruins on Base" (BB)

Vol. 20, No. 2, Summer 1949. Stories: 6
Cover: Baseball by Earle Bergey
William O'Sullivan, "Second Time at Bat" (BB)

Vol. 20, No. 3, Fall 1949. Stories: 7
Cover: Football by Earle Bergey
William Campbell Gault, "The Hard Way" (FB)
Joe Gregg, "Man of Iron" (FB)

Vol. 21, No. 1, Winter 1950. Stories: 7
Cover: Football by Earle Bergey
Ivan Gladstein, "Utility Player" (BB)
Herbert L. McNary, "I've Got Army in My Blood" (FB)

Vol. 21, No. 2, Spring 1950. Stories: 8
Cover: Baseball
John Wilson, "Borrowed Base Hits" (BB)
Kenny Kenmare (Will F. Jenkins), "The First Faith" (BB)

Vol. 21, No. 3, Fall 1950 (no Summer issue). Stories: 8
Cover: Baseball
T.W. Ford, "Bigger Than the Game" (BB)
Duane Yarnell, "Hit and Run" (BB) (reprinted from *Exciting Sports*, Spring 1943)
Harrison Hendryx, All American, "Brother" (FB)

Vol. 22, No. 1, Winter 1951. Stories: 8
Cover: Football
John Wilson, "Coffin Corner Coach" (FB)
Nelson S. Bond, "Front Page Glory" (FB) (reprinted from Thrilling Football, Fall 1939)
Bill Erin, "Face the Facts" (FB)
Francis L. Fugate, Hick, Hike, "Hoax" (FB)
Robert Sidney Bowen, "Coach of the Year" (FB)

Vol. 22, No. 2, Spring 1951. Stories: 7
Cover: Baseball
T.W. Ford, "Spikes in the Sunlight" (BB)
Jack Terry, "Behind the Plate" (BB) (reprinted from *Exciting Sports*, Spring 1941)
William O'Sullivan, "Touchdowns by the Yard" (FB)

Totals: 63 issues, 367 stories, 78 baseball stories, 53 football stories.

Thrilling Baseball

Vol. 1, No. 1, Summer 1949. Stories: 10
Cover: Earle Bergey
Cosmo Bennett, "The Firecracker Kid"
John Wilson, "Mound Magic"
Will Urbanna. "The Ten-Cent Brain"
H.C. Butler, "Bush-League Manager"
Sam Merwin, Jr., "Action at First"
T.W. Ford, "Fireman, Fireman!"
Perry Dixon (house name), "Brain Ball Chucker"
William O'Sullivan, "The Grandstander"
Arthur William Rickard, "Take It Easy"
Tom Tucker (Don Tracy), "Bat Boy"

Vol. 1, No. 2, Spring 1950. Stories: 10
Cover: Earle Bergey
Stewart Sterling (Prentice Winchell), "The Platinum Bat"
Herbert L. McNary, "Ride That Rookie"
Richard Brister, "Fifth Man in the Infield"
Roger Fuller (Don Tracy), "The Sorehead"
Cosmo Bennett, "Hit 'Em Where They Ain't"
Scott Morgan (house name), "Strikes in His Blood"
William O'Sullivan, "Man with a Glove"
Robert Sidney Bowen, "A Certain Something"
Harrison Hendryx, "Low Pitch"
Joe Gregg, "Old Catchers Never Die"

Vol. 1, No. 3, Spring 1951. Stories: 8
Cover: Unsigned, uncredited
John Wilson, "The Road Back to Glory"
T.W. Ford, "The Team Player"
Bill Erin, "Return to the Wars"
W.S. Peacock, "Final Victory"
Cosmo Bennett, "Anything Can Happen"
Lt. R.G. Emery, "Curtis of Central" (reprinted from *Popular Sports*, December 1937)
William Heuman, "The Million Dollar Arm" (reprinted from *Thrilling Sports*, Winter 1944)
Robert Sidney Bowen, "Fielder's Choice" (reprinted from *Popular Sports*, Summer 1942).

Totals: 3 issues, 28 baseball stories.

Thrilling Football

Vol. 1, No. 1, 1939 issue. Stories: 7
Cover: Earle Bergey

Nelson S. Bond, "Front Page Glory"
Sam Merwin, Jr., "Pro Payoff"
Sam Carson, "Sixty Minute Kicker"
John Easterly, "Tide of Battle"
Jack Kofoed, "Block That Girl"
Nelson Hutto, "Show-Off Quarterback"
Lamoine E. Boyle, "The Devastating Devine"

Vol. 2, No. 1, Fall 1940. Stories: 6
Cover: Earle Bergey
T.W. Ford, "No More Touchdowns"
David Brandt, "The Gridiron Foreign Legion"
Forrest Kleiman, "Pariah Pards"
Sam Carson, "The Three Aces"
Nelson S. Bond, "Wings for the Flying Dutchman"
Herbert L. McNary, "Pigskin Specialist"

Vol. 3, No. 1, Fall 1941. Stories: 8
Cover: Earle Bergey
Alexis Rossoff, "Hard Knocks Grad"
Herbert L. McNary, "Touchdown Navy"
C. Paul Jackson, "It's Fun to Block"
W.H. Temple, "Hit That Paydirt!"
Cosmo Bennett, "Take a Chance"
Duane Yarnell, "Rose Bowl Bound"
Sam Merwin, Jr., "Tough to Be Tough"
David Brandt, "Viva La Football"

Vol. 4, No. 1, Fall 1942. Stories: 8
Cover: Earle Bergey
Tracy Mason (Don Tracy), "Shavetail Drawback"
Ted Roemer, "Tiger Tackle"
Sam Carson, "Halfback Headlines"
Bertrand L. Shurtleff, "Hired Hands"
Cosmo Bennett, "Lug That Ball, Soldier"
Ted Stratton, "Half a Halfback"
T.W. Ford, "Sideline Star"
Ralph Yergin, "The Alkali Special"

Vol. 4, No. 2, Fall 1943. Stories: 7
Cover: Earle Bergey
Joe Archibald, "Gridiron Steel"
Sam Merwin, Jr., "Lazy Rivers, Fullback"
Theodore J. Roemer, "Green Kid"
Eugene Pawley, "Stars and Spinners"
W.H. Temple, "Play for Pay Palooka"
Carter Sprague (Sam Merwin, Jr.), "The Shock of Combat"
Sam Carson, "Game End Game"

Vol. 4, No. 3, Fall 1944. Stories: 7
Cover: Earle Bergey
Theodore J. Roemer, "Backfield Dynamo"
Sam Merwin, Jr., "Backs in Motion"
C. Paul Jackson, "Mr. Football"
W.H. Temple, "Dream Team's Destiny"
John Gartner, "High School Coach"
Richard Brister, "Hula Hip Hero"
Carter Sprague (Sam Merwin, Jr.), "Quick Kick"

Vol. 5, No. 1, Fall 1945. Stories: 6
Cover: Earle Bergey
William J. O'Sullivan, "This Is the Navy"
William Heuman, "Bush Town Bouncers"
Joe Archibald, "Front Lines of Autumn"
Nelson Hutto, "Backfield Bruiser"
Richard Brister, "Eleven Through Center"
Robert Sidney Bowen, "Wings Over the Gridiron"

Vol. 5, No. 2, Fall 1946. Stories: 6
Cover: Earle Bergey
Tracy Mason (Don Tracy), "Glamour Back"
William J. O'Sullivan, "Freshwater Big-Times"
Richard Brister, "Drawback"
Jackson Cole (house name), "The Glory Foot"
John Pershing McAllister, "Hades Takes a Hand"
Jack Terry, "Ham Halfback"

Vol. 5, No. 3, Winter 1948. Stories: 7
Cover: Earle Bergey
William O'Sullivan, "Navy Captain"
Joe Archibald, "Too Big for Little Four"
Roger Fuller (Don Tracy), "On the Bench"
Sam Merwin, Jr., "Doubled in Brass"
Joe Gregg, "Positively Last Appearance"
Nelson Hutto, "Clutch Quarterback"
Richard Brister, "Backfield or Bust"

Vol. 6, No. 1, Winter 1949. Stories: 9
Cover: Sam Cherry?
Joe Archibald, "Yesterday's Touchdowns"
William O'Sullivan, "Line Wrecker"
Don Keene, "The Junkman's Son"
Louis L'Amour, "Moran of the Tigers"
C. Paul Jackson, "An Eye for a T"
Sam Merwin, Jr., "Opening Game"
Carter Sprague (Sam Merwin, Jr.), "Under Pressure"
Kenny Kenmare (Will F. Jenkins), "Are Coaches People?"
Richard Brister, "You Gotta Feel Football"

Vol. 6, No. 2, Fall 1949. Stories: 9
Cover: Earle Bergey
Roe Richmond, "Third-String All-Stars"
William Campbell Gault, "This Way to Glory"
Ted Stratton, "Clown Princes on Cleats"
Will Urbanna, "It's a Game"
Talbot Davis, "The Guy You Couldn't Hurt"
T.W. Ford, "Glory Hunter No More"
V.A. Saluda, "Makers of Men"
Reynolds Phillips, "Kill the Gridiron Ghost!"
Hal K. Wells, "Touchdowns Marinara"

Vol. 6, No. 3, Fall 1950. Stories: 8
Cover: Sam Cherry?
William O'Sullivan, "Eleven Man Burden"
William Heuman, "Million Dollar Mauler"
Nelson Hutto, "The Touchdown Tornado"
Robert Sidney Bowen, "Pass and Pray!"
Louis Trimble, "Half-Time Halfback"
Johanas L. Bouma, "Touchdown Fury"
Sam Merwin, Jr., "Take the Heir"
Scott Morgan (house name), "This One on Me"

Vol. 7, No. 1, Fall 1951. Stories: 7
Cover: Earle Bergey
Robert Sidney Bowen, "All-American Chump"
William O'Sullivan, "Whipsaw"
Sid Wilton, "You Can't Let Go"
Sam Merwin, Jr., "Ivy for Sale"
William Heuman, "Gridiron Gamble" (reprinted from *Exciting Sports*, Fall 1945)
W.H. Temple, "Pigskin Gentleman" (reprinted from *Thrilling Sports*, November 1940)

T.W. Ford, "Headline Halfbac"k (reprinted from *Popular Football*, Winter 1942)
Vol. 7, No. 2, Fall 1952. Stories: 9
Cover: Sam Cherry?
Daniel Winters (house name), "Up from Hell's Kitchen"
Robert Sidney Bowen, "Write Your Own Ticket"
Giles A. Lutz, "The System"
Robert C. Tennis, "Saturday Hero"
William O'Sullivan, "To Every Man"
Ted Stratton, "Back Up That Tackle"
John L. Benton (house name), "Young Fighting Fool"
Duane Yarnell, "The Swamp Fox" (reprinted from *Popular Football*, Fall 1943)
Burt L. Shurtleff, "One More Season" (reprinted from *Popular Sports*, April 1938)

Totals: 14 issues, 104 football stories.

Thrilling Sports

Vol. 1, No. 1, September 1936. Stories: 8
Cover: Track by Earle Bergey
Robert Sidney Bowen, "Bench Warmer" (BB)
Vic Whitman, "Old Ironsides" (FB)
Vol. 1, No. 2, November 1936. Stories: 7
Cover: Baseball by Earle Bergey
Arthur Mann, "Revolt in the Series" (BB)
Orlando Rigoni, "Two Ways to Win" (BB)
Vol. 1, No. 3, December 1936. Stories: 8
Cover: Football by Earle Bergey
Robert Sidney Bowen, "Payroll Player" (BB)
George Bruce, "The Old Army Game" (FB)
Philip L. Scruggs, "Man of Iron" (FB)
Vol. 2, No. 1, January 1937. Stories: 8
Cover: Football by Earle Bergey
Lt. R.G. Emery, "The Old College Try" (FB)
Vol. 2, No. 2, February 1937. Stories: 7
Cover: Boxing by Earle Bergey
Philip L. Scruggs, Carry On, "Cameron" (FB)
Vol. 2, No. 3, March 1937. Stories: 8
Cover: Hockey by Earle Bergey
Roe Richmond, "The Teeth of the Underdog" (BB)
Joe Archibald, "Triple Threat Man" (FB)
Vol. 3, No. 1, April 1937. Stories: 7
Cover: Basketball by Earle Bergey
William Bruner, "Baseball Buckaroo" (BB)
Vol. 3, No. 2, May 1937. Stories: 8
Cover: Track by Earle Bergey
Vic Whitman, "Cupid Hits a Fast One" (BB)
John D. Swain, "Just Like a Kid" (FB)
Vol. 3, No. 3, July 1937. Stories: 8
Cover: Baseball by Earle Bergey
Robert Sidney Bowen, "They Never Forget" (BB)
Vol. 4, No. 1, September 1937. Stories: 7
Cover: Track by Earle Bergey
Jack B. Creamer, "They Started in Haiti" (BB)
Vol. 4, No. 2, November 1937. Stories: 6
Cover: Baseball by Earle Bergey
Walter Hartmann, "Buffoon" (BB)
Clark Bodey, "Little Lord Fumbleroy" (FB)
Vol. 4, No. 3, January 1938. Stories: 6
Cover: Football by Earle Bergey
Glenn Long, "A Slide for Science" (BB)
Philip L. Scruggs, "The Way of Honor" (FB)
Vol. 5, No. 1, March 1938. Stories: 6
Cover: Basketball by Earle Bergey
Arthur K. Barnes, "Indian Johnny" (BB)
Vol. 5, No. 1 (error), May 1938. Stories: 7
Cover: Baseball by Earle Bergey
Philip L. Scruggs, "Home for Old Men" (BB)
Victor Spencer, "Just Like Pop" (BB)
Vol. 5, No. 2 (error not corrected), July 1938. Stories: 7
Cover: Boxing by Earle Bergey
Walter Roeber Schmidt, "The Keystone Twins" (BB)
Vol. 5, No. 3, September 1938. Stories: 7
Cover: Baseball by Earle Bergey
Arthur Mann, "World Series Blues" (BB)
Vol. 6, No. 1, November 1938. Stories: 7
Cover: Football by Earle Bergey
James W. Egan, "Whiskers and Wallops" (BB)
Perry Dixon (Joe Archibald), "Gridiron Feud" (FB) (series character Larry White)
Vol. 6, No. 2, January 1939. Stories: 7
Cover: Football by Earle Bergey
Robert Sidney Bowen, "Slide, Fate, Slide" (BB)
Jackson V. Scholz, "Pigskin Pressure" (FB)
Vol. 6, No. 3, March 1939. Stories: 7
Cover: Basketball by Earle Bergey
Arthur Mann, "The Singing Pitcher" (BB)
Vol. 7, No. 1, May 1939. Stories: 8
Cover: Baseball by Earle Bergey
Sam Merwin, Jr., "The Nobler Game" (BB)
Jack Kofoed, "Great Dane" (FB)
Vol. 7, No. 2, July 1939. Stories: 8
Cover: Baseball by Earle Bergey
Perry Dixon (Joe Archibald), "Diamond Dust" (BB) (series character Larry White)
William O'Sullivan, "Cellar Champs" (BB)
Victor Spencer, "School for Umps" (BB)
Allan R. Bosworth, Rah, Rah, "Rider" (FB-Rodeo)
Vol. 7, No. 3, September 1939. Stories: 8
Cover: Boxing by Earle Bergey
Jack Kofoed, "Ninth Inning Stuff" (BB)
Vol. 8, No. 1, November 1939. Stories: 8
Cover: Football by Earle Bergey
Harold de Polo, "Take-a-Tip Sysmanski" (BB)
Spencer Towne, "Backfield Sparkplug" (FB)
Vol. 8, No. 2, January 1940. Stories: 8
Cover: Football by Earle Bergey
Bob DeHaven, "Redmen Blues" (Softball)
Jackson V. Scholz, "Gridiron Horseshoes" (FB)
Perry Dixon (Joe Archibald), "Last Year's Star" (FB) (Larry White series)
Vol. 8, No. 3, March 1940. Stories: 7
Cover: Boxing by Earle Bergey
Harrison Hendryx, "Little Doc" (BB)
Toora Kanazawa, "Flagle to Shade" (FB)
Vol. 9, No. 1, May 1940. Stories: 7
Cover: Baseball by Earle Bergey
Sam Merwin, Jr., "Safe All Around" (BB)

Robert Sidney Bowen, "The Roving Renegade" (Softball)
Vol. 9, No. 2, July 1940. Stories: 8
Cover: Polo by Earle Bergey
Jackson V. Scholz, "Big League Rookie" (BB)
Vol. 9, No. 3, September 1940. Stories: 8
Cover: Baseball by Earle Bergey
Arthur Mann, "Holdout Blues" (BB)
Jack Kofoed, Baldy Simmons, "Umpire" (BB)
Duane Yarnell, "Ex-Fullback" (FB)
Vol. 10, No. 1, November 1940. Stories: 8
Cover: Football by Earle Bergey
Arthur K. Barnes, "Not for Softies" (Softball)
William R. Cox, "End of a Tradition" (FB)
W.H. Temple, "Pigskin Tradition" (FB)
Jack Kofoed, "Baldy Simmons Goes Rose Bowl" (FB)
Vol. 10, No. 2, January 1941. Stories: 9
Cover: Football by Earle Bergey
Robert Sidney Bowen, "Truthful Talbot" (BB)
Jackson V. Scholz, "The Gridiron Crusader" (FB)
Nelson A. Hutto, "Lone Wolf Lineman" (FB)
Vol. 10, No. 3, March 1941. Stories: 7
Cover: Boxing by Earle Bergey
Harold de Polo, "They Got the Jobs" (BB)
Vol. 11, No. 1, May 1941. Stories: 7
Cover: Baseball by Earle Bergey
T.W. Ford, "The Fielding Fool" (BB)
Harold de Polo, "Granny Wins a Pennant" (BB)
Jack Terry, "Stadium Stooge" (FB)
Vol. 11, No. 2, July 1941. Stories: 8
Cover: Baseball by Earle Bergey
Sam Merwin, Jr., "Diamond Dynamite" (BB)
Jackson V. Scholz, "Camp Color" (BB)
Vol. 11, No. 3, September 1941. Stories: 8
Cover: Boxing by Earle Bergey
T.W. Ford, "That Rookie" (BB)
Harold Rogers, "Bantam Backstop" (BB)
Vol. 12, No. 1, November 1941. Stories: 8
Cover: Football by Earle Bergey
Myles D. Blanchard, "Puddle from Middleville" (BB)
Walter Livingston, "Rah Rah Stuff" (FB)
Sam Carson, "Short Order Hero" (FB)
Vol. 12, No. 2, January 1942. Stories: 7
Cover: Football by Earle Bergey
Jack Kofoed, "Baldy and the Unlucky Pitcher" (BB)
Don Tracy, "Kid Ego" (FB)
Richard Brister, "Five Star Touchdowns" (FB)
Vol. 12, No. 3, April 1942. Stories: 7
Cover: Boxing by Earle Bergey
Marvin Ryerson, "Pitcher's Battle" (BB)
Jack Kofoed, "Baldy and the Idealist" (FB)
Vol. 13, No. 1, Summer 1942. Stories: 7
Cover: Baseball by Earle Bergey
Don Tracy, "Season Opener" (BB)
Joseph Bruce Fox, "Jinx Juggler" (BB)
Charles Stoddard, "The Bugback" (FB)
Vol. 13, No. 2, September 1942. Stories: 7
Cover: Baseball by Earle Bergey
T.W. Ford, "Clutch Guy" (BB)
Sam Merwin, Jr., "The Clincher" (BB)
Vol. 13, No. 3, Fall 1942. Stories: 5
Cover: Football by Earle Bergey
Sam Merwin, Jr., "Keep 'Em Rolling" (FB)
Tracy Mason (Don Tracy), "The Taming of Trucker Thompson" (FB)
Vol. 14, No. 1, Winter 1943. Stories: 7
Cover: Football by Earle Bergey
Alexis Rossoff, "Gridiron Shortstop" (BB)
Don Keene, "Lost and Found" (FB)
Herbert L. McNary, "One Play Logan" (FB)
Vol. 14, No. 2, March 1943. Stories: 7
Cover: Boxing by Earle Bergey
Laurence Donovan, "Utility Goat" (BB)
Tracy Mason (Don Tracy), "Hungry Hurler" (BB)
Vol. 14, No. 3, Summer 1943. Stories: 7
Cover: Baseball by Earle Bergey
Herbert L. McNary, "World Series Wrecker" (BB)
Don Keene, "From Rags to Riches" (BB)
Vol. 15, No. 1, Fall 1943. Stories: 6
Cover: Football by Earle Bergey
Harold de Polo, "Camouflaged Rookie" (BB)
Don Tracy, "Quick Kick" (FB)
Vol. 15, No. 2, Winter 1944. Stories: 7
Cover: Football by Earle Bergey
William Heuman, "The Million Dollar Arm" (BB)
Sam Merwin, Jr., "Toward a Distant Goal" (FB)
Davis J. Brandt, "Interference" (FB)
Harold Rogers, "Halfback War Horse" (FB)
Vol. 15, No. 3, Spring 1944. Stories: 7
Cover: Baseball by Earle Bergey
Nelson A. Hutto, "Hold 'Em, Busher" (BB)
Sam Merwin, Jr., A Matter of Nerve (Women's Softball)
Vol. 16, No. 1, Summer 1944. Stories: 7
Cover: Baseball by Earle Bergey
Joe Archibald, "The Grand Old Game" (BB)
Carter Sprague (Sam Merwin, Jr.), "Parson Island Umpire" (BB)
Jack O'Brien, "Civilian in the Lineup" (FB)
Vol. 16, No. 2, Fall 1944. Stories: 7
Cover: Football by Earle Bergey
Nelson Hutto, "The Clutch Hitter" (BB)
A.R. Thurman (Arthur Mann), "Service Weight" (BB)
Jack Kofoed, "Baldy and the Forgetful Guy" (BB)
Sam Carson, "Wrecks from Tech" (FB)
Ted Stratton, "Here's to the Joneses" (FB)
Vol. 16, No. 3, Winter 1945. Stories: 9
Cover: Football by Earle Bergey
Matt Lee (Sam Merwin, Jr.), "The Psychiatric Home Run" (BB)
C. Paul Jackson, "Triple Threat Flash" (FB)
T.W. Ford, "Traitors for a Day" (FB)
Vol. 17, No. 1, Summer 1945 (no Spring issue). Stories: 6
Cover: Boxing by Earle Bergey
T.W. Ford, "Feud Mates" (BB)
Cliff Walters, "Diamond Dust" (BB)
Vol. 17, No. 2, Winter 1946 (no Fall 1945 issue). Stories: 7
Cover: Football by Earle Bergey

William O'Sullivan, "McGowan to Cross to Fanch" (BB)
Herb Kamm, "Little Number One" (FB)
Jack Kofoed, "The Psychoanalyst" (FB) (Baldy Simmons)
David X. Manners, "All-American Bonehead" (FB)
Jackson V. Scholz, "Gridiron Screwball" (FB)

Vol. 17, No. 3, Spring 1946. Stories: 7
Cover: Baseball by Earle Bergey
Joe Archibald, "Thrown Out by McKinney" (BB)
Roy C. Rainey (house name), "Home Town Boy" (BB)
Richard Brister, "Gold to Go" (FB)

Vol. 18, No. 1, Summer 1946. Stories: 7
Cover: Baseball by Earle Bergey
Herbert L. McNary, "Pull for the Fence" (BB)

Vol. 18, No. 2, Winter 1947 (no Fall 1946 issue). Stories: 7
Cover: Football by Rudolph Belarski
Cliff Walters, "Mound Master" (BB)
Tracy Mason (Don Tracy), "Unbeaten Season" (FB)
William A. Sullivan, "Crazy for Trouble" (FB)
Will Bruce, "The Wrong Right End" (FB)

Vol. 18, No. 3, Spring 1947. Stories: 8
Cover: Boxing by Earle Bergey
John Wilson, "Touchdowns Don't Count" (FB)
Jack Kofoed, "Headlines" (FB) (Baldy Simmons)

Vol. 19, No. 1, Summer 1947. Stories: 8
Cover: Baseball by Earle Bergey
T.W. Ford, "Stranger at the Plate" (BB)
John Wilson, "Gents of the Diamond" (BB)
San Merwin, Jr., "A Needle for Brett" (FB)

Vol. 19, No. 2, Fall 1947. Stories: 8
Cover: Baseball by Earle Bergey
William O'Sullivan, "Muscles in His Head" (BB)
Bill Erin, "The Rookie from Middleton" (BB)
Robert Sidney Bowen, "Don't Give It a Thought" (BB)
T.W. Ford, "The Last Gamble" (FB)

Vol. 19, No. 3, November 1947. Stories: 7
Cover: Football by Earle Bergey
John Wilson, "Big League Busher" (BB)
Tracy Mason (Don Tracy), "The Swell-headed Soph" (FB)

Vol. 20, No. 1, January 1948. Stories: 7
Cover: Football by Earle Bergey
Arthur William Rickard, "Out at Home" (BB)
Tracy Mason (Don Tracy), "Frame-Up" (BB)
M.M. Tinney, "Single Threat Man" (FB)

Vol. 20, No. 2, March 1948. Stories: 7
Cover: Basketball by Earle Bergey
T.W. Ford, "Cluck in the Outfield" (BB)
Kenny Kenmare (Will F. Jenkins), "Hate" (FB)

Vol. 20, No. 3, May 1948. Stories: 8
Cover: Baseball by Earle Bergey
Robert Sidney Bowen, "You Can't Beat Class" (BB)
A.N. Borno, "Fast Ball" (BB)
Joe Archibald, "Pigskin Prodigal" (FB)

Vol. 21, No. 1, July 1948. Stories: 7
Cover: Baseball by Sam Cherry?
John Wilson, "A Hick in Time" (BB)
Nelson Hutto, "Sucker Play" (FB)

Vol. 21, No. 2, September 1948. Stories: 7
Cover: Baseball by Sam Cherry
John Wilson, "An Old-Fashioned Single" (BB)

Vol. 21, No. 3, November 1948. Stories: 7
Cover: Football by Sam Cherry?
Roy Lopez, "Turn on the Heat" (BB)
Jack Kofoed, Softball Preferred (Softball)
Joe Archibald, "A Coach for Cinderella" (FB)

Vol. 22, No. 1, January 1949. Stories: 7
Cover: Football by Earle Bergey
John Wilson, "Blood in the Backfield" (FB)
Ted Stratton, "Only Today Counts" (FB)

Vol. 22, No. 2, Spring 1949. Stories: 7
Cover: Baseball by Earle Bergey
T.W Ford, "The Walking Guy" (BB)
W.C. Tuttle, "More Deadly Than the Gun" (BB)
H.C. Butler, "Pitcher's Pal" (BB)

Vol. 22, No. 3, Summer 1949. Stories: 6
Cover: Baseball by Earle Bergey
T.W. Ford, "The All-Star Game" (BB)

Vol. 23, No. 1, Fall 1949. Stories: 5
Cover: Football by Earle Bergey
David X. Manners, "Someone to Win For" (BB)
John Wilson, The Coffin-Cornered Kid (FB)

Vol. 23, No. 2, Winter 1950. Stories: 6
Cover: Football by Sam Cherry?
William O'Sullivan, All American

Vol. 23, No. 3, Spring 1950. Stories: 7
Cover: Baseball by Sam Cherry?
M.M. Tinney, "Love That Umpire" (BB)

Vol. 24, No. 1, Fall 1950 (no Summer issue). Stories: 7
Cover: Baseball by Sam Cherry?
T.W. Ford, "The Diamond Tramp" (BB)
Tracy Mason (Don Tracy), "Fallen Hero" (BB) (reprinted from *Exciting Sports*, Fall 1943)

Vol. 24, No. 2, Winter 1951. Stories: 8
Cover: Football by Sam Cherry?
Bob Wilton, "Where There's Life" (BB)
John Wilson, "Goal Line Stand" (FB)
T.W. Ford, "No More Touchdowns" (FB)

Vol. 24, No. 3, Spring 1951. Stories: 7
Cover: Baseball by Sam Cherry?
Robert Sidney Bowen, "Throw Him Curves" (BB)
Will Bruce, "The Final Out" (BB) (reprinted from *Exciting Sports*, Summer 1942)
Richard Brister, "Captain of the Bench" (FB)

Vol. 25, No. 4 (error; should be Vol. 25, No. 1), Summer 1951. Stories: 8
Cover: Baseball by Sam Cherry?
T.W. Ford, "I Hit to Eat" (BB)
Jackson V. Scholz, "Big League Rookie" (BB) (reprinted from *Thrilling Sports*, July 1940)

Totals: 74 issues, 534 stories, 98 baseball stories, 70 football stories.

Thrilling Publications totals: 229 issues, 1,569 stories, 395 baseball stories, 478 football stories.

Stories Annual

1955 edition (one shot). Stories: 12.
Not a sports pulp, but includes Thrilling's final two pulp baseball stories:
T.W. Ford, Diamond Outcast
Fletchef Flora, "They're Dead at Cooperstown"

NOTE: The cover art credits for generally highly collectible artists come from a variety of sources. My own collection (all but 34 of the pulps in this index at this writing) provided most credits taken from signed covers, but with a few educated guesses followed by a question mark. In many cases, I backed up my listings with the following sources: the fabulous Fiction Mags website, maintained by Phil Stephensen-Payne; the noted artist and pulp art expert David Saunders's book on his father, titled *Norman Saunders: The Art of the Pulps,* edited by Doug Ellis, Ed Hulse and Robert Weinberg; historian and pulp dealer John Gunnison at Adventure House; and the two Bookery guidebooks by Tim Cottrill. A hearty round of thanks to all!

The Only Two All-Basketball Pulps

Basketball Stories, Vol. 1, No. 1 (one shot), Winter 1937–1938, Fiction House. Stories: 8
Cover: Unsigned
Nelson S. Bond, "Gawky for Guard"
Harold M. Sherman, "The Basket Busters"
Ted Fox, "Gangway for Glory!"
William R. Cox, "Razzle-Dazzle Racketeer"
Linton Davies, "Sureshot"
Glenn Long, "100 Per Cent Grandstander"
John Star, "Hooded Hoopsters"
Harry Goldberg, "The Two-in-One Victory"

All-Basketball Stories, Vol. 1, No. 1 (one shot), Winter 1947–1948, Marvel. Stories: 8
Cover: Allen Anderson
Roe Richmond, "Court Courage"
Theodore J. Roemer, "Hoop Demons Don't Have Hearts"
J. Phillip List, "The Basket Imp"
Flynn V. Livingston, "Take It, Tanglefoot!"
Jim Blish, "Double Trouble"
Giles A. Lutz, "Break Fast, Firebrand!"
Gardner F. Fox, "Wanted—A Hotshot Hoop Hand"
Norman Ober, "Jumping Josephus"

Bibliography

NOTE: All the pulp magazines specifically referred to in the text can be found listed by publisher in Part II—Catalog of Pulp Baseball and Football from Six Publishers.

Alexander, David T., and Robert Crestohl. *The Baseball and Sports Publications Price Guide: Listings from 1860 to 1997.* Tampa, FL: Century of Sports, 1997.

Clear, Richard E. *Old Magazines, Identification and Value Guide, Second Edition.* Paducah, KY: Collector Books, 2006.

Cottrill, Tim. *Bookery's Guide to Pulps and Related Magazines, Second Edition.* Fairborn, OH: Bookery Press, 2005.

Dinan, John. *Sports in the Pulp Magazines.* Jefferson, NC: McFarland, 1998.

Ellis, Doug, Ed Hulse, and Robert Weinberg, editors. *The Art of the Pulps: An Illustrated History.* San Diego: IDW Publishing, 2017.

Ellis, Doug, John Locke, and John Gunnison. *The Adventure House Guide to the Pulps.* Silver Spring, MD: Adventure House, 2000.

Gunnison, John. *Belarski.* Silver Spring, MD: Adventure House, 2003.

Holroyd, Graham. *Paperback Prices and Checklist.* Chattanooga, TN: Guide Media, 2003.

Hulse, Ed. *The Blood and Thunder Guide to Pulp Fiction.* Charleston, SC: Murania Press, 2013.

Leavy, Jane. *Sandy Koufax: A Lefty's Legacy.* New York: HarperCollins, 2002.

Locke, John. *Pulp Fictioneers: Adventures in the Storytelling Business.* Silver Spring, MD: Adventure House, 2004.

_____. *Pulpwood Days: Editors You Want to Know.* Elkhorn, CA: Off-Trail, 2007.

McCue, Andy. *Baseball By the Books.* Dubuque, IA: William C. Brown, 1991.

Nicholls, Peter, editor. *The Science Fiction Encyclopedia.* Garden City, NY: Doubleday, 1979.

Nolan, Michelle. *Armchair Athletics in "The Art of the Pulps: An Illustrated History."* San Diego: IDW Publishing, 2017.

_____. *Ball Tales: A Study of Baseball, Basketball and Football Fiction of the 1930s through 1960s.* Jefferson, NC: McFarland, 2010.

_____. *Covering the Boys of Summer in "The Baseball and Sports Publications Price Guide."* Tampa, FL: Century of Sports, 1997.

Oriard, Michael. *Dreaming of Heroes: American Sports Fiction, 1868–1980.* Chicago: Nelson-Hall, 1982.

_____. *King Football.* Chapel Hill: University of North Carolina Press, 2000.

_____. *Reading Football: How the Popular Press Created an American Spectacle.* Chapel Hill: University of North Carolina Press, 1993.

Parente, Audrey. *Once a Pulp Man: The Secret Life of Judson P. Philips as Hugh Pentecost.* Charleston, SC: Bold Venture Press, 2016.

Reichler, Joseph. *The Baseball Encyclopedia, Seventh Edition.* New York: Macmillan, 1988.

Reilly, John M., editor. *Twentieth Century Crime and Mystery Writers, Second Edition.* New York: St. Martin's, 1985.

Robinson, Frank, and Lawrence Davidson. *Pulp Culture: The Art of Fiction Magazines.* Portland, OR: Collectors, 1998.

Saunders, David. *Norman Saunders.* St. Louis, MO: Illustrated Press, 2008.

Server, Lee. *Encyclopedia of Pulp Fiction Writers.* New York: Checkmark Books, 2002.

Sherman, Philip. *Leo Margulies: Giant of the Pulps: His Thrilling, Exciting and Popular Journey.* Columbia, SC: Altus Press, 2017.

Index